Red Hat Ansible Automation Platform

Modernize your organization with
automation and Infrastructure as Code

Luca Berton

www.bpbonline.com

First published: 2024

Published by BPB Online
WeWork
119 Marylebone Road
London NW1 5PU

UK | UAE | INDIA | SINGAPORE

ISBN 978-93-55518-996

www.bpbonline.com

Dedicated to

*My son **Filippo** - the joy of my life*

About the Author

 **Luca Berton** is an Ansible Automation Expert who has been working with JPMorgan Chase & Co. He previously worked with the Red Hat Ansible Engineer Team for three years. He is a published author of the best-selling books "Ansible for VMware by Examples" and "Ansible for Kubernetes by Examples" as part of the Ansible By Example(s) practical book series. Luca is also the creator of the Ansible Pilot project.

With over 15 years of experience as a System Administrator, he possesses extensive expertise in Infrastructure Hardening and Automation. He is an avid supporter of the Open Source community and shares his knowledge at various public events. A geek by nature, Luca's inclination is towards Linux, particularly Fedora.

Disclaimer

Any opinions or personal views I express in this book are my own and not those of Red Hat Inc. or JPMorgan Chase & Co.

Ansible®, Red Hat® Ansible® Automation Platform, Red Hat®, JBoss®, OpenShift®, Fedora®, Hibernate®, CloudForms®, RHCA®, RHCE®, RHCSA®, Ceph®, Gluster®, the Red Hat® logo and "A" logo in a shaded circle are trademarks or registered trademarks of Red Hat, Inc. or its subsidiaries in the United States and other countries. https://www.redhat.com/en/about/brand/standards/trademarks

"JPMorgan," "JPMorgan Chase," "Chase," the JPMorgan Chase logo, and the Octagon Symbol are trademarks of JPMorgan Chase Bank, N.A. JPMorgan Chase Bank, N.A., is a wholly-owned subsidiary of JPMorgan Chase & Co. https://www.jpmorgan.com/

Linux is a registered trademark of Linus Torvalds.

Certified Kubernetes®, Certified Kubernetes Administrator®, Certified Kubernetes Application Developer®, Certified Kubernetes Security Specialist®, CloudEvents®, CloudNativeCon®, CNCF®, containerd®, etcd®, KubeCon®, Kubernetes®, LSB®, Open Container Initiative®, Prometheus®, The Linux Foundation®, Xen Project®, Cloud Native Computing Foundation logo, Kubernetes and Cloud Native Associate and Design (color), OpenTelemetry and Design (black and white), Fluentd and Design of a Carrier Pigeon (color - horizontal) are registered trademarks of The Linux Foundation in the United States and/or other countries. The marks CRI-O™, LF™, LinuxCon™, Linux Foundation™, OpenGitOps™, OpenTelemetry™, Open Container Format™, Open Virtualization Alliance™, Virtual Kubelet™, World of Open Source™ have registrations pending or trademarks in use of The Linux Foundation in the United States and/or other countries. The Linux Foundation logo. US Reg. no. 5166331 (The Linux Foundation geometric design (black and white)), The Linux Foundation logo. US Reg. no. 5166330 (The Linux Foundation geometric design (color)), Certified Kubernetes logo. US Reg. no. 5734733, Community Data License Agreement logo. US Reg. no. 5852265, fluentd logo. US Reg. no. 4734498, Kubernetes logo. US Reg. no. 4816320, Kubernetes and Cloud Native Associate and Design (color) US Reg. 6949718, SupplyChainSecurity and Design (black and white) US Reg. No. 6949717 are registered trademarks for the following logo marks in the United States and/or other countries. **https://www.linuxfoundation.org/trademark-usage/**

UNIX® is a registered trademark of The Open Group.

Acknowledgement

I would like to express my gratitude to my son, family, and friends who make life worth living and whose support and encouragement have made this work possible.

I also want to extend my appreciation to all those whom I have worked with over the years and who shared their ideas for this book. Thank you all for the knowledge you have shared.

Preface

Welcome to the world of the Ansible Automation Platform. As technology continues to evolve, the need for efficient and scalable automation solutions becomes increasingly critical. This book is your comprehensive guide to mastering the Ansible Automation Platform, offering a hands-on approach to help you navigate the complexities of modern data center management.

In the dynamic landscape of modern technology, where the pace of change is relentless, and demands for efficiency, scalability, and reliability continue to rise, the role of automation has become paramount. As organizations grapple with the complexities of managing diverse IT environments, the Ansible Automation Platform emerges as a powerful ally, offering a versatile and robust solution to streamline operations, enhance deployment processes, and automate critical tasks. This book serves as an expansive and in-depth guide, meticulously crafted to empower both novices and seasoned professionals on their journey to mastering the intricacies of the Ansible Automation Platform. This book is designed to be a practical and comprehensive resource for both beginners and experienced professionals seeking to harness the full potential of the Ansible Automation Platform. We invite you to dive in, explore, and elevate your automation capabilities. Our intent is not only to provide a roadmap but to instill a sense of curiosity and empowerment. The Ansible Automation Platform, with its vast capabilities, beckons readers not just to consume knowledge but to participate in the evolution of their automation strategies actively. We invite you to embark on this journey, armed with curiosity and a commitment to mastering the Ansible Automation Platform, as we collectively navigate the ever-evolving landscape of IT automation.

Thank you for joining us on this exciting adventure!

Chapter 1: Getting Started with the Ansible Automation Platform – Begin our journey with a solid foundation, understanding the technology, typographic usage, and the crucial role Ansible plays in modern data center management. This chapter introduces us to the Ansible Automation Platform, covering its architecture, language, and the creation of playbooks and content, setting the stage for key learnings ahead.

Chapter 2: Ansible Automation Platform Architecture – Dive deep into the core of the Ansible Automation Platform. Explore its architecture and understand the Ansible Controller, Automation Hub, and Execution Environment. Gain insights into how these components interact in common use case scenarios, setting the groundwork for a robust automation infrastructure.

Chapter 3: Platform Installation Scenarios – Embark on the installation journey, exploring various scenarios and deployment options. From single-machine setups to high-availability clusters, this chapter guides us through prerequisites, requirements, and installation scenarios, providing a comprehensive understanding of Ansible Automation Platform deployment.

Chapter 4: First Steps – Navigate the Ansible Controller Dashboard with ease. Learn essential system administrator tasks, including Ansible Controller settings, CLI usage, job management, and best practices for configuring the dashboard. This chapter empowers us to efficiently manage our automation platform from a system administrator's perspective.

Chapter 5: Settings and Authentication – Organize permissions effectively with Role-Based Access Controls. This chapter covers the creation and management of access using users and teams. Explore external authentication sources and integrate Ansible Tower with LDAP, Azure Active Directory, and SAML authentication for enhanced security.

Chapter 6: IT Operations – Take control of system metrics and logging architecture. Learn how to connect Ansible metrics to Grafana, aggregate logging with tools like Splunk, and implement backup and restore strategies. Gain valuable insights into maintaining the health and performance of our Ansible Automation Platform.

Chapter 7: App Deployments – Unlock the power of automation in deploying cloud-native applications using containers. Dive into Ansible playbook development, automation of application deployments, and the distribution of applications in containers, streamlining our deployment workflows.

Chapter 8: Hybrid Cloud and Kubernetes – Explore how the Ansible Automation Platform simplifies hybrid cloud environments. Learn to build, provision, and manage applications across different cloud providers, leverage Kubernetes for container orchestration, and scale containerized applications seamlessly.

Chapter 9: Automate IT Processes – Discover the art of automating IT processes to enhance efficiency and security. This chapter covers the management of network and IT processes, automation of installations, upgrades, and day-to-day tasks, as well as responding to security threats with automated scripts.

Chapter 10: Wrap-Up – As we conclude this journey, recap the basics, install scenarios, role management, integration, authentication, and use cases. Reflect on key administration practices and express our gratitude for joining us on this exploration of the Ansible Automation Platform.

Whether you're a seasoned automation professional or just starting, this book provides a roadmap to mastering the Ansible Automation Platform and leveraging its capabilities to transform the way you approach IT automation. Let's embark on this exciting journey together!

Development Environment

The code provided in this book is compatible with any text editor or integrated development environment (IDE). An IDE is a software tool that offers comprehensive features for software development, such as code editing, debugging, compilation, and project management.

The base environment for reproducing the code examples of this book:

- A text editor: graphical (VS Code, Atom, Geany, etc.) or terminal (VIM, Emacs, Nano, Pico, etc.).

- A workstation with either the `ansible` or `ansible-core` installed packages.

We recommend using Visual Studio Code as the preferred IDE, which can be freely downloaded at **https://code.visualstudio.com**.

Conventions Used in the Book

Throughout the book, we encounter numerous examples and terminal commands. The Ansible language primarily utilizes YAML and INI formats for syntax. When not specified in the text, assume the file format is YAML. The code adheres to the latest YAML specification. YAML, known for its simplicity, readability, and broad compatibility with programming languages, allows for a concise representation of complex data structures. It is widely used for configuration files and data exchange, similar to JSON but with Python-style indentation and a more compact format for lists and dictionary statements.

The INI format is frequently used for inventory and the Ansible configuration file. It is a straightforward configuration file format utilizing key-value pairs and sections for storing settings and preferences in a human-readable manner.

Many terminal commands are standard Linux commands, indicated inline (e.g., ansible `[command]`) or in a code block (with or without line numbers). For instance:

```
$ echo Hello World
```

The provided terminal commands follow POSIX conventions and are compatible with Unix-like systems, including Linux, macOS, and BSD. Each command assumes usage by a standard user account when prefixed with the **$** (dollar) symbol or by the root user when prefixed with the **#** (number sign) symbol.

Each Ansible resource (playbook, role, plugin, and collection) adheres to the latest Ansible best practices, validated with the latest release of the Ansible Linter.

However, it's worth noting that specific code snippets intentionally diverge from best practices to reproduce specific behaviors or use cases accurately. This ensures a comprehensive understanding of Ansible, encompassing ideal techniques and real-world scenarios.

Code Bundle and Coloured Images

Please follow the link to download the
Code Bundle and the *Coloured Images* of the book:

https://rebrand.ly/70ltl91

The code bundle for the book is also hosted on GitHub at
https://github.com/bpbpublications/Red-Hat-Ansible-Automation-Platform.
In case there's an update to the code, it will be updated on the existing GitHub repository.

We have code bundles from our rich catalogue of books and videos available at **https://github.com/bpbpublications**. Check them out!

Errata

We take immense pride in our work at BPB Publications and follow best practices to ensure the accuracy of our content to provide with an indulging reading experience to our subscribers. Our readers are our mirrors, and we use their inputs to reflect and improve upon human errors, if any, that may have occurred during the publishing processes involved. To let us maintain the quality and help us reach out to any readers who might be having difficulties due to any unforeseen errors, please write to us at :

errata@bpbonline.com

Your support, suggestions and feedbacks are highly appreciated by the BPB Publications' Family.

Piracy

If you come across any illegal copies of our works in any form on the internet, we would be grateful if you would provide us with the location address or website name. Please contact us at **business@bpbonline.com** with a link to the material.

If you are interested in becoming an author

If there is a topic that you have expertise in, and you are interested in either writing or contributing to a book, please visit **www.bpbonline.com**. We have worked with thousands of developers and tech professionals, just like you, to help them share their insights with the global tech community. You can make a general application, apply for a specific hot topic that we are recruiting an author for, or submit your own idea.

Reviews

Please leave a review. Once you have read and used this book, why not leave a review on the site that you purchased it from? Potential readers can then see and use your unbiased opinion to make purchase decisions. We at BPB can understand what you think about our products, and our authors can see your feedback on their book. Thank you!

For more information about BPB, please visit **www.bpbonline.com**.

Join our book's Discord space

Join the book's Discord Workspace for Latest updates, Offers, Tech happenings around the world, New Release and Sessions with the Authors:

https://discord.bpbonline.com

Table of Contents

CHAPTER 1

Getting Started with the Ansible Automation Platform

Introduction

This chapter introduces us to the Ansible Automation technology and tools. We are going to approach the evolution of automation for the enterprise audience of the Ansible Automation Platform.

Structure

In this chapter, we will discuss the following topics:

- Brief introduction and reference
- Overview of Ansible Automation Platform
- What is Ansible
- Ansible architecture
- Ansible language
- Create Ansible Playbooks and Content

Objectives

After studying this chapter, you should be able to understand what Ansible is, its architecture, and how to write Ansible code. These are the foundation of the Ansible Automation Platform that we are going to learn in the following chapters.

Brief introduction and reference

Welcome to this book about the Ansible Automation Platform. We are going to explore the most interesting automation platform in the market. Ansible is the automation technology adopted by many organizations worldwide.

Worldwide analysts see growth in the adoption of automation technologies in every industry and sector. **Infrastructure and operations (I&O)** leaders are rethinking how infrastructures are utilized and managed. Gartner predicts 70% of organizations to implement infrastructure automation by 2025[1]. A prediction of a digital revolution with automation is mentioned in the *European DevOps software tools forecast, 2021–2025* of IDC[2]. All the major information technology analysts agree that automation is going to play a central role in the IT infrastructure of tomorrow.

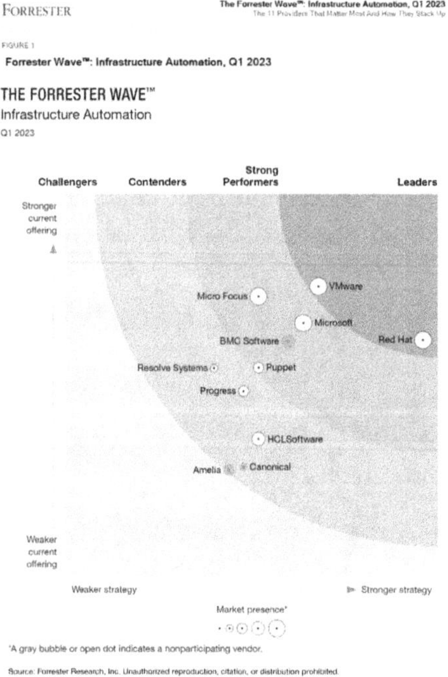

Figure 1.1: Forrester Wave™ Infrastructure Automation report.

---

[1] https://www.gartner.com/en/newsroom/press-releases/2022-10-03-gartner-survey-finds-85-percent-of-infrastructure-and-operations-leaders-without-full-automation-expect-to-increase-automation-within-three-years

[2] https://www.idc.com/getdoc.jsp?containerId=EUR148592321

Red Hat, specifically focused on the Ansible Automation Platform, has been named a leader in the *Q1, 2023 Forrester Wave™* infrastructure automation report, as shown in *Figure 1.1*. The competition was between the top 11 vendors: *Amelia, BMC Software, Canonical, HCL Software, Micro Focus, Microsoft, Progress, Puppet, Red Hat, Resolve Systems*, and *VMware*. The evaluation of each vendor on 30 different criteria ranging from a comprehensive breadth of native capabilities to integrations and ecosystems.

Overview of Ansible Automation Platform

Ansible Automation Platform is a comprehensive IT automation platform designed to simplify and accelerate complex IT tasks across hybrid and multi-cloud environments. It combines the power of Ansible Automation with enterprise-grade features, such as role-based access control, workflow automation, and analytics, to help organizations automate their IT processes and streamline their operations. Please refer to the following figure:

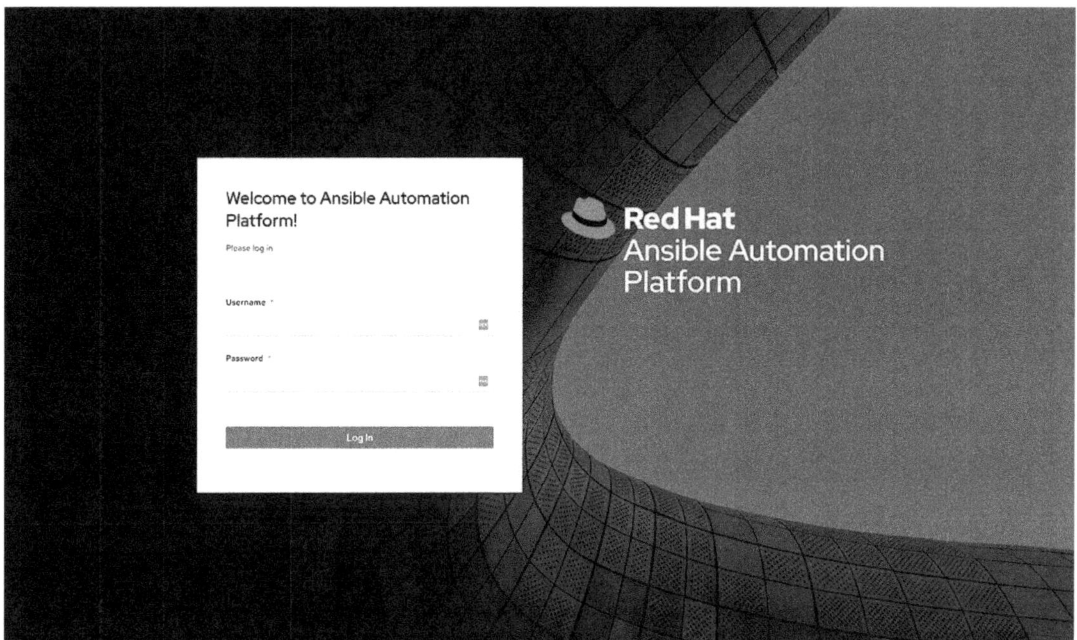

Figure 1.2: *The login screen of the Ansible Automation Platform*

The platform consists of several components, including the Ansible Core, which is the automation engine that executes Ansible Playbooks; the Ansible Automation Controller, which is a web-based GUI that provides a centralized interface for managing Ansible Playbooks, roles, and inventory; and the Ansible automation hub, which is a hub for finding, reusing, and sharing Ansible resources and content.

With the Ansible Automation Platform, organizations can automate their IT infrastructure and application delivery, enforce security and compliance policies, and collaborate and share their automation content with their teams. It supports a wide range of IT operations use cases, including configuration management, application deployment, network automation, and security automation.

IT leaders use every day the Ansible Platform to implement **Infrastructure as Code (IaC)**, **Configuration as a Code (CaC)**, Policy as a Code, Code Pipelines, Orchestration (K8s), DevSecOps, self-healing infrastructure, and event-driven automation.

The first release of the Ansible Automation Platform was in 2020, previously known as **Ansible Tower**. Ansible Tower gives every IT department the ability to securely store inventories, credentials, projects, and playbooks and manage **role-based access control (RBAC)** in a RESTful API and web user interface. The Ansible Tower is based on the open-source AWX project supercharged with much commercial integration with many enterprise-grade technologies.

The automation controller was completely redesigned since release 2.0, implementing a new container design.

The platform is expanded with additional components that integrate together for a great automation experience.

The main components of the Ansible Automation Platform are:

- **Automation controller**: The control plane for the Ansible Automation Platform.

- **Automation hub**: Find, use, and extend Ansible resources.

- **Automation execution environments**: Packaged as containers, portable environments for executing Ansible playbooks and roles.

- **Automation mesh**: Automate at scale in a cloud-native way.

- **Ansible content collections**: Ready-to-use certified modules.

- **Ansible content tools**: Tools to create custom Automation execution environments.

- **Red Hat insights for Ansible Automation Platform**: Acquire statistics and metrics on our automation savings.

IT Professionals and organizations take advantage of the full experience with the Red Hat Ansible Automation Subscription and all the connected resources. It also includes the full power of Red Hat's award-winning Customer Portal in the Standard business day (8 AM to 5 PM) or Premium 24x7. It is possible to try the Red Hat Ansible Automation Platform with the 60-day trial self-supported subscription, which includes a subscription to Red Hat Enterprise Linux, Red Hat Insights for Red Hat Ansible Automation Platform, Red Hat Smart Management, and Red Hat Ansible Automation Platform hosted services on Red Hat Hybrid Cloud Console. Independent developers take advantage of the Red Hat Developer Subscription for Individuals (SKU RH00798) program. It is a single subscription renewable every year that allows them to install on a maximum of 16 Red Hat Enterprise

Linux systems, physical or virtual, regardless of system size. Those 16 nodes might be used for demos, prototyping, QA, small production uses, and cloud access.

What is Ansible

Ansible is an open-source software platform for automating and managing IT infrastructure, including deploying applications and configuring systems. It allows us to write playbooks, which are sets of tasks in YAML (a human-readable language) that describe how to perform tasks on one or more remote servers. The first release of Ansible was on February 20, 2012. *Michael DeHaan* created the Ansible tool and started advertising the first initial community. Please refer to the following figure:

Figure 1.3: The Ansible logo

Ansible uses a client-server architecture, with a central control server (the Ansible control machine) and managed nodes (the servers that we want to automate tasks on). The control machine connects to the managed nodes over SSH (a secure network protocol) and runs the playbooks on them.

One of the key benefits of Ansible is that it uses a simple, easy-to-learn syntax and does not require any special programming skills. This makes it an appealing choice for IT professionals who need to automate tasks but may not have much programming experience.

Ansible can be used to automate a wide range of tasks, including the deployment of applications, the configuration of systems, the provisioning of cloud infrastructure, and the management of security and compliance. It is commonly used in DevOps (a software development methodology that emphasizes collaboration between development and operations teams) to automate the build, test, and deployment of applications.

The Ansible Automation Platform includes a full installation of Ansible underneath the Ansible Automation Controller.

The Ansible open-source project and community are supported by Red Hat (part of IBM). Red Hat actively works with other organizations and individuals committed to open-source software and automation. The community is constantly growing and evolving, with new contributors and users joining every day.

Ansible architecture

The Ansible architecture includes two machines: the controller and the target node. The Ansible Controller has Ansible installed and executes the automation against the target nodes. The Ansible Automation Controller includes a full installation of Ansible.

The target nodes do not need any Ansible agent or special tool installed. Ansible is so-called **agentless**. The connection parameters vary depending on the target operating systems. Ansible connects to target machines using the following protocols:

- OpenSSH for Unix-like operating systems: Linux, macOS, and so on.

- WinRM for Windows operating systems.

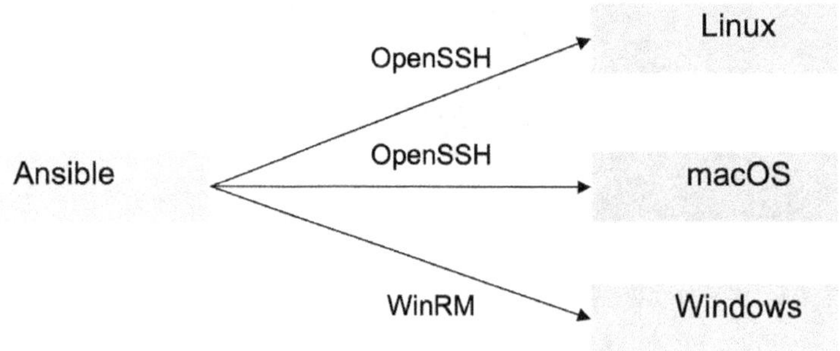

Figure 1.4: The Ansible architecture

Linux and macOS target

Ansible connects to any POSIX, Unix-like operating system in managed hosts using the OpenSSH protocol. The long list includes any Linux distributions, Unix, macOS, BSD, and so on. OpenSSH is a free, open-source implementation of the **Secure Shell (SSH)** protocol. It is a network protocol that provides secure communication between computers, allowing us to remotely log in to another computer, execute commands, and transfer files securely over a network.

The SSH protocol uses encryption to secure the connection between the client (our computer) and the server (the remote computer). It authenticates the client and server using public key cryptography and establishes a secure channel over which data can be transmitted.

OpenSSH is widely used to access remote servers and systems, and it is the default SSH implementation on most Linux and Unix-based systems. It is also available as third-party software on other operating systems, such as Windows and macOS.

OpenSSH provides various tools and utilities for managing SSH connections, such as ssh for establishing an SSH connection, SCP for securely transferring files between computers, and SFTP for transferring files over an SSH connection. It also includes a **secure copy (SCP)** utility for transferring files between computers and a **secure file transfer protocol (SFTP)** for transferring files over an SSH connection.

Windows Target

Ansible connects to Windows-managed hosts using **Windows Remote Management (WinRM)**. This Microsoft technology allows us to execute commands remotely on a Windows machine. This is based on the WS-Management protocol, which is a standard protocol for the remote management of devices and systems. At the moment of writing this book, Ansible supports the most commonly used Windows client and servers: Windows Server 2008, Windows Server 2008 R2, Windows Server 2012, Windows Server 2012 R2, Windows Server 2016, Windows Server 2019, Windows Server 2022, Windows 7, Windows 8.1, Windows 10, and Windows 11.

WinRM allows us to run scripts remotely, perform system administration tasks, and manage Windows servers remotely. It can be used to remotely manage a single machine or a group of machines in a network.

To use WinRM, we need to enable it on the remote machine and then use a tool such as Windows PowerShell or a third-party tool like Ansible to connect to the remote machine and execute add the following text at the end of the sentence "using Enable-PSRemoting PowerShell cmdlet".

Overall, WinRM is a useful tool for remotely managing and automating tasks on Windows machines. It can save time and effort by allowing us to manage multiple machines from a single location. It can be especially useful in large organizations where there may be hundreds or thousands of servers to manage.

Ansible nowadays expanded the connection capabilities to storage & network devices, container technologies, virtualization (VMware), orchestration technologies (Kubernetes), and cloud providers.

Tip: We can run our Ansible Playbook in the current machine using the setting ansible_connection variable to the "local" value.

Ansible language

Ansible is an open-source infrastructure automation tool. It enables us to manage and control a large number of systems in an automated and standardized way. The main use cases are infrastructure automation and configuration management, but they can be used to configure operating systems, deploy applications, and perform other tasks on remote servers.

The architecture of Ansible consists of a few key components:

- **Control machine**: The machine that runs the Ansible commands and playbooks. It can be any machine with Ansible installed, a server, or a local desktop or laptop.

- **Inventory**: The inventory is a list of target hosts for Ansible. It can be a static file or a dynamic inventory that is generated at runtime.

- **Modules**: Modules are the execution blocks of Ansible. They are small programs that perform a specific task, such as installing a package or starting a service.

- **Playbooks**: Playbooks are written in YAML format and contain a series of tasks. They can be used to automate complex processes and are a key component of Ansible Automation.

- **Plugins**: Plugins are programs that extend Ansible's core functionality. They can be used to modify the behavior of Ansible modules or to add new features.

In a nutshell, Ansible connects to the systems in our inventory and runs the tasks specified in our playbooks. It is coded in the YAML format using a simple, human-readable syntax.

Let us break down one by one the Ansible components. An Ansible Controller could be any computer with Ansible installed on it. The installation of Ansible is easy for any modern operating system. We can check a successful installation and the currently running version using the command:

```
ansible --version
```

The ansible command executes one module on the inventory. This behavior is called **Ansible Ad-hoc**.

The Ansible platform includes many command line tools and utilities (for example **ansible**, **ansible-playbook**, **ansible-galaxy**, **ansible-inventory**, and so on). Every Ansible installation also includes the Ansible collection **ansible.builtin** where all the main modules reside.

The inventory is the list of target hosts. More often, is the text file stored in the default location **/etc/ansible/host.** Most of the Ansible tools support the inventory overriding specifying the **-i** parameter. The Ansible inventory file formats supported are INI, JSON, and YAML. We can also have multiple files and combine them together in execution time. In some use cases, such as virtual machines, container orchestrators, or cloud computing providers, the inventory could be generated dynamically using an external script that returns a JSON inventory format. The dynamic inventory feature is very useful in fast-paced environments where the enumeration of running services is critical and fast-changing.

After the initial configuration, we only require an inventory and a playbook. The playbook is a YAML file that contains the sequence of tasks to achieve a common goal. The minimal playbook has some sections where we could specify the target host(s) and a sequence of tasks. There are also additional sections to specify the additional steps or local variables. Each task is performed by Ansible modules.

An Ansible module is the key component that executes an Ansible action of a target host. There are so many Ansible modules that are easy to perform any action without reinventing the wheel.

Additionally, we can extend the core functionality by creating some plugins to expand the native functionality or connect to a new service or API.

We can implement code reuse in our organization by creating some roles or collections. The code could be created by ourselves, our colleagues, vendors, or third parties.

There are different types of plugins based on the type of integration that we would like to achieve.

We can distribute our code and plugins to our IT department or the internet. There is a great selection of roles and collections on the Ansible Galaxy website.

Create Ansible playbooks and resources

We can create Ansible resources in our favorite text editor. Ansible does not require to use of a specific IDE. However, the VS Code is the favorite choice by automation professionals nowadays.

The minimal development environment consists of the following:

A text editor: Terminal (VIM, Emacs, Nano, Pico, and so on) or GUI (VS Code, Atom, Geany, and so on).

A workstation with the **ansible** or **ansible-core** installed packages.

Let us deep dive into the first Ansible Playbook to display the **Hi!** message on the screen:

```
---

- name: Message example
  hosts: all
  tasks:
    - name: Display a message
      ansible.builtin.debug:
        msg: "Hi!"
...
```

Let us navigate line by line through the Ansible playbook:

- Beginning of the file (**---**)

- Name of the play (**Message example**)

- Target hosts of execution (**all** of the inventory)

- Beginning of tasks

- The first task is named **Display a message**.

- Module **ansible.builtin.debug** (to display messages onscreen)

- Argument **msg** of module debug (the message that we would like to display)

- End of file (**...**)

We can execute the Hello World Ansible Playbook using the following **ansible-playbook** command:

```
ansible-playbook -i inventory.ini hi.yml
```

With:

- **ansible-playbook** is the command line utility included in every ansible installation.

- The **-i** parameter specifies which inventory file to use. In this case, the **inventory.ini** file is in the current directory.

- The **hi.yml** parameter is the name of the Ansible Playbooks file.

The easiest Ansible inventory is against localhost, which even is very convenient in the development stage, but it is rarely used in the production stage.

The local inventory in the INI format:

```
localhost ansible_connection="local"
```

The command produces the following output:

```
PLAY [Message example] ********************************************************

TASK [Gathering Facts] ********************************************************

ok: [localhost]
TASK [Display a message] ******************************************************

ok: [localhost] => {
    "msg": "Hi!"
}
PLAY RECAP ********************************************************************

localhost: ok=2    changed=0    unreachable=0    failed=0    skipped=0
rescued=0    ignored=0
```

Each line of the output highlights a step of the execution.

In the output of the execution of the **hi.yml** via the command **ansible-playbook**. The first parameter is the inventory file, and the second is the playbook.

The play executes against the target host **localhost** node. The output is self-explanatory in the step-by-step implementation.

When the command is successful, the outcome highlights in green color. Orange is an indicator of a warning message, and red for an error.

Let us go line by line:

- The automation executes the first **PLAY** named **Message example**. It simply prints the play name for easy debugging of the code. The following line in the output is the first **TASK** called **Gathering Facts**, which means acquiring some system information (facts in Ansible jargon) from the remote hosts.

- The result of the operation is an **ok** status followed by the target node name, **localhost**, in this case. The green color confirms that the operation was successful.

- The second **TASK** is actually the one that we defined in the code, displaying the **"Hi!"** message on the screen. We usually see the **ok** status and the **localhost** target node.

- The last line is a **PLAY RECAP** table that summarizes the target host(s) and the task reported status. In this case, only two **ok** statuses against **localhost**.

The **PLAY RECAP** shows how many **TASK** terminated in the statuses: **ok**, **changed**, **unreachable**, **failed**, **skipped**, **rescued**, and **ignored**.

Tip: The extra task called Gathering Facts acquired system information about the target node and made it available as Ansible Facts.

Conclusion

Ansible Automation Platform is a modern platform to enable our IT department team to save time and reduce human errors. It takes advantage of the container's design and integrates many state-of-the-art features for our hybrid cloud infrastructure. In the following chapters, we are going to learn what are the installation scenarios and how to extract the best value from the system. Integrating with the most common technologies in the market.

Points to remember

- The Ansible Controller executes the automation against the target host.

- Ansible executes a common operation to target hosts using modules.

- Ansible Automation Platform simplifies the management of inventories and playbook projects.

- Ansible automates Unix-like operating systems (Linux, macOS, and so on) and Windows.

Multiple choice questions

1. **What is not a characteristic of a modern data center?**

   a. Scalability

   b. None of these

   c. Flexibility

   d. High availability

2. **What protocol is used by Ansible to communicate with Linux target hosts?**

   a. WinRM for Windows operating systems

   b. We can use `ansible_connection=local` for current hosts

   c. None of these

   d. OpenSSH for Unix-like operating systems: Linux, macOS, and so on

3. **Is it possible to use Windows as an Ansible Controller?**

   a. True

   b. False

4. **What is the expected output of the ping module?**

   a. `ping: ping`

   b. no route to host

   c. `ping: 1`

   d. `ping: pong`

Answers

1. b

2. d

3. b

4. d

Questions

1. What is an Ansible inventory?

2. How to write an Ansible Playbook?

3. Explain what the Ansible Galaxy is.

4. What are the components of the Ansible Automation Platform?

Key terms

- **Control machine:** This is the machine where we run the Ansible commands and playbooks. It can be any machine with Ansible installed, such as our local desktop or laptop.

- **Inventory:** The inventory is a list of the systems that Ansible will manage. It can be a static file or a dynamic inventory that is generated at runtime.

- **Modules:** Modules are the building blocks of Ansible. They are small programs that perform a specific task, such as installing a package or starting a service.

- **Playbooks:** Playbooks are written in YAML and contain a series of tasks to be executed. They can be used to automate complex processes and are a key component of Ansible's automation capabilities.

- **Plugins:** Plugins are small programs that extend Ansible's core functionality. They can be used to modify the behavior of Ansible modules or to add new features.

Join our book's Discord space

Join the book's Discord Workspace for Latest updates, Offers, Tech happenings around the world, New Release and Sessions with the Authors:

https://discord.bpbonline.com

CHAPTER 2

Ansible Automation Platform Architecture

Introduction

This chapter introduces us to the Ansible automation architecture. We are going to explore the key components of the platform architecture and the main design of the Ansible Automation Platform.

Structure

In this chapter, we will discuss the following topics:

- Ansible Automation Platform architecture
- Ansible controller
- Ansible automation hub
- Ansible execution environment
- Key learning

Objectives

After studying this unit, we should be able to understand the Ansible automation design and the key component of the Ansible Automation Platform. These topics are fundamental for understanding the installation scenarios of the following chapter.

Ansible Automation Platform architecture

The Ansible Automation Platform architecture is designed to provide a comprehensive solution for managing and automating IT infrastructure. The official logo of the product is a trademark of Red Hat, as shown in *Figure 2.1*:

Figure 2.1: *Ansible Automation Platform logo*

It consists of several components that work together to enable efficient automation and orchestration of tasks.

The architecture of the Ansible Automation Platform is formed by the following components, as shown in *Figure 2.2:*

- Automation controller (formerly Ansible Tower)

- Automation hub

- Automation mesh

- Execution environment

Please refer to the following figure:

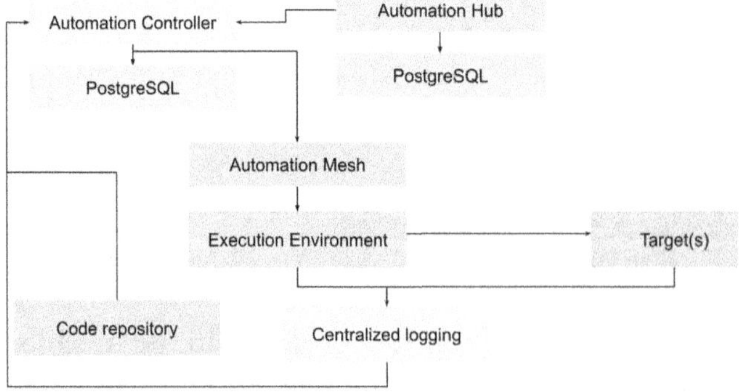

Figure 2.2: *Ansible Automation Platform architecture*

The automation controller is the key element of the Ansible Automation Platform. It was formerly the Ansible Tower with a new container-oriented design. We can clearly see this design pattern in the Ansible execution environment that execute our code connecting to the target node(s).

Learn about the installation scenarios and the system requirement in *Chapter 3, Platform Installation Scenarios.*

Ansible Automation Platform also includes additional cloud components beneficial for our organization. Please refer to the following figure:

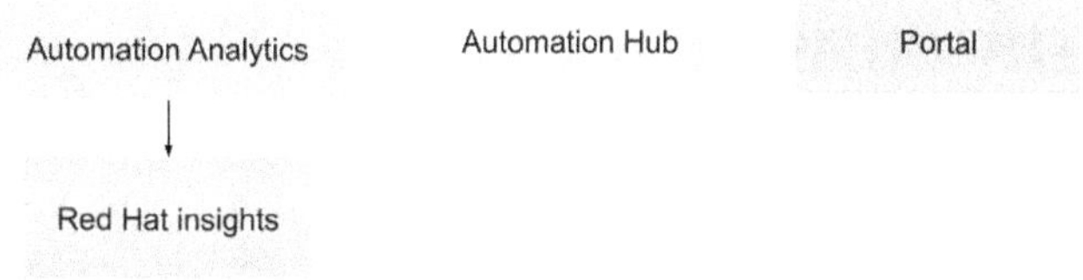

Figure 2.3: Red Hat online services

The following three Red Hat online services are available when we subscribe to the Ansible Automation Platform subscriptions:

- Automation analytics (connected with Red Hat Insight)

- Automation hub

- Red Hat portal

Automation analytics collects data from Ansible Tower/automation controller and provides insights and reporting capabilities. It helps in tracking and analyzing automation job runs, inventory changes, and other automation-related metrics. Automation analytics enables organizations to gain visibility into their automation activities, identify trends, and make data-driven decisions to improve efficiency and troubleshoot issues.

Key features and benefits of automation analytics include:

- **Insights and visibility**: Automation analytics offers a centralized dashboard that provides a visual representation of automation activities, job status, and performance metrics. It enables users to gain insights into their automation environment and track the efficiency and effectiveness of automation workflows.

- **Reporting and trend analysis**: Automation analytics generates reports and visualizations based on the collected data. It helps organizations identify trends, patterns, and bottlenecks in their automation processes. These Insights can be used to optimize automation workflows, improve resource allocation, and make data-driven decisions.

- **Troubleshooting and issue resolution**: With automation analytics, users can analyze historical data to troubleshoot issues, identify root causes, and take proactive measures to prevent similar problems in the future. It provides a historical view of job runs, inventory changes, and other automation events, making it easier to investigate and resolve issues.

- **Customization and integration**: Automation analytics allows users to create custom reports and visualizations based on their specific requirements. It also provides integration capabilities with other analytics and monitoring tools, enabling organizations to incorporate Ansible automation data into their existing monitoring and analytics workflows.

Automation controller

In today's fast-paced digital landscape, organizations are constantly seeking ways to streamline and scale their automation processes. Red Hat Ansible Automation Platform's automation controller offers a comprehensive solution for defining, operating, scaling, and delegating automation across our organization. The automation controller is the masterpiece of the AAP because it executes our automation code that revolutionizes our automation workflows.

The following are the key features and benefits of the automation controller:

- **Enhanced control and efficiency**:

   The automation controller serves as the control plane for the Ansible Automation Platform, replacing Ansible Tower. With its intuitive **user interface (UI)**, **role-based access control (RBAC)**, and advanced workflows, the automation controller empowers teams to scale their automation initiatives with greater efficiency and flexibility. It helps standardize automation deployment, delegation, and auditing, reducing sprawl and ensuring consistent processes.

- **Centralized management**:

   Managing automation becomes more streamlined with the automation controller. It provides a centralized user interface and RESTful API for managing inventory, launching and scheduling workflows, tracking changes, and integrating reporting. This centralized approach simplifies administration, enhances visibility, and enables collaboration across teams.

- **Automation topology visualization**:

   The automation controller introduces the automation topology viewer, a powerful feature that visually represents complex automation topologies. It graphically showcases various nodes, including hop, execution, hybrid, and control nodes, across multiple sites. This visualization empowers administrators to understand and optimize their automation workflows, improving overall efficiency and reliability.

- **Enhanced architecture and performance**:

  The automation controller features a decentralized, modular application architecture. It separates the control and execution planes, allowing for greater scalability and flexibility. The platform leverages execution environments, providing isolation and resource allocation for running automation tasks efficiently. With improved performance, enhanced job output filters, and stricter content security policies, the automation controller ensures a seamless and secure automation experience.

- **Upgraded user experience**:

  The automation controller's WebUI has been refactored to the design pattern PatternFly 4.0, offering a modern and intuitive user experience. The UI redesign increases usability, making it easier for users to navigate and interact with the platform. Additionally, distinct **edit** and **read** views enhance security and control, allowing administrators to define granular access permissions.

- **Reliable infrastructure and integration**:

  The automation controller leverages the latest release of the PostgreSQL database, providing a robust and scalable database foundation for storing execution data. It is installed from RHEL modules, ensuring compatibility and ease of installation. Furthermore, partitioned access enhances performance, enabling concurrent access to the platform by multiple users without compromising efficiency.

The automation controller product is an excellent tool for organizations seeking to streamline and scale their automation processes. By providing a centralized control plane, intuitive UI, advanced workflows, and enhanced scalability, it enables enterprises to automate with confidence, reducing variance and increasing efficiency. With features like automation topology visualization and improved architecture, the automation controller empowers organizations to take their automation initiatives to new heights. Embrace the power of automation controllers and unlock the full potential of our enterprise automation journey. The Ansible controller is based on the open-source project AWX actively maintained by Red Hat. The difference between Ansible controller and AWX is that the first incorporate many integration and enterprise technologies that the open-source project.

Dashboard

The dashboard is accessible using every modern browser and presents statistical data about the execution of automation scripts in our environment. The initial window presents the login authentication, as shown in *Figure 1.2*. The connection is encrypted using the HTTPS protocol with a self-signed certificate for the initial connection that we can customize with the certification authority used in our organization. Many organizations use a commercial certificate for a trustful connection to avoid man-in-the-middle attacks. See *Chapter 5,*

Integrate Authentication, for **role-based access control** (**RBAC**) integration with popular enterprise authentication such as Active Directory and LDAP.

We can easily verify the current version of the Ansible Automation Platform via the user interface, as shown in *Figure 2.4*, which displays version 4.3.6. The hackly visualization uses the cowsay command line tool as in the early days of the Ansible tool.

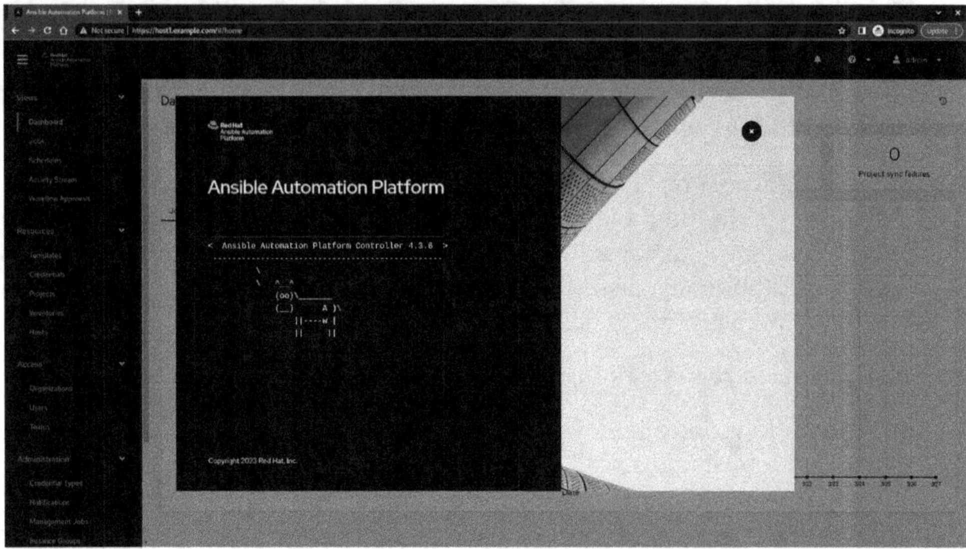

Figure 2.4: *The current version of the Ansible controller*

The dashboard of the Ansible controller is similar to the one displayed in *Figure 2.5*:

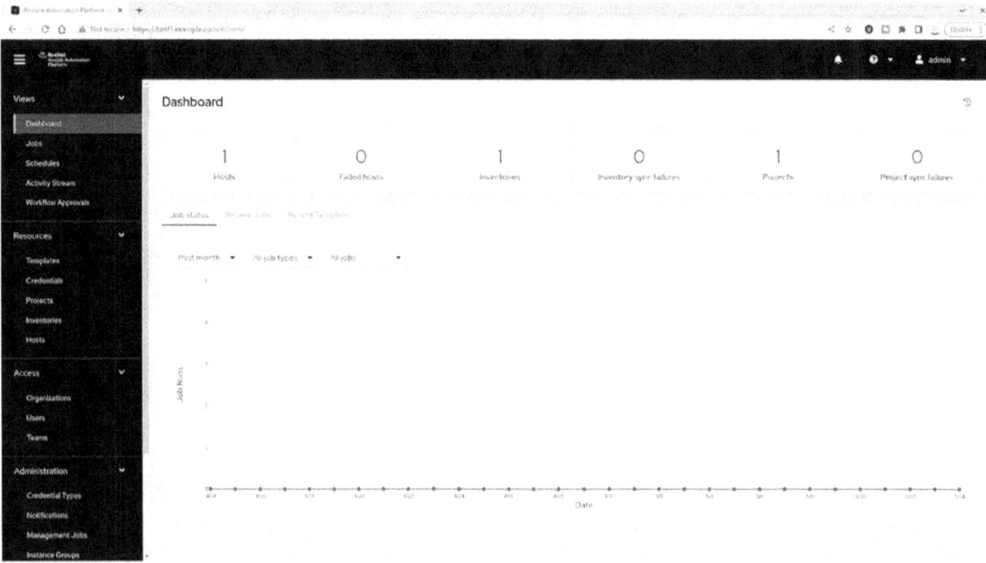

Figure 2.5: *The dashboard of the Ansible automation controller*

Projects

In the Ansible controller, a project refers to a logical group of Ansible Playbooks, roles, and other related files that are used to automate tasks and manage infrastructure. Projects provide a structured way to organize and manage our Ansible code and resources.

Ansible Playbooks and playbook directories can be managed within a project by either placing them manually under the project base path on our server or by utilizing a **source code management** (**SCM**) system supported by an automation controller, such as Git, Subversion, or Red Hat Insights.

When manually managing playbooks, we create one or more directories to store the playbooks under the project base path. We can then create or copy playbook files into the playbook directory. It is important to ensure that the playbook directory and files are owned by the same UNIX user and group that the automation controller service runs as and that the permissions are appropriate for the playbook directories and files.

If using source control, we can configure our playbooks to use a specific SCM type, such as Git or Subversion, by providing the SCM URL, branch/tag/commit details and the necessary credentials. The project preferred to implement the GitOps directory structure standard for storing contents. Each project could have an actual directory structure slightly different, but this is the commonly recommended by Ansible best practices:

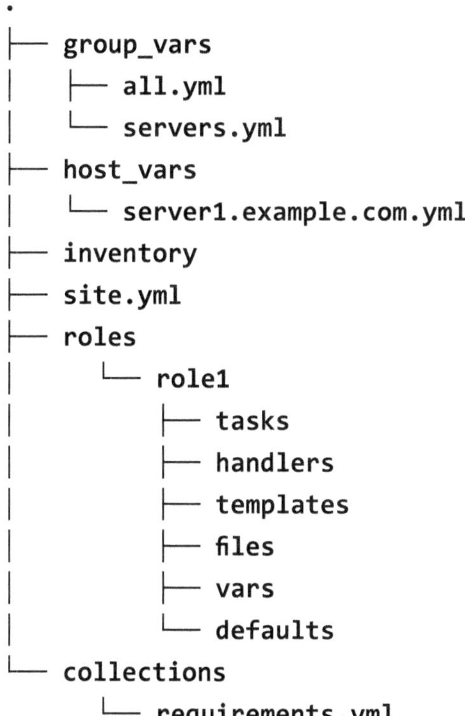

```
.
├── group_vars
│   ├── all.yml
│   └── servers.yml
├── host_vars
│   └── server1.example.com.yml
├── inventory
├── site.yml
├── roles
│   └── role1
│       ├── tasks
│       ├── handlers
│       ├── templates
│       ├── files
│       ├── vars
│       └── defaults
└── collections
        └── requirements.yml
```

The directories structure contains the **group_vars** and **host_vars** directories to specify Ansible variables specific for different groups or hosts. In this case, there are two groups: **all** and **servers**. There is also one single host, **server1.example.com**.

The **inventory** file is the Ansible inventory in INI format containing the hosts and groups. The main playbook is called **site.yml** and is usually the first Ansible Playbook to be executed with all the important tasks.

Under the **roles** directory, we can store custom role(s) for the project. In the example, there is the **role1**.

It is possible to specify the **collections** directory with a **requirements.yml** file with the required Ansible collections to be retrieved via the automation hub.

This directory structure helps to maintain a well-organized codebase and represents the standard adopted by the majority of the organization worldwide because it adheres to the Ansible best practices.

The GitOps directory structure stored in a **source code management** (**SCM**) system enables us to keep our playbooks version-controlled and easily update them when changes are made to the source control repository.

Projects have various statuses that indicate their current state. The following statuses are for any project:

- **Pending**: The source control update has been created but has yet to be queued or started.

- **Waiting**: The source control update is in the queue waiting to be executed.

- **Running**: The source control update is currently in progress.

- **Successful**: The last source control update for this project succeeded.

- **Failed**: The last source control update for this project failed.

- **Error**: The last source control update job failed to run at all (deprecated).

- **Canceled**: The last source control update for the project was canceled.

- **Never updated**: The project is configured for source control but has never been updated.

- **OK**: The project is not configured for source control and is correctly in place (deprecated).

- **Missing**: Projects need to be present in the project base path (applicable for manual or source control managed projects).

To update an existing SCM-based project, we can select the project and initiate a refresh to fetch the latest details from the configured source control repository.

The following *Figure 2.6* shows an example of **Projects** in the automation controller dashboard.

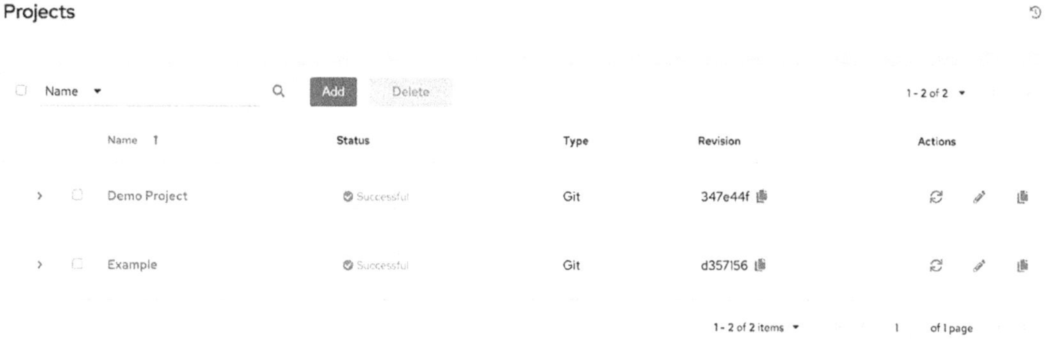

Figure 2.6: Projects in automation controller

When using Red Hat Insights as a source, we can apply the so-called **remediation** Ansible Playbook that executes updates or corrective operations in our fleet.

Jobs

Each automation script in our automation controller that executes an Ansible Playbook in our **Project** is managed as a **Job Template**. Please refer to the following figure:

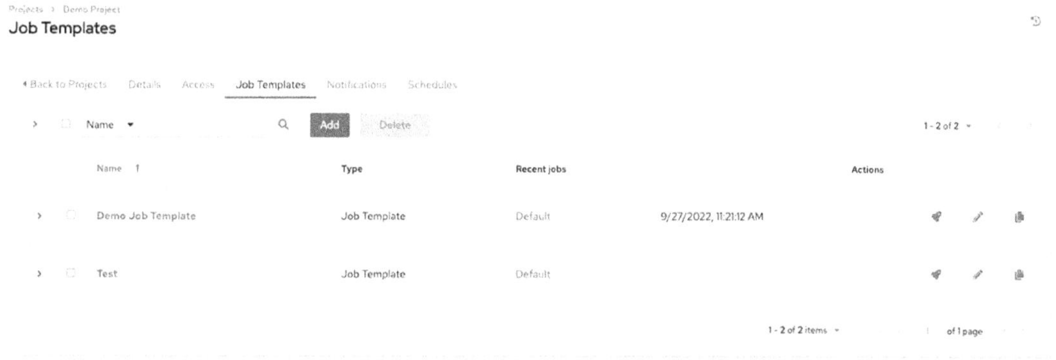

Figure 2.7: Job Templates list in automation controller

A job template specifies exactly the Ansible Playbook to execute, all the parameters, the credentials needed to connect to the target host(s) or additional resources, and the inventory. We can even decide to request some parameter from the user using the Prompt on launch feature. The window has many parameters, but the mandatory fields are only the project, playbook, and inventory, as shown in *Figure 2.8*:

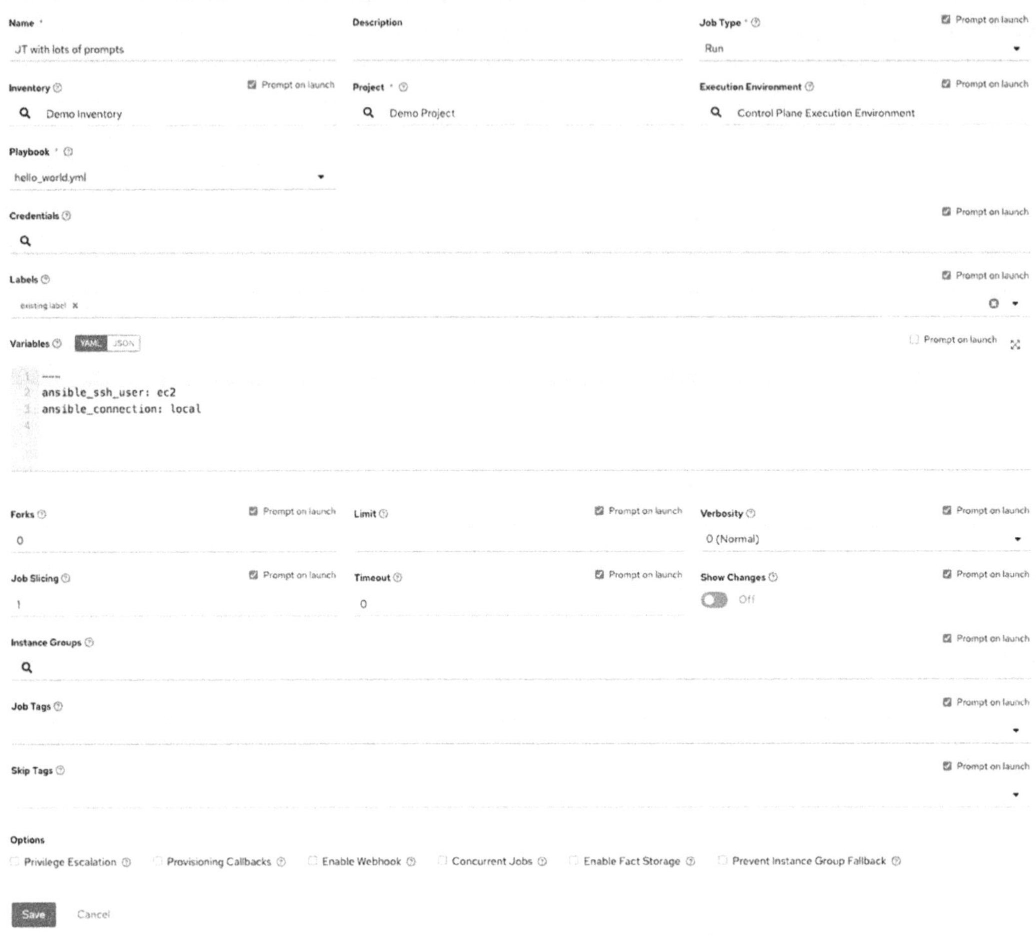

Figure 2.8: *Job Template creation in automation controller*

Advanced users can take advantage of fine-tuning of all the others. For example, we can specify a specific Ansible execution environment for each job or build a custom according to the requirements of our organization.

We can even schedule the programmatic execution of our jobs with a specific cadence, as shown in *Figure 2.9*:

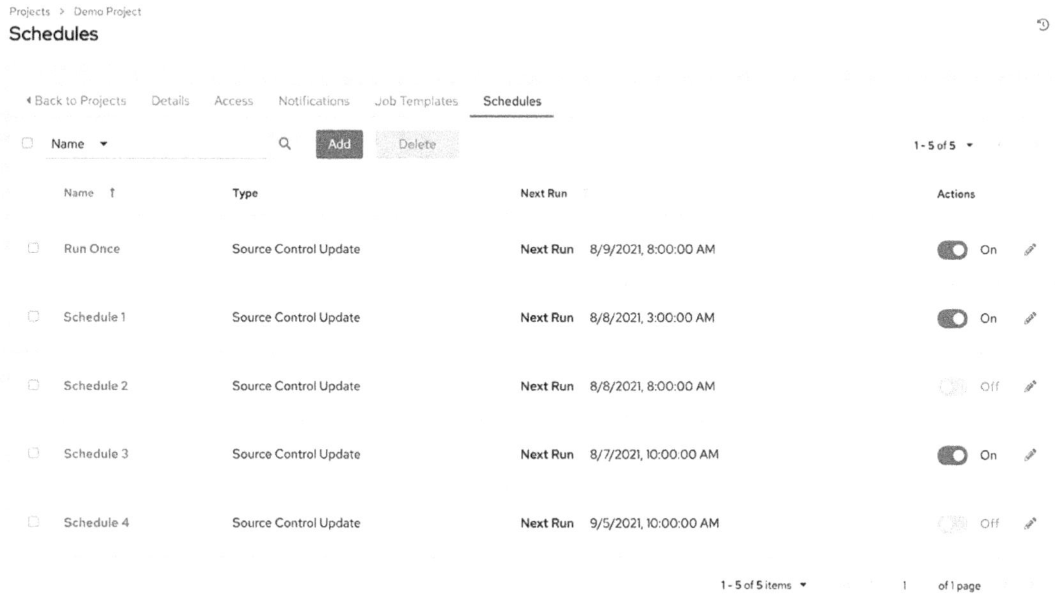

Figure 2.9: Scheduled Job Templates in automation controller

After each execution, with can trigger the execution of a notification using traditional email or more advanced integration with Slack or other instant messaging systems.

A special type of job is the callback job designed for the initial configuration of instances. The remote host can interact with a special endpoint that triggers the execution of a job.

We can combine multiple jobs together in a workflow so the execution can be concatenated or executed only when a specific return code happens. For example, we can trigger a specific job only on successful execution, on failure or always. Another advantage is that the successor job has full visibility of the variables defined by the predecessor job. Please refer to the following figure:

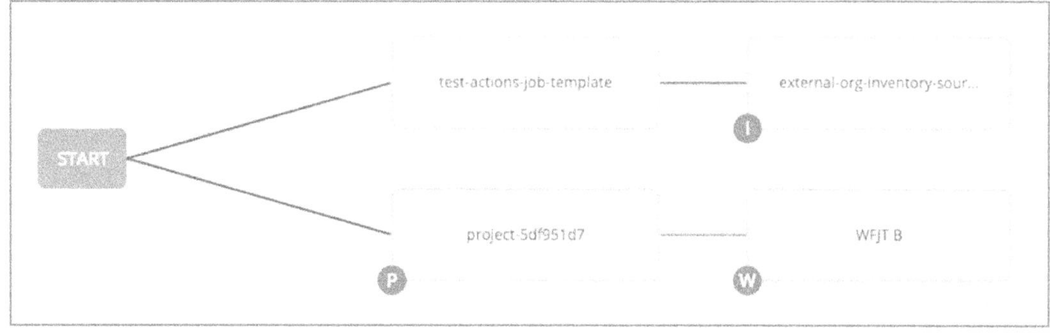

Figure 2.10: The Workflow management

Advanced users typically run every night fact gathering job and cache the results so they can boost the performance in daytime jobs using that data.

API

The Ansible controller exposes a RESTful API that presents the same information as the dashboard. It is used by large organizations to automate, perform and interact programmatically with every single component of the automation controller. The **awx-cli** command line tool and the **ansible.controller** Ansible collection interacts directly with the API to create resources or trigger jobs.

We can also interact via a modern browser by adding the endpoint **/api/v2/** to the automation controller address, as shown in *Figure 2.11*. The API interface accepts all the **HTTP** methods **GET**, **POST**, **PUT**, **DELETE**, and **HEAD**. The endpoint is preferred over an HTTPS connection using the same certification authority certificate of the automation controller dashboard. Some areas of the API require authentication. We can apply using Bearer authentication (also called token authentication) or interactive via our favorite browser.

Please refer to the following figure:

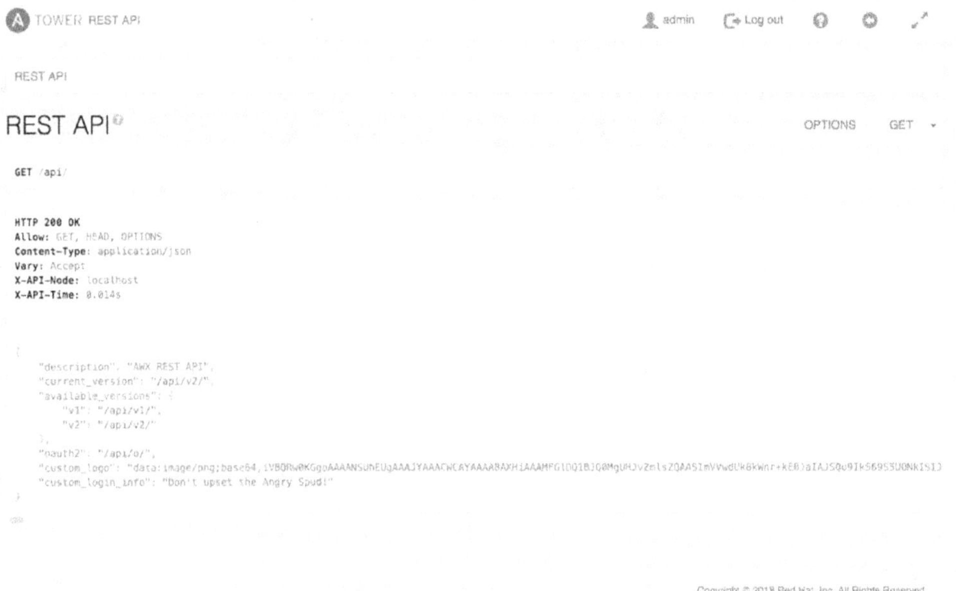

Figure 2.11: The automation controller API

Automation hub

Code reuse is a central theme in every automation journey. Rather than manually maintaining a bunch of code, repositories, and projects, we can use Ansible's standard role and collection to distribute content across our organization. These two formats are also suitable for integrating code created by Red Hat, partners, and third parties.

Roles and collections

Ansible roles and collections are two cornerstones concepts in Ansible that help organize and share reusable automation content.

Ansible roles are a way to organize and package automation content into reusable units. A role is a directory structure containing Ansible tasks, variables, templates, files, and other resources needed to perform a specific automation task. Roles provide a modular and structured approach to organizing automation code, making it easier to reuse, share, and maintain. The Ansible roles are:

- **Reusable**: Roles encapsulate a specific set of tasks and configurations related to a particular automation scenario. They can be reused across different playbooks and projects, promoting code modularity and reducing duplication.

- **Structure and organization**: Roles provide a predefined directory structure that helps organize automation content into logical components. It separates tasks, variables, templates, and other resources, making the automation code more maintainable and easier to understand.

- **Encapsulation**: Roles encapsulate all the necessary tasks, variables, and configurations needed to perform a specific automation task. This encapsulation makes it easier to share and distribute automation content, as roles can be packaged and shared as self-contained units.

- **Role dependencies**: Roles can have dependencies on other roles, allowing for role composition and reuse. This enables the creation of complex automation scenarios by combining and reusing existing roles.

- **Parameterization**: Roles support parameterization through variables, allowing users to customize the behavior of the role by providing values for specific variables during playbook execution.

Ansible collections are a more recent addition to Ansible and provide a way to package and distribute Ansible content, including roles, modules, plugins, and other automation artifacts and resources. Collections offer a centralized and standardized approach to managing and sharing Ansible content across teams and organizations.

Key features and benefits of Ansible collections include:

- **Content distribution**: Collections allow for the distribution of reusable Ansible content as a single package. They provide a convenient way to share and consume roles, modules, plugins, and other automation resources.

- **Namespace and versioning**: Collections introduce a namespace and versioning scheme to ensure content integrity and compatibility. They enable users to easily identify and manage different versions of collections, providing more control over the automation content being used.

- **Extensibility**: Collections provide a mechanism for extending Ansible's core functionality by including custom modules, plugins, and other extensions. This allows users to enhance Ansible's capabilities and tailor it to their specific needs.

- **Collaboration**: Collections facilitate collaboration among Ansible users and contributors. They enable multiple contributors to collaborate on a collection, share their work, and contribute to a standard set of automation content.

- **Centralized management**: Ansible collections can be managed and distributed through a centralized source, such as Ansible Galaxy. This makes it easier to discover, install, and update collections, simplifying the management of automation content within an organization.

Ansible roles provide a modular and reusable approach to organizing automation content within a playbook, while Ansible collections offer a centralized and standardized way to package, distribute, and share Ansible content, including roles, modules, and plugins. Both roles and collections contribute to the scalability, maintainability, and collaborative nature of Ansible automation.

Ansible Galaxy and automation hub

Ansible Galaxy and Ansible automation hub are both platforms that provide a repository for sharing and discovering Ansible content, but they serve different purposes and target different user needs. Here is an explanation of Ansible Galaxy and Ansible automation hub, highlighting their key differences:

Ansible Galaxy is a community-driven platform that allows users to share and find Ansible roles, playbooks, and other content. It is an open-source platform where community members can contribute their Ansible content for others to use. Ansible Galaxy is not part of the Ansible Automation Platform. Ansible Galaxy offers a wide range of community-contributed content, making it a valuable resource for quickly finding and reusing Ansible automation solutions.

Key features of Ansible Galaxy include:

- **Community-contributed content:** Users can access a vast collection of community-developed Ansible roles, playbooks, and collections.

- **Ratings and reviews:** Content in Ansible Galaxy can be rated and reviewed by users, providing insights into the quality and usability of the shared content.

- **Easy integration:** Ansible Galaxy content can be easily integrated into Ansible Playbooks and projects, enabling users to leverage existing automation solutions.

On the other hand, Ansible automation hub is a platform provided as part of the Red Hat Ansible Automation Platform subscription. It offers a curated collection of Ansible Content Collections that are certified, validated, and supported by Red Hat and its partners. Automation hub focuses on providing enterprise-grade content with enhanced security, reliability, and support.

Key features of Ansible automation hub include:

- **Certified and validated content**: Ansible automation hub offers a collection of Ansible Content Collections that have undergone rigorous testing, validation, and certification processes. This ensures that the content meets high-quality standards and can be relied upon in enterprise environments.

- **Red Hat support**: The content available in Ansible automation hub is backed by Red Hat's support and expertise, providing users with reliable technical assistance and guidance.

- **Private automation hub**: Automation hub also offers a private automation hub feature, allowing organizations to securely store and manage their own user-generated content within their infrastructure, ensuring control and governance over their automation assets.

Ansible Galaxy is a community-driven platform with a broad range of community-contributed content, while Ansible automation hub is a subscription-based platform provided by Red Hat, offering certified, validated, and supported content. Ansible Galaxy is ideal for quickly finding and reusing community-developed content, while Ansible automation hub is focused on delivering enterprise-grade content with enhanced support and security.

Ansible automation hub serves as a trusted central repository where users can discover and download Ansible Content Collections. This article explores the features and benefits of Ansible automation hub, including the availability of Red Hat Ansible Certified Content and a private automation hub for enhanced control and security.

As part of the Red Hat Ansible Automation Platform subscription, Ansible automation hub offers a comprehensive range of Ansible Content Collections. These collections are carefully curated and include both Red Hat Certified Content and contributions from over 60 leading industry partners. By leveraging these collections, organizations can accelerate their automation projects, ensuring efficiency and reliability.

Within Ansible automation hub, users gain access to an extensive library of Red Hat Ansible Certified Content Collections. These collections are developed by reputable partners such as *Arista*, *Aruba*, *CheckPoint*, *Cisco*, *CyberArk*, *Dynatrace*, *IBM*, *SAP*, and *ServiceNow*. Each collection undergoes rigorous testing and validation to ensure enterprise-grade quality, providing users with fully supported roles and modules.

Ansible automation hub also features Ansible validated content, which is created and maintained by Red Hat and its partners. This content delivers a trusted, expert-guided approach to managing platforms, guaranteeing improved consistency and performance. Users can deploy Ansible validated content as-is or customize it to suit their specific enterprise environment requirements.

For organizations seeking greater control over their automation content, Ansible automation hub offers a private automation hub feature. This on-premises capability allows users to store and manage user-generated content within their own infrastructure, ensuring data privacy and governance. By leveraging the private automation hub, organizations can securely share internally developed content alongside Red Hat Ansible Certified Content and Ansible validated content with their teams. Please refer to the following figure:

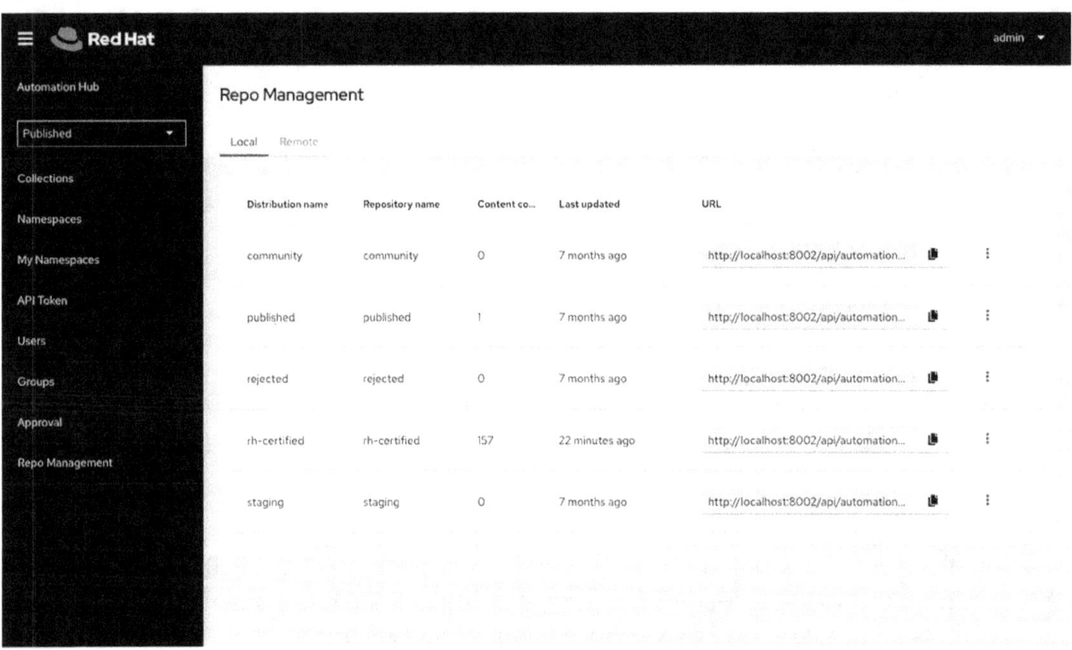

Figure 2.12: The dashboard of the automation hub

Private automation hub goes beyond content management and extends support for automation execution environments. This feature enables users to build and share container images with defined, consistent, and portable environments. By ensuring standardized execution environments, organizations can achieve better reproducibility and reliability in their automation workflows.

Ansible automation hub serves as a trusted source for Ansible Content Collections, providing users with a wide range of certified and validated content to accelerate their automation projects. Whether leveraging Red Hat Ansible Certified Content, Ansible validated content, or the private automation hub, organizations can streamline their automation efforts, ensuring consistency, security, and enhanced control over their content. With Ansible automation hub, automating new projects becomes faster, more reliable, and more accessible than ever before.

Private automation hub refers to a node instance of automation hub deployed within the infrastructure of our organization, offering the same capabilities but limited to the organization's specific content and accessible only to its members. A private automation hub can also act as a local registry for Ansible execution environments.

Large organizations also obtain performance advancement and high availability because the most used contents are cached in the local private automation hub and not fetched every time from the network.

Ansible execution environment

Ansible heavily relies on Python computer programming language and data types. Python has long been a popular choice for automation tasks, allowing users to write scripts and programs to automate various processes. Traditionally, Python virtual environments were used to manage dependencies and create isolated environments for running automation tasks. However, the introduction of Ansible execution environments has revolutionized the way we build and deploy automation workflows. In this article, we will explore execution environments in Ansible and understand how they simplify the process of building and using customized Python environments for automation.

Building an execution environment

When working with Ansible, it is common to rely on various dependencies and collections that are not part of the default Python environment. Managing these dependencies across multiple nodes can be challenging, as they need to be installed and synchronized on each machine. Previously, Ansible jobs ran inside a virtual environment, which required manual setup and maintenance.

With execution environments, Ansible introduces a container-based approach to building customized Python environments. Instead of relying on virtual environments, execution environments are container images that include system-level dependencies and collection-based content. This means that each execution environment contains only what is necessary to run a specific job, reducing the overhead and ensuring consistency across different nodes. In this way, the creator of the execution environment can integrate as much code as needed in a development environment and perform all the necessary tests in a UAT or PERF environment before deploying to production.

Custom execution environments are usually required in our organization to integrate certification authority and custom Ansible contents, such as Ansible collections or plugins.

To build an execution environment, we need to use the **ansible-builder** command line tool. First, ensure that we have either Podman or Docker installed on our system, along with the **ansible-builder** Python package. Once the prerequisites are in place, we can proceed with building the execution environment.

Building an execution environment involves creating a definition file (usually a **.yml** file) that specifies the content to include in the environment. This can include collections, Python requirements, system-level packages, and custom dependencies. If we have already migrated from a virtual environment, we can extract the required data from the migration output and use it in the definition file. Collection developers can also declare requirements for their content by providing appropriate metadata.

Once we have the definition file, we can use the **ansible-builder** command line tool to build the execution environment. The **ansible-builder** build command takes the definition file as input and generates a build context for the environment image. It then builds the image using the build context. The resulting image can be used directly or rebuilt later using the build context.

Using an execution environment

We can execute our jobs using a standard or a custom execution environment. To use an execution environment in a job, we need to ensure that it has been created using **ansible-builder**. We can specify the execution environment in our job templates using the automation controller user interface. Please refer to the following figure:

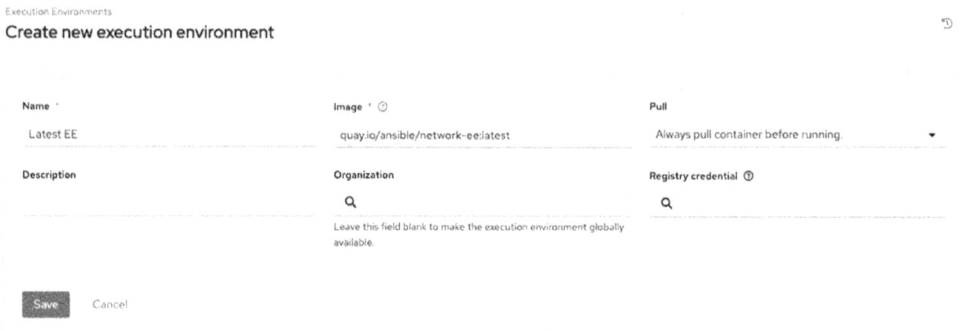

Figure 2.13: Create a new execution environment

The Ansible automation platform actively maintains three execution environments:

- **ee-supported**: A comprehensive execution environment with the collection most often used by the Red Hat customers.

- **ee-minimal**: A small footprint execution environment with only the minimum content included.

- **ee-2.9**: Ansible version 2.9 for legacy workload and network devices.

Depending on whether an execution environment is available globally or tied to a specific organization, we need the appropriate administrator privileges to use it in a job. Execution environments tied to an organization require organization administrators to run jobs within those environments.

Before running a job or job template with an execution environment, make sure that the associated credential contains the required information, such as username, host, and password.

To add an execution environment to the automation controller, navigate to the **Execution Environments** section in the user interface. Click on the Add button and enter the required details such as name, image name, pull options, description, organization assignment, and registry credential. Once added, the execution environment will be available for selection in our job templates.

By associating an execution environment with a job template, we can easily specify which environment to use for each specific job. This allows us to customize the runtime environment for different tasks and ensure consistency across our automation workflows.

Execution environment mount options

Sometimes we may need to add additional certificates or customize the execution environment further. Ansible provides options for mounting external paths into the execution environment, allowing us to inherit certificates in OpenShift or Kubernetes containers as HostPath.

Ansible automation mesh

Automation mesh is an essential feature of Red Hat Ansible Automation Platform that enables the distribution of work across a network of nodes. It relies on the open-source receptor project (ref: **https://receptor.readthedocs.io/en/latest/**). It utilizes existing networks to establish peer-to-peer connections between nodes, creating an overlay network that simplifies the deployment and management of automation tasks. This chapter provides an overview of automation mesh and offers guidance on planning and designing automation mesh topologies.

Automation mesh serves as an overlay network that facilitates the efficient distribution of work across a large and geographically dispersed collection of workers. It introduces dynamic cluster capacity, enabling the creation, registration, grouping, ungrouping, and deregistration of nodes with minimal downtime. Automation mesh separates the control and execution planes, allowing independent scaling of playbook execution capacity from the control plane capacity. We can visualize the current topology using the automation topology visualization tool integrated into the automation controller user interface, as shown in *Figure 2.14, Topology view*:

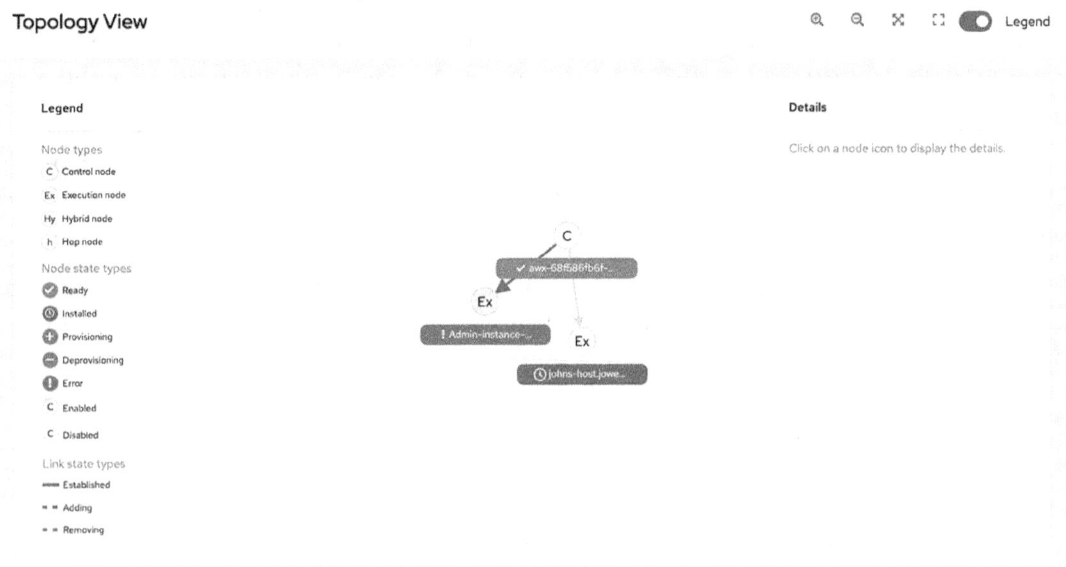

Figure 2.14: Topology view in automation controller

It offers resilient deployment choices, supports bi-directional and multi-hopped mesh communication, and complies with **Federal Information Processing Standards (FIPS)** for secure connectivity. The following *Table 2.1* summarizes the network ports used by the automation mesh.

Port	Protocol	Service	Ansible variable	Usage
22	TCP	SSH	`ansible_port`	Installation
27199	TCP	Receptor	`receptor_listener_port`	Listening port for receptor connection.
443*	TCP	Podman	N/A	Access to a container registry for execution environments.

Table 2.1: Network ports of Ansible automation mesh

Control and execution planes

To effectively plan an automation mesh deployment, it is essential to understand the control and execution planes and their corresponding Ansible automation mesh node types.

The control plane comprises hybrid nodes and control nodes. Hybrid nodes, which are the default node type for the control plane, handle automation controller runtime functions, project updates, management jobs, and **ansible-runner** task operations. On the other hand, control nodes focus on project and inventory updates and system jobs without executing regular jobs. Control nodes do not have execution capabilities.

The execution plane consists of **execution** nodes and **hop** nodes. Execution nodes execute automation tasks on behalf of the control plane and do not possess control functions. These nodes leverage the **ansible-runner** command line utility with **podman** container engine for isolation of job execution. Hop nodes, similar to jump hosts, facilitate routing traffic to other execution nodes but do not execute automation tasks themselves.

Peers define the node-to-node connections within the automation mesh. We can establish peer relationships within the **[automationcontroller]** and **[execution_nodes]** groups or by using the **[automationcontroller:vars]** or **[execution_nodes:vars]** groups.

Automation mesh node types

Defining the node types for the hosts in our inventory file is crucial for configuring automation mesh. We can set the **node_type** variable in the Ansible inventory for individual nodes or entire groups of nodes.

- **Hybrid node**: This example demonstrates the inventory for a single hybrid node in the control plane:

  ```
  [automationcontroller]

  control-plane-1.example.com
  ```

- **Control node**: This example illustrates a single control node in the control plane:

  ```
  [automationcontroller]

  control-plane-1.example.com node_type=control
  ```

- **Execution node**: The following stanza defines a single execution node in the execution plane:

  ```
  [execution_nodes]

  execution-plane1.example.com
  ```

- **Hop node:** This example showcases a **hop** node and an **execution** node in the execution plane. Note that the **node_type** variable is set for each individual node:

  ```
  [execution_nodes]

  execution-plane-1.example.com node_type=hop

  execution-plane-2.example.com
  ```

To set the node type at the group level, we can create separate groups for **execution** nodes and **hop** nodes:

```
[execution_nodes]
execution-plane-1.example.com
execution-plane-2.example.com
[execution_group]
execution-plane-2.example.com
[execution_group:vars]
node_type=execution
[hop_group]
execution-plane-1.example.com
[hop_group:vars]
node_type=hop
```

Establishing peer connections between nodes is crucial for communication within the automation mesh. We can create node-to-node connections using the **peers= host** variable. The following example connects **control-plane-1.example.com** to **execution-node-1.example.com** and **execution-node-1.example.com** to **execution-node-2.example.com**:

```
[automationcontroller]
control-plane-1.example.com peers=execution-node-1.example.com
[automationcontroller:vars]
node_type=control
[execution_nodes]
execution-node-1.example.com peers=execution-node-2.example.com
execution-node-2.example.com
```

By defining the appropriate peer connections, we establish the communication paths necessary for efficient automation mesh operation.

Till Ansible Automation Platform 1.2 was commonly used, the jump host technique that used a Python virtual environment and special Linux machine with SSH called **jump host** to connect different networks. The jump hosts are Linux machines used to forward the connection across the different networks using an SSH TCP port on the local side. The Ansible automation mesh is more robust as it dynamically routes the traffic in case of failure of a peer node.

Key learning

In this chapter, we explored the architecture of the Ansible Automation Platform and highlighted the key components. We learned that the Ansible controller coordinates the execution of the automation scripts in our IT infrastructure, connecting to the target nodes via the automation mesh that executes a container image (Ansible execution environment). Moreover, the automation hub is the center for code reuse, deploying roles, and collections.

Points to remember

- The automation controller provides a web user interface and a RESTful API.

- Automation controller key management of our content are projects, jobs, and workflow.

- Automation hub stores Ansible content, roles, playbooks, and collections for our organization.

- We can build our custom Ansible execution environment with a combination of the system software, Python libraries, and Ansible collections.

- Ansible Automation mesh enables complex network topology with different node types.

Multiple choice questions

1. **What component of the Ansible Automation Platform connects to the target node?**

    a. Automation controller

    b. Ansible Galaxy

    c. Automation hub

    d. Ansible automation mesh

2. **What tool of the automation controller enables us to execute one playbook after another?**

    a. Jobs

    b. Workflow

    c. Project

    d. Credentials

3. **How many Ansible execution environments are included in the Ansible Automation Platform?**

   a. One

   b. Two

   c. Three

   d. Four

4. **How can we configure a node-to-node connection using automation mesh?**

   a. `node_type=control`

   b. `node_type=hop`

   c. `peers= 1`

   d. `[execution_group]`

Answers

1. d

2. b

3. c

4. c

Questions

1. What is the difference between the automation controller and AWX?

2. What is the difference between the Ansible Galaxy and automation hub?

3. What is the difference between the automation mesh and receptor?

Key terms

- **Control machine**: This is the machine where we run the Ansible commands and playbooks. It can be any machine with Ansible installed, such as our local desktop or laptop.

- **Automation controller**: It is a centralized platform for managing and orchestrating Ansible automation tasks and workflows across an organization.

- **Ansible automation hub:** It is a repository for sharing, discovering, and collaborating on Ansible content, including roles, playbooks, and collections.

- **Ansible execution environment:** It provides a standardized runtime environment for running Ansible Playbooks and roles.

- **Ansible automation mesh:** It is a distributed architecture that enables efficient management and coordination of Ansible-based automation across multiple environments and locations.

Join our book's Discord space

Join the book's Discord Workspace for Latest updates, Offers, Tech happenings around the world, New Release and Sessions with the Authors:

https://discord.bpbonline.com

CHAPTER 3

Platform Installation Scenarios

Introduction

This chapter delves into the various installation scenarios for the Ansible Automation Platform, offering a comprehensive overview of deployment options, from single-machine setups suitable for rapid lab or development environments to more complex high-availability configurations with external PostgreSQL databases.

Structure

In this chapter, we will discuss the following topics:

- Overview of the installation scenarios
- Prerequisites and requirements
- Installer
- Installation scenarios
- Load balancer
- OpenShift
- Containerized

Objectives

The objectives of this chapter include providing an overview of various installation scenarios for an automation controller system, ranging from single-machine installations for quick setup to high-availability configurations with external PostgreSQL databases, optimized storage, and containerized options.

Overview of the installation scenarios

The most straightforward installation scenarios are single-machine installations. This installation scenario becomes handy when we would like to quickly start up a laboratory, a development environment, or a minimal installation. The easiest installation scenario is the automation controller with the internal PostgreSQL database. The most complex is an installation with high availability nodes with an external PostgreSQL database. A high-availability solution generally has more nodes performing the same task in an active-active scenario, so we can distribute the load using a load balancer or reverse proxy in front of our fleet. Either the automation controller or the automation hub supports high availability. An external PostgreSQL database enables us to assign the machine to a most performant storage class to provide sustainable read and write IOPS.

People usually prefer to store database node(s) in **solid state disk** (**SSD**) that deliver better performance and non-database nodes in mechanical/traditional **hard disk drives** (**HDD**) for cost-effective results.

Prerequisites and requirements

In each installation scenario, the amount of resources in our IT infrastructure needed by the Ansible Automation Platform depends on the installation scenarios. At the moment, of writing this book, for every single node of the installation, we need to allocate the following resources. The resources are (usually) provided via virtual machine instances or (rarely) via on-premises machines. Please refer to the following figure:

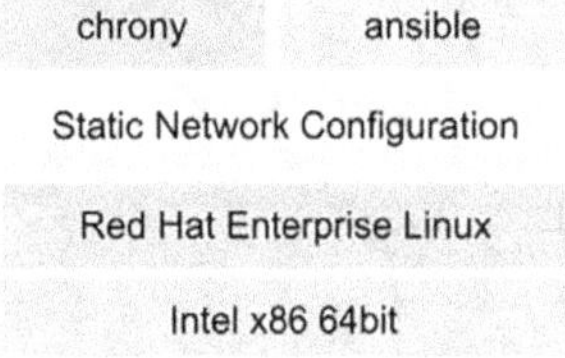

Figure 3.1: Diagram of the prerequisites for AAP

The following are the requirements for all the nodes:

* 64-bit processor architecture

* Red Hat Enterprise Linux operating system

- Network configured with a static IP address or DHCP reservations with infinite lease and DNS records.

- NTP client **chrony** service configured

- **ansible-core** latest version installed

The Ansible Automation Platform supported only x86-compatible (codename **x86_64/amd64** for Intel or AMD processors). Still, since Ansible Automation Platform version 2.4 was released in June 2023, a wide range of processor architectures were available. The most important is the support of the Ansible Automation Platform for ARM architectures (codename **aarch64/pp64le**), offering seamless integration, scalability, and performance. The release also introduced technology preview support for Linux on IBM Power and IBM Z (codename **s390x**) server hardware.

The following are the minimum requirements for automation controller and execution nodes:

- 16 GB of RAM for automation controller nodes and execution nodes

- 4 CPUs for automation controller nodes and execution nodes

- Database node 20+ GB storage

- Non-database nodes 40+ GB storage

The following are the minimum requirements for a private automation hub:

- 8 GB of RAM

- 2 CPUs

- Database node 20+ GB storage

- Non-database nodes 40+ GB storage

These are the minimum requirements for our node(s), which we need to adjust based on the number of automation scripts, network connections, CPU, and memory used by our system. As a rule of thumb, more resources usually return more performance in the platform. However, most virtualization technologies do not allow easy scaling down the assigned resources, especially for storage space. My recommendation is to execute some tests in development and test environments in order to have some real-life statistics before deploying our system in the production environment.

Please note that an Ansible **fork** value of 5 is used as a default for every installation. Refer to *Chapter 4, Setting Dashboard*, for more information about Ansible performance tuning.

As we noticed, the suggested database node size is 20+ GB, depending on the amount of information that we need to store. The exact size depends on many factors, such as the many Ansible resources we need to interact with, the number of executions per day, and the log retention data. The suggested space for a non-database node is 40+ GB as they need to operate with Ansible execution environment container images that are impactful on the file system size. Storage volumes must rate at least a minimum baseline of 1500 IOPS for the automation controller and automation hub, and PostgreSQL nodes. Please note that the automation controller and the automation hub use different tables in the database. The latest release of the Red Hat Ansible Automation Platform includes the latest release of PostgreSQL. At the moment of writing this book is PostgreSQL 13 is available. This release of PostgreSQL takes advantage of the table partitioning for optimized data storage and information retrieval. From the security perspective all user passwords are hashed before stored in the database using the SCRAM-SHA-256 hashing algorithm.

Ansible Automation Platform use **Red Hat Enterprise Linux (RHEL)** as operating system that requires a valid subscription entitlement. The subscription manager automatically manages and enables the needed software repositories for the YUM/DNF package manager. We can use the `subscription-manager` command to register and manage any instances to the **Red Hat Network (RHN)** using the following command:

```
subscription-manager register --username Username --password 'Password'
```

The username and password are placeholder for our Red Hat customer portal credentials. A successful registration returns a similar output message on the screen:

```
The system has been registered with id: a1b2c3d4-a1b2-a1b2-a1b2-acdf1234567
```

We can attach the instance to an entitlement pool during the registration process or use the default for our Red Hat account. The large organization uses Red Hat Satellite (based on the Foreman project) to register and maintain up-to-date consistently the operating system Red Hat Enterprise Linux and apply security patches. Ansible Automation Platform used to run only on Intel-compliant x86 64-bit processors. However, ARM and IBM Power architectures have been supported since release 2.4. The product exclusively supports the Red Hat Enterprise Linux operating system. This is necessary to provide the award-winning best support from Red Hat, as they are able to trace all the software stacks in our systems. Usually, every Ansible troubleshooting session begins with sharing the **sos-report** archive with an engineer of the Ansible support team. The network configuration requires a static IP address or a DHCP reservation with infinite lease. Each name needs to be registered as a DNS record in the DNS server of our organization or a **fully qualified domain name (FQDN)**. The DNS hostname is preferred rather than specifying the IP address in the inventory file directly. Please note that **localhost** is not an accepted hostname for the instances. It requires time synchronization via the NTP protocol. We can easily perform the time clock synchronization by configuring the **chrony** service to connect when needed to the NTP server of our organization or the closest internet pool available. The AAP also requires the latest version of the **ansible-core** package installed in all the nodes. The Ansible installation tool is going to check the installation status and execute the installation as one of the first steps.

As we successfully allocated the resources and installed the software prerequisites, we are ready to execute the Ansible Platform installer.

Installer

As we learned in the previous chapter, many components must be harmonized to run our infrastructure automation smoothly. The Ansible Automation Platform provides an installation tool to simplify user onboarding and set up the necessary components. The **Setup** tool is officially called **Red Hat Ansible Automation Platform installer**. The tool is included in every release of the Ansible Automation Platform and assists the IT professional in the initial installation of the system. It also produces a handful of installation log files if we need to review the installation status. Please refer to the following figure:

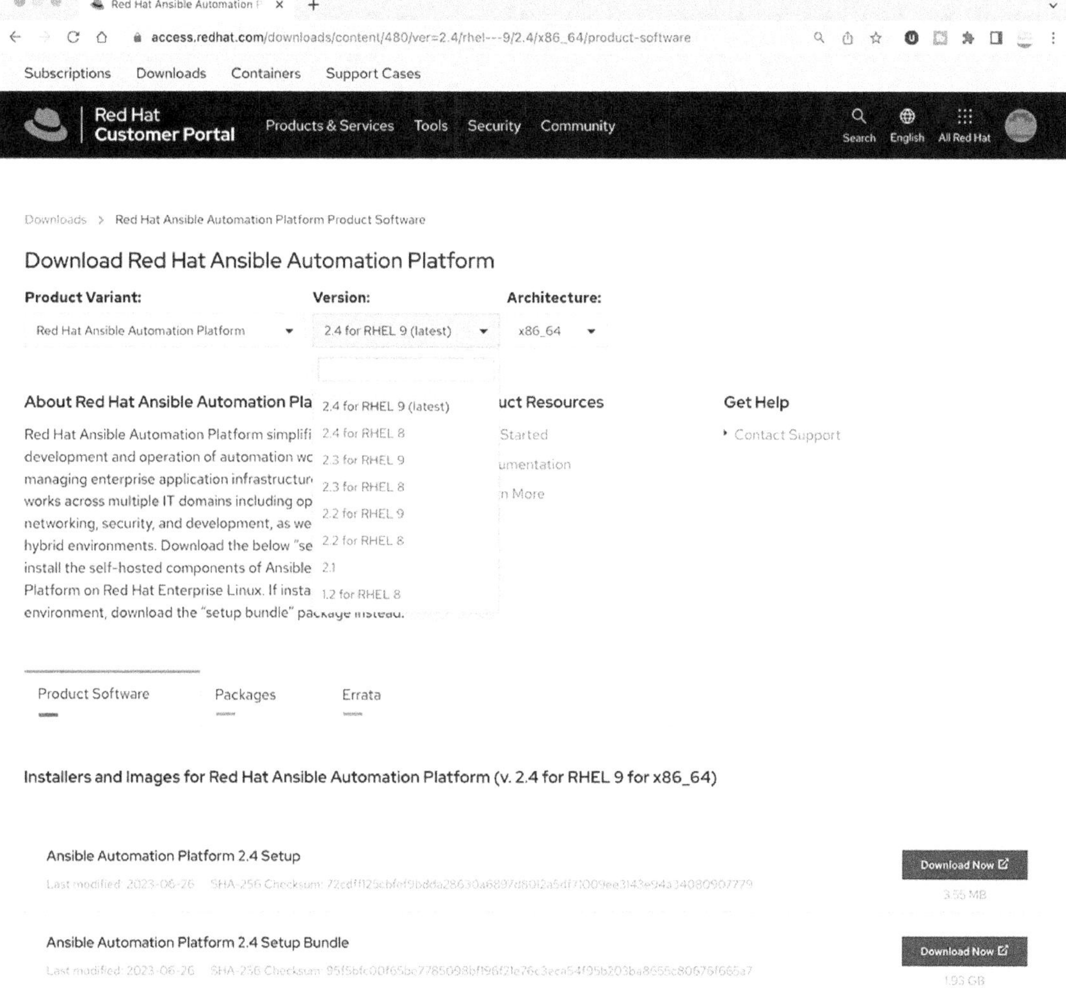

Figure 3.2: *AAP download from the Red Hat customer portal*

The installation tool could be downloaded via our Red Hat customer portal in two different formats: Online and bundle, as shown in *Figure 3.1*. For reference, for the AAP 2.4 for RHEL9, the online installer package is ~3.55MB, and the bundle is ~ 1.93 GB. AAP 2.3 for RHEL9, the online installer package is ~7.53 MB versus the bundle package of ~1.35 GB.

Please note to upgrade the Ansible Automation Platform components only using the installation tool provided.

The installation tool expects the inventory file to be configured according to the following use case and perform a successful platform installation.

The online installation enables the Ansible Automation Platform repositories in our system to download the latest release of the software packages and configure our system according to the parameters specified in the inventory file.

Whereas the bundled installation contains all the files needed for a successful offline installation of the system. All the necessary software and dependencies are provided for our Red Hat Enterprise Linux version. Many users prefer this way of installing the system using the bundle installer, even if they are not in an air-gapped use case. The air-gapped environment is usually used by highly regulated industries such as financial institutions, transportation companies, and so on, where a node is completely isolated from the internet.

Every installation of the Ansible Automation Platform requires the following steps:

1. Access our Red Hat customer portal.

2. Download the Ansible Automation Platform installer online or bundle. A verification hash is provided for the most common algorithm (SHA-256 checksum at the moment).

3. Decompress the tarball archive. The installer is stored in a compressed way to save disk space and download time. Execute the following command on the terminal to decompress the archive:

```
tar zxvf ansible-automation-platform-setup-*.tar.xz
```

4. Enter in the decompressed folder. The folder name is slightly different when we use the online or the bundle installation method.

   - **bundled installer: `ansible-automation-platform-setup-bundle-<aap-version>`**

   - **online installer: `ansible-automation-platform-setup-<aap-version>`**

   Now that we know the installation directory, we can easily access it using the **cd** command. We can access the directory of the bundled installer using the command:

   ```
   cd ansible-automation-platform-setup-bundle-<aap-version>
   ```

5. Customize the **inventory** file according to our installation scenarios.

6. The installation begins when we execute the following command on the terminal:

   `./setup.sh`

   Please note that this step requires an administrative user as we are going to install the AAP packages in our system and create specific users (`'awx'` and **receptor**) and apply system configuration parameters.

Note: The Installer fails with the following error message displayed on the screen when the "localhost" instance name is used.

`The system hostname cannot be localhost, receptor requires it to be set to something other than localhost"`

Note: The Installer fails with the following error message displayed on the screen when the memory allocated to the current instance doesn't meet the minimum criteria.

`This machine does not have sufficient RAM to run Ansible Automation Platform.`

We can override the minimum amount of memory, for example, to be able to run on Apple Silicon processors hardware with limited available memory by customizing the value of the following file:

`collections/ansible_collections/ansible/automation_platform_installer/ roles/preflight/defaults/main.yml`

Red Hat highly discouraged this practice as it ended up in an unsupported installation scenario, but we might consider it only in the development environment. *Figure 3.3* demonstrates editing with the VIM text editor in a terminal window:

```
---
## Operational parameters

required_ram: 7400
ignore_preflight_errors: false

## Configurable parameters
```

```
<_platform_installer/roles/preflight/defaults/main.yml" 7L, 109B          4,15                All
```

Figure 3.3: AAP pre-flight customization

7. Connect to the web interface and apply the license manifest file.

    This file validates our Red Hat Ansible Automation subscription and enables the full feature of the Ansible Automation Platform. We can obtain the manifest file for our Ansible Automation Platform from the subscription allocations page in the Red Hat customer portal associated with our Ansible Automation Platform entitlement(s) plan. Please note that a 30-day trial license is available.

A successfully installed Ansible Automation Platform is expected at the end of the AAP installer execution.

Installation scenarios

The following installation scenarios simplify our installation by providing the **inventory** file for the Ansible Automation Platform installer. In most cases, we only need to customize the name of our host(s), the database password, and the administrative user (username: admin) to be able to proceed with the installation of the AAP.

The following three installation scenarios are supported for a single automation controller:

- Standalone with internal PostgreSQL database

- Single with external installer-managed PostgreSQL database

- Single with external PostgreSQL database

The following three installation scenarios are supported for the private automation hub:

- Standalone with internal PostgreSQL database

- Single with external installer-managed PostgreSQL database

- Single with external PostgreSQL database

The Ansible Automation Platform 2.4 introduced the **Event-Driven Ansible** controller (**EDA**) that could be installed similarly to automation controller or private automation hub. This book will teach the installation scenario of a standalone EDA controller with an internal PostgreSQL database.

The following three installation scenarios are supported for the complete Ansible Automation Platform:

- All the nodes with an external installer-managed database

- All the nodes with an external PostgreSQL database

- Installation on Red Hat OpenShift Container Platform (Kubernetes based)

In the following sections, we explore each use case and explain when it is commonly used for each scenario. Please note that the unused lines of the **inventory** file are redacted.

Setup automation controller

The automation controller is the control plane for the Ansible Automation Platform (formerly Ansible Tower). It provides a user interface, role-based access control, workflows, and CI/CD capabilities to manage the automation lifecycle across the organization. The automation controller helps standardize automation deployment, auditing, and management while reducing sprawl and variance. It features a centralized web user interface and RESTful API for inventory management, workflow scheduling, change tracking, and reporting. The latest versions include an automation topology viewer for visualizing complex automation setups. It can be deployed on physical or virtual environments without requiring Red Hat OpenShift. Red Hat Ansible Automation Platform offers a comprehensive solution for automating processes, fostering collaboration, and accelerating growth.

We can easily set up an automation controller running the Ansible Automation Platform installer. It is an easy task as the default inventory file is provided out of the box in the downloaded package.

Standalone automation controller with internal database

A single automation controller can be deployed with an internal PostgreSQL database. This scenario simplifies deployment, enhances data security, improves deployment speed in the development environment, streamlines maintenance, simplifies configuration and management, and ensures better availability for managing automation workflows and data within the organization. It is preferred for development environments and small organizations with limited automation executions. Please refer to the following figure:

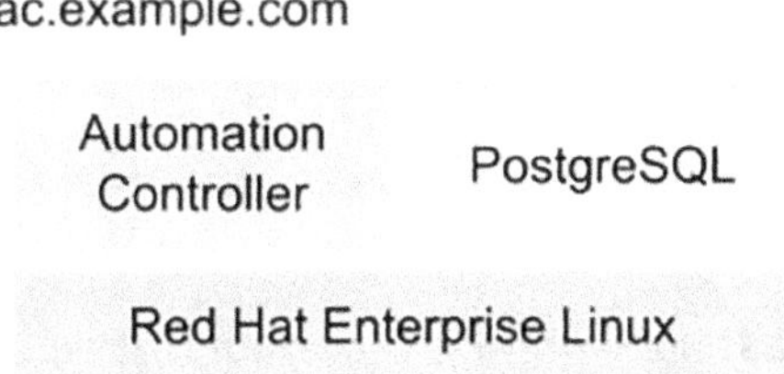

Figure 3.4: Standalone automation controller with internal database

The following Ansible **inventory** file is used to install a single Ansible automation controller on **ac.example.com** with an internal PostgreSQL database.

```
[automationcontroller]
ac.example.com
[all:vars]
admin_password='<password>'
pg_host=''
pg_port='5432'
```

```
pg_database='awx'
pg_username='awx'
pg_password='<password>'
pg_sslmode='prefer'
registry_url='registry.redhat.io'
registry_username='<registry username>'
registry_password='<registry password>'
```

Let us break down the contents of the **inventory** file:

1. **[automationcontroller]**: This is a group name used to identify the automation controller node. In this case, the only node specified is **ac.example.com**, which is the hostname of the automation controller.

2. **[all:vars]**: This section includes variables that are applied to all hosts in the inventory. It is a group in the Ansible inventory.

3. **admin_password='<password>'**: This variable sets the password for the Ansible Automation Platform admin user with administrative rights.

4. **pg_host=''**: This variable specifies the hostname or IP address of the PostgreSQL database server. In this example, it is left empty, indicating that the database is running on the same node as the automation controller.

5. **pg_port='5432'**: This variable sets the port number for the PostgreSQL database server.

6. **pg_database='awx'**: This variable specifies the name of the PostgreSQL database used by the Ansible Automation Platform.

7. **pg_username='awx'**: This variable sets the username for connecting to the PostgreSQL database.

8. **pg_password='<password>'**: This variable specifies the password for the PostgreSQL database user.

9. **pg_sslmode='prefer'**: This variable determines the SSL mode for the PostgreSQL database connection. In this case, it is set to **'prefer'**, meaning SSL is preferred but not enforced.

10. **registry_url='registry.redhat.io'**: This variable sets the URL of the container registry from which Ansible Automation Platform components will be downloaded. People keep the default **registry.redhat.io** if the organization does not have a private container registry.

11. **registry_username='<registry   username>'**: This variable specifies the username for authenticating with the container registry. Please enter the same username as the credential of our Red Hat customer portal profile.

12. **registry_password='<registry password>'**: This variable sets the password for authenticating with the container registry. Please enter the same password as the credential of our Red Hat customer portal profile.

Single automation controller with installer-managed database

Separating the database by the automation controller node enables us to assign resources individually to the frontend machine or the database machine. It is common to assign a premium storage class to the database machine and a cost-effective storage class to the frontend machine. Please refer to the following figure:

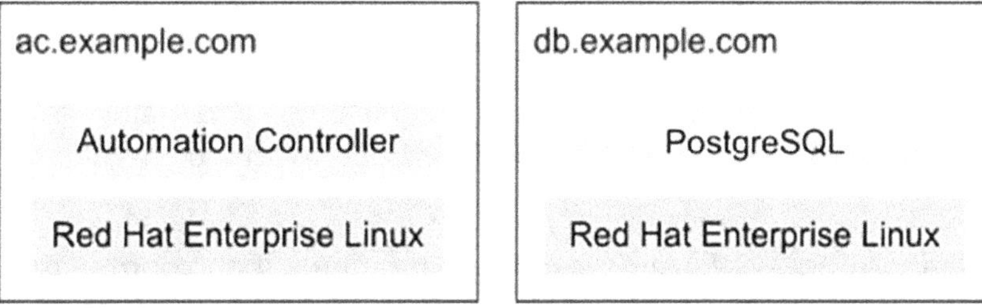

Figure 3.5: *Single automation controller with installer-managed database*

The following example represents an inventory file for installing a single automation controller deployed with an external PostgreSQL database on a separate node. The database is going to be deployed by the installer on a separate node **db.example.com**.

```
[automationcontroller]
ac.example.com
[database]
db.example.com
[all:vars]
admin_password='<password>'
pg_host='db.example.com'
pg_port='5432'
pg_database='awx'
pg_username='awx'
pg_password='<password>'
pg_sslmode='prefer'
registry_url='registry.redhat.io'
registry_username='<registry username>'
registry_password='<registry password>'
```

Let us go through the contents of the **inventory** file:

1. **[automationcontroller]**: This group name is used to identify the automation controller node. In this case, the only node specified is **ac.example.com**, which represents the hostname or IP address of the automation controller.

2. **[database]**: This group name is used to identify the database node. In this example, the node is specified as **db.example.com**, representing the hostname or IP address of the separate database node.

3. **[all:vars]**: This section includes variables applied to all hosts in the inventory.

4. **pg_host='db.example.com'**: This variable specifies the hostname or IP address of the PostgreSQL database server. In this case, it points to the separate node designated for the database.

    The remaining variables have the same meaning and value as the previous installation scenario of the automation controller with the internal database.

    By populating this **inventory** file with the appropriate values and running the installation process, we can set up a single automation controller node with an external database on a separate node using the Red Hat Ansible Automation Platform.

Configure external database

When the workload is intense, or we would like to fine-tune the performance of the database, we can manage a database node by ourselves. If desired, we can configure the PostgreSQL database as independent nodes not controlled by the Automation Platform installer. This is also useful when we manage multiple database servers. The typical use cases are multiple database servers that work together to allow a second server to take over quickly if the primary server fails (high availability) or to allow several computers to serve the same data (load balancing). Ideally, database servers could work together seamlessly. The following deployments are usually implemented: Primary-secondary replication, shared disk failover, file system (block-device) Replication, warm standby using **point-in-time recovery (PITR)**, statement-based replication middleware, asynchronous or synchronous multi-master replication. For a more intense workload consider using externally maintained databases (explored in the following section). Please refer to the following figure:

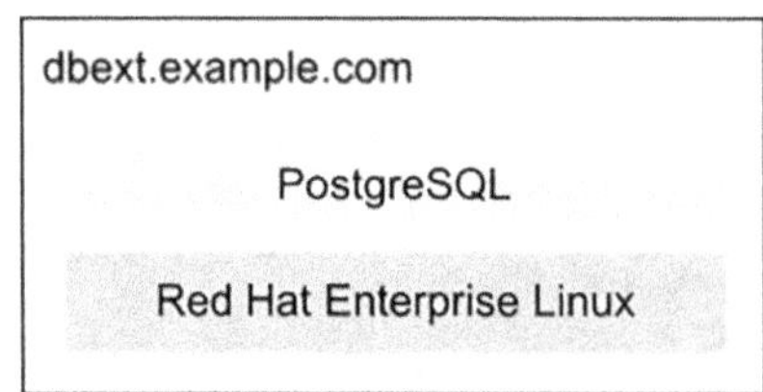

Figure 3.6: Diagram of the external database

We must install a standard Red Hat Enterprise Linux instance with PostgreSQL database and the **ansible** core packages. At the moment of writing this book, the latest supported version of PostgreSQL for AAP 2.4 is version 13 of PostgreSQL. To access the database used by the automation controller and automation hub, the **rh-postgresql13 software collections** (**SCL**) must be enabled because they use the Red Hat PostgreSQL Software Collections.

Tip: Administrators have the option to utilize the "awx-manage dbshell" command, which will automatically enable the PostgreSQL SCL.

1. **Install the PostgreSQL server packages on Red Hat Enterprise Linux:**

   We can install the Red Hat PostgreSQL database server on a machine using the DNF package manager:

   ```
   # dnf install postgresql-server
   ```

   ```
   # dnf module install postgresql:13/server
   ```

2. **Initialize the database cluster:**

   ```
   # postgresql-setup --initdb
   ```

   Red Hat recommends storing the database data in the (default) **/var/lib/pgsql/ data** directory. We can set up the **/var** in a separate partition to implement the zoning/segregated file system design.

3. **Start the PostgreSQL service:**

   ```
   # systemctl start postgresql.service
   ```

4. **Enable the PostgreSQL service to start at boot:**

   ```
   # systemctl enable postgresql.service
   ```

5. **Create a new user for our installation:**

   The following commands are used to switch to the **postgres** user, access the PostgreSQL command-line interface (**psql**), and then create a new user called **aap_mydbuser** with the password **mypasswd**, granting them the roles of creating roles and databases.

   ```
   # su - postgres
   ```

   ```
   $ psql
   ```

   ```
   postgres=# CREATE USER aap_mydbuser WITH PASSWORD 'mypasswd' CREATEROLE CREATEDB;
   ```

   We can log out from the **psql** interactive terminal by using the **\q** meta command:

   ```
   postgres=# \q
   ```

6. **Login using the aap_mydbuser**:

```
# psql -U aap_mydbuser -h 127.0.0.1 -d postgres
```

The provided command is used to access the PostgreSQL command-line interface (**psql**) with the specified parameters:

- **-U aap_mydbuser** specifies the username as **aap_mydbuser** to connect to the database.

- **-h 127.0.0.1** specifies the host as **127.0.0.1** (localhost) to connect to the database server.

- **-d postgres** specifies the name of the database to connect to as **postgres**.

By default, the AAP installer sets up the database server with recommended defaults for typical workloads. However, we can modify these settings for a PostgreSQL database server node, considering that **ansible_memtotal_mb** represents the total memory size of the database server instance. The **ansible_memtotal_mb** parameter is to calculate the value for the PostgreSQL configuration file, but we can use it as a reference for our setup. The following parameter is set in the PostgreSQL configuration files stored in the **/var/lib/pgsql/data/** directory, under the **postgresql.conf** file. These are the crucial parameters:

```
max_connections == 1024

shared_buffers == ansible_memtotal_mb*0.3

work_mem == ansible_memtotal_mb*0.03

maintenance_work_mem == ansible_memtotal_mb*0.04
```

The given expressions are configuration settings related to the PostgreSQL database, commonly used with the Ansible Automation Platform:

- **max_connections == 1024**: This sets the maximum number of concurrent connections that can be made to the database. In this case, the value is set to **1024**, meaning that the database can handle up to **1024** simultaneous connections.

- **shared_buffers == ansible_memtotal_mb*0.3**: Shared buffers are an important resource in PostgreSQL that stores frequently accessed data in memory to improve performance. This expression sets the size of the shared buffers as a fraction of the total available memory (**ansible_memtotal_mb**). It is set to 30% (**0.3**) of the total memory available in this case.

- **work_mem == ansible_memtotal_mb*0.03**: Work mem is used for sorting and hashing operations in PostgreSQL. This expression sets the amount of memory allocated per session for such operations. The value is set to 3% (**0.03**) of the total memory available (**ansible_memtotal_mb**).

- `maintenance_work_mem == ansible_memtotal_mb*0.04`: Maintenance work mem is used for maintenance operations like vacuuming and index rebuilding. This expression sets the amount of memory allocated per session for these maintenance tasks. The value is set to 4% (`0.04`) of the total memory available (`ansible_memtotal_mb`).

By setting these configuration parameters based on the available memory (`ansible_memtotal_mb`), it optimizes the database's performance and resource allocation for the Ansible Automation Platform.

Single automation controller with external database

Setting up a single automation controller with an external (customer-provided) database offers several benefits:

- **Scalability**: By separating the automation controller and the database into different nodes, we can distribute the workload and scale each component independently. This allows for better performance and capacity management, especially in large and complex environments.

- **Flexibility**: Using an external database gives us the freedom to choose a database system that aligns with our organization's requirements and preferences. We can leverage existing database infrastructure, utilize specific features or optimizations of the chosen database, and have more control over its configuration and maintenance.

- **Data management**: With an external database, we can centralize and manage automation-related data more effectively. The database serves as a repository for storing automation playbooks, inventory information, job histories, and other metadata. It provides a reliable and scalable solution for organizing and accessing this data, facilitating efficient searching, versioning, and tracking of automation assets.

- **Separation of concerns**: Keeping the automation controller and the database separate ensures a clear separation of responsibilities. The automation controller focuses on managing and executing automation workflows, while the external database is dedicated to data storage and retrieval. This separation enhances modularity, simplifies troubleshooting, and allows for more granular control over each component.

- **High availability**: By having the database on a separate node, we can implement high availability measures such as database replication, clustering, or failover mechanisms. This helps ensure data integrity and availability, minimizing the risk of downtime or data loss.

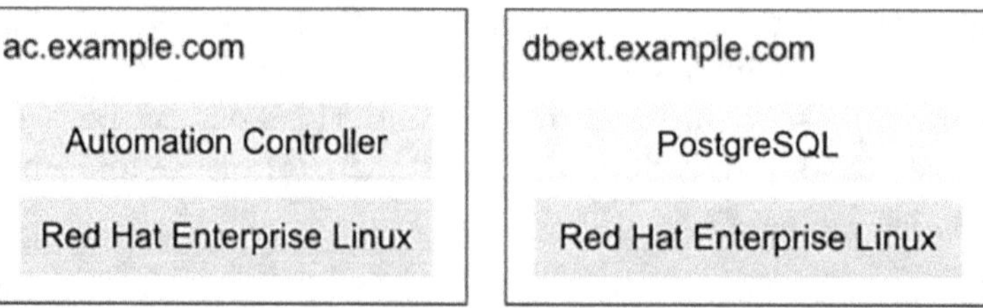

Figure 3.7: Single automation controller with external database

The external database options are:

- A customer-deployed high-availability or disaster recovery configuration using PostgreSQL packages provided by Red Hat.

- A customer-provided PostgreSQL database provided by a customer-internal team.

- A cloud-hosted PostgreSQL database.

- A third-party PostgreSQL offering (for example Crunchy Postgres).

For best performance, it is recommended to use lower than 5ms latency.

Setting up a single automation controller with an external database provides flexibility, scalability, and efficient data management. This enables organizations to optimize their Ansible Automation Platform deployment according to their needs and infrastructure requirements. The following **inventory** file deploys one automation controller, **ac.example.com**, connected to the database **db.example.com**.

```
[automationcontroller]
ac.example.com
[database]
[all:vars]
admin_password='<password>'
pg_host='dbext.example.com'
pg_port='5432'
pg_database='awx'
pg_username='awx'
pg_password='<password>'
pg_sslmode='prefer'
registry_url='registry.redhat.io'
registry_username='<registry username>'
registry_password='<registry password>'
```

The given configuration file represents an **inventory** file used for installing the Red Hat Ansible Automation Platform with a single automation controller node and an external (customer-provided) database on a separate node. Let us examine the contents of the inventory file:

- **[automationcontroller]**: This group name is used to identify the automation controller node. In this case, the only node specified is **ac.example.com**, representing the hostname or IP address of the automation controller.

- **[database]**: This group name is used to indicate the presence of a database, but no specific node is provided. The absence of a node under this group indicates that the database already exists and is managed elsewhere, not by the platform installer.

- **[all:vars]**: This section includes variables applied to all hosts in the inventory.

- **admin_password='<password>'**: This variable sets the password for the Ansible Automation Platform **admin** user.

- **pg_host='dbext.example.com'**: This variable specifies the hostname or IP address of the externally managed PostgreSQL database server. It indicates where the platform should connect to the existing database.

The remaining variables have the same meaning and value as the other automation controller installation scenarios.

We can set up an Ansible automation controller instance with an external PostgreSQL database on a separate node by populating the **inventory** file with the appropriate values and running the installation process.

Additional options

We can also add additional optional lines to the **inventory** file, as commented below (preceded by the **#** character), that provide additional optional configuration options for SSL-related settings, such as custom CA certificate installation, web server SSL certificates, and PostgreSQL SSL settings. These are the relevant keys in the **inventory** file:

```
# SSL-related variables
# If set, this will install a custom CA certificate to the system trust store.
# custom_ca_cert=/path/to/ca.crt
# Certificate and key to install in nginx for the web UI and API
# web_server_ssl_cert=/path/to/tower.cert
# web_server_ssl_key=/path/to/tower.key
# Server-side SSL settings for PostgreSQL (when we are installing it).
# postgres_use_ssl=False
# postgres_ssl_cert=/path/to/pgsql.crt
# postgres_ssl_key=/path/to/pgsql.key
```

Setup private automation hub

The automation hub is a cloud-based service providing the Red Hat Ansible Certified Content Collections from a wide range of partners (Arista, Aruba, Checkpoint, Cisco, CyberArk, Dynatrace, IBM, SAP, ServiceNow, and so on). The contents are collections, roles, and modules enterprise-certified and production ready Ansible resources.

Organizations that would like to develop Ansible-validated content with their teams and want to cache the most often used content should adopt one or more instances of private automation hub.

The private automation hub is a Red Hat Ansible Automation Platform component and serves as an on-premises repository for Ansible collections. These are the main advantages of deploying the automation hub in our organization:

- **Ansible private automation hub deployment**: Install and configure the private automation hub by following the official documentation. Modify the **inventory** file variables to suit our environment, including the hub URL, database settings, and API token.

- **Configure and sync the repositories**: Access the private automation hub's URL and navigate to the **Repository Management** option. Configure the community and **rh-certified** repositories by providing the necessary details such as the repository URL, YAML requirements file, Ansible Galaxy username, and password. Sync the repositories to fetch the collections.

- **Connect to the private automation hub as a content source**: Authenticate with an API token target machine. We can generate the API token in the WebUI to create a new token via the **Collection** option and API token management. Copy the CLI configuration parameters from the **Repository Management** option and paste them into the **/etc/ansible/ansible.cfg** file on the target machine or in the WebUI of the automation controller.

- **Pull and install collections from private automation hub**: Use the **ansible-galaxy** command to install collections from the private automation hub. The process is like installing collections from Ansible Galaxy. After installation, we can use the **ansible-doc** command to check the available modules in the installed collections or the **ansible-navigator** command.

The following installation scenarios provide detailed instructions about how to set up and utilize the private automation hub for managing Ansible collections in their on-premises environment.

Standalone automation hub with internal database

Setting up a single private automation hub with an internal PostgreSQL database enables us to deploy a self-contained and independent environment for managing automation content. With an internal database, the private automation hub can store and organize all the necessary information and metadata related to automation resources, such as playbooks, roles, and modules. This allows for efficient searching, versioning, and tracking of automation assets within the automation hub. Additionally, a standalone setup with an internal database offers increased control and security over the data, as it eliminates the need for external dependencies and potential connectivity issues. It provides a reliable and self-sufficient solution for organizations to manage and share their automation content within their infrastructure. Please refer to the following figure:

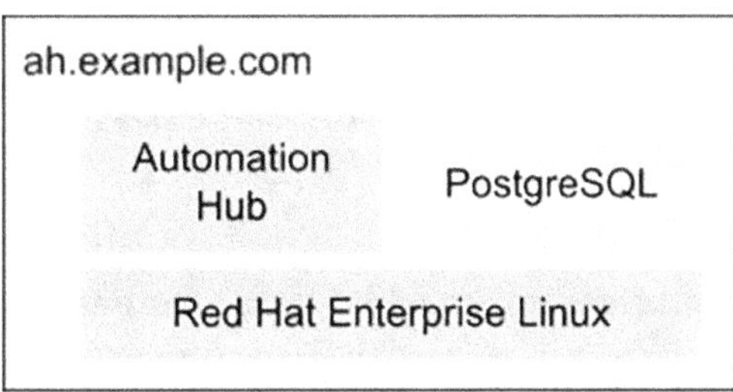

Figure 3.8: *Standalone automation hub with internal database*

The following **inventory** file deploys a single instance **ah.example.com** of the private automation hub with an internal PostgreSQL database (installer-manged).

```
[automationcontroller]
[automationhub]
ah.example.com
[all:vars]
registry_url='registry.redhat.io'
registry_username='<registry username>'
registry_password='<registry password>'
automationhub_admin_password= <PASSWORD>
automationhub_pg_host=''
automationhub_pg_port='5432'
automationhub_pg_database='automationhub'
automationhub_pg_username='automationhub'
automationhub_pg_password=<PASSWORD>
automationhub_pg_sslmode='prefer'
```

Let us break down the contents of the **inventory** file:

- **[automationcontroller]**: this group name is empty, indicating no automation controller nodes specified in this deployment.

- **[automationhub]**: this group name is used to identify the automation hub node. **ah.example.com** is specified as the hostname for the private automation hub.

`ansible_connection=local` indicates that the connection to the automation hub will be made locally on the machine where the inventory file is being executed.

- **[all:vars]**: this section includes variables applied to all hosts in the **inventory**.

- Container registry variables:

  o **registry_url**, **registry_username**, and **registry_password** specify the credentials for accessing the container registry.

- These parameters are specific for the configuration of the private automation hub:

  o **automationhub_admin_password** sets the password for the automation hub admin user.

  o **automationhub_pg_host** is left empty, indicating that the internal database will be hosted on the same machine as the automation hub.

  o **automationhub_pg_port** specifies the port number for the PostgreSQL database (default 5432 TCP).

  o **automationhub_pg_database** sets the name of the internal database as **'automationhub'**.

  o **automationhub_pg_username** and **automationhub_pg_password** specify the credentials for accessing the internal database.

  o **automationhub_pg_sslmode** defines the SSL mode for the database connection (set to **'prefer'** in this example).

- SSL-related parameters:

  o The remaining lines in the **inventory** file provide optional configuration options for SSL-related settings.

  o **automationhub_disable_https** determines whether the automation hub deployment will be TLS-enabled.

  o **automationhub_ssl_validate_certs** controls whether self-signed certificates generated by the default installation will be validated.

  o The lines related to custom CA certificates, **automationhub_ssl_cert**, and **automationhub_ssl_key** allow us to provide SSL certificates for the automation hub node.

By populating this inventory file with the appropriate values, we can deploy a single instance of the private automation hub with an internal PostgreSQL database. If enabled, the deployment will use the specified configuration, including the provided passwords, registry credentials, and SSL settings.

Single automation hub with installer-managed database

A single private automation hub with an installer-managed database offers the same benefits as a single automation controller. It centralizes the storage of Ansible resources, simplifies deployment and database maintenance, facilitates integration and collaboration, and streamlines maintenance and upgrades. It provides organizations with efficient and reliable automation operations, helping them streamline processes and achieve automation goals. It is the perfect solution for development environments and small organizations. Please refer to the following figure:

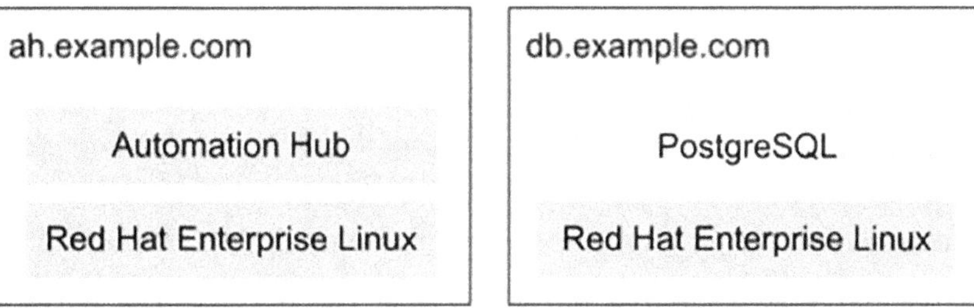

Figure 3.9: Single automation hub with installer-managed database

The provided **inventory** file is used to deploy a single instance of the private automation hub **ah.example.com** with an external PostgreSQL database **db.example.com**.

```
[automationcontroller]
[automationhub]
ah.example.com
[database]
db.example.com
[all:vars]
registry_url='registry.redhat.io'
registry_username='<registry username>'
registry_password='<registry password>'
automationhub_admin_password= <PASSWORD>
automationhub_pg_host='db.example.com'
automationhub_pg_port='5432'
automationhub_pg_database='automationhub'
automationhub_pg_username='automationhub'
automationhub_pg_password=<PASSWORD>
automationhub_pg_sslmode='prefer'
```

The only differences between the previous scenario in the content of the **inventory** file:

- **[database]**:

  o This group name is used to specify the external database node that the installer manages.

  o **db.example.com** is provided as the hostname for the external database.

- **[all:vars]**:

  o This section includes variables applied to all hosts in the inventory.

- **Automation Hub configuration**:

  o **automationhub_admin_password** sets the password for the automation hub admin user.

  o **automationhub_pg_host** specifies the hostname of the external database.

  o **automationhub_pg_port** sets the port number for the external database (default 5432 TCP).

  o **automationhub_pg_database** sets the name of the external database as **'automationhub'**.

  o **automationhub_pg_username** and **automationhub_pg_password** specify the credentials for accessing the external database.

  o **automationhub_pg_sslmode** defines the SSL mode for the database connection (set to **'prefer'** in this example).

Using this **inventory** file and providing the necessary values, we can deploy an instance of the automation hub with an external (installer-managed) database. If enabled, the deployment will utilize the specified configuration, including the provided passwords, registry credentials, external database information, and SSL settings.

Single automation hub with external database

A single automation hub with an external database involves using an external database system to store and manage automation-related data. The automation hub serves as the central control point for managing automation tasks. This setup provides benefits such as centralized control, data separation and management, scalability, data persistence and integrity, integration capabilities, and flexibility in sizing the database host. It enhances the efficiency and reliability of automation processes and enables organizations to manage and scale their automation operations effectively. Please refer to the following figure:

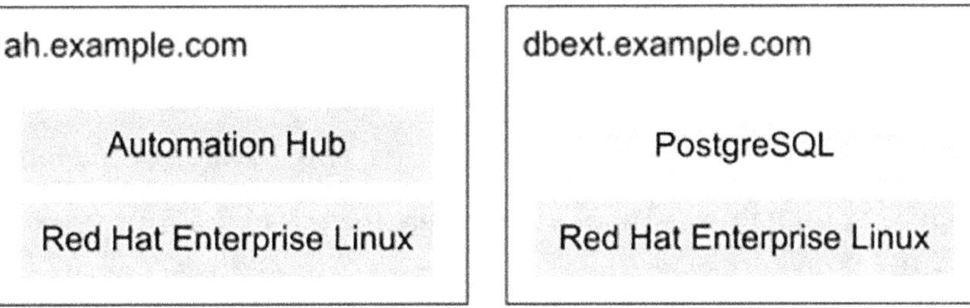

Figure 3.10: Single automation controller with installer-managed database

This example does not have a host under the database group. This indicates to the installer that the database is an external PostgreSQL database managed by the customer. The following inventory file configures a private automation hub **ah.example.com** with an external database **dbext.example.com**.

```
[automationcontroller]
[automationhub]
ah.example.com
[database]
[all:vars]
registry_url='registry.redhat.io'
registry_username='<registry username>'
registry_password='<registry password>'
automationhub_admin_password= <PASSWORD>
automationhub_pg_host='dbext.example.com'
automationhub_pg_port='5432'
automationhub_pg_database='automationhub'
automationhub_pg_username='automationhub'
automationhub_pg_password=<PASSWORD>
automationhub_pg_sslmode='prefer'
```

The provided **inventory** file example is used to deploy a single instance of the private automation hub with an external PostgreSQL database not managed by the platform installer. The only differences between the previous scenarios in the content of the **inventory** file:

- **[database]**:
  - o This group name is empty, indicating no host specified under the database group.
  - o This signifies that the external database exists and is being managed elsewhere.

- **[all:vars]**:
  - o This section includes variables applied to all hosts in the inventory.
- **The configuration of the private automation hub via the parameters:**
  - o **automationhub_admin_password** sets the password for the automation hub admin user.
  - o **automationhub_pg_host** specifies the hostname of the external database.
  - o **automationhub_pg_port** sets the port number for the external database (default 5432 TCP).
  - o **automationhub_pg_database** sets the name of the external database as **'automationhub'**.
  - o **automationhub_pg_username** and **automationhub_pg_password** specify the credentials for accessing the external database.
  - o **automationhub_pg_sslmode** defines the SSL mode for the database connection (set to **'prefer'** in this example).

By using this inventory file and providing the necessary values, we can deploy an instance of the private automation hub with an external PostgreSQL database. The platform installer does not manage the database.

Setup Event-Driven Ansible controller

Event-Driven Ansible, a Red Hat Ansible Automation Platform feature, enables event-driven automation to streamline IT operations, reduce manual tasks, and foster innovation. By processing events and intelligently responding to changing conditions, Event-Driven Ansible automates a range of tasks in the IT environment, including ticket enhancement, remediation, and user management. It provides a unified platform for manual and automatic automation, empowering teams to focus on critical work and deliver value to the business. With flexibility and adaptability, Event-Driven Ansible can be applied across diverse IT domains, ensuring consistency while minimizing human errors. It connects event sources with corresponding actions through Ansible Rulebooks, allowing for precise execution and leveraging existing playbooks and templates. With comprehensive features and content collections, Event-Driven Ansible accelerates event-driven automation initiatives and enhances IT responsiveness and efficiency.

To illustrate the power of Event-Driven Ansible, consider a scenario where an observability tool detects an unresponsive network router. This event triggers Event-Driven Ansible, which locates the corresponding Ansible Rulebook and matches the event with the desired action. This action could involve re-applying a configuration, resetting the router, or creating a service ticket. Event-Driven Ansible then executes the instructions from the rulebook, resetting the router and restoring normal function — without manual intervention, even during off-hours.

The Event-Driven Ansible relies on the Ansible Rulebook command-line interface for running Ansible Rulebooks. It monitors events and delegates the execution of playbooks to Ansible Automation Platform's existing tooling. On the other hand, the Event-Driven Ansible controller provides management, scaling, and observability functionality that effectively utilizes Event-Driven Ansible across various environments, including the cloud, on-premises, and hybrid setups.

Event-Driven Ansible controller was released since Ansible Automation Platform 2.4 and supports ARM and IBM Power processor architectures. It requires an Ansible automation controller to be successfully installed to connect. At the moment of writing this book it is possible to use only one event-driven controller per Ansible Automation Platform but the team is working to implement more than one. It is based on the Drools open source decision making technology. At the moment it was tested by 7000 rulebook concurrently however the actual limit might be superior as it is a new product.

Note: The Installer fails with the following error message displayed on the screen when is not specified any automation controller.

An automation controller host is required for automation EDA controller. A host must exist in **[automationcontroller]** group or **automation_controller_main_url** must be set when setting up automation EDA

The following **inventory** file deploys one Event-Driven Ansible controller, **eda.example. com**, connected to automation controller with internal database **ac.example.com**.

```
[automationcontroller]
ac.example.com
[automationcontroller:vars]
peers=execution_nodes
[execution_nodes]
[automationhub]
[automationedacontroller]
eda.example.com
[database]
[sso]
[all:vars]
admin_password='redhat'
pg_host=''
pg_port=5432
pg_database='awx'
```

```
pg_username='awx'
pg_password='redhat'
automationedacontroller_admin_password='redhat'
automationedacontroller_pg_host='ac.example.com'
automationedacontroller_pg_port=5432
automationedacontroller_pg_database='automationedacontroller'
automationedacontroller_pg_username='automationedacontroller'
automationedacontroller_pg_password='redhat'
```

The lines provided are a set of configuration parameters for the Event-Driven Ansible controller and automation controller. Please refer to the automation controller section. For the initial parameters. Let us focus only on the parameters of the Event-Driven Ansible controller:

- **automationedacontroller_admin_password='redhat'**: This parameter sets the administrator password for the Event-Driven Ansible controller. In this case, the password is set to **'redhat'**, but it can be customized to meet the organization's security requirements.

- **automationedacontroller_pg_host='ac.example.com'**: This parameter specifies the PostgreSQL database host where the Event-Driven Ansible controller will store its data. In this example, the host is set to **'ac.example.com'**, the same as the Ansible controller. We must specify our PostgreSQL database server's hostname, IP address, or external database.

Note: The Installer fails with the following error message displayed on the screen when the "automationedacontroller_pg_host" parameter is empty.

automationedacontroller_pg_host is currently empty, ensure **automationedacontroller_pg_host** is defined and pointing to a database.

- **automationedacontroller_pg_port=5432**: This parameter sets the port number for the PostgreSQL database. By default, PostgreSQL uses port 5432 for communication. If our PostgreSQL database runs on a different port, we can modify this value accordingly.

- **automationedacontroller_pg_database='automationedacontroller'**: This parameter specifies the name of the PostgreSQL database where the Event-Driven Ansible controller will store its data. In this example, the database name is set to **'automationedacontroller'**. We can choose a different name if desired.

- **automationedacontroller_pg_username='automationedacontroller'**: This parameter sets the username for connecting to the PostgreSQL database. Here, the username is set to **'automationedacontroller'**. We may need to modify it based on our PostgreSQL configuration.

- **automationedacontroller_pg_password='redhat'**: This parameter sets the password for the PostgreSQL database user specified in the **automationedacontroller_pg_username** parameter. In this case, the password is set to **'redhat'**, but we should replace it with a strong and secure password.

These configuration parameters are essential for connecting the Event-Driven Ansible controller to the PostgreSQL database and managing its administrative settings and access. Ensuring that the values provided align with our specific environment and security requirements is important.

As a result of a successful installation, we can access the Web user interface of the **eda. example.com** server with any browser. We can connect to the Web UI using the **admin** user and the selected password (**'redhat'**). A successful installation and login result on the dashboard is shown in *Figure 3.11*:

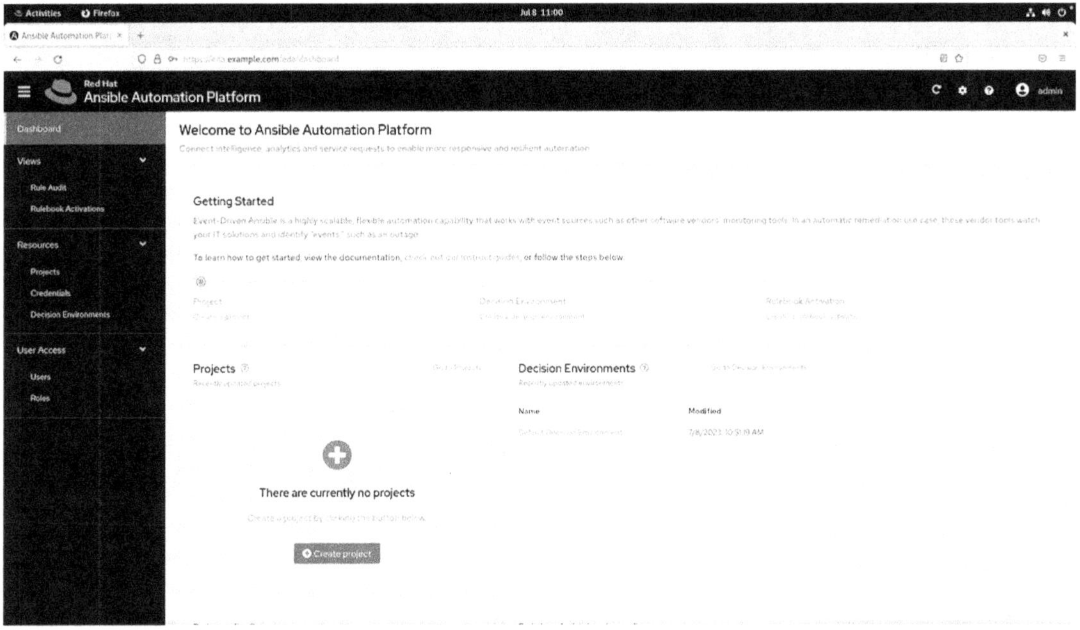

Figure 3.11: *The Dashboard of the Ansible Event-Driven controller*

Setup Ansible Automation Platform

A full installation of the Ansible Automation Platform involves deploying the automation controller and the automation hub instances and additional execution instances as shown in the following installation scenarios. We can also fine-tune the automation environment specifying the execution nodes using the Ansible mesh technology.

Ansible Automation Platform with installer-managed database

The Ansible Automation Platform with installer-managed database provides several advantages, including simplified installation and deployment, centralized automation and orchestration, extensive automation capabilities, efficient database management, enhanced collaboration and governance, integration and extensibility, and scalability and performance. This platform streamlines automation workflows, improves infrastructure management, and increases operational efficiency for organizations. Please refer to the following figure:

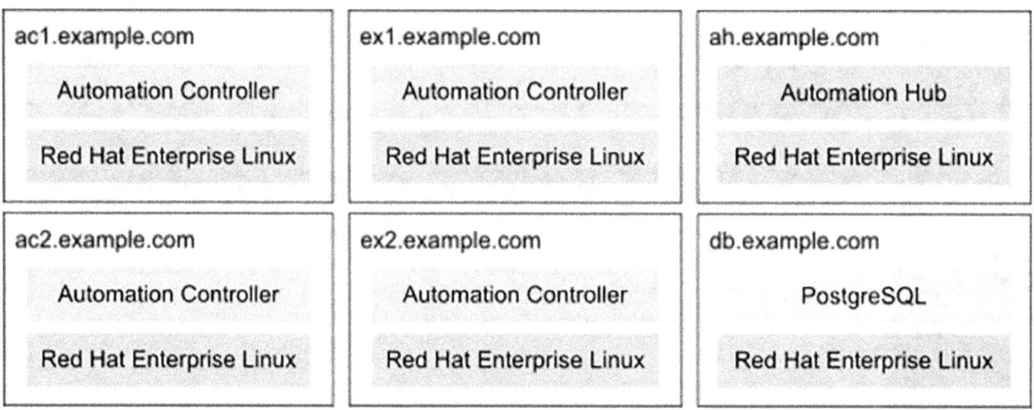

Figure 3.12: Ansible Automation Platform with installer-managed database

The example represents an **inventory** file for installing the Ansible Automation Platform with multiple automation controller nodes, execution nodes, and an automation hub, all connected to an external (installer-managed) database, as shown in *Figure 3.12*.

```
[automationcontroller]
ac1.example.com node_type=control
ac2.example.com node_type=control
[execution_nodes]
ex1.example.com node_type=execution
ex2.example.com node_type=execution
[automationhub]
ah.example.com
[database]
db.example.com
[all:vars]
admin_password='redhat'
pg_host='db.example.com'
```

```
pg_port='5432'
pg_database='awx'
pg_username='awx'
pg_password='redhat'
pg_sslmode='prefer'  # set to 'verify-full' for client-side enforced SSL
registry_url='registry.redhat.io'
registry_username='<registry username>'
registry_password='<registry password>'
receptor_listener_port=27199
automationhub_admin_password='redhat'
automationhub_pg_host='db.example.com'
automationhub_pg_port='5432'
automationhub_pg_database='automationhub'
automationhub_pg_username='automationhub'
automationhub_pg_password='redhat'
automationhub_pg_sslmode='prefer'
```

The given an example represents an **inventory** file used to deploy a standalone instance of the automation hub with an internal database. Let us break down the contents of the **inventory** file:

- **[automationcontroller]**: This group name is empty, indicating there are no automation controller nodes specified in this deployment.

- **[automationhub]**: This group name is used to identify the automation hub node. The **ah.example.com** is specified as the hostname for the automation hub. The **ansible_connection=local** indicates that the connection to the automation hub will be made locally on the machine where the inventory file is being executed.

- **[all:vars]**: This section includes variables that are applied to all hosts in the inventory.

- **Container registry variables**: **registry_url**, **registry_username**, and **registry_password** specify the credentials for accessing the container registry.

- **Automation hub configuration**: **automationhub_admin_password** sets the password for the automation hub **admin** user. The **automationhub_pg_host** is left empty, indicating that the internal database will be hosted on the same machine as the automation hub. The **automationhub_pg_port** specifies the port number for the internal database (default is **5432**). The **automationhub_pg_database** sets the name of the internal database as **'automationhub'**. The **automationhub_pg_username** and **automationhub_pg_password** specify the credentials for accessing the internal database. The **automationhub_pg_sslmode** defines the SSL mode for the database connection (set to **'prefer'** in this example).

- **SSL-related variables**:

  o The remaining lines in the inventory file are commented out and provide optional configuration options for SSL-related settings.

  o These options include installing a custom CA certificate, providing a certificate and key for the automation hub node, and configuring SSL settings for the automation hub.

  o By populating this inventory file with the appropriate values, we can deploy a standalone instance of the automation hub with an internal database. The deployment will use the specified configuration, including the provided passwords, registry credentials, and SSL settings if enabled.

Ansible Automation Platform with external database

The Ansible Automation Platform with the external-managed database refers to an installation or configuration setup where the platform's data is stored and managed in an external database system. Instead of using an internal PostgreSQL database, the platform is configured to utilize a separate and dedicated external PostgreSQL database for storing its data. This configuration allows for scalability, improved performance, and easier management of the Ansible Automation Platform's data, as it is stored in a reliable and robust database system. This scenario is for large organizations with a team that can use a fully managed PostgreSQL database or cluster. Please refer to the following figure:

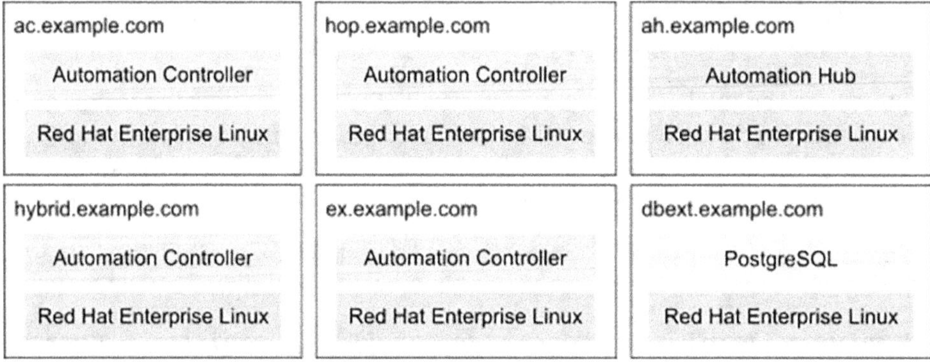

Figure 3.13: Ansible Automation Platform with an external database

The following **inventory** file sets up an Ansible Automation Platform with an external (customer-provided) database. It specifies the configuration for different platform components, including the automation controller, execution nodes, and automation hub.

```
[automationcontroller]
hybrid.example.com node_type=hybrid
ac.example.com node_type=control
[execution_nodes]
```

```
hop.example.com node_type=hop
ex.example.com node_type=execution
[automationhub]
ah.example.com
[database]
[all:vars]
admin_password='redhat'
pg_host='dbext.example.com'
pg_port='5432'
pg_database='awx'
pg_username='awx'
pg_password='redhat'
pg_sslmode='prefer'
registry_url='registry.redhat.io'
registry_username='<registry username>'
registry_password='<registry password>'
receptor_listener_port=27199
automationhub_admin_password='redhat'
automationhub_pg_host='dbext.example.com'
automationhub_pg_port='5432'
automationhub_pg_database='automationhub'
automationhub_pg_username='automationhub'
automationhub_pg_password='redhat'
automationhub_pg_sslmode='prefer'
```

The given example represents an **inventory** file used for installing the Ansible Automation Platform with four different node types (**control**, **hybrid**, **hop**, and **execution**), an instance of private automation hub, and an external customer-provided PostgreSQL database. Let us go through the contents of the **inventory** file:

- **[automationcontroller]**:

    o   This group name is used to identify the automation controller nodes.

    o   Two nodes are specified: **hybrid1.example.com** and **ac.example.com**.

    o   **hybrid.example.com** is assigned **node_type=hybrid**, indicating it can run everything.

    o   **ac.example.com** is assigned **node_type=control**, indicating it can only run project and inventory updates but not regular jobs.

- **[execution_nodes]:**
    - o This group name is used to identify the execution nodes.
    - o Two nodes are specified: **hop.example.com** and **ex.example.com**.
    - o **hop.example.com** is assigned **node_type=hop**, indicating it forwards jobs to an execution node.
    - o **ex.example.com** is assigned **node_type=execution**, indicating it can run jobs.
- **[automationhub]:**
    - o This group name is used to identify the automation hub node.
    - o **ah.example.com** is specified as the automation hub host.
- **[database]:**
    - o This group name indicates the absence of a specific database node.
    - o The installer assumes that the database exists and is managed externally, not by the platform installer.
- **[all:vars]:**
    - o This section includes variables applied to all hosts in the inventory.
- **`admin_password='<password>'`:**
    - o This variable sets the password for the Ansible Automation Platform admin user.
- **PostgreSQL database variables:**
    - o `pg_host`, `pg_port`, `pg_database`, `pg_username`, `pg_password`, and `pg_sslmode` specify the connection details for the external database.
- **Container registry variables:**
    - o `registry_url`, `registry_username`, and `registry_password` specify the credentials for accessing the container registry.
- **Receptor configuration:**
    - o `receptor_listener_port` sets the port for the receptor listener.
- **Automation hub configuration:**
    - o `automationhub_admin_password` sets the password for the private automation hub admin user.

o PostgreSQL database parameters (`` `automationhub_pg_host` ``, `` `automationhub_pg_port` ``, `` `automationhub_pg_database` ``, `` `automationhub_pg_username` ``, `` `automationhub_pg_password` ``, and `` `automationhub_pg_sslmode` ``) specify the connection details for the private automation hub's external database.

Load balancer

Configuring a load balancer enables us to distribute the workload in multiple instances. The benefit is in the amount of workload we can actively process (active-active scenario) and fault tolerance. The second property is crucial in the enterprise environment to guarantee the business continuity of our Ansible Automation Platform. Another common usage is for SSL terminators. This way, we can handle the encrypted traffic via the load balancer and process our workload faster in the nodes. Setting the following parameters we configure the proxy support for the Red Hat Ansible Automation Platform. Proxy servers act as intermediaries between clients and servers, simplifying and controlling the complexity of requests. The typical proxy servers in front of the automation controller and private automation hub are Amazon **Application Load Balancer** (**ALB**), **Amazon Network Load Balancer** (**NLB**), HAProxy, Squid, Nginx, and Tinyproxy. Please refer to the following figure:

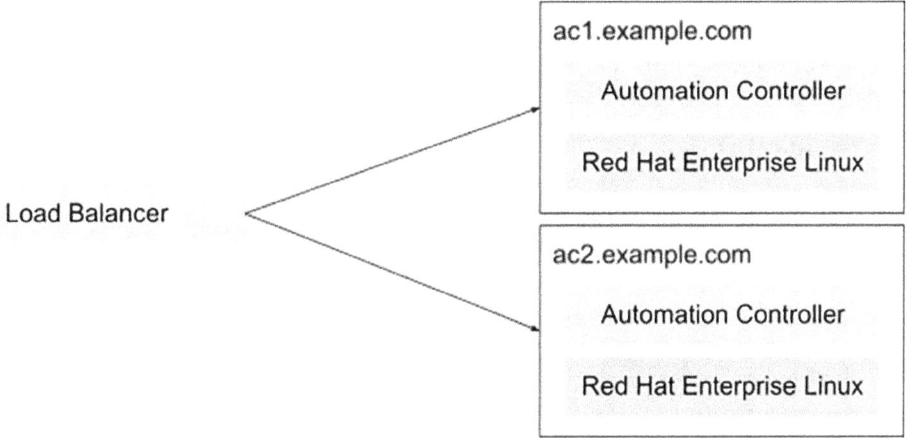

Figure 3.14: Ansible Automation Platform load balancer

We need to perform the following steps:

1. **Enable AAP proxy support**:

   To enable proxy server support, we need to set the **REMOTE_HOST_HEADERS** parameter in the settings page of our automation controller. The **REMOTE_HOST_HEADERS** variable determines the enabled remote host's IP address by searching through a list of headers. By default, it is set to **["REMOTE_ADDR", "REMOTE_HOST"]**.

2. **Available proxies**:

   When the automation controller instance(s) is configured with **REMOTE_HOST_HEADERS = ['HTTP_X_FORWARDED_FOR', 'REMOTE_ADDR', 'REMOTE_HOST']**, it assumes that the value of **X-Forwarded-For** originated from the proxy or load balancer in front of the automation controller. However, this can be vulnerable to falsified IP addresses. To mitigate this, we can configure a list of known proxy servers using the **PROXY_IP_ALLOWED_LIST** field in the settings menu of our automation controller. Requests from load balancers or hosts not on the available proxies list will be rejected.

3. **Configuring known proxies**:

   To configure a list of the available proxies in our network, we need to add their IP addresses to the **PROXY_IP_ALLOWED_LIST** field on the settings page of our automation controller. The IP addresses should be entered following the provided syntax, such as **"example.proxy.com:8080"**. It is important to ensure that the proxies in the list properly sanitize header input and set the **X-Forwarded-For** value to the real source IP of the client.

4. **Configuring a reverse proxy**:

   To support a reverse proxy server configuration, we can add **HTTP_X_FORWARDED_FOR** to the **REMOTE_HOST_HEADERS** field in our automation controller settings. The **X-Forwarded-For (XFF)** header identifies the originating IP address of a client connecting to a web server through an HTTP proxy or load balancer.

5. **Enable sticky sessions**:

   By default, an **Application Load Balancer (ALB)** routes each request independently based on the load-balancing algorithm. However, to avoid authentication errors when running multiple instances of private automation hub behind a load balancer, we must enable the sticky session feature (also known as session affinity). This involves setting a custom application cookie that matches the cookie configured on the load balancer, enabling stickiness. The custom cookie can include any required cookie attributes.

Websockets

The automation controller nodes of the Ansible Automation Platform are interconnected through web sockets to distribute messages (Websocket emitted) across the system. This setup allows any browser to subscribe as a Websocket client to any job running for any automation controller node. Websocket clients are not directed to specific nodes; any automation controller node can handle any Websocket request. All automation controller nodes must know Websocket messages intended for all clients.

The Websocket configuration is performed in the **/etc/tower/conf.d/websocket_ config.py** file on all automation controller nodes. After making the changes, the service must be restarted for the configuration to take effect.

The automation controller automatically discovers other automation controller nodes through the instance record in the database.

To enable the automation controller to discover other nodes automatically, we can configure the Websocket connections. This involves editing the Websocket information for the port and protocol and specifying the verification of the SSL certificates (**True** or **False**) for the Websocket connections.

Example configuration:

```
BROADCAST_WEBSOCKET_PROTOCOL = 'http'

BROADCAST_WEBSOCKET_PORT = 80

BROADCAST_WEBSOCKET_VERIFY_CERT = False
```

These settings define the protocol as HTTP, the port as 80, and disable certificate verification for the Websocket connections.

OpenShift

Another option is the installation of the Ansible Automation Platform on the Red Hat OpenShift Container Platform (Kubernetes based).

The Ansible Automation Platform operator is a tool that facilitates the seamless deployment of the Ansible Automation Platform instances within our OpenShift environment. It leverages cloud-native technologies and provides a straightforward, push-button deployment process. With the Ansible Automation Platform operator, we can easily deploy and manage automation controller and private automation hub instances and define and launch automation controller jobs.

By utilizing the Kubernetes native operator, deploying Ansible Automation Platform instances simplifies the Red Hat **OpenShift Container Platform (OCP)** lifecycle maintenance. These advantages include simplified upgrades and comprehensive lifecycle support for our Red Hat Ansible Automation Platform deployments. The latest Ansible Automation Platform operator can install the Ansible Automation Platform on the latest versions of the OpenShift Container Platform. After successfully installing the Ansible Automation Platform operator, the Kubernetes operators and pods of *Table 3.1* are running in our cluster:

Operator manager controllers	Automation controller	Automation hub

`automation-controller-operator-controller-manager`
 	
`automation-hub-operator-controller-manager`
 	
`resource-operator-controller-manager`
	`controller`
	
	`controller-postgres`
		`hub-api`
		
		`hub-content`
		
		`hub-postgres`
		
		`hub-redis`
		
		`hub-worker`

Table 3.1: Operators included in Ansible Automation Platform operator

The Ansible Automation Platform operator is a great tool for managing the lifecycle of the automation controller, automation hub instances, and all the dependents resources, as shown in the user interface displayed in *Figure 3.15*:

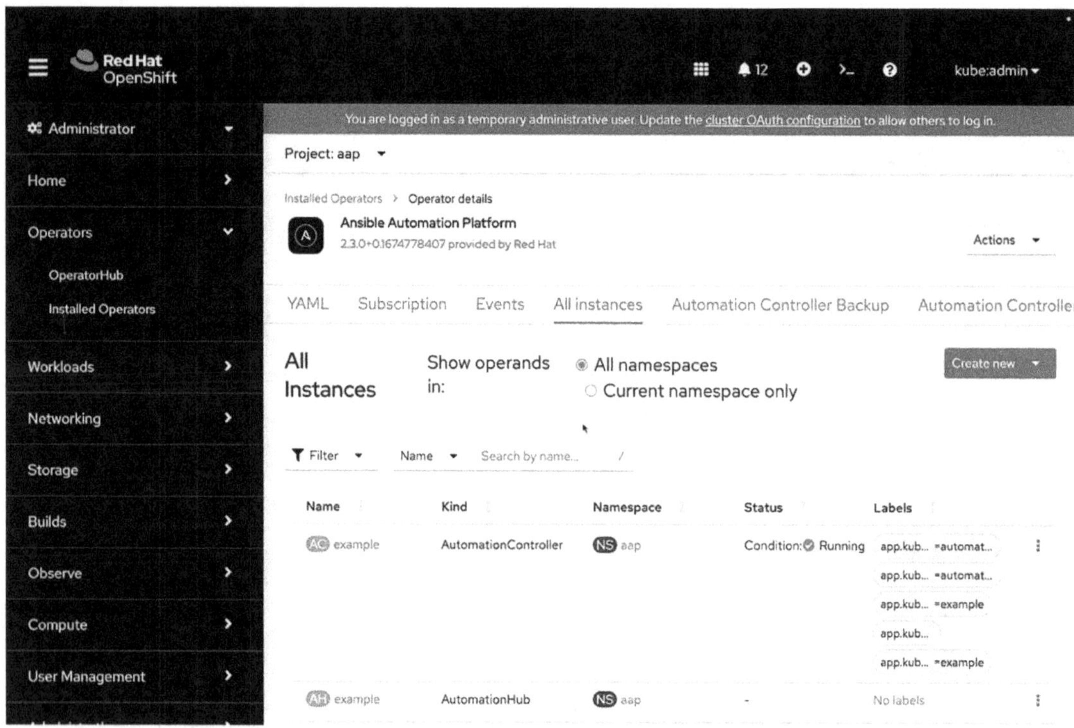

Figure 3.15: Manage AAP via operator

Operator installation

Installing the Ansible Automation Platform operator in a Red Hat OCP cluster is easy using the native OperatorHub.

First, we must log into our OpenShift cluster via the web console with a user with administrative privileges (**kubeadmin** for example). Alternatively, it is possible to install the command line.

To install the Ansible Automation Platform operator, we can access the Red Hat operators catalog in OperatorHub, the marketplace integrated into the OpenShift cluster, where we will find the necessary resources for installation, as shown in *Figure 3.16*:

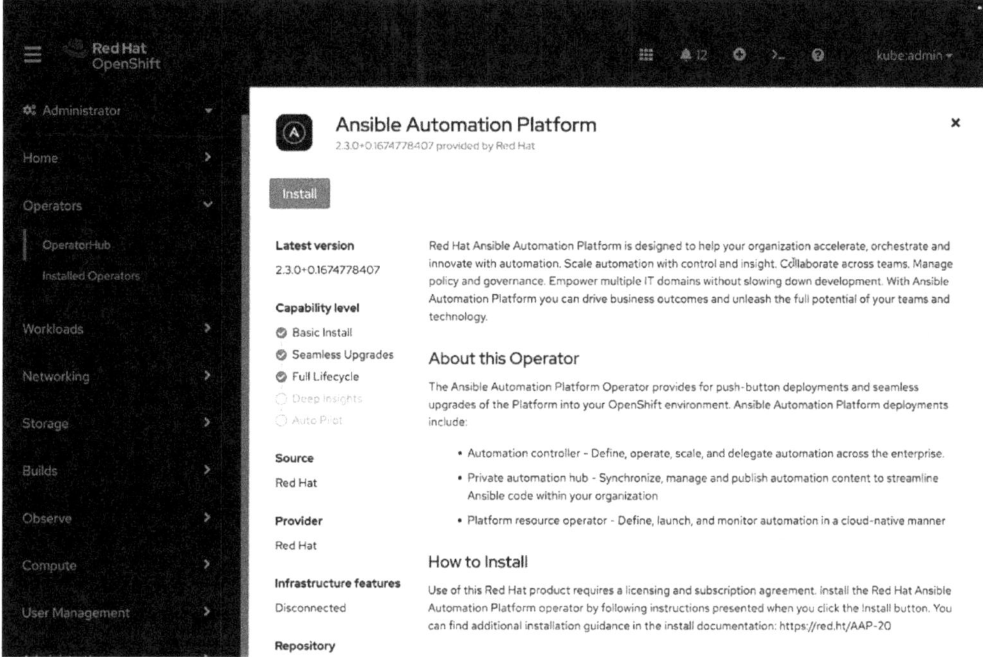

Figure 3.16: Install Ansible Automation Platform operator

The Ansible Automation Platform operator enables streamlined management and deployment of Ansible Automation Platform instances, enhancing the efficiency and effectiveness of our automation workflows within our OpenShift environment.

The installation options for the Ansible Automation Platform operator are shown in *Figure 3.14*. We need to choose the update channel, the installation mode, and the update approval. For the **Update** channel, we have the following choices:

- **stable-2.x**: Installs a namespace-scoped operator, limiting automation hub and automation controller instances to the namespace where the operator is installed. This is suitable for most scenarios, requiring fewer resources and no administrator privileges.

- **stable-2.x-cluster-scoped**: Deploys automation controller and private automation hub and across multiple namespaces in the cluster, necessitating administrator privileges for all namespaces.

Additionally, select the installation mode, installed namespace, and approval strategy, as displayed in *Figure 3.17*:

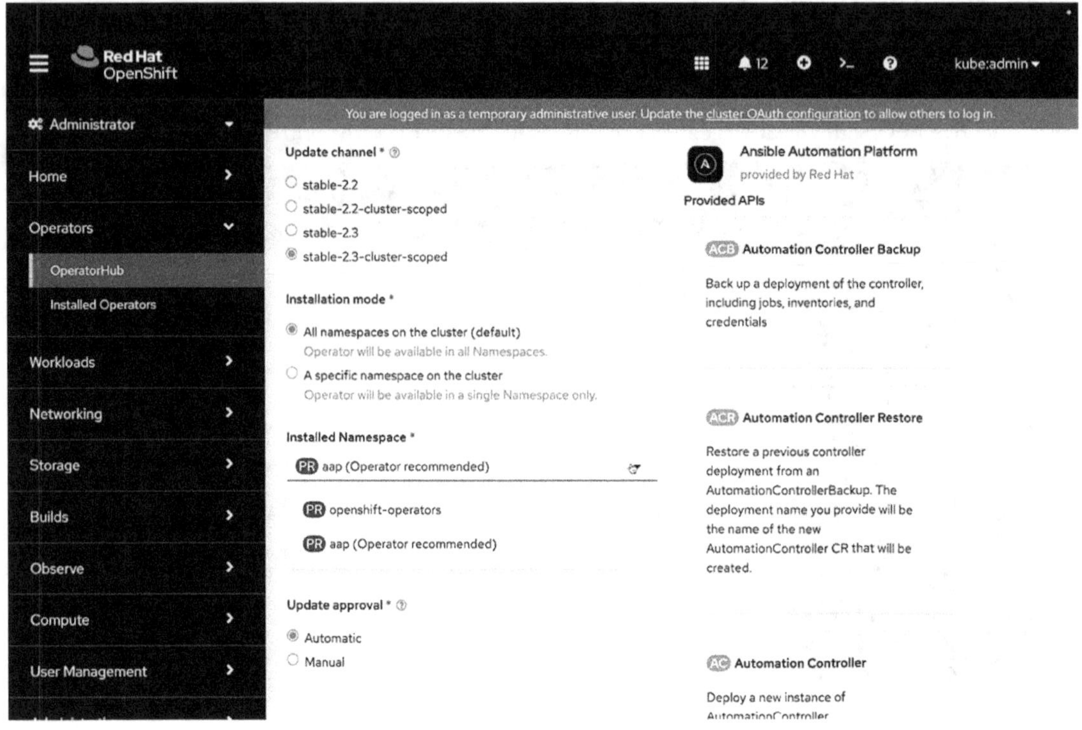

Figure 3.17: Ansible Automation Platform operator installation options

When we are ready, we can hit the **Install** button. After a few minutes, the Ansible Automation Platform operator is going to be installed in our OpenShift cluster. We obtain the `installed operator - ready to use` message on the screen. We can check the installed operators in our OpenShift cluster at every moment via the **Installed Operators** drop-down menu. The operator provides an easy way to install and maintain the software lifecycle of the automation controller and automation hub deeply integrated into OpenShift, allocating the necessary resources for the PostgreSQL databases and shared secrets. There are also specific options for backup and restoration of each instance. Whenever we start a template, all the dependent containers are allocated: PostgreSQL database, Redis, control plane, execution environment, web container, and so on. The operators of *Table 3.1* are running in our cluster.

Automation controller

The Ansible Automation Platform operator provides an easy way to install and configure the automation controller instances on the Red Hat **OpenShift Container Platform** (OCP). We can install the automation controller specifying custom resources and deploying the Ansible Automation Platform with an external PostgreSQL database. It provides the prerequisites (CPU cores, memory, storage limits, and requests), creates an automation controller instance using the form view or YAML view, configures image pull policies, sets resource requirements, and defines replicas and other options. It is important to note that configurations made in the **extra_settings** take precedence over those made in the user interface, and manual removal of old **Persistent Volume Claims** (**PVCs**) is recommended before deploying a new automation controller instance in the same Kubernetes/ OCP namespace. The user interface for creating the automation controller is shown in *Figure 3.18*:

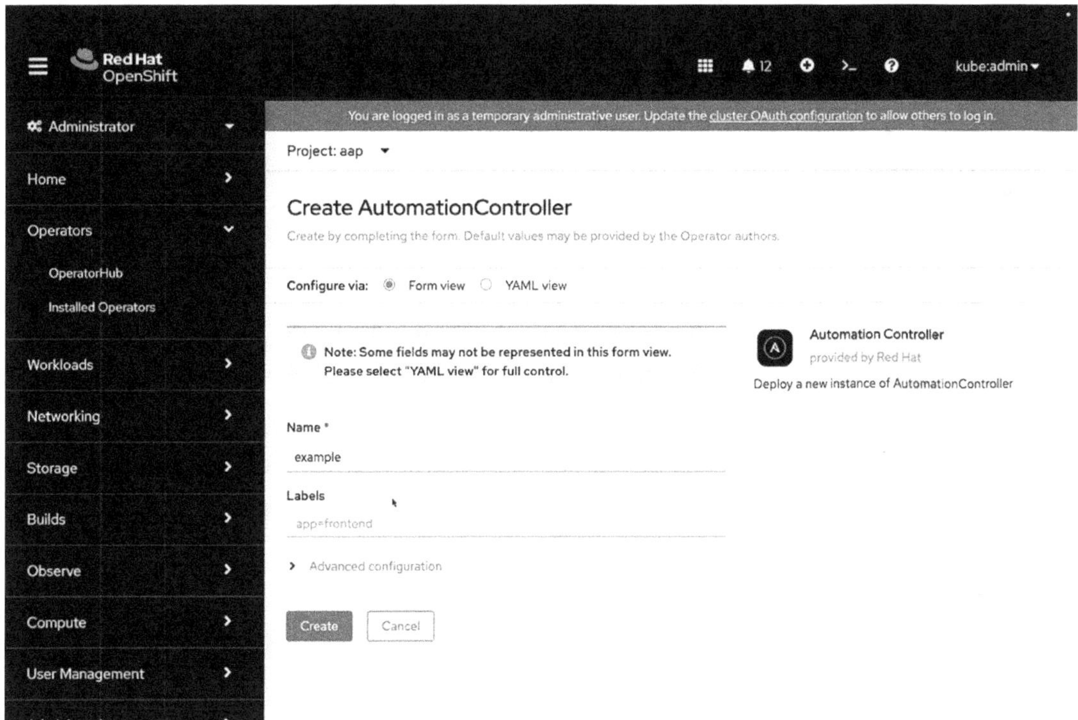

Figure 3.18: Install automation controller via AAP operator

Power users can customize the configuration using the **Advanced configuration** with LDAP settings, PostgreSQL container resources, web container resources, used secrets, EE control plane container resources, preload instance with data upon creation, Ingress network configuration, and so on.

Automation hub

The Ansible Automation Platform operator provides install and configures the automation hub on the Red Hat OpenShift Container Platform web console. It covers installing the automation hub operator, specifying custom resources, and deploying the Ansible Automation Platform with an external PostgreSQL database. The configuration of the automation hub can be done through the **pulp_settings** or the user interface after deployment, with the **pulp_settings** taking precedence. It is recommended to manually remove old Persistent Volume Claims before deploying a new private automation hub instance in the same namespace. It also provides prerequisites for installation and discusses storage options such as ReadWriteMany file-based storage, Azure Blob storage, and Amazon S3-compliant storage for the automation hub operation. Additional parameters are possible to set up advanced parameters such as storage configurations as displayed in *Figure 3.19*:

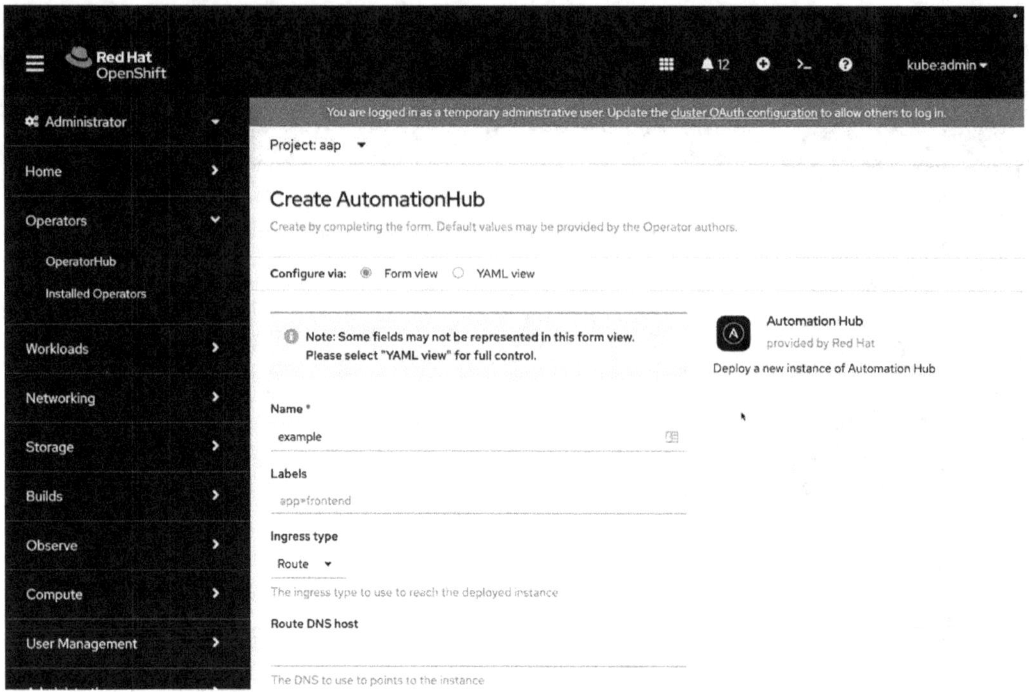

Figure 3.19: Install automation hub via AAP operator

Containerized

On 28 September 2023, Red Hat proudly announced the technical preview of a containerized version of its Ansible Automation Platform. This innovative solution marks a significant milestone in streamlining and enhancing the management of Ansible services. The evolution of the Ansible Automation Platform led to the inclusion of various services and components. While this expanded the platform's capabilities, it also introduced complexities related to maintenance, installation, and support. These challenges became the driving force behind the development of the containerized Ansible Automation Platform. Containerization represents the first step toward achieving a more streamlined and efficient platform management experience, aligning with Red Hat's vision and long-term strategy. Underneath it takes advantage of the Podman technology integrated on Red Hat Enterprise Linux.

The containerizing version of the Ansible Automation Platform goes beyond merely adapting existing services. Red Hat set several ambitious goals to provide a holistic solution that benefits users in multiple ways:

- **Slimmed down installation**: The installation process has been simplified, making it more accessible for users with varying levels of technical expertise.

- **Layered installation approach**: The approach allows for greater flexibility and customization, ensuring that users can tailor the platform to their specific needs.

- **Security out of the box**: The containerized solution employs rootless Podman containers, enhancing security immediately.

- **New features**: This technical preview introduces several new features, such as applying Ansible Automation Platform licenses during installation and pre-seeding automation controller configurations as code.

- **Lighter footprint**: The containerized platform caters to a wide range of markets and solutions, ensuring a lighter footprint that can meet the demands of diverse users.

The setup process is designed to be straightforward, even for users with limited experience. It involves a few essential tasks:

1. **Download and unpack the installation bundle**: Users can access the installation bundle through the **Red Hat Network (RHN)** portal. The package is available in both online (internet access required) and offline bundle forms, catering to diverse installation scenarios.

2. **Edit the supplied inventory file**: The installation directory contains an **inventory** file preconfigured with essential information. Users can edit this file, modifying configurations as needed and filling in the required variables. The following **inventory** file installs the full containerized Ansible Automation Platform (database, automation controller, Ansible automation hub, and Event-Driven Ansible controller) on the **aap.example.com** host.

```
[automationcontroller]
aap.example.com ansible_connection=local
[automationhub]
aap.example.com ansible_connection=local
[automationeda]
aap.example.com ansible_connection=local
[database]
aap.example.com ansible_connection=local
[all:vars]
postgresql_admin_username=postgres
```

```
postgresql_admin_password=redhat
registry_username=RHN_USERNAME
registry_password=RHN_PASSWORD
controller_admin_password=redhat
controller_pg_host=aap.example.com
controller_pg_password=redhat
hub_admin_password=redhat
hub_pg_host=aap.example.com
hub_pg_password=redhat
eda_admin_password=redhat
eda_pg_host=aap.example.com
eda_pg_password=redhat
controller_main_url=https://aap.example.com
```

Additionally, we can enable these two options for post-installation applying the manifest license and the config-as-code directory by uncommenting and setting accordingly the following two variables.

```
#controller_postinstall=true
#controller_license_file=<full path to your manifest .zip file>
#controller_postinstall_dir=<full path to your config-as-code directory>
```

3. **Set environment variables**: Users need to specify the location of the installer collections using the **ANSIBLE_COLLECTIONS_PATH** environment variable.

```
export ANSIBLE_COLLECTIONS_PATH=/full-path-to-installer/collections
```

4. **Run the installer**: The installation process involves running the installer collections playbook using the **ansible-playbook** command. This step can be customized with various options, including increasing verbosity or privilege escalation.

```
ansible-playbook -i inventory ansible.containerized_installer.
install
```

The installation process is going to take a while as many components are installed in the target system. Once the installation is complete, users can access the Ansible Automation Platform services via their web browsers. The services are deployed on our instance on specific ports. The following are the one used in the Technology Preview version (they might change in the future):

- Automation controller on port 443

- Ansible automation hub on port 444

- Event-Driven Ansible controller on port 445

Please refer to the following figure:

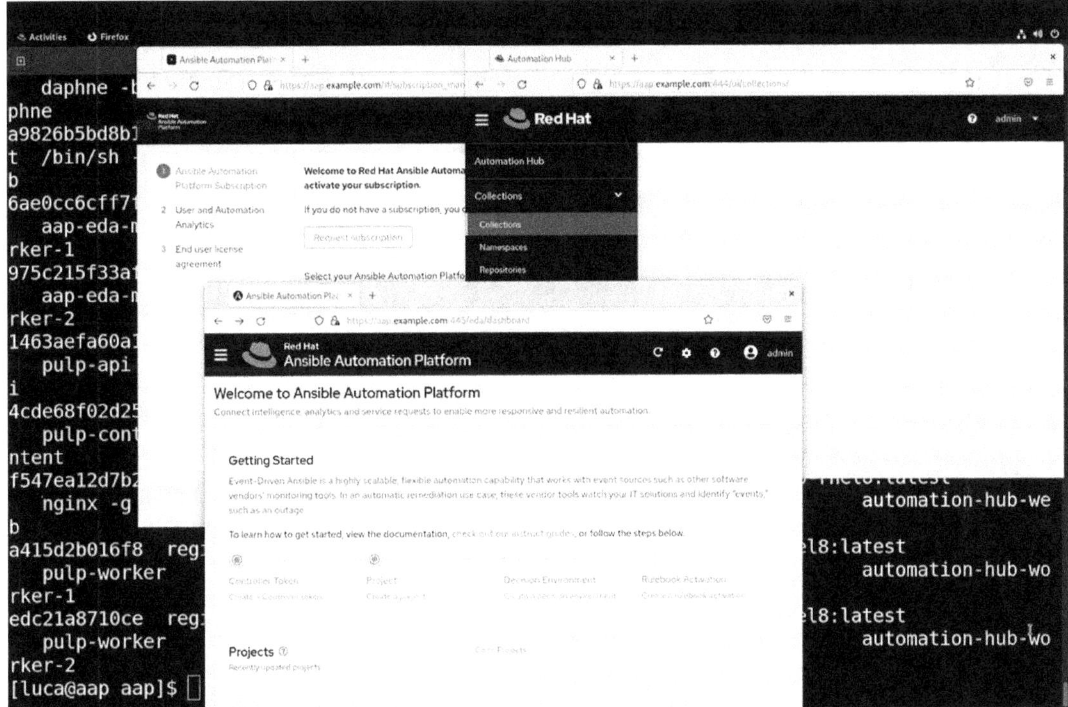

Figure 3.20: Containerized AAP

In the follow the full list of running containers in a fully containerized Ansible Automation Platform:

```
$ podman ps
CONTAINER ID  IMAGE                                                         COMMAND
CREATED          STATUS                      PORTS          NAMES
45079e0f8b65 registry.redhat.io/rhel8/redis-6:latest                          run-
redis            3 days ago      Up Less than a second           redis
0e686ba496a7               registry.redhat.io/rhel8/postgresql-13:latest
run-postgresql     37 minutes ago  Up 35 minutes                   postgresql
631bd7c95a48             registry.redhat.io/ansible-automation-platform-24/ee-
supported-rhel8:latest           /usr/bin/receptor...   35 minutes ago   Up 6
minutes                    receptor
7507d7732073   registry.redhat.io/ansible-automation-platform-24/controller-
rhel8:latest             /usr/bin/launch_a...   19 minutes ago   Up 6 minutes
automation-controller-rsyslog
6190a2861e06   registry.redhat.io/ansible-automation-platform-24/controller-
rhel8:latest             /usr/bin/launch_a...   8 minutes ago    Up 6 minutes
automation-controller-task
```

```
120a89253743    registry.redhat.io/ansible-automation-platform-24/controller-
rhel8:latest             /usr/bin/launch_a...   8 minutes ago    Up 6 minutes
automation-controller-web
06d289e13a85             registry.redhat.io/ansible-automation-platform-24/eda-
controller-rhel8:latest    gunicorn --bind 1...  6 minutes ago   Up 3 minutes
automation-eda-api
69734ae71fe8             registry.redhat.io/ansible-automation-platform-24/eda-
controller-rhel8:latest    daphne -b 127.0.0...  5 minutes ago   Up 3 minutes
automation-eda-daphne
a9826b5bd8b1             registry.redhat.io/ansible-automation-platform-24/eda-
controller-ui-rhel8:latest  /bin/sh -c nginx ...  5 minutes ago   Up 3 minutes
automation-eda-web
6ae0cc6cff7f             registry.redhat.io/ansible-automation-platform-24/eda-
controller-rhel8:latest    aap-eda-manage rq...  4 minutes ago   Up 3 minutes
automation-eda-worker-1
975c215f33af             registry.redhat.io/ansible-automation-platform-24/eda-
controller-rhel8:latest    aap-eda-manage rq...  4 minutes ago   Up 3 minutes
automation-eda-worker-2
1463aefa60a1             registry.redhat.io/ansible-automation-platform-24/hub-
rhel8:latest                 pulp-api              3 minutes ago   Up About a
minute                   automation-hub-api
4cde68f02d25             registry.redhat.io/ansible-automation-platform-24/hub-
rhel8:latest                 pulp-content          2 minutes ago   Up About a
minute                   automation-hub-content
f547ea12d7b2         registry.redhat.io/ansible-automation-platform-24/hub-web-
rhel8:latest                 nginx -g daemon o...  2 minutes ago   Up About a
minute                   automation-hub-web
a415d2b016f8             registry.redhat.io/ansible-automation-platform-24/hub-
rhel8:latest                 pulp-worker           2 minutes ago   Up About a
minute                   automation-hub-worker-1
edc21a8710ce             registry.redhat.io/ansible-automation-platform-24/hub-
rhel8:latest                 pulp-worker           2 minutes ago   Up About a
minute                   automation-hub-worker-2
```

The introduction of the containerized Ansible Automation Platform represents a major advancement in the world of IT management. Red Hat's commitment to streamlining and enhancing the platform's management experience is evident in this technical preview. Customers now have a secure and flexible variety of deployment scenarios. The software is available for download from the Red Hat portal under the downloads section, with comprehensive documentation provided for a detailed installation walkthrough. As the future unfolds, Red Hat continues to innovate, with the promise of more exciting features and enhancements on the horizon.

Key learning

This chapter provides a comprehensive overview of the Ansible Automation Platform installation scenarios. It covers the prerequisites and requirements for installation, compares the online and bundle installer options, and explores various installation scenarios. The chapter guides readers through the setup of the automation controller, private automation hub, the Event-Driven Ansible controller, and Ansible Automation Platform. It also discusses the setup of a load balancer specific to the Ansible Automation Platform and provides information on deploying the platform on OpenShift. Overall, the chapter offers valuable insights into the installation process for the Ansible Automation Platform in a range of different scenarios.

Points to remember

- The Ansible Automation Platform includes the Red Hat Ansible Automation Platform installer tool to simplify user onboarding and component setup.

- The installation is available in online or bundle formats according to the needs of our organization.

- There are many installation scenarios based on workload, high availability, and resiliency of the system.

Multiple choice questions

1. **What is not a correct pre-requisite or requirement for the Ansible Automation Platform node?**

    a. x86-compatible 64-bit processor Intel or AMD

    b. Red Hat Enterprise Linux operating system

    c. 1 CPU for controller nodes

    d. NTP client **chrony** service configured

2. **What are the two supported modes for the Red Hat Ansible Automation Platform installer?**

    a. Online and offline

    b. Online and bundle

    c. Standalone and cluster

    d. Standalone and online

3. **What is not a supported automation controller scenario?**

    a. Single automation controller with installer-managed external database

    b. Standalone automation controller with internal database

    c. Single automation controller with installer-managed database

    d. Single automation controller with external database

4. **How can we deploy the Ansible Automation Platform in the Red Hat OpenShift Container Platform?**

    a. Ansible namespace

    b. AAP YAML manifest

    c. Manually deploy automation controller and automation hub

    d. Ansible Automation Platform operator

Answers

1. c

2. b

3. a

4. d

Questions

1. What are the pre-requisite and requirements for automation controller nodes, execution nodes, and automation hub nodes?

2. How can the Red Hat Automation Platform be deployed in an air-gapped scenario using the Red Hat Ansible Automation Platform installer?

3. What are the supported automation controller scenarios?

4. What are the supported automation hub scenarios?

5. How can we deploy the Ansible Automation Platform in the Red Hat OpenShift Container Platform?

6. What tools to set up a load balancer for the Ansible Automation Platform?

Key terms

- **Online versus bundle**: The Ansible Automation Platform offers two installation options: Online installation, which simplifies user onboarding and component setup, and the bundle installer, which assists IT professionals with the initial system installation and provides installation log files for review.

- **Air-gapped**: It refers to a secure environment or system physically isolated from external networks, preventing direct communication or data transfer between the isolated system and the outside world.

- **Internal database**: An internal database is a data storage system built into a software application or system and used for storing and managing data internally within the application or system itself.

- **External database**: An external database is a separate data storage system accessed by an application or system to store and manage data outside the application or system itself.

- **Standalone instance**: A standalone instance refers to a single, independent, and self-contained deployment of a software or service that operates independently without being part of a larger system or cluster.

- **Red Hat OpenShift Container Platform**: It is a comprehensive enterprise-grade Kubernetes container platform for deploying, managing, and scaling applications.

- **WebSockets**: These communication protocols enable real-time, two-way data exchange between a client and a server over a single, long-lived connection.

Join our book's Discord space

Join the book's Discord Workspace for Latest updates, Offers, Tech happenings around the world, New Release and Sessions with the Authors:

https://discord.bpbonline.com

CHAPTER 4
First Steps

Introduction

After successfully installing the Ansible Automation Platform in this chapter, we move the first steps to the automation controller, automation hub, and Event-Driven Ansible controller. We will explore the key components of each, interacting with the software dashboards and the most important options to execute our Ansible automation code (playbook, rulebook, and collection) most efficiently and successfully.

Structure

In this chapter, we will discuss the following topics:

- Subscription activation
- Automation controller dashboard
- Ansible controller API
- Automation controller CLI
- Execution environments
- Jobs
- Managing log

- Dynamic inventory

- Automation hub dashboard

- Event-Driven Ansible

- Best practices

Objectives

By the end of this chapter, we will be able to successfully execute our code in the automation controller and take advantage of the Ansible Automation Platform's main components.

Ansible subscription

The Red Hat Ansible Automation Platform subscription support is necessary to use the platform effectively. Organizations gain access to full enterprise life cycle support, enabling them to manage and expand their automation initiatives effectively. There are two subscriptions: standard (8 AM to 5 PM SLA technical support) or premium (24x7 SLA technical support). There is also a 60-day trial for new customers. Our automation controller needs a subscription manifest file that we can upload manually or using Ansible code. Alternatively, we can use our Satellite credentials if our cluster nodes are registered to Red Hat Satellite through Subscription Manager. We can obtain the manifest file for our Ansible Automation Platform via the **subscription allocations** page in the Red Hat customer portal associated with our Ansible Automation Platform entitlement(s) plan.

We can manually retrieve our subscription by typing our Red Hat customer portal or Satellite credentials on the first connection to the Ansible automation controller. The screen dialog is shown in *Figure 4.1* below:

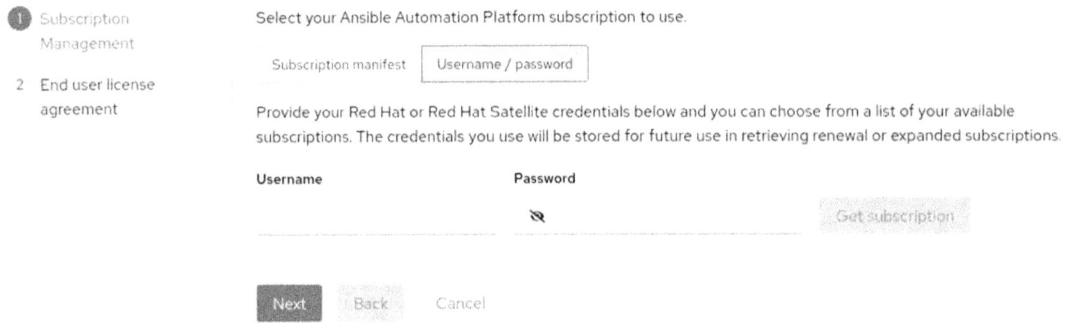

Figure 4.1: License credentials

Suppose we have a subscription manifest downloaded for the Red Hat customer portal. In that case, we can upload it either through the Red Hat Ansible Automation Platform interface or an Ansible Playbook. The screen dialog is shown in *Figure 4.2* below:

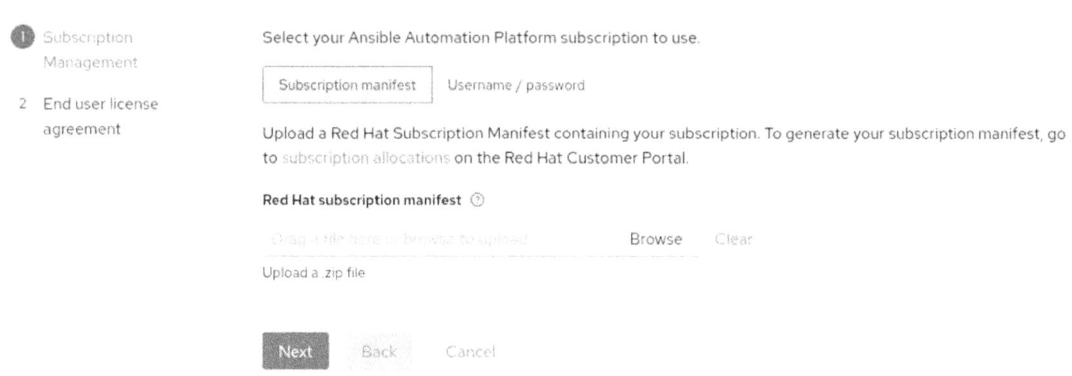

Figure 4.2: License manifest

By following these activation procedures, we can successfully activate the Red Hat Ansible Automation Platform using credentials or a manifest file. This ensures proper authorization for using the Ansible Automation Platform and allows us to access its features and functionalities.

Activate with Ansible

We can activate the Ansible controller by providing the manifest file automatically using the Ansible **license** module in the **ansible.controller** collection. For further information, refer to the official *Red Hat Hybrid Cloud Console* documentation, as shown in *Figure 4.3*:

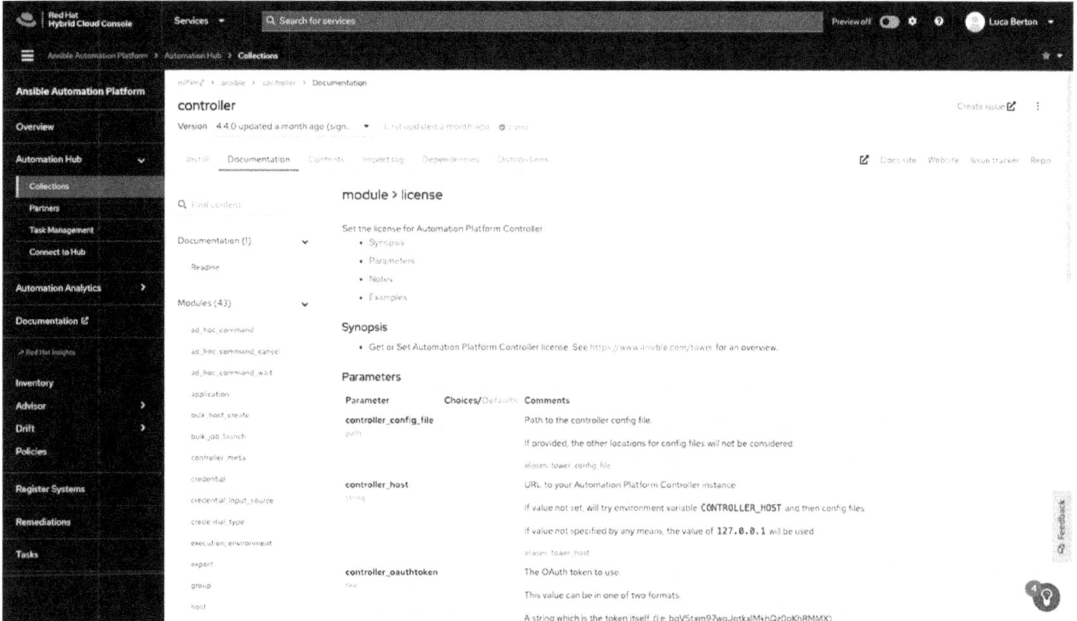

Figure 4.3: Documentation for the ansible.controller collection

The following **aap_activate.yml** Ansible Playbook to set the license using the manifest file specified in the **manifest** variable:

```
---

- name: Activate License
  hosts: all
  vars:
    manifest: "/tmp/my_manifest.zip"
  tasks:
  - name: Set the license using manifest file
    ansible.controller.license:
      manifest: "{{ manifest }}"
      controller_host: ac.example.com
      controller_username: admin
      controller_password: redhat
```

These are the key areas of the Ansible playbook:

- **vars:** section defines variables used within the playbook. In this case, it sets the manifest variable to **/tmp/my_manifest.zip**. We can modify the path according to the location of the manifest file or use an extra variable to override the parameter.

- **ansible.controller.license**: It is a module provided by the **ansible.controller** collection, specifically designed for managing licenses in the Ansible Automation Platform.

- **manifest**: This parameter specifies the path to the subscription **manifest** file. In this case, it uses the value of the manifest variable defined earlier.

- **controller_host**: This parameter specifies the hostname or IP address of the Ansible Automation Platform controller. Modify this value to match our automation controller host.

- **controller_username** and **controller_password**: These parameters are used to provide the credentials required to access the Ansible Automation Platform. Modify these values according to our environment's **admin** username and password or provide the OAuth token using the **controller_oauthtoken** parameter.

We can execute the Ansible Playbook using the **ansible-playbook** command included in every Ansible installation:

```
ansible-playbook aap_activate.yml
```

By running this playbook, Ansible activates the license using the provided manifest file and the specified credentials to authenticate with the Ansible automation controller.

Automation controller

The automation controller **Dashboard** provides a user-friendly graphical interface for our IT orchestration needs. Here is a breakdown of the key elements on the Dashboard:

- **Navigation menu**: Located on the left side, the navigation menu allows us to easily access different views, navigate resources, grant access, and manage the automation controller features in the user interface, as shown in *Figure 4.4:*

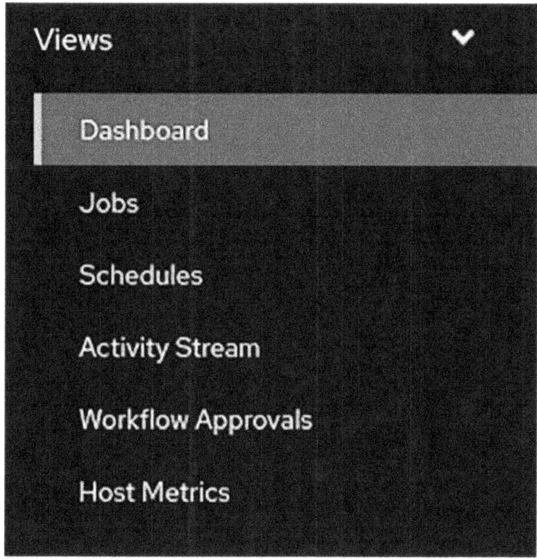

Figure 4.4: Automation controller navigation menu

- **Menu icon**: Clicking on the **Menu** icon at the top of the left navigation hides or displays the navigation bar, providing more space on the screen, as shown in *Figure 4.5:*

Figure 4.5: Automation controller menu icon

- **Main Dashboard view**: The **Dashboard** view summarizes our current job status. We can filter the job status by time period or job type. The **Recent Jobs** and **Recent Templates** tabs provide summaries of recently executed jobs and used templates, which various attributes can sort, as shown in *Figure 4.6:*

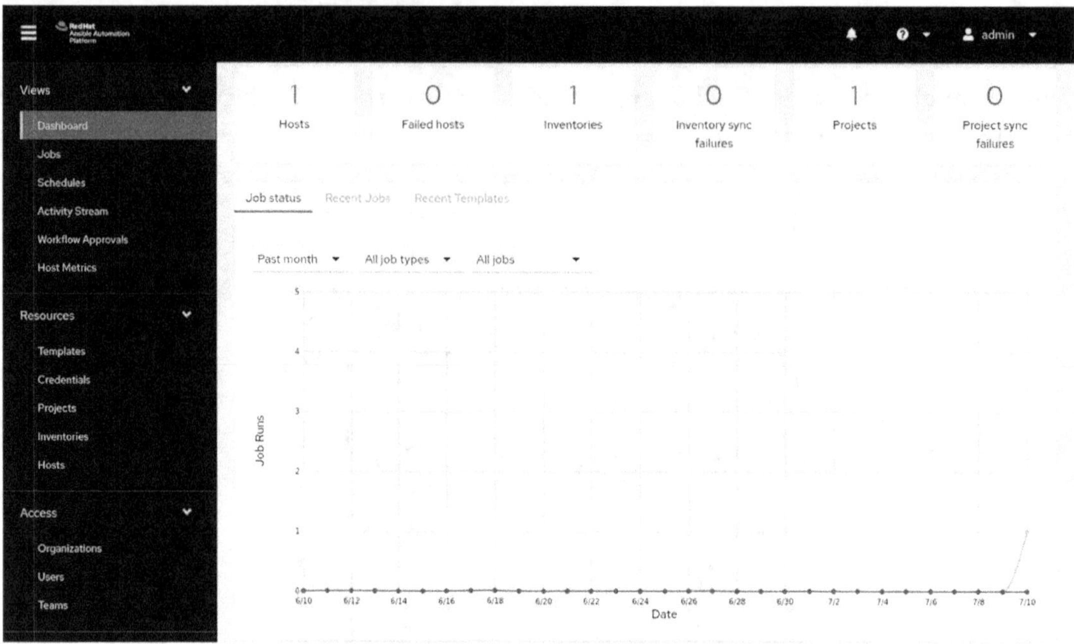

Figure 4.6: Automation controller main Dashboard view

- **Settings**: The **Settings** option, located at the end of the navigation bar as shown in *Figure 4.7*, allows administrators to configure authentication, jobs, and system-level attributes, customize the user interface, and access product license information. Refer to the *Automation Controller Settings* in *Chapter 5, Settings and Authentication*, for detailed configuration options. Please refer to the following figure:

Figure 4.7: Automation controller Settings

- **About icon**: Regardless of the window or action we are performing, the About icon (represented as **About**) is located at the top of each page next to our **User** icon. Clicking on it provides information about the versions of the automation controller and Ansible currently in use as shown in *Figure 4.8:*

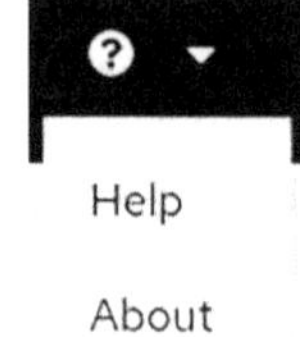

Figure 4.8: Automation controller About icon

- **User icon**: The user icon (represented as a person) is located at the top right of each page next to the **About** icon. Clicking on it provides information about the current user of the automation controller and the logout option, as shown in *Figure 4.9:*

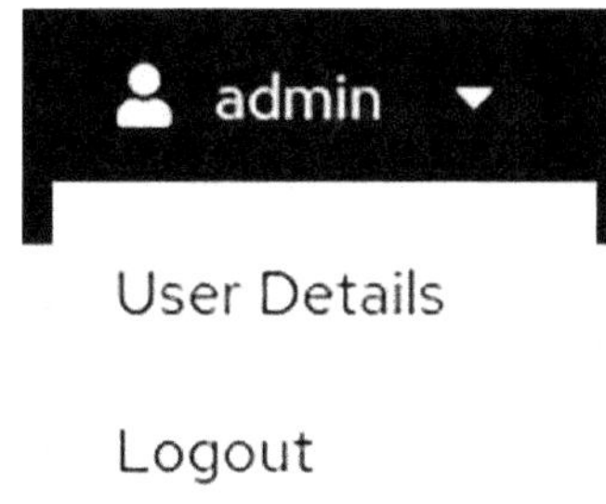

Figure 4.9: *Automation controller User icon*

Note: The new automation controller user interface (UI) is available for tech preview and may change in a future release.

- To enable the new UI, go to the **Settings** menu, select **Miscellaneous System**, and toggle the **Enable preview of new user interface** option to **On**. After saving, log out and log back in to access the new UI from the preview banner. We can return to the previous UI by clicking the link on the top banner. See *Chapter 5, Settings and Authentication*, section *Automation Controller Settings*, for more information.

By familiarizing ourselves with the automation controller dashboard and its various features, we can efficiently navigate the interface and leverage its capabilities for managing our IT orchestration tasks.

Organization

An **Organization** within the automation controller object hierarchy is a logical collection of users, teams, projects, and inventories. It serves as the highest-level object in the hierarchy, as shown in *Figure 4.10*. The **Job Template** under **Resources | Organizations** is found in the user interface. Please refer to the following figure:

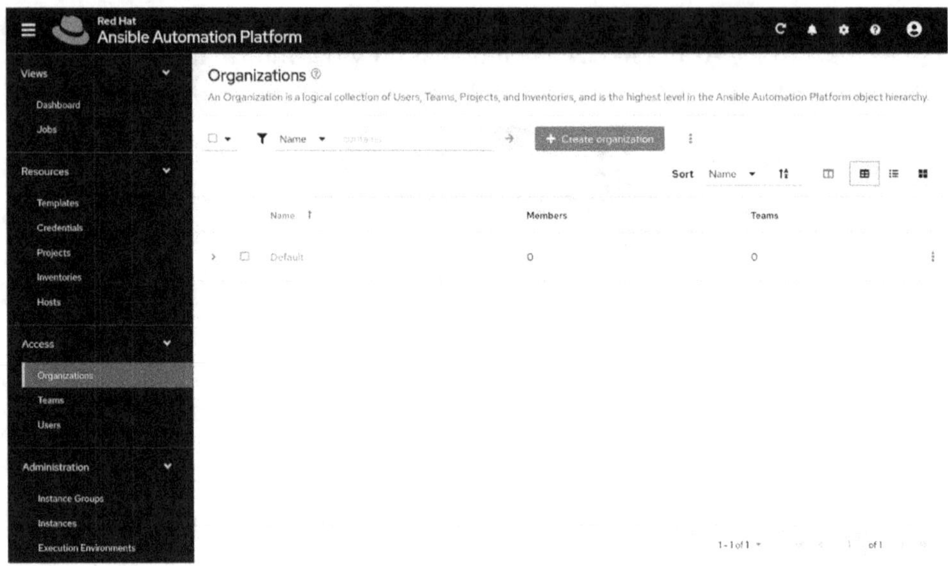

Figure 4.10: List of organization hierarchy

We can review and manage **Organizations** in the automation controller by selecting Organizations via the left navigation bar. Users with a self-support level license and Basic subscription should not delete the default organization as it is essential for Ansible controller functionality. Enterprise or premium license holders can edit and add new organizations using the wizard displayed in *Figure 4.11*. Reviewing the organization settings and ensuring they are properly configured enables us to manage users, teams, projects, and inventories within our automation controller effectively. Please refer to the following figure:

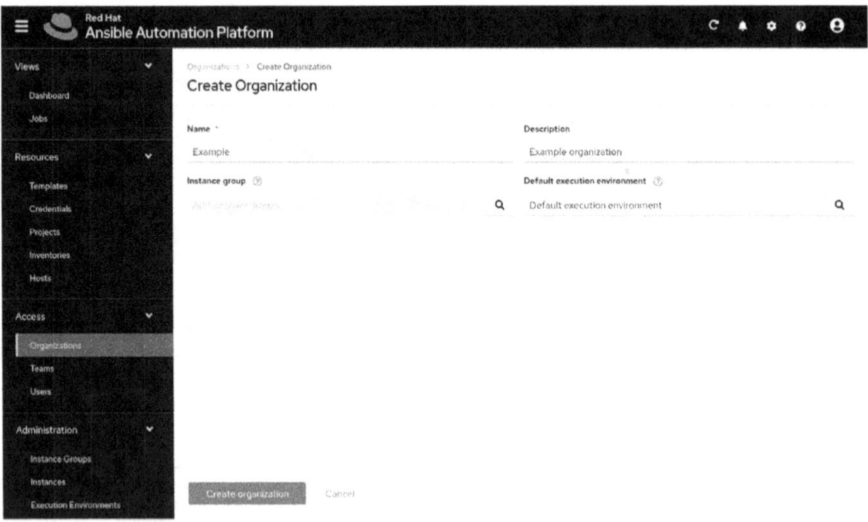

Figure 4.11: New organizations

Inventory

An inventory in the automation controller is a list of hosts that are managed by the system. **Organizations** are assigned to inventories, and permissions to launch playbooks against inventories are controlled at the user or team level. We can define the username, password, or SSH key to log in to each host or group of the inventory using the **Credentials**. To access the inventories in the automation controller, click on **Inventories** from the left navigation bar to view existing inventories.

Note: The automation controller provides out-of-the-box demo inventory. We delete or make edits as needed.

The listed inventories are displayed in a view similar to *Figure 4.12*. We can find the **Job Template** under **Resources | Inventories** in the user interface. Please refer to the following figure:

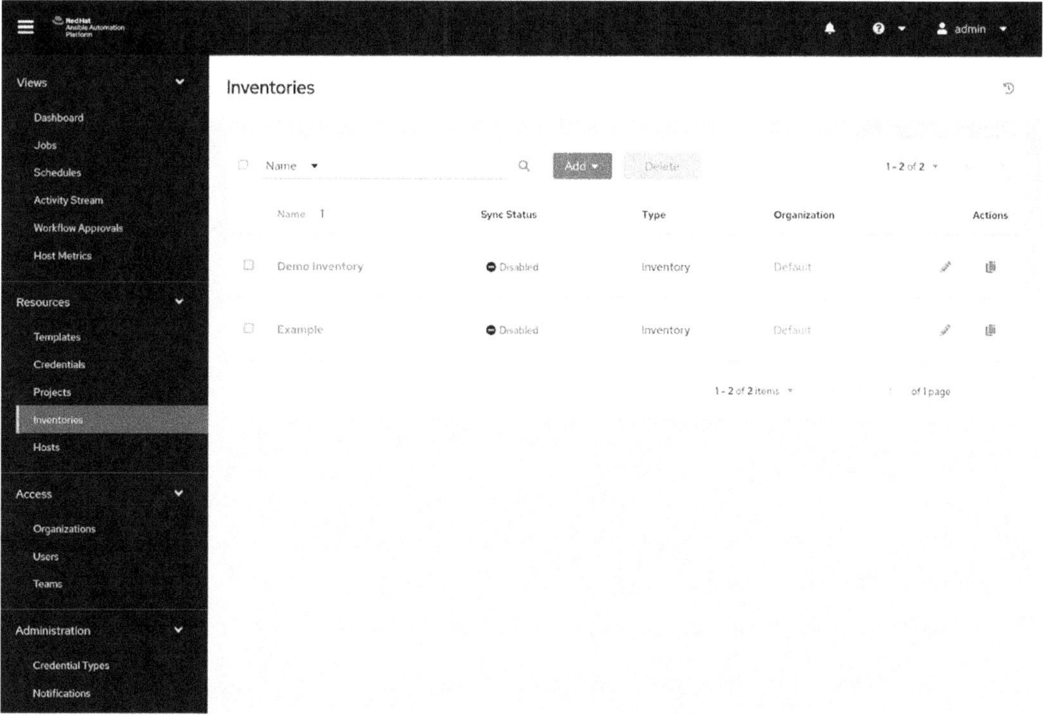

Figure 4.12: List inventories

To create an additional inventory, click the **Add** button, select **Add Inventory** from the dropdown menu, specify the **Name** and **Organization**, and save the new inventory using the **Save** button, as shown in *Figure 4.13*.

Note: Similar to organizations, inventories also have associated users and teams. we can view them through the Access tab.

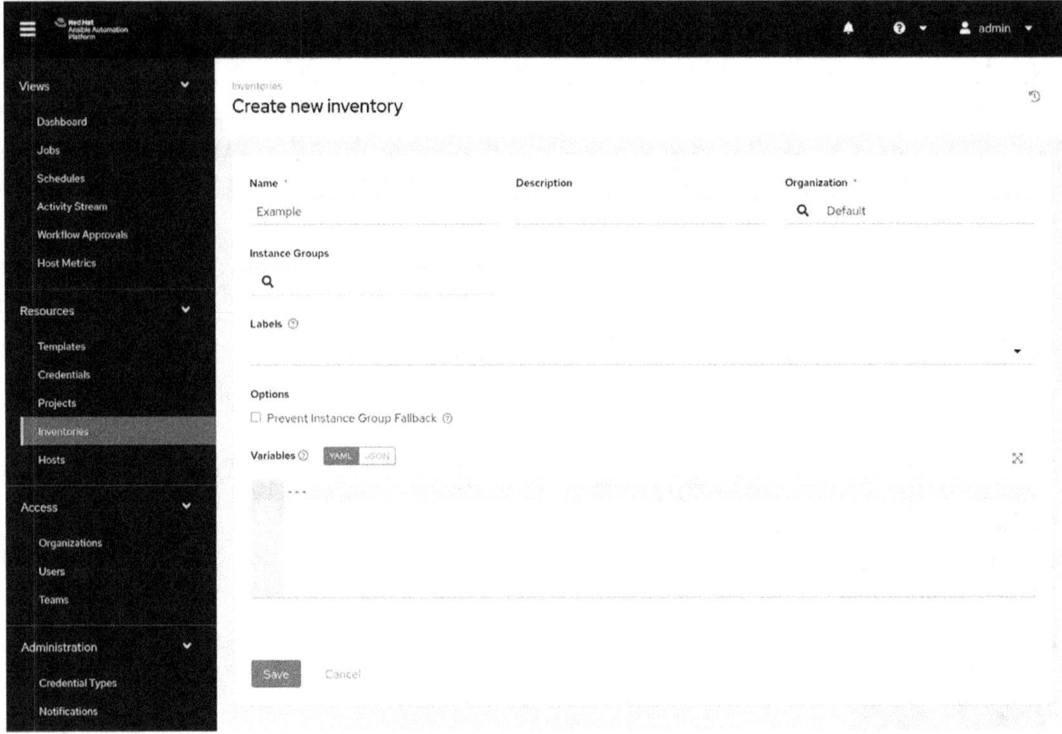

Figure 4.13: List inventories

1. A default admin user with the role of **System Administrator** is automatically assigned to the **Demo Inventory**.

2. **Groups** and **Hosts**: Inventories are divided into groups and hosts. Groups can represent specific environments, server types, or organizational structures. The groups and hosts belonging to the **Demo Inventory** are displayed in the **Groups** and **Hosts** tabs, respectively.

3. Click the **Add** button in the **Groups** screen to add new groups.

4. In the **Hosts** tab, click the **Add** button to add hosts to groups.

5. Suppose the organization we created earlier has a group of web server hosts supporting a particular application. To add these hosts to the inventory, create a group and add the web server hosts.

6. Click **Cancel** (if no changes are made) or use the breadcrumb navigation links at the top of the automation controller browser to return to the Inventories list view. Clicking **Save** does not exit the **Details** dialog.

By following these steps, we can create a new inventory, manage groups and hosts, and associate users and teams with the inventory. This allows for effective organization and control of hosts within our automation controller.

Dynamic inventory

Ansible dynamic inventory is a feature in Ansible automation controller that allows us to generate inventory information for our projects dynamically. It provides a way to dynamically manage and retrieve host information from external sources, such as cloud providers, virtualization platforms, databases, or custom scripts. With dynamic inventory, we can define scripts or plugins that gather information about our infrastructure in real-time and present it to Ansible as an inventory. This eliminates the need to manually maintain static inventory files, especially in large or rapidly changing environments. In Ansible automation controller, dynamic inventory is configured by creating inventory sources. An inventory source specifies the external source from which the dynamic inventory is generated. It can be a cloud provider like AWS or Azure, a virtualization platform like VMware or OpenStack, or any other custom source that provides an API or script to retrieve host information. It relies on additional Ansible inventory plugins. When configuring an inventory source in Ansible automation controller, we specify the necessary parameters to connect to the external source and retrieve inventory data. This can include authentication credentials, API endpoints, filters, and other relevant information. Once the inventory source is set up, Ansible automation controller periodically polls the source to update the inventory information. It retrieves host data, such as IP addresses, hostnames, groups, variables, and other attributes, and makes it available to Ansible for playbook execution, as shown in *Figure 4.14*:

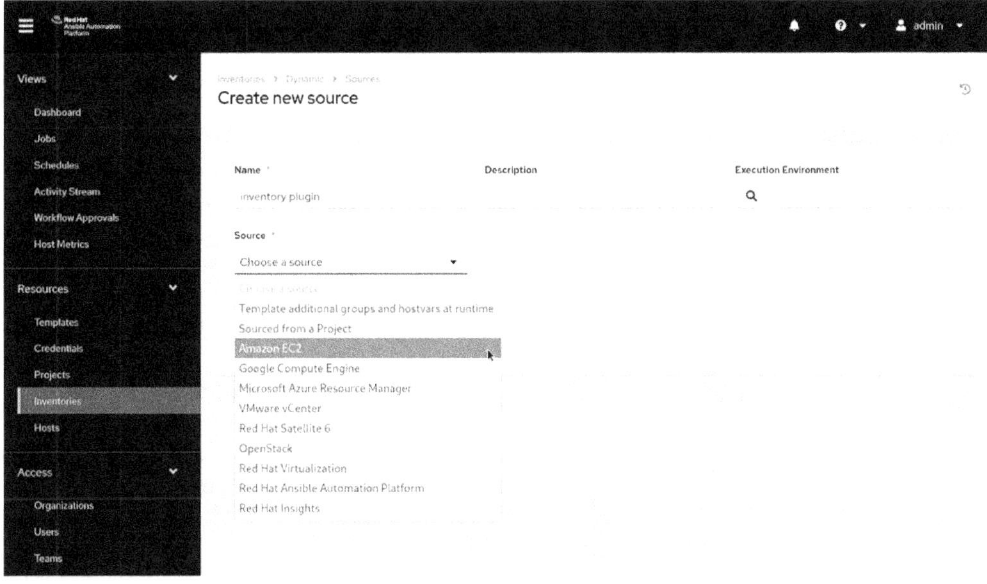

Figure 4.14: Dynamic inventory

Dynamic inventory in Ansible automation controller offers several advantages: **Automatic real-time inventory updates, Scalability, and flexibility, Integration with external platforms, Grouping, and variable assignment.** By leveraging dynamic inventory in Ansible automation controller, we can automate the management of inventory information, streamline playbook execution, and ensure that our Ansible Playbooks are always executed against the latest infrastructure configuration.

Credential

Credentials are used to authenticate the controller user for launching Ansible Playbooks against inventory hosts. They can include passwords, SSH keys, or other authentication methods. The most common credential type is **Machine** which specifies the credentials to connect to a target machine. We can list all the available credentials using the view displayed in *Figure 4.15*. The **Job Template** under **Resources | Credentials** is found in the user interface. Please refer to the following figure:

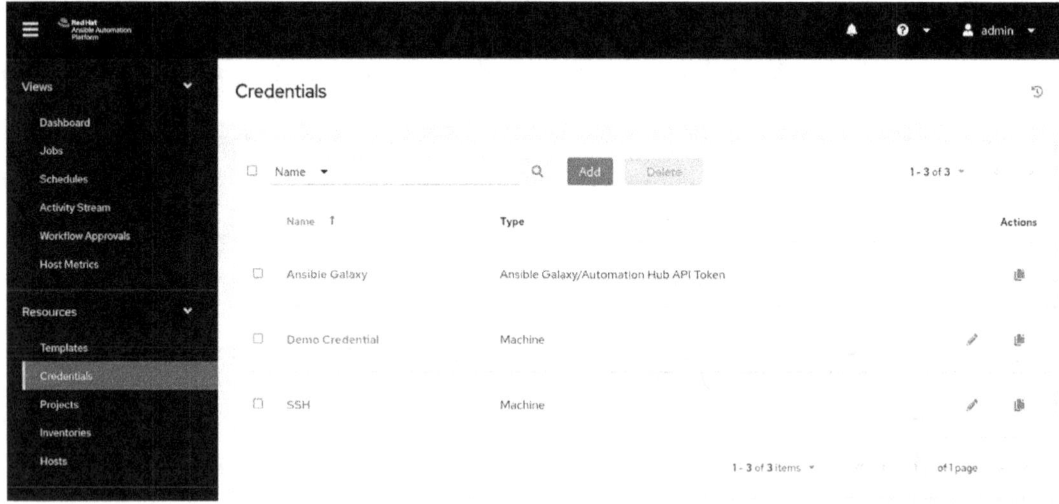

Figure 4.15: List Credentials

To create a new credential, navigate to the **Credentials** section in the left navigation bar, access the list of existing credentials, and add a new credential by following the instructions in the "**Add a New Credential**" section. For future edits, click **Edit** from the **Details** tab or use the **Edit** button (represented by a pencil icon) next to the credential name in the Credentials list view, make the required changes, and save the updates as needed.

Note: When setting up additional credentials, ensure the assigned user has the necessary privileges, such as root access or SSH connectivity to the host machine.

We successfully created and managed credentials within the automation controller by following these steps. These credentials are essential for authenticating the controller user when executing Ansible Playbooks against inventory hosts.

Figure 4.16 shows the creation of a new **Machine** credential type:

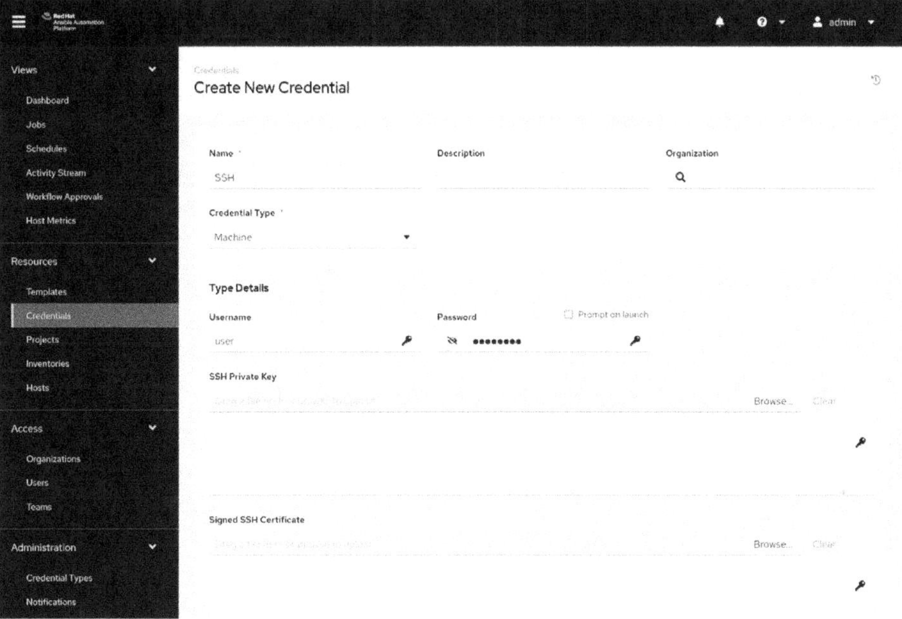

Figure 4.16: *New Credential (part 1)*

As the page is long, *Figure 4.17* shows the remaining part and the **Save** button.

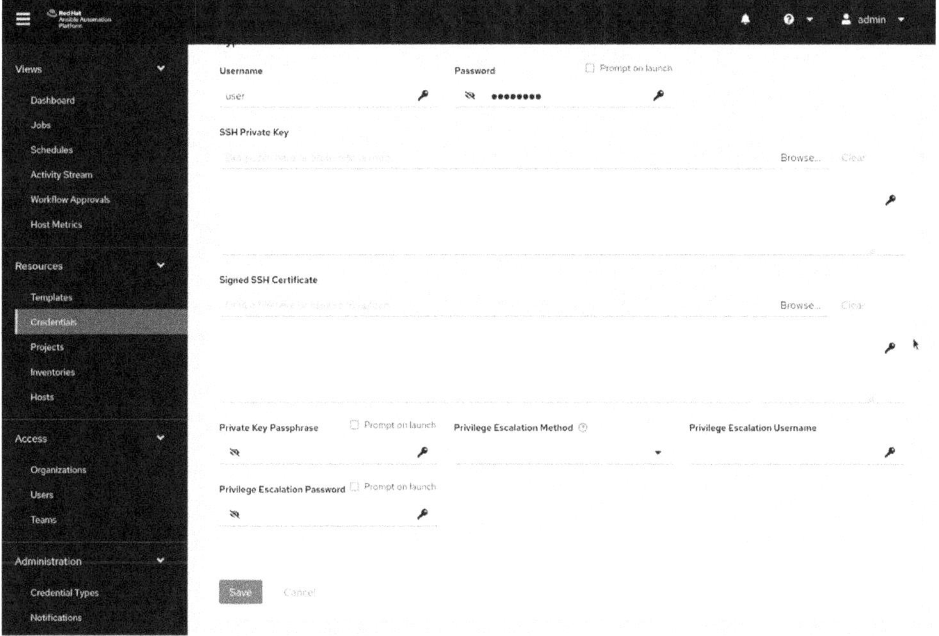

Figure 4.17: *New Credential (part 2)*

Ansible Vault is a feature available in the Ansible Automation Platform that provides encryption and security for sensitive data used in Ansible Playbooks and roles. It allows us to encrypt variables, files, and other content within our playbooks, ensuring that sensitive information such as passwords, API keys, and other secrets are securely stored and transmitted. With Ansible Vault, we can create encrypted files or individual variables within our playbooks. The encrypted data is stored in an encrypted format and can only be decrypted by authorized users with the appropriate decryption key or password. This ensures that even if our playbooks or files are accessed by unauthorized individuals, they would not be able to access sensitive information without the decryption key. To use Ansible Vault, we can create an encrypted file using the **ansible-vault create** command. This will prompt us to enter a password that will be used to encrypt the file. We can then edit the file using the **ansible-vault edit** command, which will decrypt the file temporarily for editing and re-encrypt it when we save the changes.

When running our playbooks manually, we can specify the decryption password using the **--ask-vault-pass** option of the **ansible-playbook** command, or we can store the password in a file and specify it using the **--vault-password-file** option. Ansible Vault also integrates with external credential management systems, allowing us to retrieve credentials from external sources securely. The Ansible Automation Platform provides additional features for managing and sharing encrypted content. We can manage access to encrypted files and variables using **role-based access control** (**RBAC**) to control who can view and modify sensitive information. Using the platform's collaboration features, we can also securely share encrypted content with other team members. Overall, Ansible Vault in the Ansible Automation Platform offers a robust and secure solution for managing sensitive data in our automation workflows. This ensures that our secrets are protected from unauthorized access while still being easily accessible by authorized users and processes.

Project

A project in the automation controller represents a logical collection of Ansible Playbooks. It allows us to organize and manage our playbooks effectively. We can list all the available **Projects** using the view shown in *Figure 4.18*. We can find the **Job Template** under **Resources | Projects** in the user interface. Please refer to the following figure:

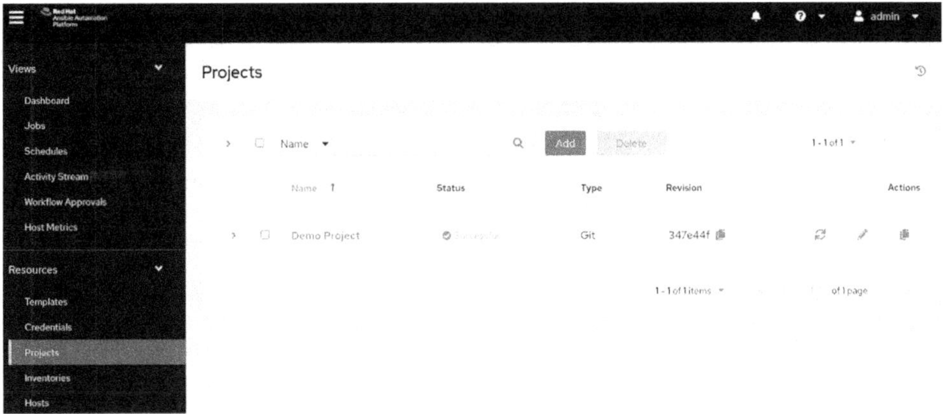

Figure 4.18: List Projects

Here is how we can set up a project:

1. We can manage playbooks and playbook directories in two ways:

    -   Manually place them under the **Project Base Path** on our controller server.

    -   Place our playbooks in a **source code management** (**SCM**) system supported by the controller, such as Git, Subversion, or Mercurial.

Note: Using source control whenever possible to manage our playbooks is recommended. This best practice aligns with treating infrastructure as code and supports DevOps principles for production.

2. To review existing projects, click on **Projects** from the left navigation bar.

3. The **Projects** view will display, and we will find a **Demo Project** provided by the automation controller for us to work with initially.

4. Click on **Demo Project** to view its details, as shown in *Figure 4.19:*

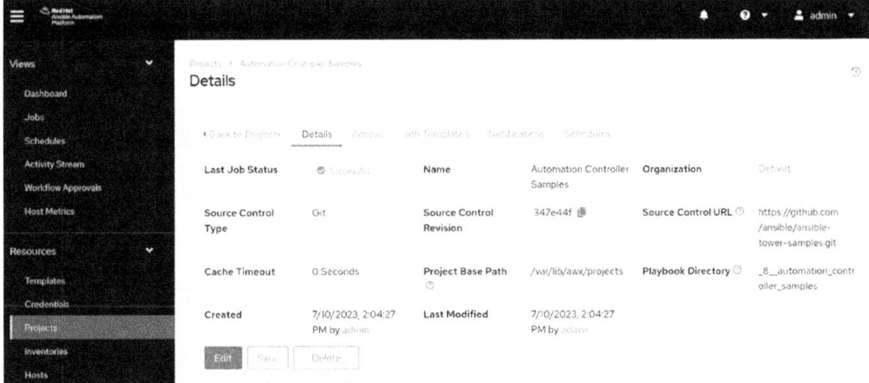

Figure 4.19: Project Details

Note: If we need to edit the default project later, we can click on Edit from the Details tab or click the Edit button (represented by a pencil icon) next to the project name in the Projects list view. Make the desired changes and save them.

5. If we want to fetch the latest changes for the project, we can manually start an SCM sync. To do this, navigate to the **Details** tab of the SCM-based demo project and click on **Sync**. Alternatively, in the **Projects** list view, click the **Sync** button (represented by a sync icon) next to the project name.

Note: After adding new projects set up to use source control, an automatic sync process initiates to fetch the project details from the configured source control. Figure 4.20 shows the view to create a new project.

Please refer to the following figure:

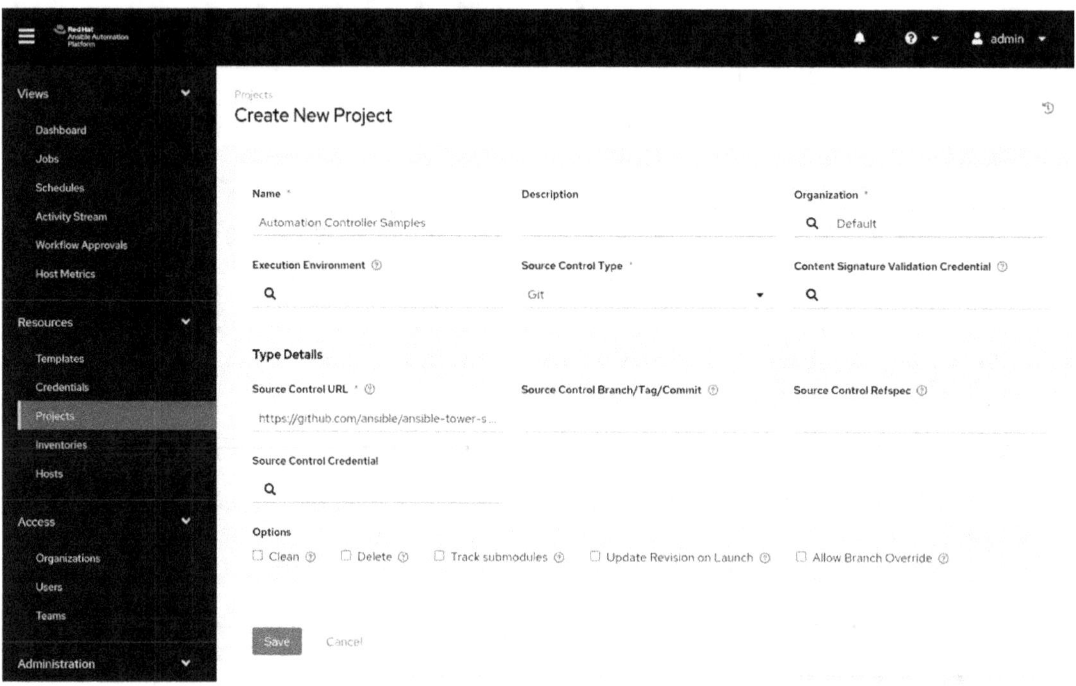

Figure 4.20: New Project

By following these steps, we can set up and manage projects in the automation controller, allowing us to organize and utilize our Ansible Playbooks efficiently.

Playbook

An Ansible Playbook for the Ansible Automation Platform is a file written in YAML format that contains a series of tasks and instructions for Ansible to execute. Playbooks are at the core of Ansible and are used to define the desired state of the system and automate configuration management, application deployment, and other IT tasks.

Every Ansible automation script is a YAML document composed of Ansible Playbooks containing one or more plays. We can execute the same code that we execute manually using the **ansible-playbook** command using the **Job Template** in the automation controller.

In the context of the Ansible Automation Platform, a playbook can be associated with a **Project** in the automation controller, which is a logical container of Playbooks. Playbooks can be stored in a project's directory within the Ansible Automation Platform, or they can be stored in a source code management system like Git, Subversion, or Mercurial. In the **Project** directory, we can store additional Ansible files, such as **requirements.yml** for roles and collections and custom Ansible resources.

Playbooks consist of a list of plays, where each play consists of a set of tasks to be executed on specific hosts or groups of hosts. Tasks can include executing commands, running scripts, managing files, installing packages, and more. Playbooks can also define variables, conditions, and loops to customize their behavior.

When executing a playbook in the automation controller, we can specify the hosts or groups of hosts on which the playbook should run. we can also pass extra variables to the playbook to customize its execution based on specific requirements.

Ansible Automation Platform provides a user-friendly interface for managing and executing playbooks. We can create and configure job templates that associate a playbook with specific settings, such as **inventory**, **credentials**, and **notifications**. These **Job Templates** can then be used to launch playbooks and track their execution status.

By using Ansible Playbooks in the Ansible Automation Platform, organizations can automate and streamline their IT operations, ensure consistency across environments, and improve efficiency in managing infrastructure, applications, and services.

The playbook might require any privilege escalation if the tasks are supposed to be executed by another user or a privileged user (usually **root** in Linux systems). In a traditional playbook, this operation is performed by the **become** optional statement that can be set to true or yes to enable privilege escalation using an Ansible **become** plugin. The Ansible **become** plugin executes commands with elevated privileges on Unix-like systems, which are integrated inside the Ansible Automation Platform. Let us explain each of them:

- **sudo** (short for **superuser do**) allows a user to run commands as the superuser or another user based on the configuration. It provides fine-grained control over privilege escalation, allowing authorized users to execute specific commands with elevated privileges after providing their own password.

- **su** (short for **switch user**) is used to switch to another user account or become the superuser. By default, when we run **su** without specifying a username, it switches to the superuser account (**root**). We can provide the username as an argument to switch to a different user or use the credentials.

- **pfexec** is a command used in the Solaris and OpenSolaris operating systems. It provides privilege elevation similar to **sudo**, allowing users to execute specific commands with elevated privileges after authenticating with their password.

- **doas** (short for **do as**) is a command used in some BSD-based systems, such as OpenBSD and NetBSD. After providing their password, it allows authorized users to execute commands with elevated privileges. The configuration for **doas** is typically defined in the **/etc/doas.conf** file.

- **pbrun** is a command used in the PoourBroker software suite (also known as **BeyondTrust PoourBroker**). It allows users to run commands with elevated privileges by authenticating with their password or using other authentication mechanisms, such as Active Directory or LDAP.

- **dzdo** is a command used in the Quest Privilege Manager for Sudo software. It is similar to **sudo** and allows users to execute commands with elevated privileges based on the configuration. Users authenticate with their password or other authentication methods supported by Privilege Manager.

- **ksu** is a command used in some Unix systems, such as AIX and HP-UX. It allows users to obtain a shell with the privileges of another user, typically the superuser, after providing their password.

These commands provide different privilege elevation and access control methods, allowing users to perform administrative tasks or execute commands with elevated privileges while maintaining security and control over system access. The specific command available on a system may vary depending on the operating system and its configuration.

Job Template

A Job Template in Ansible automation controller combines an Ansible Playbook from a **Project** with the necessary settings to execute it. To manage existing job templates, navigate to the **Templates** section in the left navigation bar. *Figure 4.21* list the available Job Templates. We can find the **Job Template** under **Resources | Templates** in the user interface. Please refer to the following figure:

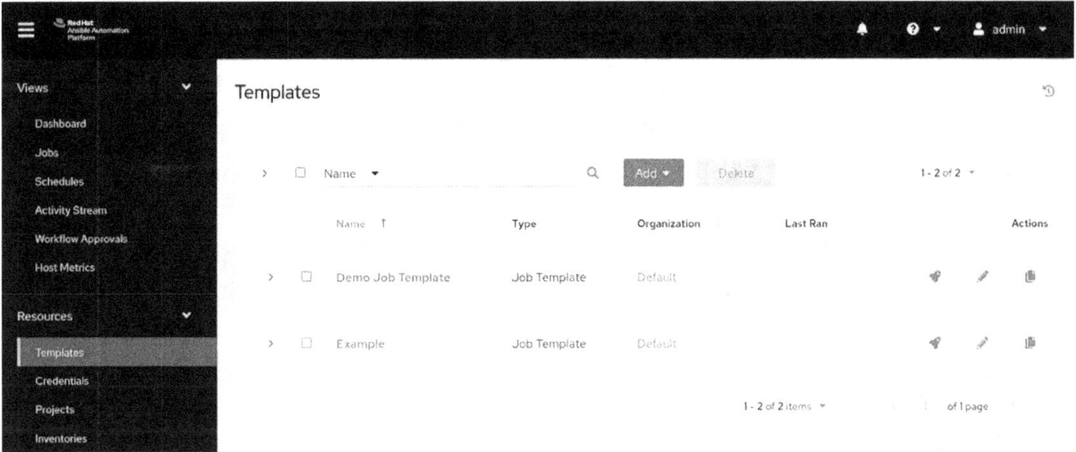

Figure 4.21: List Job Templates

On the **Job Templates** home page, we will find a pre-configured **Demo Job Template** for our convenience.

To view the details of the **Demo Job Template**, click on its name, as shown in *Figure 4.22*:

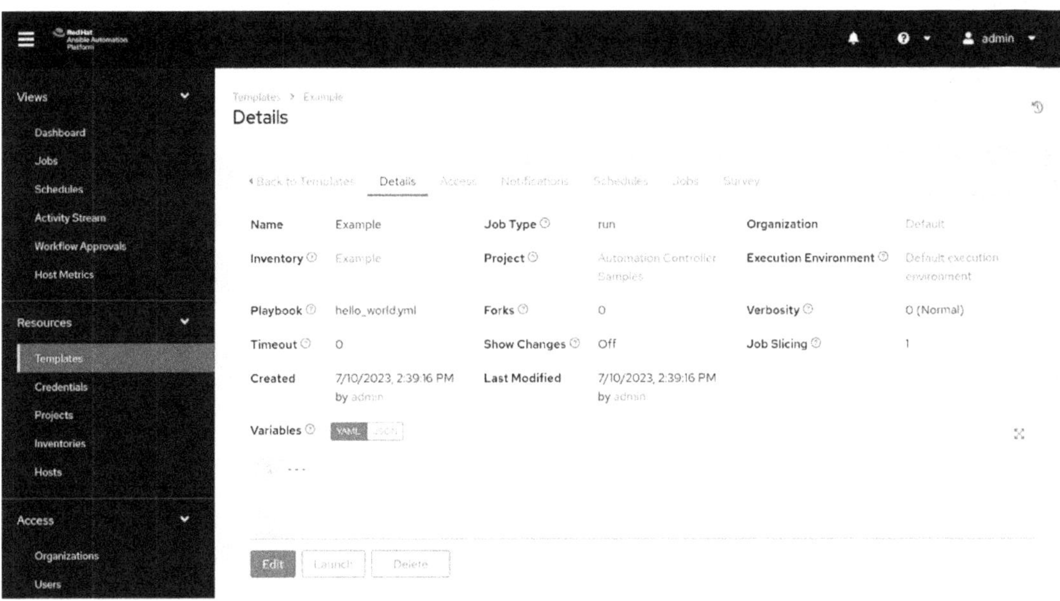

Figure 4.22: Job Template Details

On the Job Template details page, we can review the settings and configurations of the template. However, if we need to modify the template later, we can click on the **Edit** button in the **Details** tab. Alternatively, in the **Templates** list view, we can click the **Edit** button next to the template name to make the necessary changes.

After making any modifications, we can either click **Save**, and then **Cancel** (if no changes are made), or use the breadcrumb navigational links at the top of the automation controller browser to return to the **Templates** list view. It is important to note that clicking **Save** does not exit the **Details** dialog.

We can create a new Job Template using the **Add Template** view, as shown in *Figure 4.23* and *Figure 4.24*:

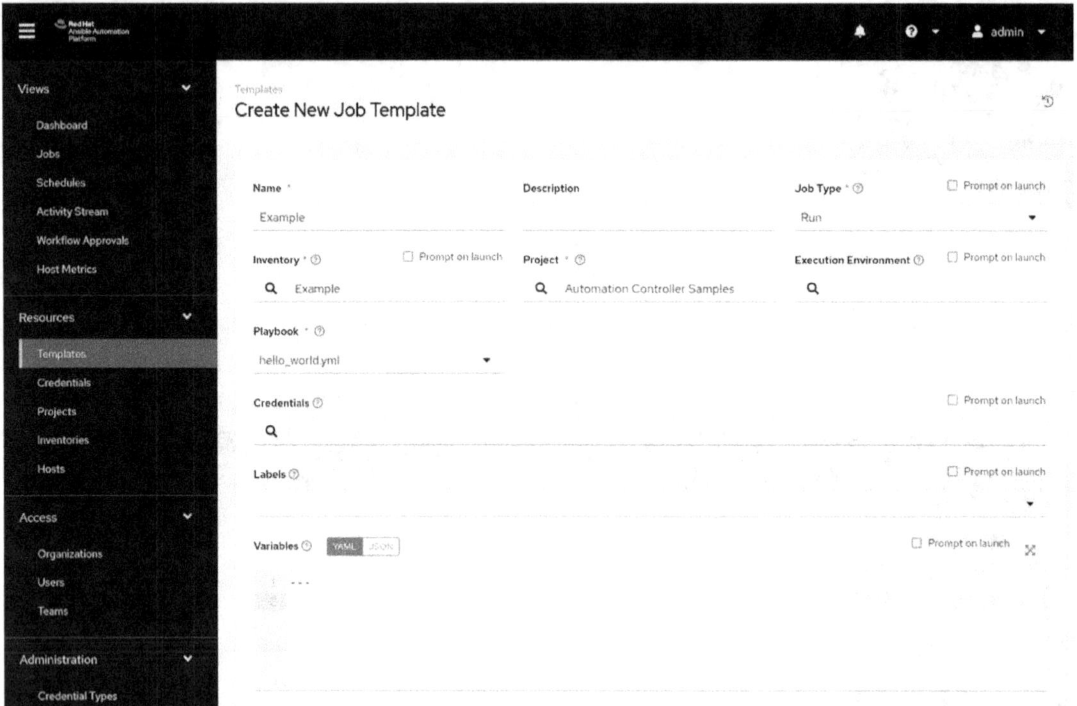

Figure 4.23: New Job Template (part 1)

As the page is long, *Figure 4.24* shows the remaining part and the **Save** button.

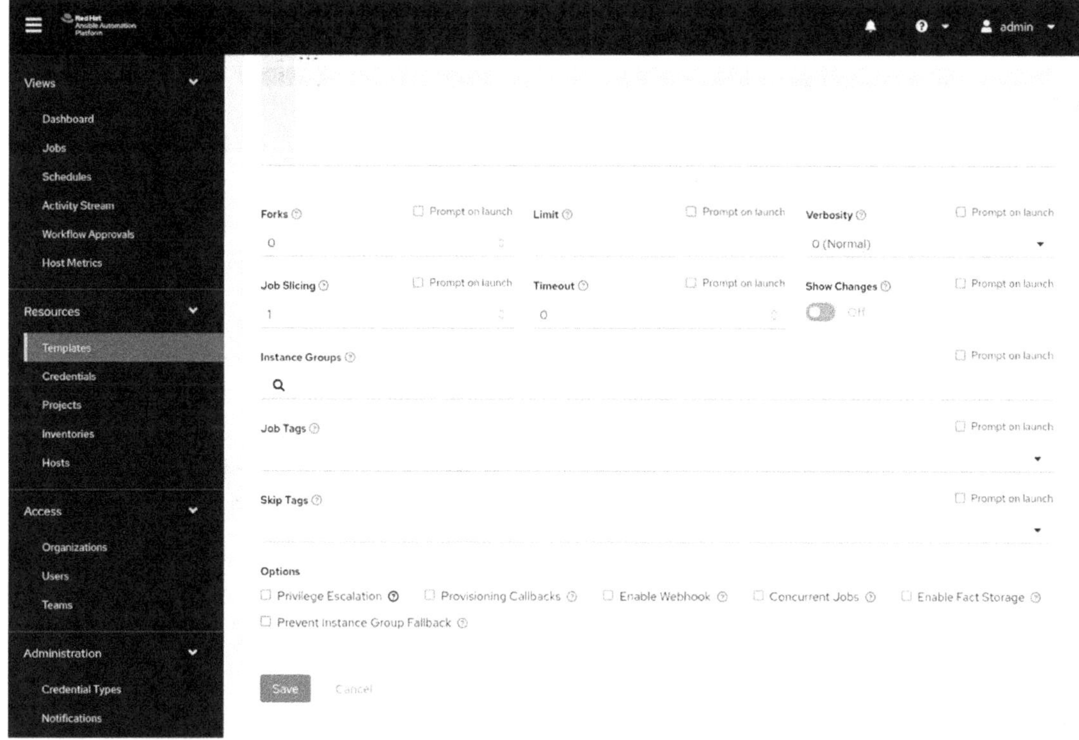

Figure 4.24: New Job Template (part 2)

When the Job Template is executed we can keep track of the progress and result in the **Jobs** section of the user interface, as shown in *Figure 4.25*:

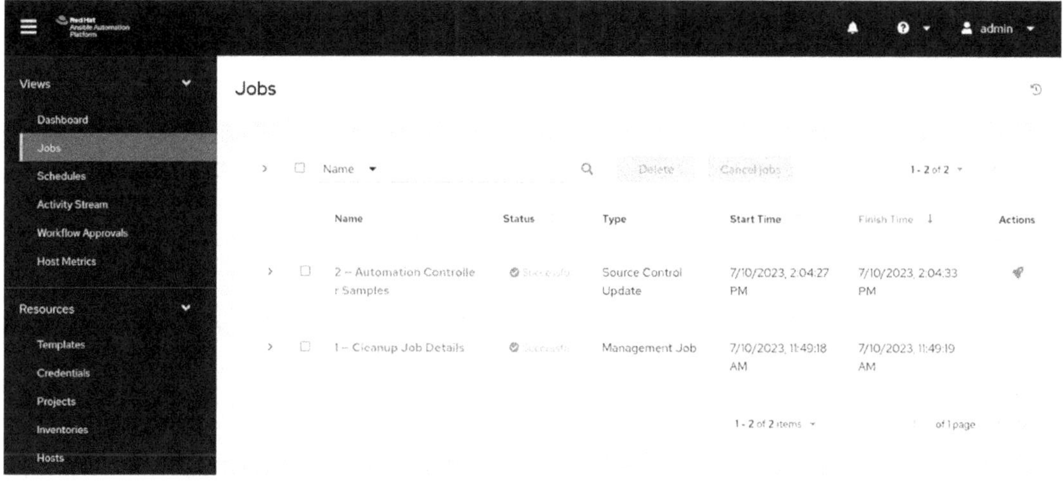

Figure 4.25: Jobs

Workflow Template

We can combine the execution of more than one Job Template in a Workflow Template. Workflows in automation controller allow us to configure a sequence of Job Templates or Workflow Templates that can be connected in a graph-like structure called nodes as shown in *Figure 4.26*. These nodes can represent individual jobs, project syncs, or inventory syncs. Workflows provide a way to track and manage a series of jobs as a single unit, such as in a release process. Workflows can consist of job templates that share or do not share inventory, playbooks, or permissions. They have both **admin** and **execute** permissions, similar to job templates. When a workflow is launched, a copy of the graph structure is saved as a **Workflow Job**. During the execution of a workflow, jobs are spawned based on the linked templates in each node. If a node is linked to a job template with prompt-driven fields (for example, **job_type**, **job_tags**, **skip_tags**, **limit**), those fields will be inherited by the node and will not be prompted again during the workflow launch. However, job templates with promptable credentials or inventory without defaults cannot be included in a workflow. Overall, workflows provide a way to organize and execute a series of related jobs or tasks in a coordinated manner, allowing for more efficient management and tracking of complex processes or release cycles. Please refer to the following figure:

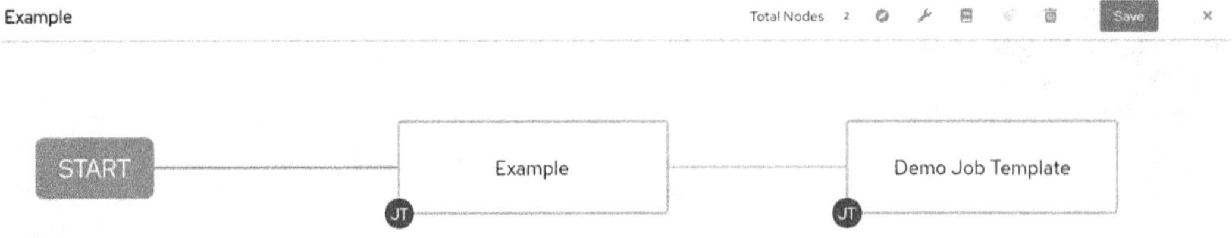

Figure 4.26: Workflow Template

Notification

A Notification Template in Ansible controller is a predefined configuration for sending notifications using different channels such as email, Slack, or webhooks. Each template has specific requirements depending on the notification type. A Notification is an instance of a Notification Template that is triggered when a specific event occurs, such as a job failure. It uses the configuration defined in the associated Notification Template.

The typical flow of the notification system involves creating a **Notification Template** through the user interface. Then, the template is assigned to relevant objects such as job templates, organizations, or projects, specifying the trigger level for which the notification should be sent (for example, job start, job success, or job error).

Notification Templates can be assigned at different levels and will inherit templates defined on parent objects. For example, Job Templates inherit notification templates from the associated Project and Organization. Project Updates inherit templates from the Project and its associated Organization. Inventory Updates use notification templates from the associated Organization.

Users and teams also have the flexibility to define their own notifications that can be attached to specific jobs.

Overall, the notification hierarchy allows for flexible configuration and inheritance of notification templates to ensure appropriate notifications are sent based on specific events and objects within the automation controller. We can create a new **Notification Template** in the **Administration | Notifications** section of the user interface, as shown in *Figure 4.27*:

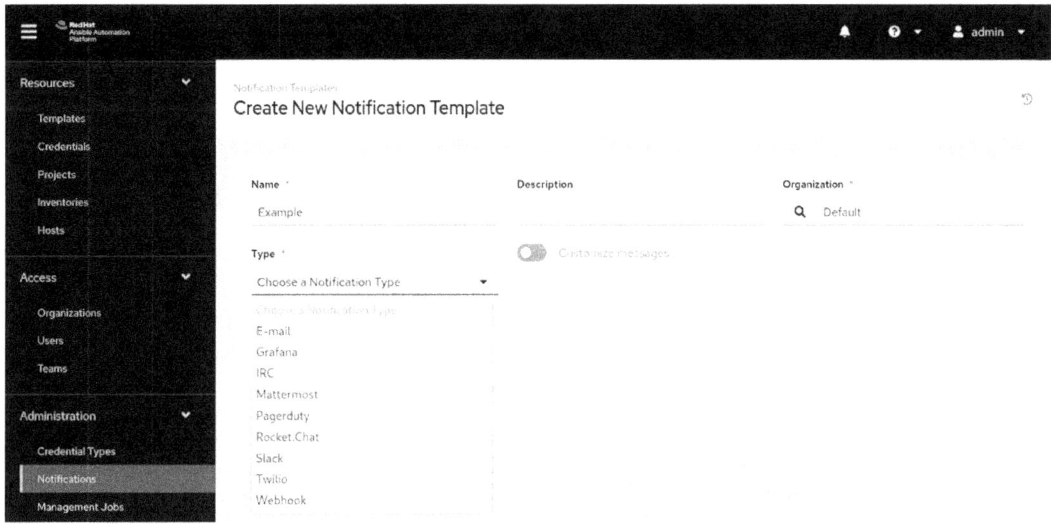

Figure 4.27: Notifications

Project signature

Since the Ansible Automation Platform 2.3 was released in November 2022, the Ansible controller has supported the project signature feature using the **ansible-sign** command line utility. We can use the utility to sign a project in our SCM repository, usually GIT. The list of files for signature is specified in the **MANIFEST.in** file, where we can specify what files to include or exclude, commonly used in many open-source projects.

The full command to sign our project via the command line is:

```
ansible-sign project gpg-sign PROJECT_ROOT
```

In the same way, we could verify our project manually using the command:

```
ansible-sign project gpg-verify PROJECT_ROOT
```

A signed project has an additional **.ansible-sign** directory with two files inside. The first is the **sha256sum.txt** which contains the SHA256 hash of each file. This is already an industry standard for our content. And the second is **sha256sum.txt.sig**, which contains the GPG signature of the previous file.

With the contents signature and verification, we succeed when the signature verification is valid: Two files exist, the checksum is valid, and the signature is valid.

We might receive one of the other scenarios when something is not correct:

- checksum invalid when files are tampered with or invalid,

- signature invalid when the signature is tampered or invalid,

- signature mismatch when the signature is wrong, expired, or inaccessible.

To be able to use the **Project signature** feature, we just need to add the GPG signature credential to the **Project** in the automation controller.

API

The automation controller **representational state transfer** (**RESTful** API) is a set of endpoints and methods provided by the automation controller that allows users to interact with and automate various tasks within the platform programmatically. It enables users to manage and control resources, such as job templates, inventories, playbooks, and notifications, using HTTP requests to retrieve or send data to the automation controller. The RESTful API provides a way to integrate the Ansible Automation Platform with other systems, build custom automation workflows, and automate administrative tasks. The Web user interface and the **command line interface** (**CLI**) are actually built around the API. The API interface act as a backend infrastructure implementing the **model–view–controller** (**MVC**) software design pattern using the Python Django framework. The browsable API in automation controller allows users to access and explore the available resources and endpoints of the REST API through a web browser. Version 2 of the API was introduced in automation controller 3.2 (For reference, Ansible Automation Platform incorporates ansible controller 4.4.0) and can be accessed by clicking the corresponding link. Version 1 of the API, endpoint **/api/v1/**, has been discontinued since automation controller version 3.6. By navigating through the API links, users can discover and explore related resources and access documentation on the available access methods and returned data for each API endpoint. Users can also perform PUT and POST operations by providing JSON data in the respective text fields. Additionally, the API provides information on changing settings modified through the API browser, not from static settings files.

We can access all the available resources of the **Dashboard** via the RESTful API by accessing the endpoint **/api/v2/** of our automation controller, as shown in *Figure 4.28*. Please note that this endpoint requires authentication using automation controller credentials. Some areas of the API are accessible only after a successful login operation. The API support Session Authentication, Basic Authentication, OAuth 2 Token Authentication, and **Single sign-on** (**SSO**) authentication methods like Google SSO, Azure SSO, SAML, or GitHub SSO. Please refer to the following figure:

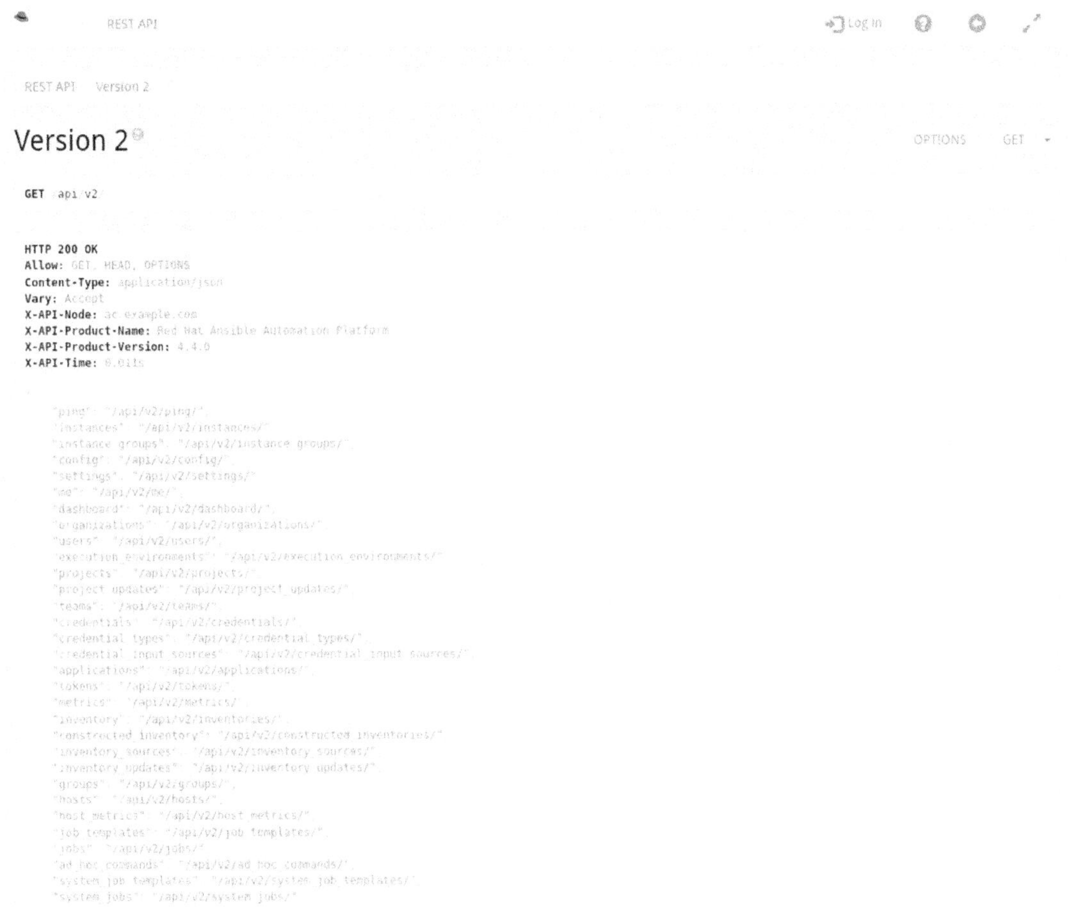

Figure 4.28: *Automation Controller API*

CLI

Automation controller CLI refers to the command-line interface provided by Ansible automation controller. It allows users to interact with the automation controller and perform various operations and tasks using command-line commands. With the automation controller CLI, users can execute commands to manage inventories, run playbooks, configure settings, create job templates, manage credentials, and perform other administrative tasks within the automation controller environment. The CLI provides a convenient and efficient way to automate tasks, integrate with other systems and tools, and perform bulk operations. It allows users to leverage the pous of the command line to interact with automation controller and perform actions programmatically. Using the CLI, users can script and automate routine tasks, schedule jobs, and perform complex operations, enabling more efficient and streamlined management of their automation workflows. Overall, the automation controller CLI is a powerful tool for managing and controlling the Ansible automation controller from the command line. It provides flexibility and automation capabilities for managing infrastructure and orchestrating IT processes. The automation controller CLI, known as **awx-manage** (formerly **tous-manage**), is a command-line utility used to access detailed internal information of the Ansible automation controller. It is recommended to run **awx-manage** commands as the **awx** or **root** user. The CLI provides various functionalities for managing Ansible controller, including inventory import, cleanup of old data, cluster management, token and session management, and analytics gathering. For inventory import, the **awx-manage inventory_import** command allows importing inventory directly into automation controller by synchronizing an automation controller inventory object with a text-based inventory file, dynamic inventory script, or a directory of inventory sources. It supports options such as specifying the source path and inventory identifier and overwriting existing inventory data. The **awx-manage cleanup_jobs** and **awx-manage cleanup_activitystream** commands are used to clean old data from Toour, permanently deleting job details, job output, and activity stream data that exceed a specified number of days. For cluster management, the **awx-manage** utility provides commands like **provision_instance** and **deprovision_instance**, which are explained in the **Clustering** section of the documentation. Token and session management commands, such as **create_oauth2_token**, **revoke_oauth2_tokens**, **cleartokens**, **expire_sessions**, and **clearsessions**, enable administrators to manage OAuth2 tokens and user sessions.

Additionally, the **awx-manage gather_analytics** command allows gathering analytics data on-demand outside the predefined window. It is important to note that running **awx-manage** commands via a playbook is not recommended or supported. Only run **awx-manage** commands as instructed by Ansible Support. Overall, the automation controller CLI provides a range of commands for managing and administering automation controller through the command line, offering flexibility and control over various aspects of the system, as shown in *Figure 4.29:*

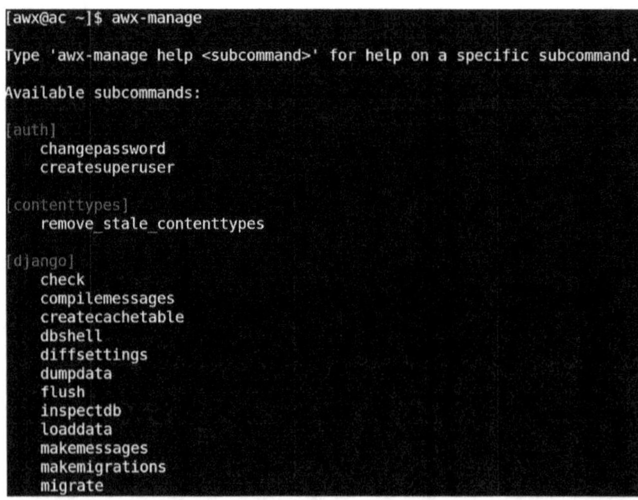

Figure 4.29: Automation controller CLI

Execution environments

Ansible execution environments replaced traditional Python virtual environments and the Ansible Tower **bubblewrap** technology. Execution environments are container images that allow for the inclusion of system-level dependencies and collection-based content. Each execution environment is customized to contain only the necessary components for running a job, resulting in a more streamlined and efficient execution process. To build an execution environment, Ansible provides the **ansible-builder** tool. This tool creates an execution environment based on a YAML definition file (**.yml**) that specifies the required content, such as Ansible, Ansible Runner, Ansible collections, Python requirements, and system-level packages. The execution environment can be built using the **ansible-builder** build command, which inputs the definition file and generates a build context necessary for building the execution environment image.

Once an execution environment is created, it can be used in jobs. In the automation controller user interface, as shown in *Figure 4.30*, administrators can specify the execution environment for **Job Templates**. Please refer to the following figure:

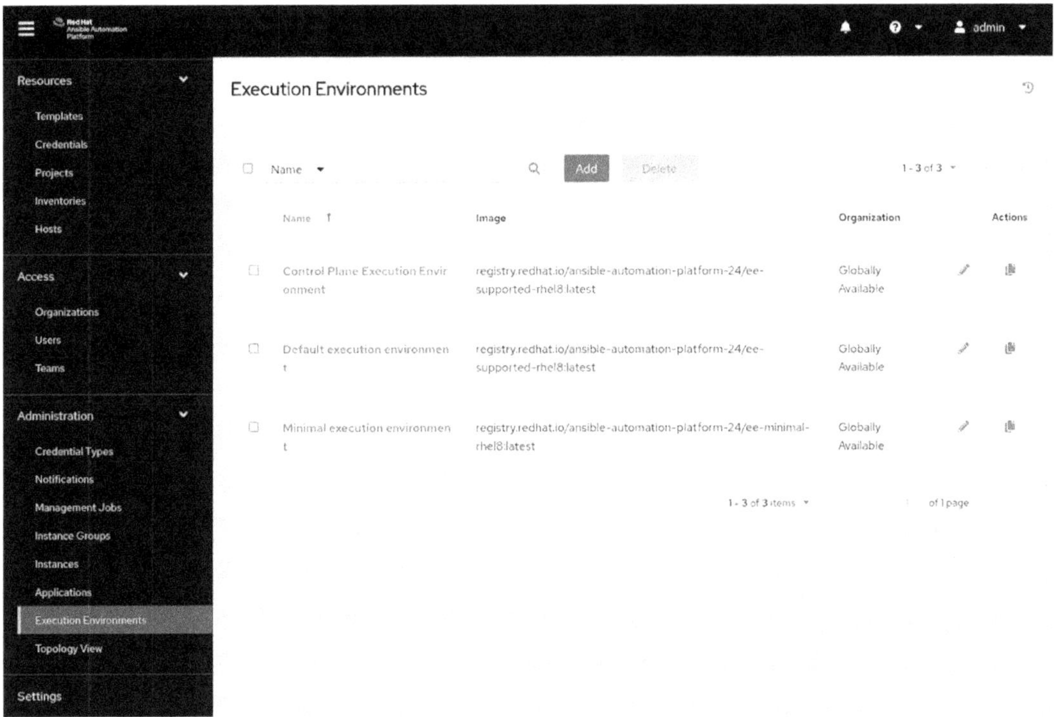

Figure 4.30: Ansible Execution Environments

Execution environments can be tied to an organization or made available globally, and the appropriate level of administrator privileges is required to use them in jobs. Execution environments can be added to automation controller through the **Execution**

Environments section of the user interface. Administrators can provide details such as the name, image name, pull options, description, organization assignment, and registry credential for the execution environment. Once added, the execution environment can be selected in job templates, enabling the use of specific execution environments for different jobs. Additional options for execution environments include mount options and mount paths. These options allow for customization and configuration, such as mounting system trust stores or exposing specific paths to isolated jobs. The mount options and paths can be configured in the **Job Settings** page of the user interface using postman-style volume mount syntax. Automation execution environments can be retrieved by container registries (such as `registry.redhat.io`) or published in the private automation hub. Overall, Ansible execution environments provide a containerized approach to running jobs, allowing for better management of dependencies, streamlined execution, and increased flexibility in customizing the execution environment for different Job requirements. The following three Ansible execution environments are available for every automation controller installation:

- **Default execution environment**: contains the latest Ansible Core release along with Ansible Runner plus all Red Hat-supported collections and dependencies.

- **Minimal execution environment**: contains the latest Ansible Core release along with Ansible Runner but contains no collections or other additional content.

- **Control plane execution environment**: used for the Project sync runs from the **source code management** (**SCM**), like GitLab or GitHub.

These are the key components of the automation execution environments included in the Ansible Automation Platform 2.4: Red Hat Enterprise Linux **Universal Base Image** (**UBI**) base image, Ansible Core, Python, Ansible collections, and Python or binary dependencies. We can create custom execution environments using the `ansible-builder` utility.

Automation hub dashboard

The private automation hub dashboard is the user interface to interact with the private automation hub that provides a centralized repository for discovering, downloading, publishing, and managing Ansible Content Collections. All of these contents are downloaded by the automation hub cloud services and made available for our internal users. The automation controller can actually download contents from the automation hub cloud services or private automation hub cloud. Most often is configured to download contents only by the private **Automation Hub**.

It offers several features to help automate projects more efficiently: a trusted **source for Ansible Content Collections (including** Ansible Certified Content from Red Hat and over 60 industry-leading partners), a **Private automation hub** (store and control custom-generated content access), **store and manage container images, Red Hat Ansible Certified Content, and Ansible validated content and Automation execution environments.** The private automation hub dashboard offers a comprehensive solution for managing Ansible

Content Collections, facilitating collaboration and governance within organizations, and providing the ability to store and share container images and content in a controlled manner.

At the moment of writing this book, **Automation Hub** has 146 collections from 70 partners, as shown in *Figure 4.31:*

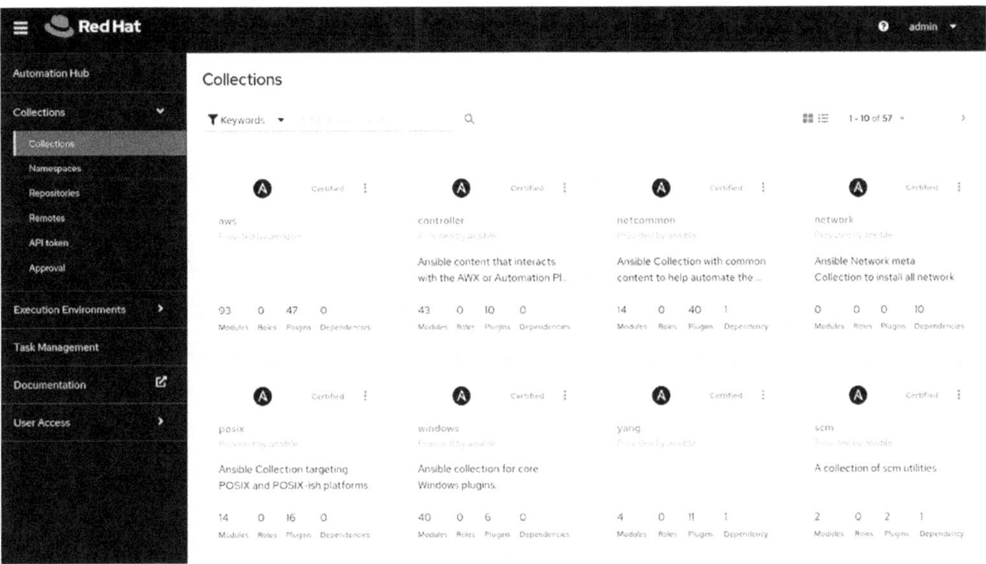

Figure 4.31: *Private automation hub dashboard*

The private automation hub has a RESTful API to connect to in the same way as the automation controller API. However, it is not browsable, so we need to access the correct endpoint.

Ansible validated contents

The corporate world relies on the Ansible automation hub to provide Ansible resources and content ready to use. Ansible automation hub manages resources from Red Hat product teams, **independent software vendor** (ISV) partners, and community and private contributors. The partner list in Ansible automation hub is getting lengthier day by day. It includes, at the moment: Amazon, Arista, Aruba Networks, Check Point, Cisco, Citrix, CyberArk, Dell EMC, Dynatrace, F5 Networks, Fortinet, HPE, IBM, Juniper Networks, Kubernetes, Microsoft, NetApp, Nvidia, 1Password, SAP, ServiceNow, Splunk, TrendMicro, and VMware. Since version 2.3 Ansible Automation Platform of November 2022, take advantage of the validated contents feature. Content in automation hub can be certified and signed via a GPG key. The GNU Pretty Good Privacy, or GPG, the popular program, is used to authenticate contents with digital signatures of stored files. We could choose a key that validates all the code we download to our servers to certify the software chain from the creator to the final users.

Custom execution environment

The automation hub can store a container as a container registry. This feature is very useful for Ansible execution environment. First of all, we need to generate our execution environment and assign a tag. To push a tagged container image to a private automation hub and populate the container registry, follow these steps:

1. Log in to Podman using our private automation hub fully qualified domain name (FQDN) or IP address and credentials. Run the following command:

```
podman login -u=<username> -p=<password> <automation_hub_url>
```

2. Push our container image to our automation hub container registry. Use the following command:

```
podman push <automation_hub_url>/<container_image_name>
```

Note: Pushing signed images to the automation hub container registry requires the --remove-signatures flag. The push operation re-compresses image layers during the upload, which can result in changes to the image-layer digest and a failure error message.

We can find all the container images in the private automation hub, as shown in *Figure 4.32*:

1. Log in to our **Automation Hub**.

2. Navigate to the **Container Registry** section.

3. Locate the container in the container repository list.

Please refer to the following figure:

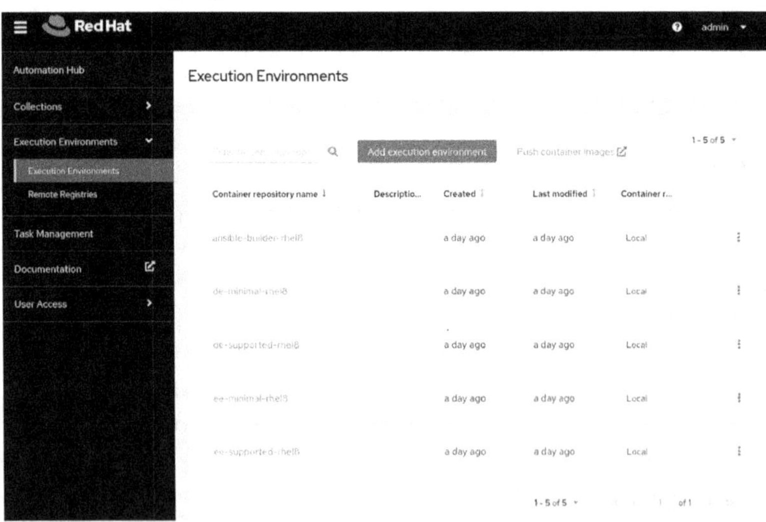

Figure 4.32: Automation hub execution environments

By following these steps, we can successfully push a container image to our private automation hub and ensure it is available in the container registry for use.

Event-Driven Ansible

We can execute Event-Driven Ansible code using the Event-Driven Ansible controller dashboard. Please refer to the following figure:

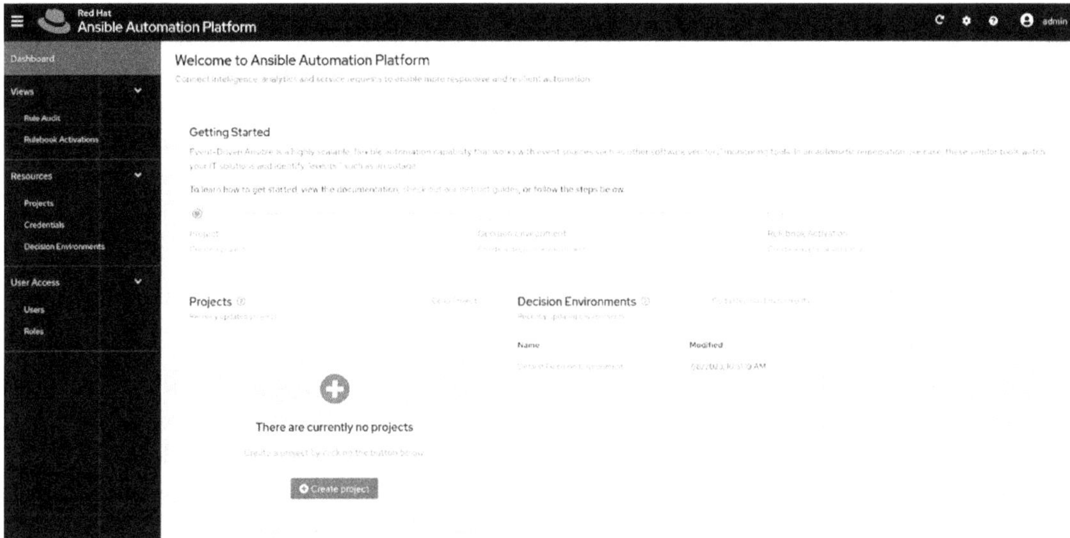

Figure 4.33: *The Dashboard of the Ansible Event-Driven controller*

Project

Projects in the Event-Driven Ansible Controller Dashboard serve as organized collections of rulebooks, facilitating efficient management of automation tasks. Rulebooks must be located within the rulebooks directory of the project. To create a new project, ensure prerequisites such as logging in as a content consumer, setting up necessary credentials, and having a repository with integrated rulebooks and playbooks are met. Follow the steps by logging in, selecting Projects from the navigation panel, and choosing to create a new project. Input project details such as name, optional description, Git as the only available **SCM type**, **SCM URL** pointing to the repository, and optional **credential** for the SCM URL. After creating the project, it can be managed on the Projects screen, allowing users to edit or delete as needed.

Note: The SCM URL cannot be edited after project creation.

Decision environment

Decision environments serve as container images for executing Ansible Rulebooks, providing a standardized platform for automation tasks with seamless management of dependencies. Users can create custom environments while the default Ansible Rulebook decision environment is available. To import a decision environment into the Event-Driven Ansible Controller Dashboard, prerequisites such as logging in as a content consumer and setting up necessary credentials must be met. Follow the steps by navigating to the Dashboard, selecting Decision Environments, and choosing to create a new environment. Input details like the environment name, optional description, image location (including registry, name, and version tag), and optional credentials. After creating the environment, it can be managed on the Decision Environments screen, allowing users to edit or delete as needed. These steps facilitate the integration and utilization of decision environments for effectively executing automation tasks.

Automation controller token authentication

To authenticate and access the Ansible Automation Controller, setting up a token granting the necessary permissions for executing automation tasks is crucial. To do this, ensure prerequisites like logging into the Event-Driven Ansible Controller Dashboard as a content consumer are met. Follow the steps by logging in, selecting the user profile, navigating to **User** details, and choosing **Create Controller token**. Input details such as the token name, optional description, and the token generated in the automation controller with write-scope permissions. After creating the token, it can be managed or deleted from the Controller Tokens tab. These steps establish a secure authentication mechanism, laying the foundation for effectively initiating and managing automation tasks within the Event-Driven Ansible Controller Dashboard.

Rulebook activation

Rulebook activation involves the initiation of configured rulebooks within the Event-Driven Ansible Controller Dashboard. Prerequisites for this process include logging into the Event-Driven Ansible Controller Dashboard as a content consumer, setting up a project, configuring a decision environment to run Ansible Rulebooks, and creating an authentication token for Ansible Automation Platform controller access. To set up a rulebook activation, users need to navigate to the Dashboard, select Rulebook Activation, and choose to create a new activation. Details such as activation name, optional description, project selection, associated rulebook, decision environment, and restart policy are specified, with options for automatic activation and variable configuration. Once entered, the activation is created and can be managed in the Rulebook Activations screen, allowing users to edit or delete the activation as needed.

Best practices

There are many Ansible best practices that can help us write successful code and avoid the most common pitfalls in our automation journey. Enforcing Ansible best practices using the **ansible-lint** command line utility involves running the tool on Ansible Playbooks and roles to identify and address potential issues. Here is a step-by-step guide:

1. **Install ansible-lint**: Begin by installing **ansible-lint** on our system. we can use a package manager like **pip** or install it as a Python package. For example, using **pip**:

   ```
   pip install ansible-lint
   ```

2. **Run ansible-lint**: Execute **ansible-lint** against us Ansible Playbooks or roles to analyze them for best practice violations. Provide the path to the playbook or role directory as an argument:

   ```
   ansible-lint playbook.yml

   ansible-lint roles/

   ansible-lint collections/
   ```

3. **Analyze the output**: **ansible-lint** will process our code and generate a list of issues, warnings, or suggestions based on predefined rules. Each violation will be accompanied by a message explaining the issue and providing guidance on how to fix it.

   Carefully review the output and address the identified issues. Some violations may be simple coding style suggestions, while others could be critical best practice violations that should be resolved.

4. **Customize rules**: **ansible-lint** provides a set of default rules, but we can customize them to match our specific needs. Create a configuration file, **.ansible-lint**, in us project directory or use the **--exclude`** or **`--include** options to ignore or include specific rules, respectively.

   Tailor the rules to our requirements to focus on the particular best practices and coding standards relevant to our project.

5. **Integration with CI/CD**: To enforce Ansible best practices consistently, integrate **ansible-lint** into our CI/CD pipeline. Configure our pipeline to run **ansible-lint** automatically whenever there are changes to the Ansible code. This ensures violations are caught early, preventing non-compliant code from being deployed.

By incorporating **ansible-lint** into our development workflow, we can enforce best practices and maintain code quality across our Ansible projects. Regularly running **ansible-lint** helps catch potential issues, improves readability, and ensures adherence to recommended standards, ultimately leading to more robust and maintainable Ansible playbooks and roles. In the same way, we use **molecule** tool to execute Ansible role tests:

dependency, cleanup, destroy, syntax, create, prepare, converge, idempotence, side_effect, and verification.

Configuration as code

Advanced users could consider managing automation controller **configuration as code** (**CaC**) using Ansible. The major benefits of treating configurations as code are easier replication, bug tracking, and deployment management. The automation controller and CaC integration is achieved through the **ansible.controller** and **infra.controller_configuration** Ansible collections that provide modules and roles to connect, manage, and configure the automation controller. We need to define a Git repository to store the configuration, use a logical directory structure to organize the configuration and leverage Ansible Vault to encrypt sensitive data. Creating a consistent and well-defined directory structure is important, using Git branching features to handle multiple environments and promoting configuration between branches representing specific environments. The flow of configuration implementation involves making changes to configuration files in a Git repository, triggering events through Git hooks, processing the changes, and executing tasks based on Job Templates in the automation controller. For example, the following Ansible playbook creates a project and job template in automation controller:

```
---

- name: Set Up a Project and Job Template
  hosts: all
  tasks:
    - name: Create a Project
      ansible.controller.project:
        name: Automation Controller Samples
        state: present
        scm_type: git
        scm_url: https://github.com/ansible/ansible-toour-samples.git

    - name: Create a Job Template
      ansible.controller.job_template:
        name: my-job-1
        project: Job Template Test Project
        inventory: Demo Inventory
        playbook: hello_world.yml
        job_type: run
        state: present
```

Other services

Ansible Automation Platform subscription includes other interesting services Red Hat provides as cloud services.

Web console

The **Web Console Dashboard** (codename `gateway`) has been introduced since the release of Ansible Automation Platform 2.5. It provides a unified view and access to all the platform resources, including the automation controller, automation hub, and Event-Driven Ansible controller. It eliminates the need to remember and manage separate login credentials for each component, making it more convenient for users to switch between different areas of the Ansible Automation Platform. The web console is based on the Envoy open-source edge and service proxy designed for cloud-native applications. This framework addresses the networking and observability challenges that arise when transitioning to a distributed architecture, serving as a high-performance C++ distributed proxy for individual services and applications and a universal data plane for large microservice service mesh setups. It supports advanced features like HTTP/2 and gRPC, load balancing, and dynamic configuration management, enhancing observability with deep traffic insights and distributed tracing. It simplifies microservices management, making it easier to debug, optimize performance, and add features across a network of services. Envoy is also the foundation of the Istio service in a Kubernetes cluster. The web console enhances the user experience, simplifies management, and improves efficiency when working with the Ansible Automation Platform.

Automation analytics

The online components of the Red Hat Ansible Automation Platform report feature (part of Red Hat Insights) are **called automation analytics**. This platform cloud service gives users a visual overview of their automation efforts across different Ansible teams. Each report is designed to help users monitor various aspects of their automation environment. The most common used reports are: license count, vulnerability and compliance, Infrastructure data, Execution, and task reports. The reports feature within the Ansible Automation Platform offers users a comprehensive view of their automation environment. It covers a wide range of information, including license counts, vulnerability data, infrastructure details, execution statistics, and task-specific reports. These insights empower users to make data-driven decisions, optimize their automation workflows, and ensure the smooth operation of their Ansible deployments.

Key learning

Using Dashboard, CLI, and API interfaces, we learned how to move our initial steps inside the automation controller, automation hub, and Event-Driven Ansible controller.

Points to remember

- Automation controller manages our content and executes using Projects, Jobs, Credentials, Inventory, and Workflow.

- Automation controller, automation hub, and Event-Driven controller provide a web user interface, RESTful API, and a CLI interface.

- Automation hub stores Ansible content, roles, playbooks, collections, and Ansible execution environment.

- We can activate our Ansible Automation Platform subscription using Red Hat portal credentials, manifest file, or automate using Ansible.

Multiple choice questions

1. **How can we activate our Ansible Automation Platform subscription?**

    a. Red Hat portal credentials

    b. Manifest file

    c. Automate using `ansible.controller` collection

    d. All the previous options

2. **What tool of the automation controller enables us to execute one playbook after another?**

    a. Jobs

    b. Workflow

    c. Project

    d. Credentials

3. **How can we interact with automation controller in the Ansible Automation Platform?**

    a. Web interface

    b. API

    c. CLI

    d. All the previous options

4. **How can we create Ansible reusable contents for our organization?**

   a. Automation controller

   b. Automation hub

   c. Private automation hub

   d. Ansible Event-Driven controller

Answers

1. d

2. b

3. d

4. c

Questions

1. How can we connect to the automation controller from the command line terminal?

2. What are the three Ansible execution environments included in the Ansible Automation Platform?

3. How can we check that our code adheres to the Ansible best practices?

Key terms

- **Workflow Template**: A Workflow Template in the Ansible automation controller is a configuration that defines a sequence of job templates or tasks to be executed as a single unit in a predefined order.

- **ansible-lint** is a static analysis tool for Ansible Playbooks and roles that helps enforce best practices and coding standards.

- **ansible-sign** is a command-line tool used to sign Ansible artifacts, such as playbooks or roles, with a digital signature to ensure authenticity and integrity.

- **Ansible rulebook** is a framework that defines the structure and guidelines for Event-Driven Ansible automation, consisting of rulesets with sources, rules, and conditions.

Join our book's Discord space

Join the book's Discord Workspace for Latest updates, Offers, Tech happenings around the world, New Release and Sessions with the Authors:

https://discord.bpbonline.com

CHAPTER 5

Settings and Authentication

Introduction

We are going to learn how we can customize the settings in the Ansible Automation Platform to personalize the response of the role-based access controls, authentication integrations, and centralized authentication to configure and manage user permissions, security, and authentication methods efficiently.

Structure

In this chapter, we will discuss the following topics:

- Automation controller settings
- Users, Teams, and RBAC
- Authentication integrations
- Ansible Automation Platform Central Authentication

Objectives

In this chapter, we are going to familiarize ourselves with the most used options in the settings to execute our Ansible jobs better and the most common authentication integrations.

Automation controller settings

Customizing the Ansible controller settings, we can fine-tune any Ansible controller behavior. We can access the automation controller settings via the **Settings** options in the web user interface, as shown in *Figure 5.1* below.

Accessing the **Setting** section of the user interface is organized into five sections that appear on our screen: **Authentication, Jobs, System, User Interface,** and **Subscription.**

Some **Settings** parameters can be literal values that we can review and modify (like the **fork value**), and some are toggles (like the **New User Interface**).

For example, a common job performance tweak is to increase the Ansible fork value, as explained in the following section. Please refer to the following figure:

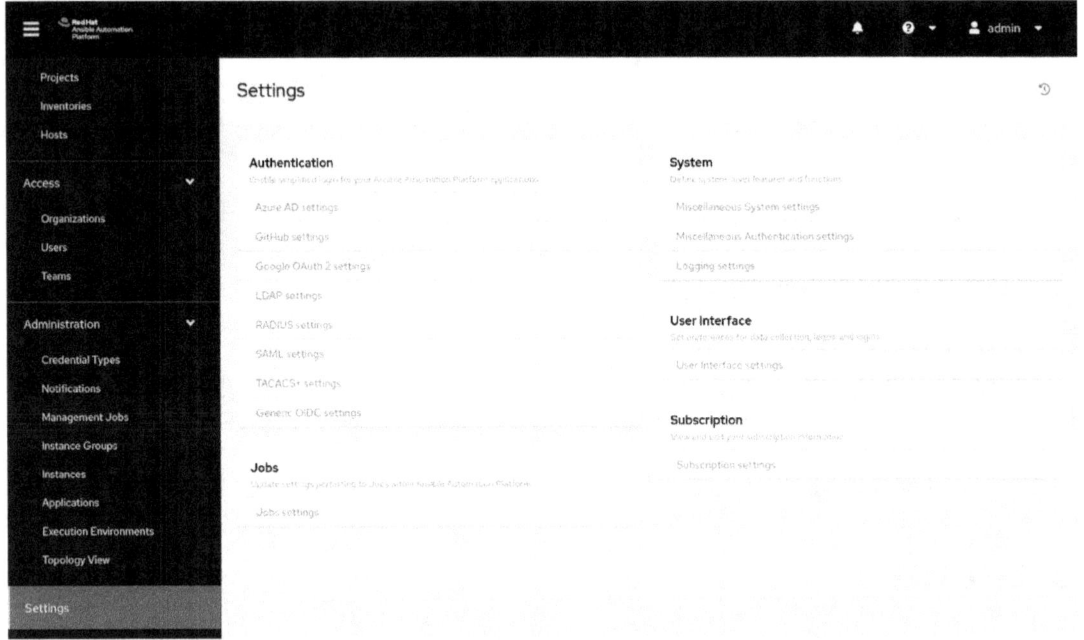

Figure 5.1: Automation controller web settings

In the same way, we have access to all the available settings parameters via the RESTful API accessing the endpoint **/api/v2/settings/** of our automation controller, as shown in *Figure 5.2* below. Please note that this endpoint requires authentication using automation controller credentials. Please refer to the following figure:

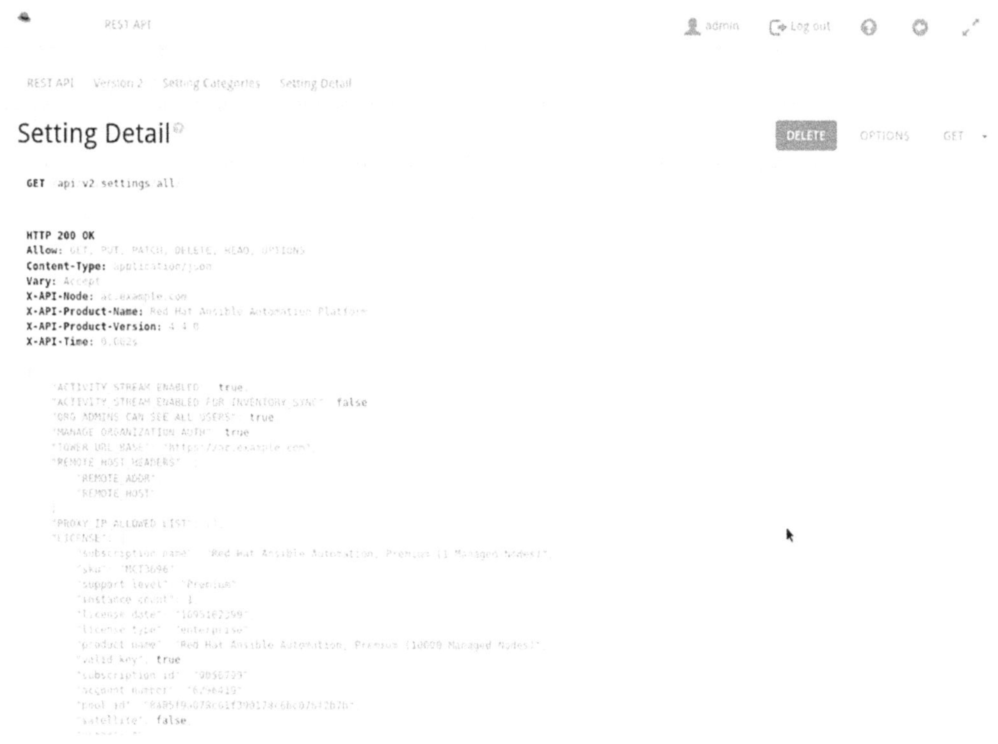

Figure 5.2: Automation controller API settings

New User Interface

The updated user interface in **Technology Preview** in Ansible Automation Platform 2.4 is a preview of the new **graphical user interface (GUI)** designed to enhance the management and scalability of features within the Ansible Automation Platform. The ultimate goal is to provide a unified user experience across various platform components, including automation controller, private automation hub, and Event-Driven Ansible controller. In the initial release, the updated GUI is available only for automation controller, with plans to expand it to other components in the future.

The updated user interface offers several new capabilities, such as support for dark mode, which can be customized to match our operating system preferences. The **Web User Interface** is more responsive, customizable, and user-friendly. However, it is important to note that the updated interface is in the technical preview stage to gather customer feedback and further improve it. Some capabilities from the previous webUI may still need to be fully matched at this stage, but they will be enhanced over time.

We can enable the new user interface in Ansible Automation Platform 2.4 by enabling the **Enable Preview of New User Interface** button in the **Settings | Miscellaneous System**. Please refer to the following figure:

Figure 5.3: Enable or disable the New User Interface feature

After saving and reloading the Ansible controller user interface looks like the following *Figure 5.4*:

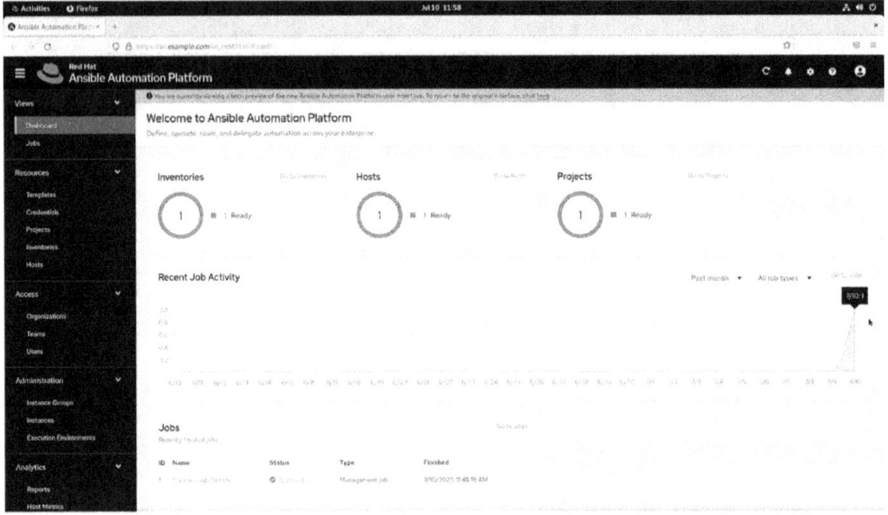

Figure 5.4: Ansible automation controller New UI

One of the advantages of the **New User Interface** is the support of a dark theme, as shown in *Figure 5.5*:

Figure 5.5: Ansible automation controller New UI dark theme

Job Settings

In Ansible, the term **fork** refers to the number of parallel processes or connections that the tool utilizes to manage hosts simultaneously. By default, Ansible is set to use 5 forks for every job execution, determining the number of target hosts it can operate on concurrently. This number could be suboptimal for our execution, especially in a large inventory. This value can be adjusted to optimize performance based on available resources and task complexity.

To modify the fork value, we can edit the **ansible.cfg** file in the current project (the **forks** key in the [**defaults**] section) or customize the relative job template. For example, setting the value of the fork to 10 would allow Ansible to use 10 parallel processes when managing target hosts resulting in better performance with a large Ansible inventory. By adjusting the fork value, we can control the level of parallelism in Ansible's host management operations, ensuring efficient resource utilization and minimizing the impact on system resources like CPU and memory during task execution. This flexibility empowers users to tailor Ansible's performance to suit their specific requirements and infrastructure. Remember to execute some tests to check the CPU and memory resource utilization for our playbook. Please refer to the following figure:

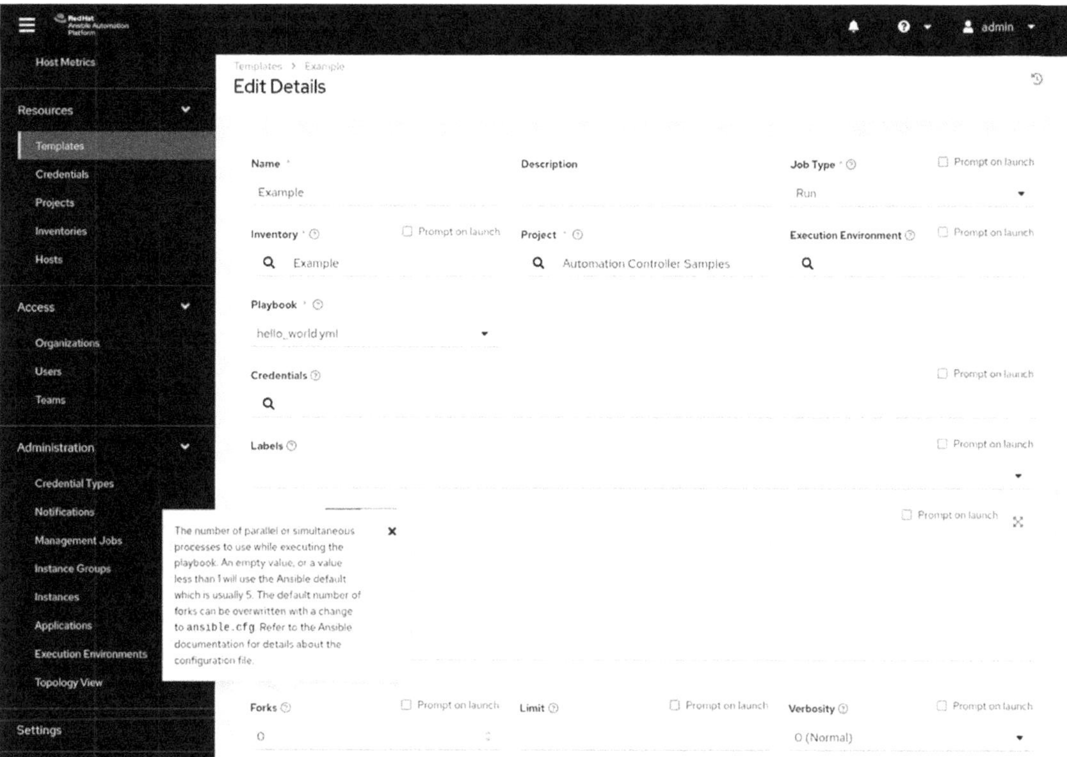

Figure 5.6: Customize Ansible fork setting

The maximum value for the fork parameter can be set in the **Settings | Jobs** setting area. By default, the maximum is 200 for the platform, as shown in *Figure 5.7*. The setting is called **Maximum number of forks per job**.

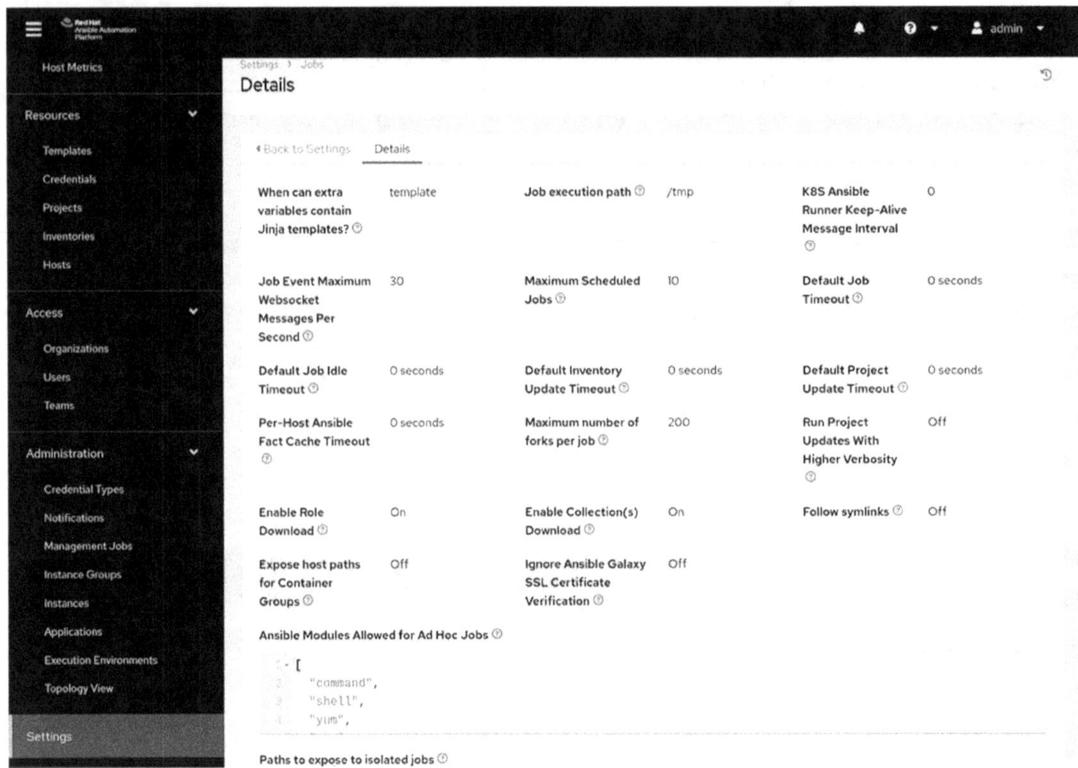

Figure 5.7: Maximum forks setting

Logging level

Sometimes we need to investigate the automation controller's behavior in debugging complex job execution or system integration with other components in our network. Increasing the log level of the platform is beneficial.

We can increase the log level from the default INFO to DEBUG at **Automation Controller Dashboard | Settings | System | Logging settings**. The output is displayed in the **log** file at **/var/log/tower/tower.log** or via any log aggregator service. Please refer to the following figure:

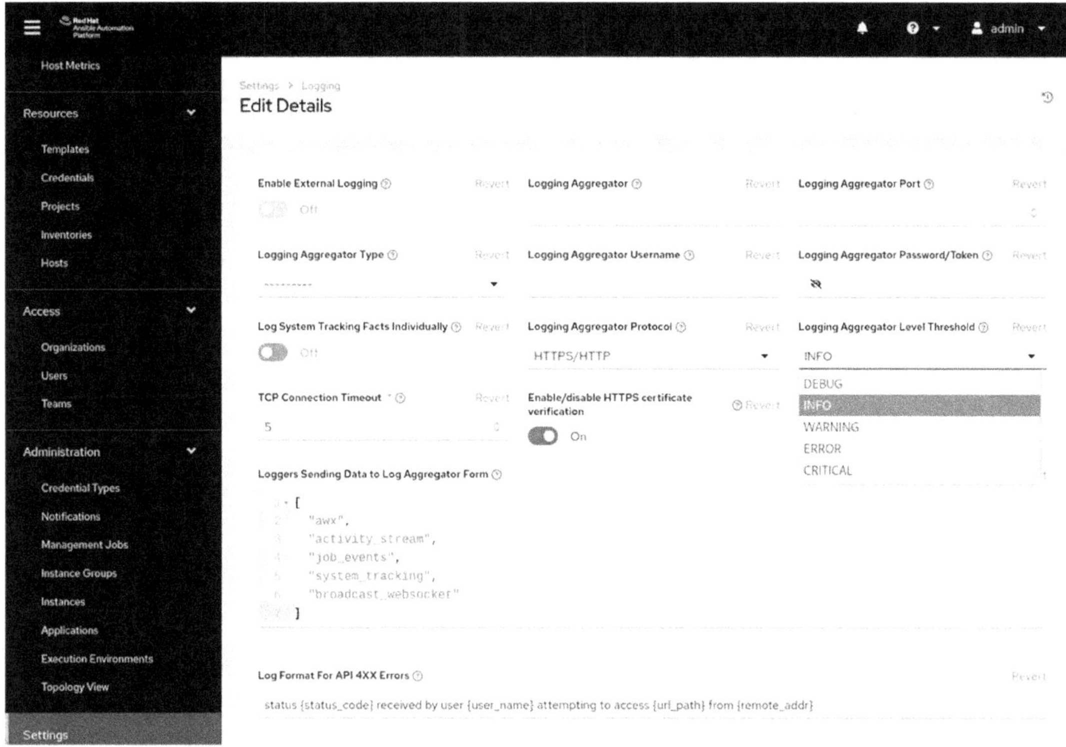

Figure 5.8: Logging level

Users, Teams, and RBAC

Automation controller is a powerful platform that facilitates efficient management of automation tasks and workflows usable by each member of our organization. Users with the appropriate permissions can seamlessly execute automation tasks, leading to a more streamlined and effective automation process. At the core of the automation controller are three essential components: **Users**, **Roles**, and **Teams**, each playing a vital role in orchestrating and securing automation processes.

Users are the individual members of our organization who interact with the automation controller. They possess specific permissions and credentials, allowing them to execute automation workflows, access resources, and manage various aspects of the system. Users are integral to the successful implementation and smooth functioning of automation processes.

Conversely, roles define the behaviors and capabilities associated with specific groups of hosts, groups, or host patterns in Ansible and automation controller. They encompass variable values, tasks, and handlers, offering a modular and redistributable approach to share and reuse behaviors across playbooks and with other users. Additionally, Roles play a crucial role in RBAC, granting access rights and permissions to users and teams, thereby ensuring a secure and controlled environment.

Teams act as sub-divisions within an Organization, providing a structured approach to manage users, projects, credentials, and permissions. Organizations can implement **role-based access control (RBAC)** schemes by utilizing Teams, enabling seamless delegation of responsibilities and access across various projects and resources.

Combining Teams, Users, and Roles, automation controller maximizes efficiency, security, and collaboration. Teams create a structured framework for managing users and their access, while Roles facilitate consistency and reusability of automation behaviors.

Creating and managing users credentials

Automation controller is a powerful tool that enables efficient management and execution of automation workflows. As an administrator, controlling who can access the system and what actions they can perform is essential. This is where managing users and their associated permissions and credentials become crucial. In this guide, we will explore the various aspects of user management in automation controller.

To begin managing users, navigate the **Automation Controller Dashboard** to the **Users** page by clicking **Users** from the left navigation bar in automation controller, as shown in *Figure 5.9*. This page displays a list of all the current users in the system. We can easily search and sort users by their **Username**, **First Name**, or **Last Name** by clicking on the respective headers. Please refer to the following figure:

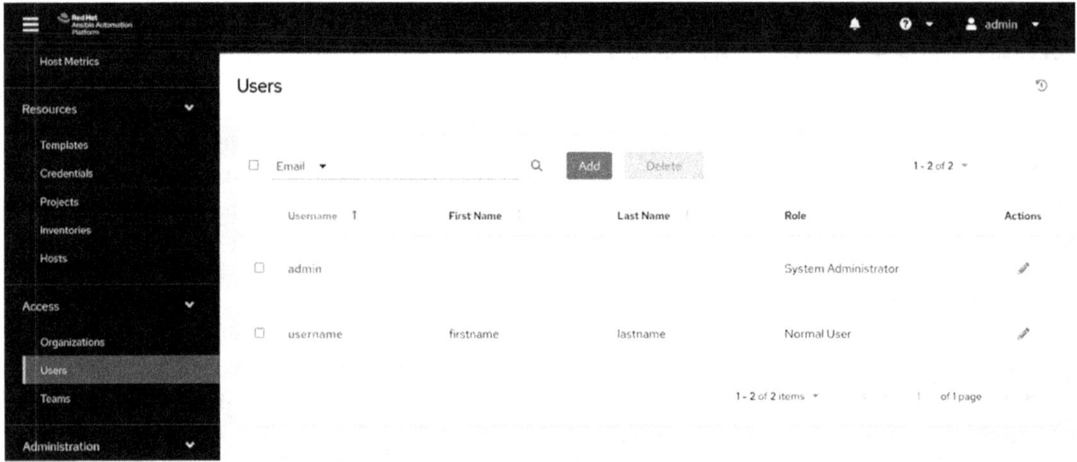

Figure 5.9: List available users

In the **User Overview** screen, we can quickly view permissions and user type information beside each user's name. This provides a snapshot of each user's access level and role.

To create a new user, follow these steps as shown in *Figure 5.10*:

1. Click the **Add** button, which opens the **Create User** dialog.

2. Enter the required details about the new user. Fields marked with an asterisk (*) are mandatory.

3. Select the appropriate user type from the three available options:

   - **Normal User**: Has read and write access limited to the resources for which they have been granted roles and privileges.

   - **System Auditor**: Inherits read-only capability for all objects within the environment.

   - **System Administrator (Superuser)**: Has full system administration privileges with read and write access throughout the platform. Assign this role cautiously, as it grants complete control over automation controller.

Note: When modifying our user password, log out and log back in again for the changes to take effect.

4. Click **Save** when finished. Once the user is successfully created, the **User** dialog opens for that user. Please refer to the following figure:

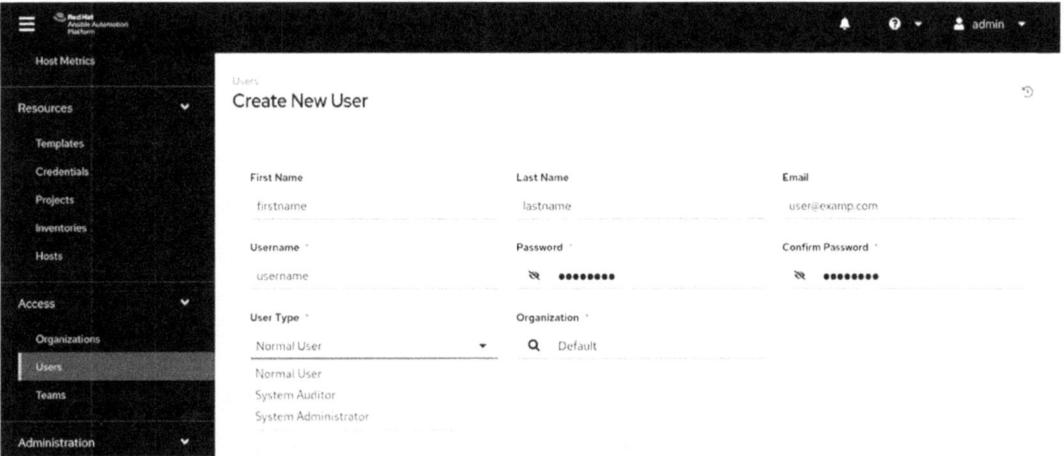

Figure 5.10: Create a new user

We can review and modify the user's organizations, teams, roles, and other membership details in the **User** dialog. For existing users, the details screen also displays the last login activity of that user.

To delete a user, we must have user permissions. Follow these steps to delete a user account:

1. Expand the **Access** menu from the left navigation bar and click **Users** to display a list of current users.

2. Select the checkbox(es) for the user(s) we want to remove and click **Delete**.

3. Confirm the action by clicking **Delete** in the confirmation warning message.

We can see the user's details by clicking on a specific username, as shown in *Figure 5.11*:

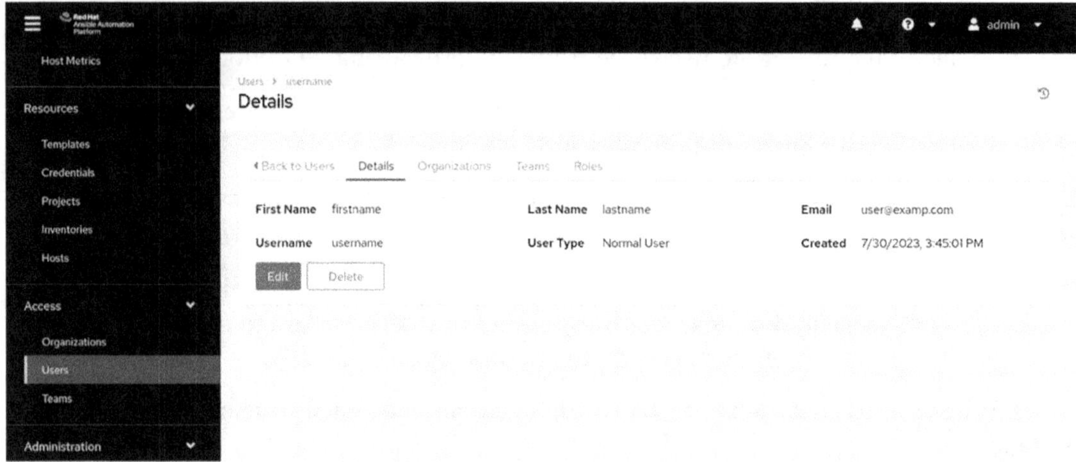

Figure 5.11: The user details

The **Users - Organizations** section displays the list of organizations to which a user is a member. This list can be searched by **Organization Name** or **Description**, but organization membership cannot be modified from this display panel.

In the **Users - Teams** section, we can view the list of teams to which a user is a member. Like organizations, this list can be searched by **Team Name** or **Description**, but team membership cannot be modified from this display panel.

The **Users - Roles** section displays the set of permissions assigned to a user through role-based access controls. These roles determine the user's ability to read, modify, and administer projects, inventories, job templates, and other elements in automation controller.

Please note that a user with a role like **Job Template Administrator** may not have access to other resources (inventory, project, credentials, or instance groups) associated with the template. System administrators can grant individual users permissions to specific resources as necessary.

To add permissions to a particular user, follow these steps:

1. Click the **Add** button, which opens the **Add Permissions Wizard**.

2. Select the object for which the user will have access and click **Next**.

3. Choose the resource to assign team roles and click **Next**.

4. Check the checkbox(es) beside the role to assign that role to the selected resource. Different resources may have different options available.

5. Click **Save** when done, and the **Add Permissions Wizard** will close, displaying the updated profile for the user with the assigned roles.

The **Users - Tokens** tab is available only for our users (ourselves). Here, we can manage tokens associated with our user profile. Tokens are used for authentication and authorization purposes within the automation controller. We can create application-specific tokens or **personal access tokens** (**PAT**s) without linking them to any application.

To create a token for our user, as shown in *Figure 5.12*:

1. Click on our user from the **Users** list view to configure the **OAuth 2** tokens.

2. Click the **Tokens** tab from the user's profile.

3. If no tokens are present, click the **Add** button to open the **Create Token** window.

4. Enter the necessary details, such as application (if applicable), description, and scope.

5. Click **Save** to create the token.

After creating a token, it will be displayed with its associated information, including the expiration date. Please refer to the following figure:

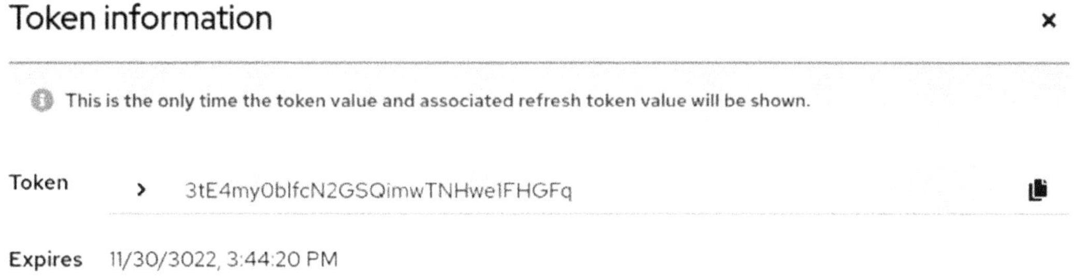

Figure 5.12: User token

Managing users and their access permissions is vital for maintaining a secure and organized automation controller environment. By following the steps outlined in this guide, administrators can effectively manage users, roles, and credentials, ensuring smooth operations and adherence to security best practices.

Managing users efficiently with Teams

In the automation controller, Teams are sub-divisions of organizations with associated Users, Projects, Credentials, and Permissions, providing a means to implement role-based access control schemes and delegate responsibilities across organizations. Each Team can be assigned permissions, allowing scalability in managing access and ownership of **Credentials**. To create a new Team, click the **Add** button, enter the required details, such as **Name**, **Description**, and **Organization**, and click **Save**, as shown in *Figure 5.13*:

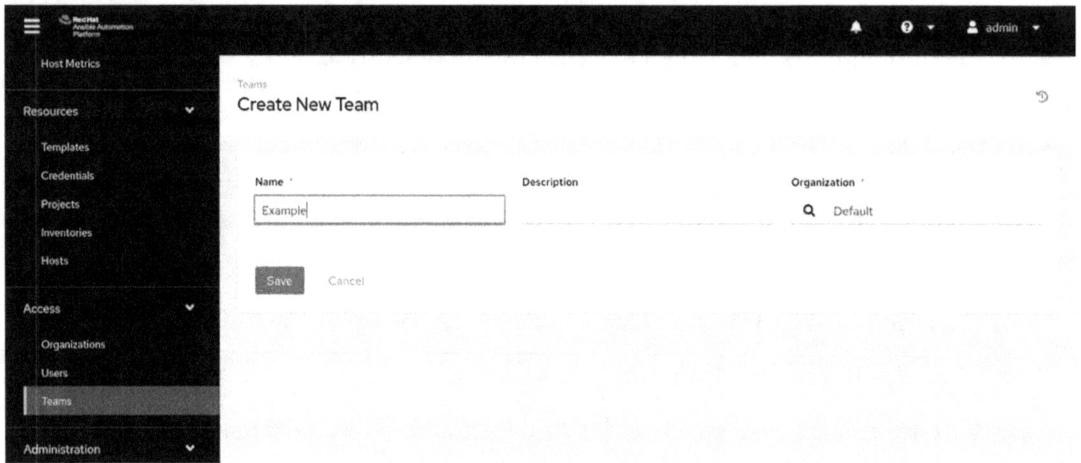

Figure 5.13: Create a new Team

The Team's **Access** tab displays the list of **Users** who are members of the Team, and adding existing users to the Team can be done by clicking the **Add** button in the **Access** tab, following the prompts, and clicking **Save** when done. We can list all the available teams in our organization, as displayed in *Figure 5.14*:

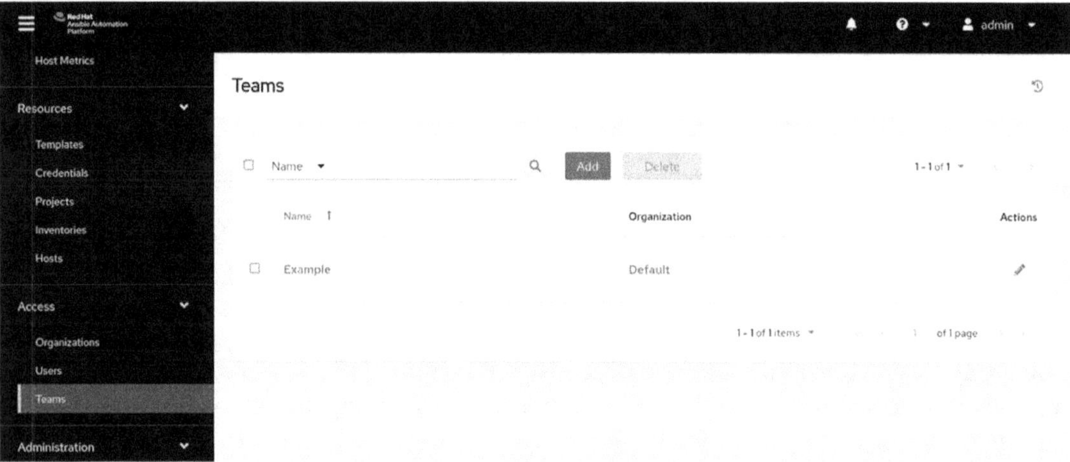

Figure 5.14: List the teams in the organization

The **Team Roles** view lists the permissions currently available for the Team, and permissions must be set explicitly via an Inventory, Project, Job template, or within the **Organization** view. Adding **team permissions** can be achieved through the **Add Permissions Wizard**, where we select the object for which the team will have access, the resource to assign team roles, and click the checkbox beside the role to assign it to the chosen type of resource, as shown in *Figure 5.15*:

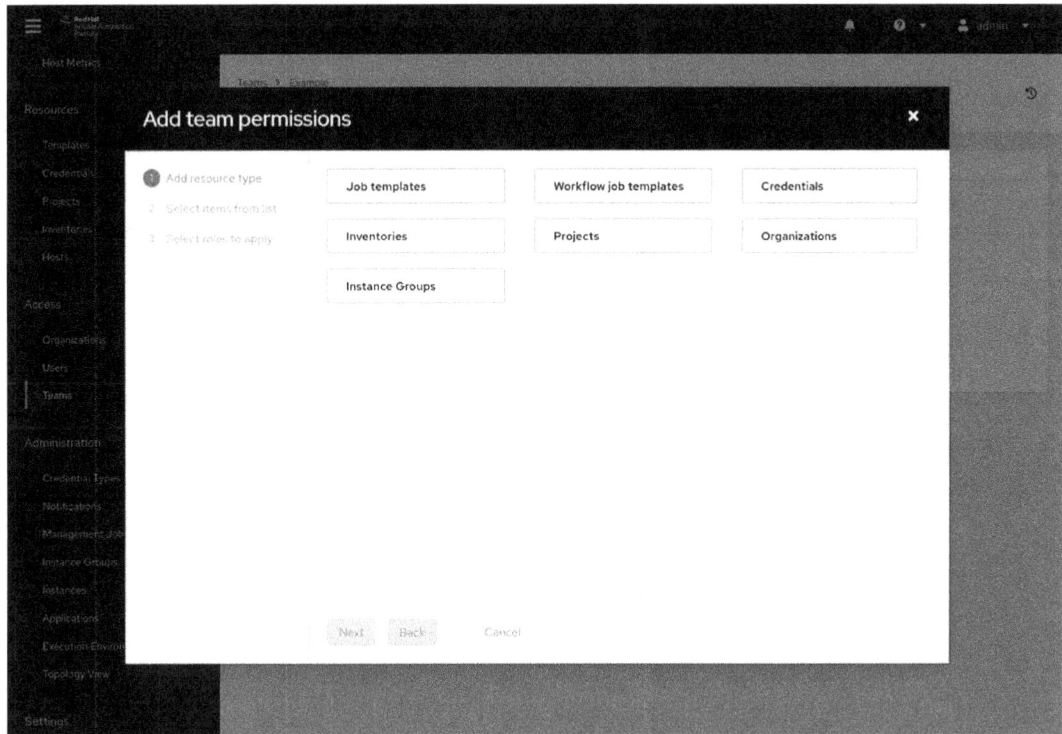

Figure 5.15: Add team permissions

Removing permissions for a resource can be done by clicking the disassociate (x) button, followed by a confirmation dialog. This allows for efficient management of user access and roles, enabling organizations to optimize performance based on available resources and the nature of the tasks being executed.

Role-based access controls

The role-based access controls feature is integrated into the automation controller and enables enhanced security and management. RBAC is a crucial feature built into automation controllers, allowing administrators to delegate access to server inventories, organizations, and more. RBAC ensures that the right users have the appropriate level of access to perform specific actions, which helps to enhance security, streamline management, and maintain a well-organized system. In this article, we will explore the concepts of RBAC and how they function within an automation controller environment. Three main concepts are central in the automation controller RBAC system: Roles, Resources, and Users.

Let us take a closer look at each of these:

- **Roles**

  A Role is a collection of capabilities defining what actions a user or team can perform within the automation controller. Roles are associated with a group of capabilities granted to users or teams. All capabilities are derived from membership within a role. Users receive capabilities through the roles they are assigned or through roles inherited via the role hierarchy.

  The automation controller provides several built-in roles, such as System Administrator, System Auditor, Admin Role, Auditor Role, Execute Role, Member Role, Read Role, Update Role, Owner Role, and Use Role, each with specific permissions and access levels.

- **Resources**

  Resources represent various components within the automation controller, such as workflows, projects, inventories, credentials, job templates, and so on. Each resource can be associated with specific roles, and the permissions granted to users or teams are based on these associations.

- **Users**

  Users are individuals or teams who interact with the automation controller. Users can be assigned one or more roles, determining their access to different resources and capabilities.

One of the key features of RBAC in automation controller is the **Role Hierarchy**. The Role Hierarchy allows roles to include all the capabilities of other roles, creating a hierarchical relationship. This means that any capability granted to a child role is implicitly granted to its parent roles, and so on.

For example, we have roles like System Administrator, Organization Administrator, and Project Administrator. If a user is assigned the Project Administrator role, they will inherit all the capabilities of both the Organization Administrator and System Administrator roles.

This hierarchical structure simplifies permissions management, as administrators can define roles with varying access levels and then easily assign these roles to users or teams. It also ensures that users have the necessary access to perform their tasks efficiently while maintaining security by not granting excessive permissions.

Let us explore how RBAC is applied in different aspects of the automation controller:

- **Editing Users**

  Automation controller administrators can assign roles like System Administrator or System Auditor to users. System Administrators have full control over all objects in the automation controller environment, while System Auditors can view all aspects of the system in read-only mode.

- **Editing Organizations**

  When editing an organization, administrators can specify various roles for users, including organization administrators, organization auditors, and organization members. Organization administrators have full control over all aspects of the organization, while organization auditors can view all aspects of the organization in read-only mode. Organization members, by default, do not have access to any aspect of the organization and require specific roles to gain access.

- **Editing Projects in an Organization**

  Administrators can assign roles to users or teams for organizational projects. Roles like project administrators and project members define the level of control and access that users have over the projects.

- **Creating Inventories and Credentials within an Organization**

  Access to inventories and credentials is handled through roles. Administrators can create inventories and credentials within organizations and grant usage capabilities to specific users or teams.

- **Editing Job templates**

  Roles like system administrators, organization administrators, and project administrators can create and modify job templates for their respective projects. Users with execution capabilities for job templates can run them against specific hosts.

- **User View**

  Users can see and execute job templates for which they have been granted execution capabilities. They can also create their own credential objects, view and be members of organizations and projects, and more, based on their assigned roles.

Automation controller support personnel often assign users different roles, referred to as personas, based on their responsibilities, access needs, and common team roles, as shown in *Figure 5.16*. Common personas are the following:

1. **Owner for Team Lead/Technical Lead**: Has control over access for other users in the organization, can add/remove users and grant specific access to projects, inventories, and job templates.

2. **Auditor for Security Engineer/Project Manager**: Can view all aspects of the organization in read-only mode, suitable for maintaining compliance and managing data.

3. **Member Team for All other users**: By default, has no access to any aspect of the organization and requires specific roles to gain access.

4. **Member Team Owner for Power users/Lead Developer**: Has administrative permissions over the organization's specific components (projects, inventories, job templates).

5. **Member Team Execute for Developers/Engineers**: Can execute job templates and has read permission for specific components.

6. **Member Team Use for Developers/Engineers**: Can use credentials, inventories, projects, and job templates in their work.

7. **Team Member Update for Developers/Engineers**: Can update projects and run SCM updates.

Please refer to the following figure:

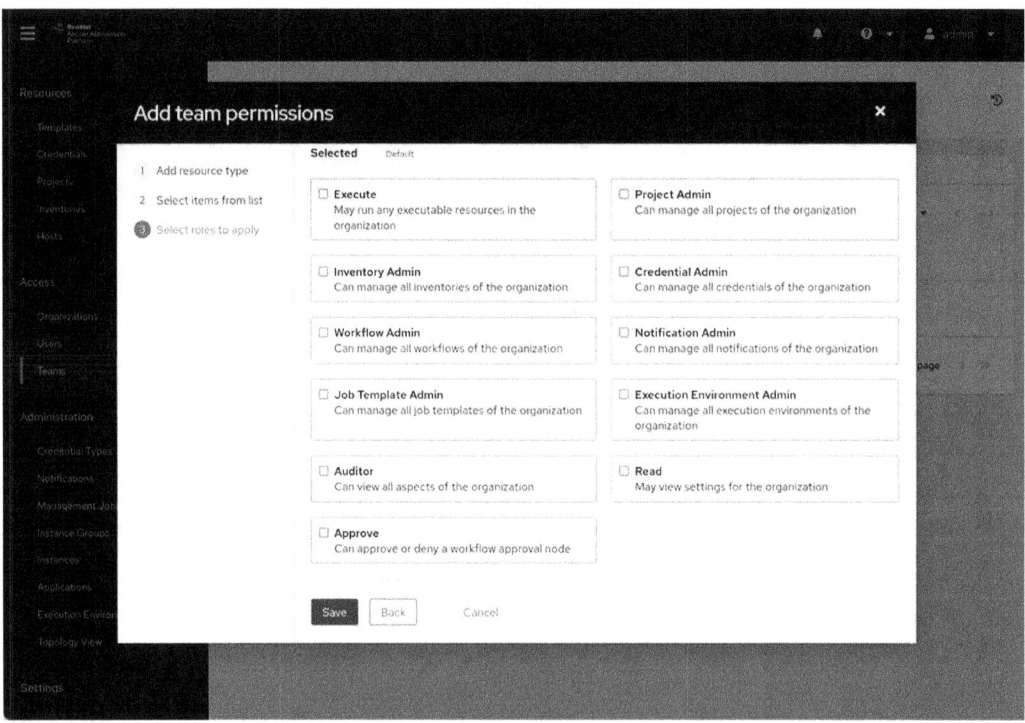

Figure 5.16: Automation controller RBAC permissions

Role-based access controls in automation controllers enable organizations to manage access, permissions, and security in a streamlined manner. By assigning appropriate roles to users and teams, administrators can ensure that the right individuals have the necessary access to perform their tasks without compromising overall system security. The role hierarchy simplifies the management of permissions, allowing for efficient delegation of capabilities. Embracing RBAC in an automation controller environment is a proactive step towards securing our automation infrastructure while enhancing collaboration and productivity.

Automation hub

Automation hub has a similar configuration as automation controller via the Dashboard for single users and groups. User access is managed through groups, where permissions are assigned to groups, and users are then added to these groups to inherit the assigned permissions. The default admin user is created in the **Admin** group with all permissions. We can create and manage groups, assign permissions to groups, create new users and super users, and add users to groups. As well it is possible to delete a user from automation hub. It is important to create a group for content curators and lists various permissions available for different objects in the private automation hub. For example, it is possible to enable view-only access for a private automation hub, which allows users to view collections and namespaces without the need to log in. This is achieved by editing the inventory file and setting specific parameters. Verification steps are provided to ensure the view-only access works as intended after the installation. We can see all the integrated roles in *Figure 5.17*:

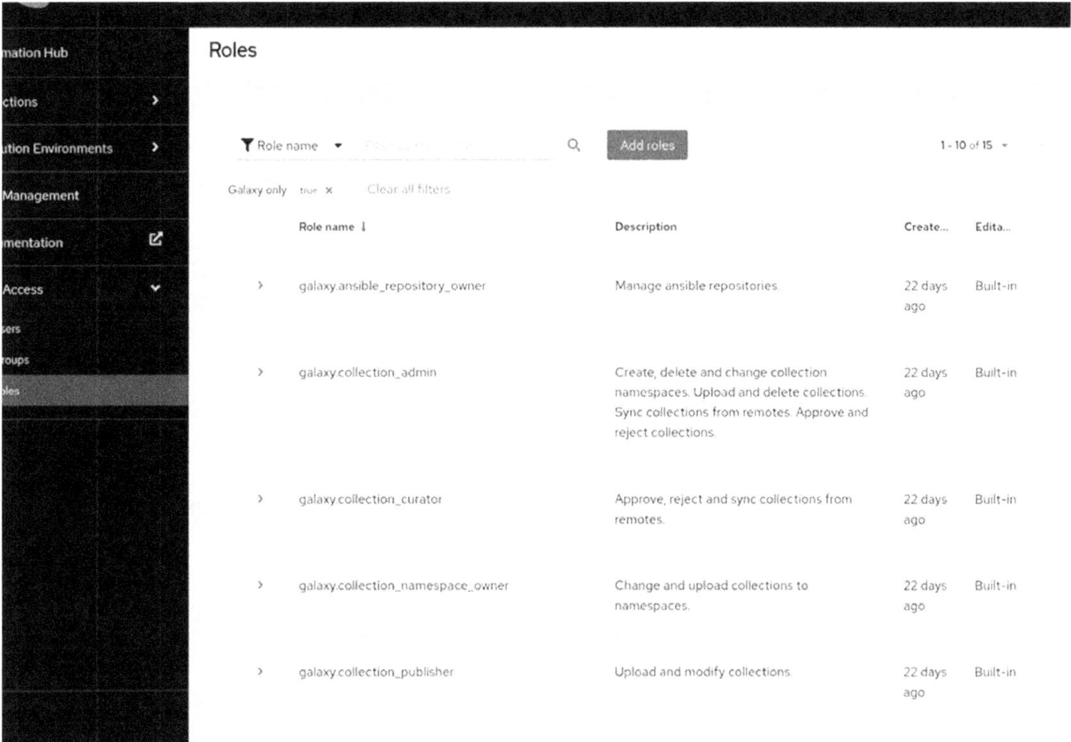

Figure 5.17: Automation Hub Roles

Authentication integrations

When the number of users in our organization grows up, we can use external authentication to manage a large number of users easily. External authentication for the Ansible Automation Platform refers to configuring an external authentication mechanism that allows users to log in and access the platform using a single set of credentials. This approach improves security, simplifies user management, and provides a seamless experience for users across multiple components of the Ansible Automation Platform, especially for large organizations. This approach enables organizations to centralize user access control and authentication using an external authentication service. The following sections cover various aspects, such as integrating the Ansible Automation Platform with an external authentication system like LDAP or Active Directory, setting up authentication plugins, and configuring roles and permissions for users and groups. The full list of supported authentication settings is Azure AD, GitHub, Google OAuth2, LDAP, RADIUS, SAML, TACACS+, and Generic OIDC settings. The SAML, RADIUS, and TACACS+ are categorized as Enterprise authentications and create Enterprise types of users. In contrast, Microsoft Azure, Google, or GitHub are called **social authentications** and are implemented using the **OAuth** standard. Enterprise users can only be created when the first successful login attempt is made from the remote authentication backend. However, if a non-enterprise user with the same name already exists in the controller, the creation/authentication of the enterprise user will not be possible. For enterprise users, their controller passwords must always remain empty and cannot be set by any user, especially if enterprise backends are enabled. On the other hand, if the enterprise backends are disabled, an enterprise user can be converted to a normal controller user by setting the password field. It is important to note that this process is irreversible, meaning the converted controller user will lose their enterprise user status and can no longer be treated as an enterprise user.

lightweight directory access protocol (LDAP) is a popular authentication mechanism to centralize user access control and manage user information across an organization in the Unix domain. This feature allows users to log in using their LDAP credentials, automatically creating accounts for them and granting access to specific organizations based on LDAP attributes. Red Hat Ansible Automation Platform provides the capability to integrate with LDAP for user authentication, making it easier for organizations to manage access to their automation controller or private automation hub instances. For the automation controller, we can configure it in the web user interface, whereas for automation hub, we need to configure specific variables in the inventory file.

LDAP is usually the underlying technology that provisions data to enable Kerberos/SSO/SPNEGO authentication in the realm of users' data.

Automation controller LDAP integration

We can easily integrate our automation controller with LDAP external authentication. In the following more information about the parameters involved in configuring LDAP integration for Ansible automation controller. The most interesting part is that we can actually use up to five concurrent LDAP servers to retrieve users' information, as shown in *Figure 5.18*:

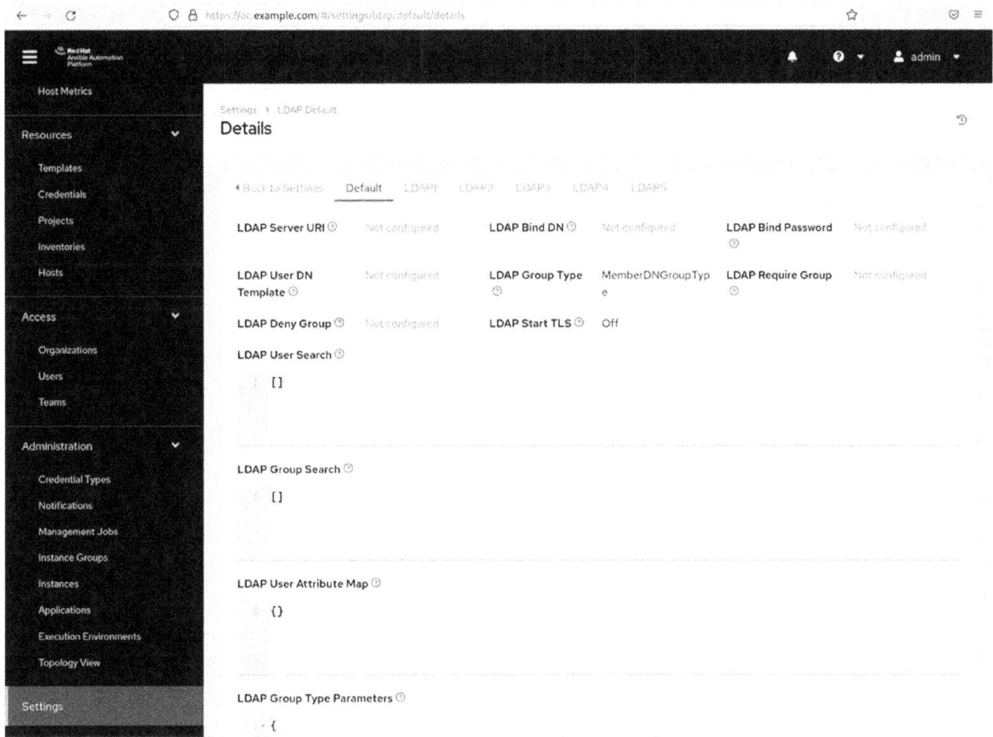

***Figure 5.18:** Automation controller LDAP settings*

To successfully configure LDAP integration, administrators need to understand the various parameters involved in the process. In this article, we will delve into the key parameters required for LDAP configuration in Ansible automation controller.

1. **LDAP Server URI**

   The **LDAP Server URI** parameter specifies the address of the LDAP server to which the controller will connect. It should be provided in the format of `ldap://<hostname>:<port>` (usually port 389) for LDAP connections and `ldaps://<hostname>:<port>` (usually port 636) for secure LDAPS connections. Multiple LDAP servers can be specified by separating each with spaces or commas.

2. **LDAP Bind DN and Bind Password**

   The **LDAP Bind DN** parameter is the distinguished name of the user that the Ansible automation controller uses to bind (connect) to the LDAP server. It should be a user account with read access to the entire LDAP structure. For example, `CN=john,CN=users,DC=example,DC=com`.

The **LDAP Bind Password** parameter is the password for the user specified in the **LDAP Bind DN**. It is essential to use a strong and secure password for this parameter.

3. **LDAP Group Type**

   The **LDAP Group Type** parameter specifies the type of LDAP groups used for managing user access in the automation controller. It supports various group types like **PosixGroupType, GroupOfNamesType, GroupOfUniqueNamesType, ActiveDirectoryGroupType,** and others. The choice of the group type depends on the LDAP server configuration.

4. **LDAP Start TLS**

   The **LDAP Start TLS** parameter enables TLS when the LDAP connection does not use SSL. It is disabled by default. Enabling TLS ensures secure communication between Ansible automation controller and the LDAP server.

5. **LDAP User Search and Group Search**

   The **LDAP User Search** parameter defines where to search for users during authentication. It includes three elements: The base DN where users are searched, the search scopxe (**SCOPE_BASE, SCOPE_ONELEVEL**, or **SCOPE_SUBTREE**), and the key name where the username is stored.

   The **LDAP Group Search** parameter specifies where to search for groups and how to search them. It also includes the base DN where groups are searched, the search scope, and the object class of a group object in the LDAP.

6. **LDAP User Attribute Map**

   The **LDAP User Attribute Map** parameter maps LDAP user attributes to the corresponding fields in Ansible automation controller. For example, mapping LDAP attributes like **givenName, sn** (surname), and **mail** (email) to the first name, last name, and email address fields in the controller.

7. **LDAP Group Type Parameters**

   The **LDAP Group Type Parameters** parameter allows specifying parameters for the selected group type. It is a dictionary that will be converted by the controller to keyword arguments and passed to the **LDAP Group Type** class selected. The common parameters include **name_attr** and **member_attr**.

8. **LDAP User Flags by Group**

   The **LDAP User Flags by Group** parameter allows setting user profile flags based on LDAP group membership. For instance, it can be used to set users as **Superusers** or **Auditors** if they belong to specific LDAP groups.

9. **LDAP Organization and Team Mapping**

   The **LDAP Organization and Team Mapping** parameters control user placement into organizations and teams based on LDAP attributes. These parameters define which users are added as admins or regular users to specific organizations and teams.

We can debug the configuration by setting the logging aggregator level threshold to **DEBUG** at **Automation Controller Dashboard** | **Settings** | **System** | **Logging** settings. The output is displayed in the log file at **/var/log/tower/tower.log** as described in the **Logging Level Settings** section.

LDAP integration in Ansible automation controller offers a powerful way to centralize user authentication and access control. By understanding and configuring the key parameters mentioned above, administrators can seamlessly connect their organization's LDAP server to Ansible automation controller, simplifying user management and enhancing security within their automation platform.

Windows Active Directory

Windows Active Directory is a requested integration, especially in the Windows Domains environment. It is possible to integrate the authentication as a specialized LDAP setting. Ansible automation controller offers seamless integration with Windows **Active Directory** (**AD**), enabling organizations to centralize user authentication and access control. By leveraging Windows AD, Ansible automation controller can efficiently manage user access to resources based on existing AD user and group information. This guides us through setting up Windows AD integration in automation controller, as shown in *Figure 5.19*:

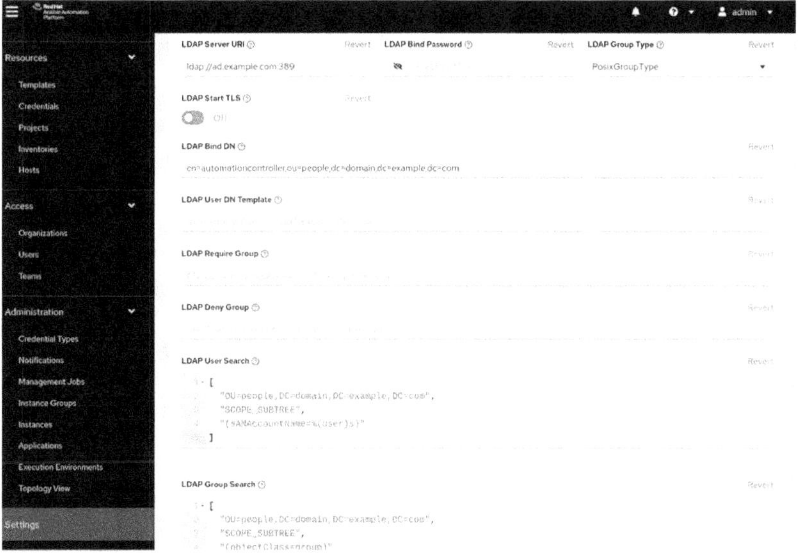

Figure 5.19: Automation controller and Windows Active Directory

Before proceeding with the configuration, gathering the required Windows AD information is essential. Below are the Windows AD settings that need to be configured in Ansible automation controller:

- **LDAP Server**: For Windows AD integration, specify the LDAP server as "LDAP" or choose from LDAP 1-5 if we have multiple LDAP configurations.

- **LDAP Server URI**: Enter the URI of the Windows AD server, including the server's hostname or IP address and the default LDAP port 389.

- **LDAP Bind DN**: Provide the **Distinguished Name (DN)** of the user account used by Ansible to authenticate against the Windows AD. This user account should have read access to the AD directory.

- **LDAP Bind Password**: Enter the LDAP Bind DN user account password.

- **LDAP Group Type**: Use the `PosixGroupType` for Windows AD integration with Linux systems. Alternatives are `ActiveDirectoryGroupType` or `NestedActiveDirectoryGroupType`.

- **LDAP User Search**: Define the search query for locating AD users. It includes the base DN and the search filter to find users based on their `sAMAccountName` (username).

```
[
  "OU=AD Users,DC=wer_ad_domain,DC=example,DC=com",
  "SCOPE_SUBTREE",
  "(sAMAccountName=%(user)s)"
]
```

- **LDAP Group Search**: Specify the search query for locating AD groups. Similar to the user search, it includes the base DN and the group search filter.

```
[
  "OU=AD Users,DC=wer_ad_domain,DC=example,DC=com",
  "SCOPE_SUBTREE",
  "(objectClass=group)"
]
```

- **LDAP User Attribute Map**: Map LDAP attributes to the corresponding user attributes in Ansible automation controller. This mapping allows the system to populate user information correctly.

```
{
  "first_name": "givenName",
  "last_name": "sn",
  "email": "mail"
}
```

- **LDAP Group Type Parameters**: Specify parameters related to the LDAP group type, such as the attribute name used for the group's common name (cn).

```
{
  "name_attr": "cn"
}
```

Automation hub LDAP integration

To enable LDAP authentication for our private automation hub, we need to set six specific variables in the Ansible Automation Platform Installer **inventory** file, as shown in *Figure 5.20*:

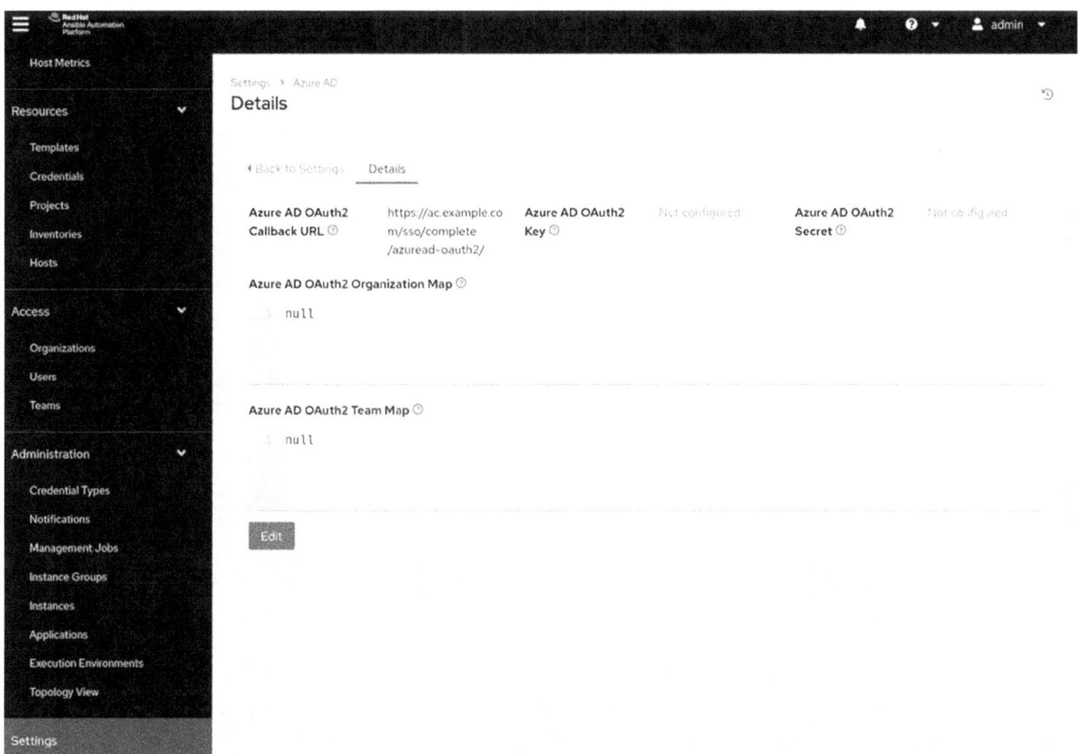

Figure 5.20: Automation hub LDAP settings

These variables provide the necessary information for the Ansible automation installer to connect to our LDAP server and authenticate users. These are the six variables that must be defined:

1. **automationhub_authentication_backend**: Set this variable to **ldap** to enable LDAP authentication for the private automation hub.

2. **automationhub_ldap_server_uri**: This variable should contain the URI of our LDAP server. If we use a non-secure connection (LDAP), set it to **ldap://ldap. example.com:389**. For a secure connection (LDAPS), use **ldaps://ldap.example. com:636**.

3. **automationhub_ldap_bind_dn**: The LDAP user's **distinguished name (DN)** that the automation hub will use to bind to the LDAP server. For example, **cn=admin,dc=example,dc=com**.

4. **automationhub_ldap_bind_password**: The password for the LDAP user specified in the **automationhub_ldap_bind_dn** variable. Make sure to use a strong and secure password.

5. **automationhub_ldap_user_search_base_dn**: The base distinguished name where the automation hub will search for user entries. For example, **ou=people,dc=example,dc=com**.

6. **automationhub_ldap_group_search_base_dn**: The base distinguished name where the Ansible Automation Platform will search for group entries. For example, **ou=people,dc=example,dc=com**.

Note: If any of these variables are missing or improperly configured, the Ansible automation installer cannot complete the installation process successfully.

In addition to the six required variables mentioned above, we can set up extra LDAP parameters to customize the LDAP integration further. These additional parameters allow us to configure features like superuser access, user groups, mirroring, and LDAP attribute mapping. To set up these extra parameters, follow these steps:

1. Create the **ldapextras.yml** YAML file containing the additional LDAP settings in a **ldap_extra_settings** dictionary.

2. We can define the extra LDAP parameters inside the YAML file based on our requirements. Here are some examples:

   - **Mapping LDAP User Attributes**: Use the **AUTH_LDAP_USER_ATTR_MAP** parameter to map LDAP user attributes to specific fields in the automation hub. These are the most common mapping:

     ```
     ldap_extra_settings:
         AUTH_LDAP_USER_ATTR_MAP: '{"first_name": "givenName",
     "last_name": "sn", "email": "mail"}'
     ```

   - **Setting Up Superuser Access**: Use the **AUTH_LDAP_USER_FLAGS_BY_GROUP** parameter to grant superuser access to members of a specific LDAP group:

     ```
     ldap_extra_settings:
         AUTH_LDAP_USER_FLAGS_BY_GROUP: {"is_superuser": "cn=pah-
     admins,ou=groups,dc=example,dc=com"}
     ```

- **Mirroring LDAP Groups**: Use the **AUTH_LDAP_MIRROR_GROUPS** parameter to mirror all LDAP groups a user belongs to:

  ```
  ldap_extra_settings:
    AUTH_LDAP_MIRROR_GROUPS: True
  ```

- **Granting or Denying Access Based on LDAP Group Membership**: Use the **AUTH_LDAP_REQUIRE_GROUP** or **AUTH_LDAP_DENY_GROUP** parameters to grant or deny access based on LDAP group membership:

  ```
  ldap_extra_settings:
    AUTH_LDAP_REQUIRE_GROUP: 'cn=pah-users,ou=groups,dc=example,dc=com'
  ```

- **Enabling LDAP Debug Logging**: Use the **GALAXY_LDAP_LOGGING** parameter to enable LDAP debug logging:

  ```
  ldap_extra_settings:
    GALAXY_LDAP_LOGGING: True
  ```

- **Configuring LDAP Caching**: Use the **AUTH_LDAP_CACHE_TIMEOUT** parameter to set the LDAP cache timeout in seconds:

  ```
  ldap_extra_settings:
    AUTH_LDAP_CACHE_TIMEOUT: 3600
  ```

3. During the private automation hub installation, run the setup command with the **-e @ldapextras.yml** option to apply the extra LDAP parameters:

   ```
   setup.sh -e @ldapextras.yml
   ```

Note: If we need to enable LDAP to debug logging, we can manually add GALAXY_LDAP_LOGGING: True to the /etc/pulp/settings.py file on our private automation hub. After making the changes, restart both pulpcore-api.service and nginx.service for the changes to take effect.

Configuring LDAP authentication for our Red Hat Ansible Automation Platform private hub enhances security and allows centralized user access control. We can seamlessly integrate our private automation hub with our LDAP server by setting the required variables in our inventory file and optionally configuring extra LDAP parameters. This enables our organization to manage user access efficiently and permissions, providing our team with a more secure and streamlined automation experience.

Integrate Azure Active Directory

We can integrate the automation controller with Microsoft Azure **Active Directory** (**AD**), part of the Microsoft Identity Platform. To set up enterprise authentication for Microsoft Azure Active Directory, follow these steps as shown in *Figure 5.21*:

1. Register wer organization-owned application in Azure to obtain an **OAuth2** key and secret. Each key and secret must be unique to the application and cannot be shared between different authentication backends. Register the application at **Register an application with the Microsoft identity platform**. Provide wer webpage URL as the Callback URL shown in the **Settings Authentication** screen.

2. Click **Settings** from the left navigation bar in the automation controller.

3. On the left side of the **Settings** window, select **Azure AD settings** from the list of authentication options.

4. The Azure AD OAuth2 Callback URL field will be pre-populated and non-editable. After registering the application in Azure, we will get the Application ID and Object ID.

5. Click **Edit** and copy the Azure Application ID to the **Azure AD OAuth2 Key** field.

6. Follow Azure AD's documentation to connect wer app to Microsoft Azure Active Directory and provide the key (shown only once) to the client for authentication.

7. Copy and paste the actual secret key created for wer Azure AD application to the **Azure AD OAuth2 Secret** field in the **Settings - Authentication** screen.

8. Complete the mapping fields following the **Organization** and **Team Mapping** guidelines.

9. Click **Save** to save the settings.

10. To verify the authentication configuration, log out of the automation controller, and the login screen will now display the Microsoft Azure logo, allowing we to log in using Azure AD credentials.

```
# If upgrading from Ansible Automation Platform 2.0 or earlier, you must either:
# - provide an existing Automation Hub token as 'automationhub_api_token' or
# - set 'generate_automationhub_token' to True to generate a new token
# Generating a new token will invalidate the existing token.
#
# automationhub_api_token=''
# generate_automationhub_token=

# Automation Hub LDAP configuration
#
# For Automation Hub to connect to LDAP directly the following variables
# need to be configured. The list of all possible configuration can be found here:
# https://django-auth-ldap.readthedocs.io/en/latest/reference.html#settings
# Extra parameters will need to be passed through an ansible ldap_extra_settings dictionary.
#
automationhub_authentication_backend = "ldap"

automationhub_ldap_server_uri = "ldap://ldap:10389"
automationhub_ldap_bind_dn = "cn=admin,dc=ansible,dc=com"
automationhub_ldap_bind_password = "GoodNewsEveryone"
automationhub_ldap_user_search_base_dn = "ou=people,dc=ansible,dc=com"
automationhub_ldap_group_search_base_dn = "ou=people,dc=ansible,dc=com"

# By default, bundle installer seeds certified and validated collections into
-- INSERT --                                                    176,1          71%
```

Figure 5.21: Automation controller and Azure AD

For more information on application registering basics in Azure AD, refer to the Azure AD Identity Platform (v2) overview on the Microsoft Azure Website.

Integrate SAML authentication

Security Assertion Markup Language (**SAML**) is an XML-based, open-standard data format for exchanging account authentication and authorization data between an identity provider and a service provider.

The configuration of SAML settings in Ansible automation controller. SAML facilitates the authentication and authorization data exchange between an **identity provider** (**IdP**) and a service provider (automation controller). Administrators need to specify various SAML-related parameters and mappings to set up SAML authentication. These include the SAML **Assertion Consumer Service** (**ACS**) URL, SAML service provider metadata URL, SAML service provider Entity ID, server certificate, and private key. Furthermore, SAML attributes can be mapped to user flags, and SAML organization and team attribute mappings can be defined. Transparent SAML logins are also possible, enabling direct access to the login page with SSO authentication buttons. It is only possible to write a comprehensive guide for all of the possible providers because many settings are involved that provide administrators with the necessary steps to configure SAML settings in Ansible automation controller and integrate it with their SAML identity providers. The setting interface is shown in *Figure 5.22*:

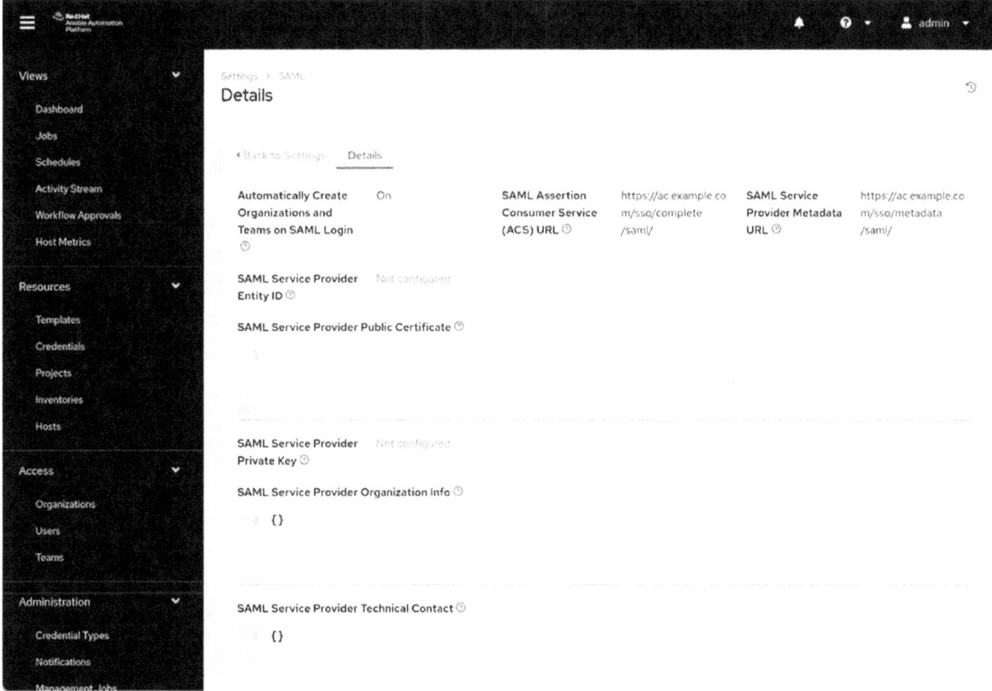

Figure 5.22: Automation controller and SAML

Ansible Automation Platform Central Authentication

The Ansible Automation Platform Central Authentication is a versatile third-party identity provider solution that offers a streamlined single sign-on experience across the entire Ansible Automation Platform. This powerful feature empowers platform administrators to leverage central authentication for essential tasks, such as testing connectivity and authentication, onboarding new users, and efficiently managing user permissions through group assignments. Apart from supporting OpenID connect-based and LDAP authentication, the central authentication system also provides a well-supported REST API, enabling seamless integration and easy customer usage initialization. With central authentication, organizations can enhance security, simplify user management, and optimize the overall user experience within the Ansible Automation Platform.

We can configure the Ansible Automation Platform Central Authentication by populating the following parameters in the Ansible Automation Platform installer of the inventory file:

- **sso_keystore_password** field define the keystore password of the Automation Platform Central Authentication,

- specify a hostname under the [**SSO**] section of the inventory file to install an instance of the central authentication,

- **sso_console_admin_password** specify the password for the user interface of the central authentication instance.

Connecting private automation hub with automation controller

The integration between Red Hat Ansible Automation Platform's private automation hub and automation controller brings a seamless and efficient automation experience to our organization. This connection allows us to access **Collections** and **Execution Environments** from the **Private Automation Hub**, enabling effective management and deployment of automation resources. In this guide, we will walk through the process of connecting our private automation hub to our automation controller. We need the following components:

1. **Private automation hub**: Make sure we have a private automation hub instance up and running.

2. **Automation controller**: Ensure we have Red Hat Ansible Automation Platform installed with a working automation controller.

3. **Automation hub API token**: Obtain an API token from our private automation hub. This token will be used for authentication.

Follow these steps to connect our private automation hub to our automation controller:

1. Collect API Token from private automation hub as shown in *Figure 5.23*:

   - Log in to our private automation hub.

     o Navigate to API token management by going to **Collections | API token management**.

     o Load our API token and click **Copy to clipboard** to save it.

     o Paste the API token into a secure file and store it in a safe location.

Please refer to the following figure:

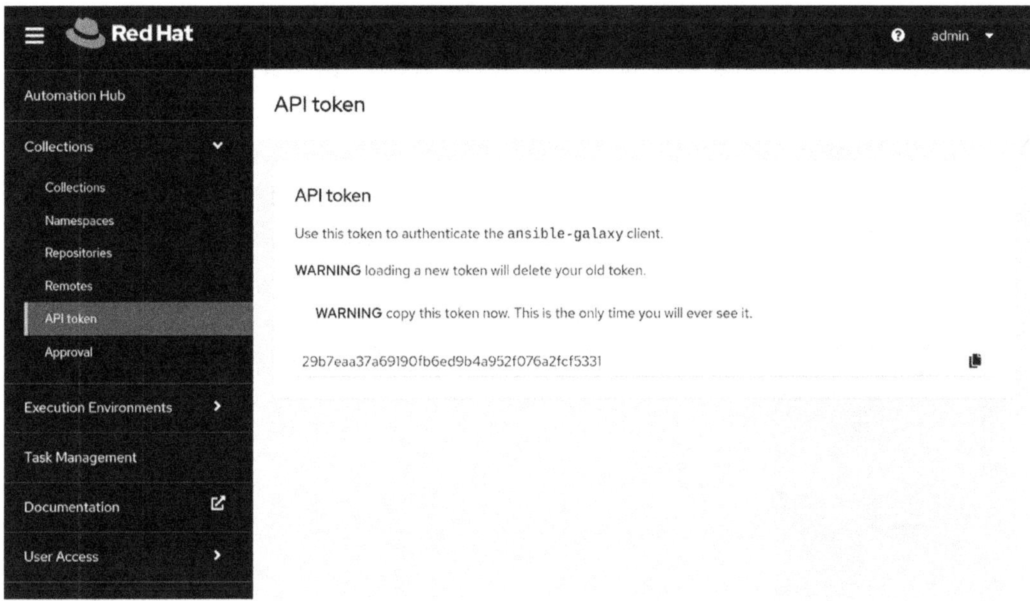

Figure 5.23: *Automation hub API token*

2. Create credentials in automation controller

   To authenticate our automation controller with our private automation hub, we need to create specific credentials, as shown in *Figure 5.24*:

   - **Private automation hub — Publish credential**:

     o **Credential Type**: Ansible Galaxy / automation hub API token.

     o **Galaxy Server URL**: **https://ah.example.com/api/galaxy/content/ published/**.

     o **API Token**: Paste the API token obtained from the private automation hub.

- **Private automation hub — RH-certified credential**:

    o **Credential Type**: Ansible Galaxy / automation hub API token

    o **Galaxy Server URL**: **https://ah.example.com/api/galaxy/content/rh-certified/**.

    o **API Token**: Paste the API token obtained from the private automation hub.

- **Private automation hub — Container registry credential**:

    o **Credential Type**: Container registry

    o **Galaxy Server URL**: **https://ah.example.com/**.

    o **Username**: Our private automation hub login username.

    o **Password or Token**: Our private automation hub login password or token.

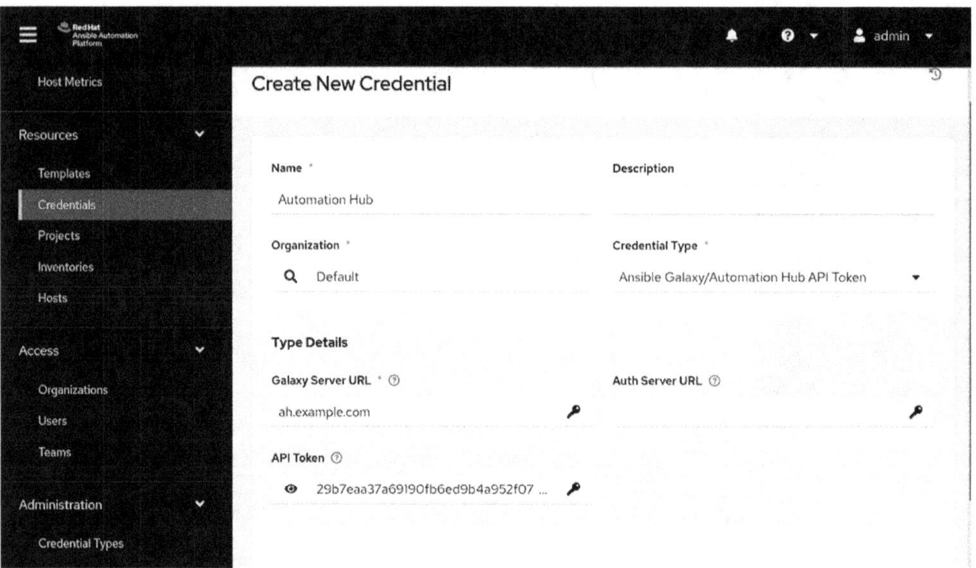

Figure 5.24: Automation controller New Credential

3. (Optional) Disable SSL verification for private automation hub in **Automation Controller** | **Settings** | **Jobs**, as shown in *Figure 5.25*:

Figure 5.25: Automation controller disable Galaxy SSL Verification

4. **Attach credentials to respective organization**

   Attach the created credentials to their respective organization within the automation controller, as shown in *Figure 5.26*:

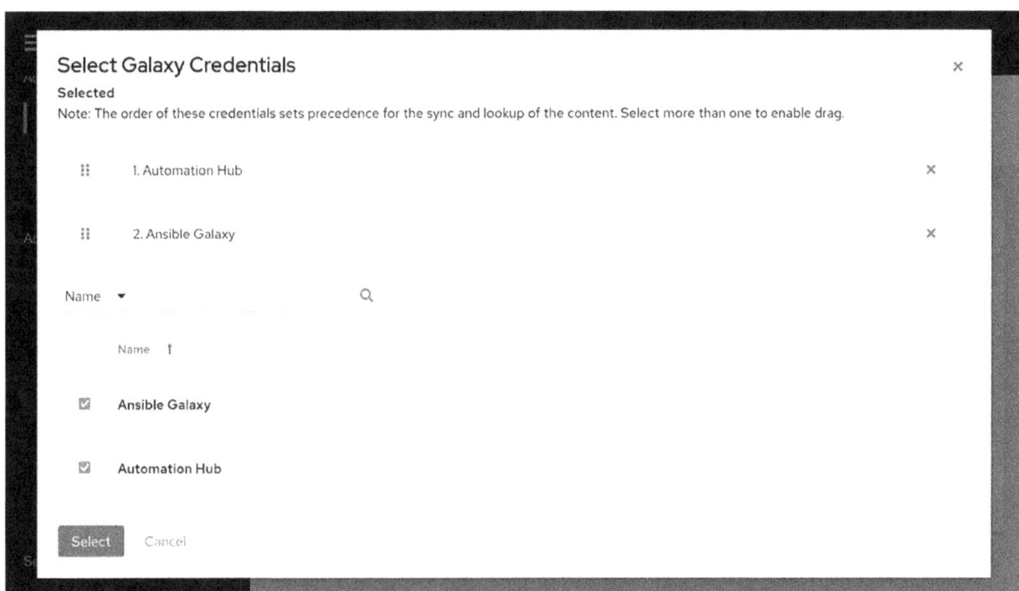

Figure 5.26: *Automation controller associate Galaxy Credentials to Organization*

The final result is the organization with the new associated credentials, as shown in *Figure 5.27*:

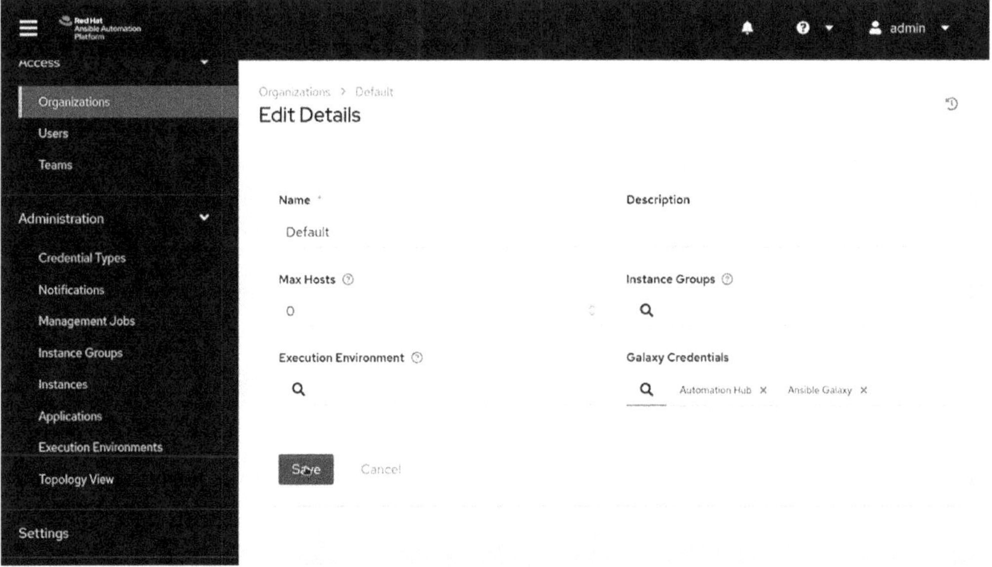

Figure 5.27: *Automation Controller Organization with Galaxy Credentials*

5. Authenticate and access resources

   Our automation controller is now successfully connected to our private automation hub. It can authenticate using the provided credentials and access **Collections** and **Execution Environments** from the **Private Automation Hub**.

Integrating our private automation hub with our automation controller enhances our organization's automation capabilities by enabling seamless access to resources and efficient management of automation assets. Following the steps outlined in this guide, we can establish a secure and effective connection between the private automation hub and the automation controller, empowering our teams to achieve more with automation.

Key learning

We learned about the main settings and configuration of the automation controller and automation hub. We integrated our systems with the most common authentication integration to better manage the users in our organization.

Points to remember

- We can customize the job execution settings in automation controller.

- We can customize the log-level settings in automation controller.

- We can define users, groups, and teams to assign permissions in our organization.

- We can integrate our Ansible Automation Platform with authentication services to manage the user's credentials.

- The Ansible Automation Platform offers many integrations with authentication services out-of-the-box but requires customization and tests.

Multiple choice questions

1. **How can we activate the New User Interface in automation controller?**

   a. **Settings | Jobs**

   b. **Settings | Authentication**

   c. Via terminal **awx-manage**

   d. **Settings | Miscellaneous System**

2. **How can we assign RBAC in automation controller?**

   a. Users

   b. Teams

   c. RBAC

   d. Groups

3. **How can we integrate automation controller with Microsoft Active Directory?**

   a. LDAP settings

   b. Azure AD settings

   c. SAML settings

   d. All the previous options

4. **How can we debug automation controller authentication integrations?**

   a. Increasing log level to DEBUG

   b. By logging in to the Dashboard

   c. Using `awx-manage` command

   d. Using Ansible Automation Platform Central Authentication

Answer

1. d

2. b

3. a

4. a

Questions

1. How can we customize job execution settings in automation controller?

2. How can we customize the logging level in automation controller?

3. What is the RBAC model, and why is it important?

4. How can we integrate the Enterprise authentication in automation controller?

5. How can we integrate social authentication in automation controller?

Key terms

- Role-based access control is a security model that grants permissions and access rights to users based on their assigned roles within an organization or system.

- Lightweight directory access protocol is a network protocol used for accessing and managing directory information, commonly used for centralized authentication and user management in network environments.

- Active Directory is a Microsoft directory service that provides authentication, authorization, and centralized management of network resources, including user accounts, computers, and group policies.

- Ansible Automation Platform Central Authentication enables users to authenticate across different services using a single centralized authentication mechanism.

Join our book's Discord space

Join the book's Discord Workspace for Latest updates, Offers, Tech happenings around the world, New Release and Sessions with the Authors:

https://discord.bpbonline.com

## CHAPTER 6

IT Operations

Introduction

In this chapter, we are going to explore the **IT operations** (**IT Ops**) part of the Ansible Automation Platform: How we can start, stop, restart, manage logs, interact with metrics API endpoint to integrate with Grafana and Splunk and how to backup and restore data.

Structure

In this chapter, we will discuss the following topics:

- Starting, stopping, and restarting
- Log files
- Overview of metrics endpoint
- Connect Ansible metrics endpoint to Grafana
- Overview of logging tools
- Connect Ansible controller logging to Splunk
- Backup and restore
- Security

Objectives

By the end of this chapter, we are going to manage the principal system administration and IT operations from start to stop the service, monitor the status using Grafana and Prometheus, as well as execute backup and restore.

Start, stop and restart

Starting, stopping, and restarting services are essential tasks from the perspective of IT operations, as they play a crucial role in maintaining the overall health, stability, and efficiency of the IT infrastructure and services. Especially when we are applying a security update to the underlying operating system, we need to restart the Ansible Automation Platform to perform the necessary updates.

Automation controller

To ensure smooth operation, it is essential to know how to start, stop, and restart the controller services. The software includes a convenient admin utility script, **automation-controller-service**, that we can use for managing the controller services. The **automation-controller-service** script, located at **/usr/bin/automation-controller-service**, offers a convenient way to handle the controller services on a single controller node. With this script, administrators can start, stop, or restart all the relevant services, including message queue components and the integrated database in non-clustered installations.

Services:

1. **automation-controller.service**: Automation controller general service

2. **postgresql.service**: PostgreSQL database server

3. **redis.service**: Redis persistent key-value database

4. **nginx.service**: The nginx HTTP and reverse proxy server

5. **supervisord.service**: Process monitoring and control daemon

6. **receptor.service**: Ansible receptor service for automation mesh

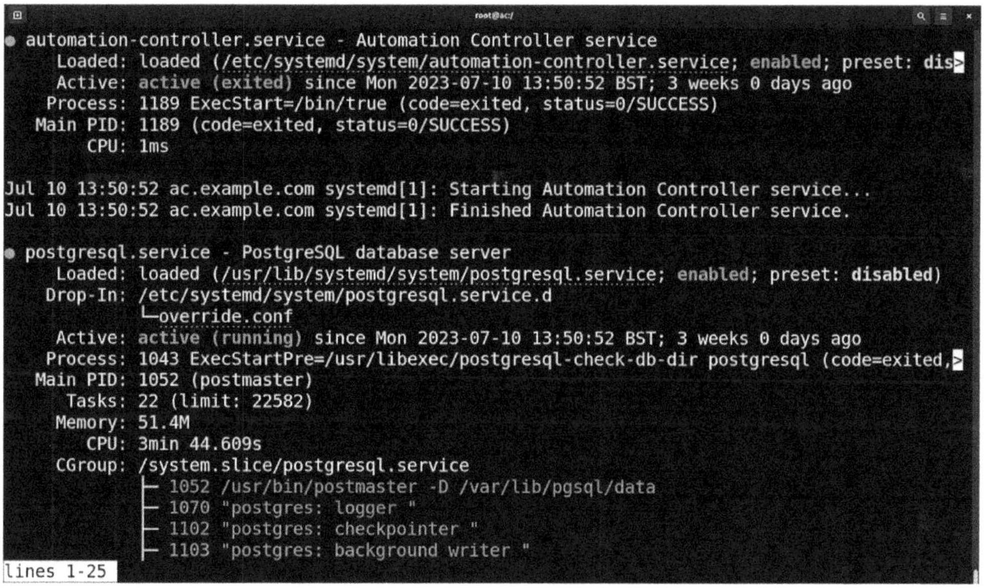

Figure 6.1: Automation-controller-service script

- Restarting the controller:

  To restart all controller services on a single node, simply execute the following command:

  ```
  automation-controller-service restart
  ```

Note: In clustered installations, PostgreSQL is not included in the services restarted by automation-controller-service. For clustered environments, use 'systemctl restart automation-controller' instead and ensure to restart of each cluster node for specific changes to persist.

- Distribution-specific service management:

  In addition to using the automation-controller-service script, some distribution packages might offer a similar service management script, often as an init script. Users can leverage their distribution's specific service management system for controlling services.

- Running the controller in a container:

  For users running the controller in a containerized environment, it is essential to avoid using the **automation-controller-service** script. Instead, restart the pod using container-specific environment settings.

  Effectively managing the starting, stopping, and restarting of the automation controller's services is crucial for maintaining a stable and efficient automation environment. By using the **automation-controller-service** script or distribution-specific service management tools, administrators can ensure the smooth operation of the controller, enabling seamless automation workflows and tasks.

Automation hub

As with any complex software, it relies on a set of services to function correctly. Understanding how to manage these services is essential for maintaining the stability and reliability of the private automation hub. In this article, we will explore the process of starting, stopping, and restarting services in a private automation hub on Red Hat Enterprise Linux. The following list of services used by private automation hub:

- **pulpcore-api**: The API service responsible for handling content requests and management.

- **pulpcore-content**: Manages content synchronization and distribution.

- **pulpcore-resource-manager**: Handles resource management and task scheduling.

- **pulpcore-worker@1 and pulpcore-worker@2**: Worker services that execute background tasks and handle content processing.

- **rh-redis-5-redis / redis**: Redis service used as a caching layer and for handling background tasks.

- **rh-postgresql-10 / postgresql**: PostgreSQL database service (standalone installation only).

- **nginx**: Web server responsible for serving web pages and handling HTTP requests.

```
● nginx.service - The nginx HTTP and reverse proxy server
     Loaded: loaded (/usr/lib/systemd/system/nginx.service; enabled; preset: disabled)
     Active: active (running) since Sun 2023-07-09 10:26:22 BST; 3 weeks 1 day ago
   Main PID: 39706 (nginx)
      Tasks: 5 (limit: 22581)
     Memory: 4.9M
        CPU: 5.250s
     CGroup: /system.slice/nginx.service
             ├─39706 "nginx: master process /usr/sbin/nginx"
             ├─46408 "nginx: worker process"
             ├─46409 "nginx: worker process"
             ├─46410 "nginx: worker process"
             └─46411 "nginx: worker process"

Jul 09 10:26:22 ah.example.com systemd[1]: Starting The nginx HTTP and reverse proxy server.
Jul 09 10:26:22 ah.example.com nginx[39704]: nginx: the configuration file /etc/nginx/nginx.
Jul 09 10:26:22 ah.example.com nginx[39704]: nginx: configuration file /etc/nginx/nginx.conf
Jul 09 10:26:22 ah.example.com systemd[1]: Started The nginx HTTP and reverse proxy server.
Jul 09 10:29:54 ah.example.com systemd[1]: Reloading The nginx HTTP and reverse proxy server
Jul 09 10:29:54 ah.example.com systemd[1]: Reloaded The nginx HTTP and reverse proxy server.

● redis.service - Redis persistent key-value database
     Loaded: loaded (/usr/lib/systemd/system/redis.service; enabled; preset: disabled)
    Drop-In: /etc/systemd/system/redis.service.d
             └─limit.conf
[root@ah ~]# systemctl status pulp* nginx.service redis.service
```

Figure 6.2: Automation hub Services status

The following managing services in automation hub:

- Stopping services:

  Stopping services is a crucial aspect of managing automation hub, especially during maintenance, updates, or issue resolution. To stop the services on Red Hat Enterprise Linux, execute the following commands in the terminal, usually by the root user:

  ```
  systemctl stop pulp* nginx.service redis.service
  systemctl stop pulpcore-worker@1.service; systemctl stop pulpcore-worker@2.service
  ```

Explanation:

- The first command stops all services with names starting with "**pulp**" (for example, `pulpcore-api`, `pulpcore-content`).

  The second command stops the individual pulpcore worker services (for example, `pulpcore-worker@1`, `pulpcore-worker@2`).

After any necessary maintenance or updates, it is essential to start the services to resume normal operations. To start the services on Red Hat Enterprise Linux, execute the following commands in the terminal, usually by the **root** user:

```
systemctl start pulp* nginx.service redis.service
systemctl start pulpcore-worker@1.service; systemctl start pulpcore-worker@2.service
```

Explanation:

- The first command starts all services with names starting with "**pulp**" (for example, `pulpcore-api`, `pulpcore-content`) plus nginx and redis services.

  The second command starts the individual **pulpcore** worker services (for example, `pulpcore-worker@1`, `pulpcore-worker@2`).

Effectively managing services in automation hub is essential for ensuring the smooth functioning of the platform. Whether we need to stop services for maintenance or start them after updates, following the commands provided will help us maintain the stability and reliability of our private automation hub installation on Red Hat Enterprise Linux. Proper management of services ensures that our organization can leverage the full potential of automation hub, enabling seamless automation content sharing and distribution within our IT environment.

Log files

In any IT environment, having access to comprehensive and well-organized log files is vital for monitoring and troubleshooting system performance and issues. For Ansible

Automation Platform administrators, log files play a crucial role in understanding the behavior of the platform and diagnosing potential problems. In this article, we will explore the centralized locations of Ansible Automation Platform log files and the valuable information they provide for managing and maintaining the automation platform.

Automation controller

Ansible controller has taken significant strides to consolidate its log files, making it more convenient for administrators to access and analyze log data, as shown in *Figure 6.3*:

```
[root@ac /]# ls /var/log/
anaconda                hawkey.log              README              tuned
audit                   hawkey.log-20230710     receptor            vmware-network.1.log
boot.log                hawkey.log-20230720     redis               vmware-network.2.log
boot.log-20230708       hawkey.log-20230730     rhsm                vmware-network.3.log
boot.log-20230710       insights-client         samba               vmware-network.4.log
boot.log-20230720       kdump.log               secure              vmware-network.5.log
btmp                    lastlog                 secure-20230710     vmware-network.6.log
chrony                  maillog                 secure-20230720     vmware-network.7.log
cron                    maillog-20230710        secure-20230730     vmware-network.8.log
cron-20230710           maillog-20230720        speech-dispatcher   vmware-network.9.log
cron-20230720           maillog-20230730        spooler             vmware-network.log
cron-20230730           messages                spooler-20230710    vmware-vgauthsvc.log.0
cups                    messages-20230710       spooler-20230720    vmware-vmsvc-root.log
dnf.librepo.log         messages-20230720       spooler-20230730    vmware-vmtoolsd-root.log
dnf.log                 messages-20230730       sssd                wtmp
dnf.rpm.log             nginx                   supervisor
firewalld               private                 tallylog
gdm                     qemu-ga                 tower
[root@ac /]#
```

Figure 6.3: Automation controller Log Files

The log files can be found in two centralized locations:

- **/var/log/tower/:**

  In this directory, we can find various log files related to different aspects of the automation controller. Let us take a look at some of the essential log files and their functions:

  o **callback_receiver.log**: Captures callback receiver logs, responsible for handling callback events during the execution of Ansible jobs.

  o **dispatcher.log**: Contains log messages for the controller dispatcher worker service, which plays a vital role in job dispatching.

  o **job_lifecycle.log**: Provides details of job runs, including any blocking conditions that might be affecting them.

  o **management_playbooks.log**: Captures logs related to management playbook runs, isolated job runs, and metadata copying.

  o **rsyslog.err**: Records **rsyslog** errors that may occur during authentication with external logging services.

- o **task_system.log**: Contains logs of background tasks executed by the controller, such as adding cluster instances and gathering information for analytics.

- o **tower.log**: Captures runtime errors and other log messages that occur during job execution.

- o **tower_rbac_migrations.log**: Logs related to **Role-Based Access Control (RBAC)** database migration or upgrade.

- o **tower_system_tracking_migrations.log**: Logs for the controller's system tracking migration or upgrade.

- o **wsbroadcast.log**: Contains logs of websocket connections on the controller nodes.

- **/var/log/supervisor/**:

  This directory holds log files managed by the supervisord process. The following log files are essential for understanding the behavior of various Tower services:

  - o **awx-callback-receiver.log**: Logs related to the callback receiver that handles events during Ansible job runs.

  - o **awx-daphne.log**: Captures logs of Websocket communication for the automation controller Web user interface.

  - o **awx-dispatcher.log**: Records logs when tasks are dispatched to controller instances.

  - o **awx-rsyslog.log**: Logs related to the **rsyslog** service.

  - o **awx-uwsgi.log**: Contains logs related to uWSGI, an application server used by Tower.

  - o **awx-wsbroadcast.log**: Logs of the websocket service used by the controller.

  - o **failure-event-handler.stderr.log**: Captures standard errors for **/usr/bin/failure-event-handler**, a subprocess of supervisord.

  - o **supervisord.log**: Contains logs related to the supervisord process itself.

Apart from the two centralized locations, Tower generates log paths for services used by the Ansible Automation Platform:

- o **/var/log/nginx/**: Contains logs for the Nginx web server used by Tower.

- o **/var/lib/pgsql/data/pg_log/**: Holds logs related to the PostgreSQL database service, provided Tower is using an integrated installation.

- o **/var/log/redis/**: Contains logs for the Redis caching layer used by Tower.

The Job executions are stored in the database and not in the local filesystem. All job logs can be retrieved from the automation controller API. For each Job, we need to access the identified endpoint. The identifier is the Job execution number. The specific endpoint can be accessed by the "**/api/v2/jobs/<id#>/**" endpoint with "**<id#>**" as a Job identifier. The output of the execution is stored in the "**stdout**" subnode of the endpoint, the "**/api/v2/jobs/<id#>/stdout/**" is the full endpoint.

Automation hub

The automation hub has a similar directory structure as shown in *Figure 6.4*:

```
[root@ah ~]# ls /var/log
anaconda                galaxy_api_access.log   private              tuned
audit                   gdm                     qemu-ga              vmware-network.1.log
boot.log                hawkey.log              README               vmware-network.2.log
boot.log-20230709       hawkey.log-20230709     redis                vmware-network.3.log
boot.log-20230710       hawkey.log-20230731     rhsm                 vmware-network.4.log
btmp                    insights-client         samba                vmware-network.5.log
chrony                  kdump.log               secure               vmware-network.6.log
cron                    lastlog                 secure-20230709      vmware-network.7.log
cron-20230709           maillog                 secure-20230731      vmware-network.8.log
cron-20230731           maillog-20230709        speech-dispatcher    vmware-network.9.log
cups                    maillog-20230731        spooler              vmware-network.log
dnf.librepo.log         messages                spooler-20230709     vmware-vgauthsvc.log.0
dnf.log                 messages-20230709       spooler-20230731     vmware-vmsvc-root.log
dnf.rpm.log             messages-20230731       sssd                 vmware-vmtoolsd-root.log
firewalld               nginx                   tallylog             wtmp
[root@ah ~]#
```

Figure 6.4: Automation hub Log Files

The private automation hub has a known problem of log flooding that we can resolve by redirecting the relevant messages to the **/var/log/pulp/** directory. However, in this environment, an issue arises with the logging configuration of the underlying component called **pulpcore**.

By default, **pulpcore** sends logs to the **/var/log/messages** file. This standard log location is shared by various system components and services, including essential OS services and performance monitoring tools like "**PCP pmie**". The logs generated by pulpcore are flooding the **/var/log/messages** file, which causes it to be cluttered and makes it difficult to identify actual OS issues or performance alerts. This log flooding may hide critical OS-related problems or performance indicators, leading to difficulties in troubleshooting and monitoring the overall system's health.

To address this log flooding issue and prevent **pulpcore** logs from cluttering the **/var/log/messages** file, the following steps are taken:

- Configuration of rsyslog:

    A custom rsyslog configuration file named "**pulp.conf**" is created in the **/etc/rsyslog.d/** directory. This file specifies rules for handling different program logs related to **pulpcore**.

Add the content of the "**pulp.conf**" file is as follows:

```
if $programname == 'pulpcore-api' then {
  *.* /var/log/pulp/pulpcore-api.log
  *.* stop

} else if $programname startswith 'pulpcore-worker' then {
  *.* /var/log/pulp/pulpcore-worker.log
  *.* stop

} else if $programname == 'gunicorn' then {
  *.* /var/log/pulp/pulp.log
  *.* stop

} else if $programname == 'pulpcore-content' then {
  *.* /var/log/pulp/pulpcore-content.log
  *.* stop

}
```

The rsyslog rules in this configuration file route logs from specific **pulpcore** components to separate log files under the **/var/log/pulp/** directory.

- Creation of the logs directory:

  To accommodate the custom log files, create a directory named "**pulp**" created under **/var/log/** using the following command performed by root user:

  mkdir /var/log/pulp/

  This directory will store the individual log files for different **pulpcore** components defined in the **rsyslog** configuration file.

- Restarting rsyslog service:

  To apply the new rsyslog configuration, the rsyslog service is restarted using the following command:

  systemctl restart rsyslog

  By implementing these steps, the issue of log flooding is addressed, and the system administrators can now efficiently monitor the health of the OS, identify OS-specific problems, and effectively manage the Ansible Private automation hub without interference from excessive logs flooding the **/var/log/messages** file.

Consolidating log files

The process of consolidating log files in centralized locations is a significant step forward in simplifying log management for Ansible Automation Platform administrators. Having access to these comprehensive log files empowers administrators to monitor, analyze, and troubleshoot issues more effectively. By regularly reviewing the log data, IT operations teams can ensure the stability, reliability, and optimal performance of their Automation Platform, ultimately enhancing the efficiency of their IT processes. In the world of IT operations, the ability to monitor and analyze system logs is critical for maintaining a stable and reliable infrastructure. Automation controller offers robust logging and aggregation features that allow IT administrators to gain valuable insights into the platform's usage, track technical trends, and monitor for anomalies. This article delves into the world of logging and aggregation in the Ansible Automation Platform, exploring the types of data collected, the loggers involved, and the integration with external log aggregation services. Ansible Automation Platform's logging feature empowers administrators to send detailed logs to various external log aggregation services, providing a centralized view of system activity. This aggregated data serves as a powerful resource for analyzing infrastructure events, correlating data across services, and monitoring the overall health of the platform.

The log data is sent in JSON format over an HTTP connection with minimal service-specific tweaks. This approach ensures compatibility with a wide range of log aggregation systems, making it versatile for different environments.

When we install the Ansible Automation Platform introduces a newer version of **rsyslog**, which replaces the version that comes with the Red Hat Enterprise Linux base. The new **rsyslog** package does not include specific modules, such as **rsyslog-udpspoof** and **rsyslog-libdbi**. It is recommended to use the version included in the Ansible Automation Platform of the **rsyslog** package for any logging outside of the automation controller that may have been done with the Red Hat Enterprise Linux provided **rsyslog** package previously.

To configure logging aggregation in the Ansible Automation Platform, administrators can access the settings in the dashboard or via the "**/api/v2/settings/logging/**" API endpoint. The API endpoint allows users to specify various parameters for log handling, including:

- **LOG_AGGREGATOR_MAX_DISK_USAGE_GB**: Sets the amount of data (in gigabytes) to store during an external log aggregator outage. This setting helps ensure logs are retained and not lost during downtime.

- **LOG_AGGREGATOR_MAX_DISK_USAGE_PATH**: Specifies the location to persist logs that should be retried after an external log aggregator outage. This ensures the logs are saved for future processing.

Ansible Automation Platform employs specialized loggers that provide structured or semi-structured data, enhancing the insights gained from the log aggregation process. Let us explore these loggers:

- **job_events**: Captures data returned from the Ansible callback module, offering valuable information about Ansible job runs.

- **`activity_stream`**: Records changes to objects within the automation controller application, providing an audit trail of user actions.

- **`system_tracking`**: Provides fact data gathered by the Ansible setup module during job template runs with Enable Fact Cache selected.

- **`awx`**: Contains generic server logs, including logs normally written to a file. It covers standard metadata but only has the message from the log statement.

The loggers primarily use the log level of **INFO**, except for the **awx logger**, which may use any given level. We can configure the log level as described in *Chapter 5, Settings & Authentication*, section *Automation Controller Settings*, subsection *Logging Level*.

Logging aggregator services

Ansible Automation Platform integrates seamlessly with several log aggregation services, including Splunk, Loggly, Sumologic, and Elastic Stack (formerly ELK Stack). System Administrators and IT Operators can configure the platform to send logs to the desired aggregator service, enabling easy analysis and monitoring of the log data.

Logging tools play a crucial role in modern IT operations by capturing and analyzing various types of data generated by software applications, systems, and networks. These tools help organizations monitor, troubleshoot, and optimize their environments, ensuring smooth functionality and security. Here is an overview of some popular logging tools and their key features:

- **Splunk**: Splunk is a leading log management and analysis platform that collects, indexes, and correlates data from various sources. It offers real-time monitoring, searching, and visualization capabilities, making it valuable for detecting and investigating security incidents, operational issues, and performance bottlenecks.

- **ELK Stack (Elasticsearch, Logstash, Kibana)**: ELK is an open-source log management solution. Elasticsearch stores and indexes data, Logstash collects and processes logs, and Kibana provides visualization and dashboarding. Together, they offer powerful log analysis and real-time insights.

- **Datadog**: Datadog is a cloud-based monitoring and analytics platform with log management. It provides real-time log processing, visualization, and correlation with other monitoring data, enabling comprehensive infrastructure and application monitoring.

- **Sumo Logic**: Sumo Logic is a cloud-native log management and analytics platform that offers real-time insights into application and infrastructure performance. It provides machine learning-powered analytics, monitoring, and security features.

- **Loggly**: Loggly is a cloud-based log management and analysis platform focusing on simplicity and ease of use. It offers real-time monitoring, dynamic dashboards, and powerful search capabilities.

- **SolarWinds Log Analyzer**: SolarWinds offers a log management solution for logging collection, analysis, and visualization. It helps identify patterns, troubleshoot issues, and maintain compliance.

- **New Relic Logs**: New Relic offers a log management and analysis solution as part of its observability platform. It provides real-time log monitoring, visualization, and integration with other monitoring data.

These logging tools empower organizations to gather insights, detect anomalies, troubleshoot issues, and enhance security across their IT infrastructure. The choice of a logging tool depends on factors like scale, complexity, budget, and specific use cases.

Splunk

The Splunk software is the leading data analysis and visualization platform awarded by Gartner as a powerful, simple, and intuitive **Security Information and Event Management (SIEM)** tool:

Figure 6.5: Splunk Logo

Splunk enables businesses to collect, index, and analyze data from diverse sources in real time, transforming raw information into actionable insights. At its core, Splunk serves as a robust and versatile tool for log management and analysis. It empowers organizations to understand their data in-depth, uncover trends, detect anomalies, and gain valuable operational intelligence. Splunk's capabilities extend beyond traditional log analysis; it can handle structured and unstructured data, providing a holistic view of an organization's digital landscape.

To integrate the Splunk logging aggregator with automation controller, administrators must provide the full URL to the **Splunk HTTP Event Collector (HEC)** host in the **Automation Controller Loggins Setting** area, as shown in *Figure 6.6*:

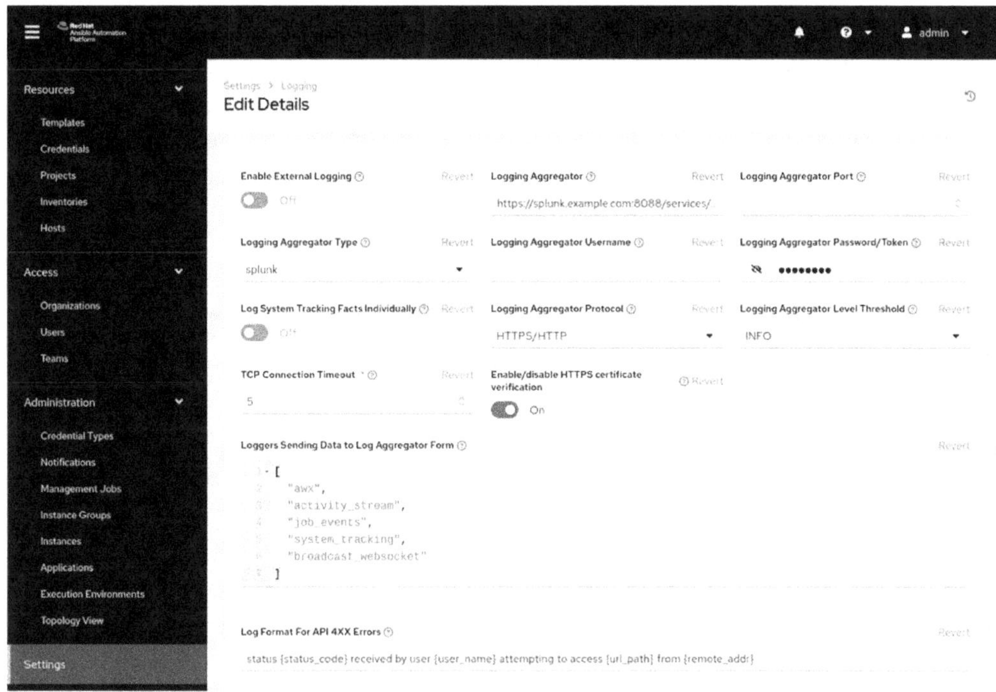

Figure 6.6: Splunk UI integration

We can configure the same settings via the automation controller API interface using the "`/api/v2/settings/logging/`" endpoint, as shown in *Figure 6.7*:

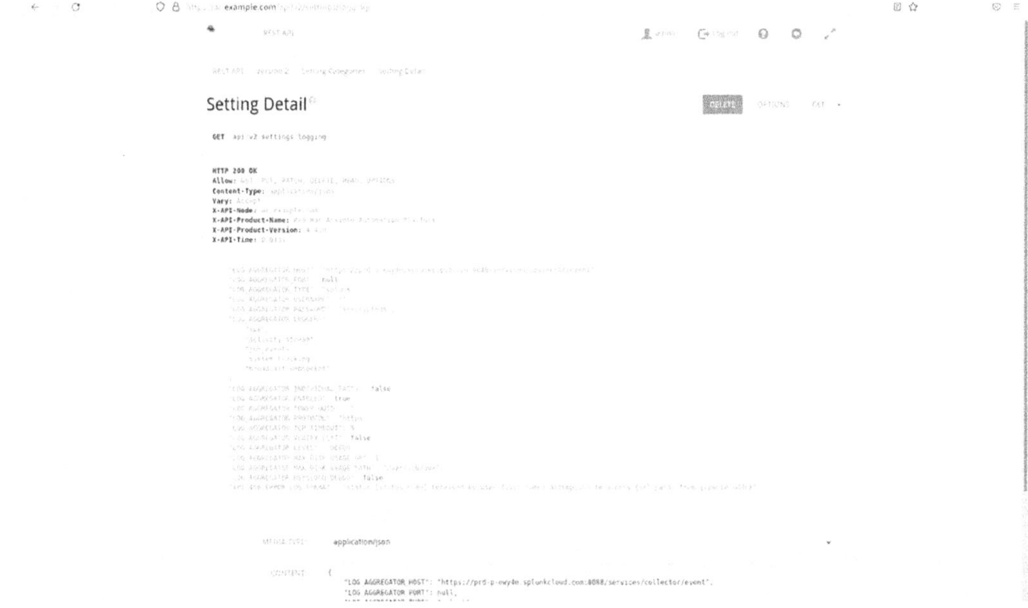

Figure 6.7: Splunk API integration

These are the setting parameters of the automation controller to integrate with Splunk:

- **LOG_AGGREGATOR_HOST**: Provide the full URL to the Splunk HTTP Event Collector host. It should follow the format: "**https://splunk.example.com:8088/services/collector/event**".

- **LOG_AGGREGATOR_TYPE**: Set the aggregator type to "**splunk**".

- **LOG_AGGREGATOR_USERNAME** and **LOG_AGGREGATOR_PASSWORD**: If required, enter the username and password for authentication. Alternatively, we can use an OAuth2 token in the **LOG_AGGREGATOR_PASSWORD.obratined** by the Splunk interface.

- **LOG_AGGREGATOR_LOGGERS**: Define the loggers we want to send data from. Common options include "**awx**", "**activity_stream**", "**job_events**", and "**system_tracking**".

- **LOG_AGGREGATOR_ENABLED**: Set this to true to enable the Splunk Logging Aggregator.

A successful integration shows the events of the automation controller in the Splunk dashboard, as shown in *Figure 6.8*:

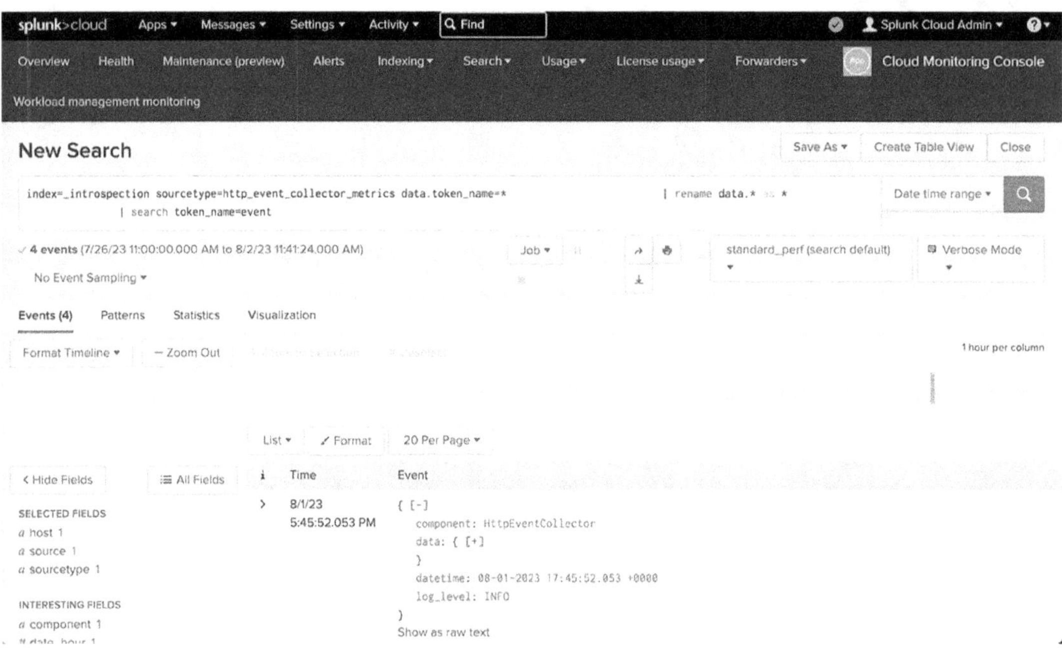

Figure 6.8: Ansible events in the Splunk interface

Similarly, each aggregator service requires specific configuration settings to establish the connection and process log data.

Logging and aggregation are indispensable tools for IT operations, allowing administrators to gain insights into their automation controller's usage, performance, and behavior. By leveraging centralized logging and external log aggregation services, administrators can efficiently monitor their infrastructure, identify potential issues, and ensure the optimal functioning of the automation platform.

With Ansible Automation Platform's robust logging capabilities and seamless integration with various log aggregation services, IT operations teams can proactively manage their environment, maintain high levels of reliability, and make informed decisions to drive business success.

ELK Stack

The ELK Stack is a powerful and widely used open-source solution alternative to Splunk for collecting, processing, storing, and analyzing large volumes of log and event data from different sources: Please refer to the following figure:

Figure 6.9: ELK Stack logo

ELK stands for Elasticsearch, Logstash, and Kibana – the three main components of the stack. Each component plays a specific role in the log management and analysis process:

- **Data collection and transformation**: Logstash is a data collection and processing pipeline tool. It is used to ingest, transform, and enrich data from different sources before sending it to Elasticsearch for indexing. Logstash supports a wide range of data inputs, including logs, metrics, events, and more. It also offers various filter plugins to parse, manipulate, and enhance the incoming data before it is indexed.

- **Data Index**: Elasticsearch is a distributed, RESTful search and analytics engine that serves as the core of the ELK Stack. It is designed to handle and index large volumes of data quickly and efficiently. Elasticsearch provides real-time search capabilities, allowing users to search, explore, and retrieve data from various sources. It also supports full-text search, geospatial queries, and complex aggregations.

- **Data visualization and analysis**: Kibana is a web-based visualization and dashboard platform that allows users to explore, visualize, and interact with data stored in Elasticsearch. It provides a user-friendly interface for creating dynamic and customizable dashboards, charts, and graphs. With Kibana, users can gain insights from their data, monitor trends, and detect anomalies.

Integrating the Elastic Stack with an automation controller can provide profound insights into the system's performance, health, and user behavior. Here, we will delve into the process of configuring Logstash, a pivotal component in the Elastic Stack, to handle JSON log data generated by the automation controller.

The JSON data format is widely used for structured log messages, and Logstash offers seamless integration for processing JSON data. To ensure smooth integration between the automation controller and the Elastic Stack, follow these steps to configure Logstash:

1. **Access the Logstash Configuration File (logstash.conf)**: Locate the Logstash configuration file, often named **`logstash.conf`**, which defines the data processing pipeline.

2. **Add the JSON Filter Plugin**: Within the configuration file, introduce the **`json`** filter plugin as shown below:

```
filter {
  json {
    source => "message"
  }
}
```

This configuration instructs Logstash to extract JSON-formatted data from the **`"message"`** field.

Alternatively, we can set up a new Logstash HTTP endpoint to input data directly in the JSON format:

```
input {
  http {
    host => "0.0.0.0"
    port => "8085"
    codec => "json"
  }
}
```

3. Configure the automation controller to send data to Logstash, as shown in *Figure 6.10*, in the same way we configured Splunk:

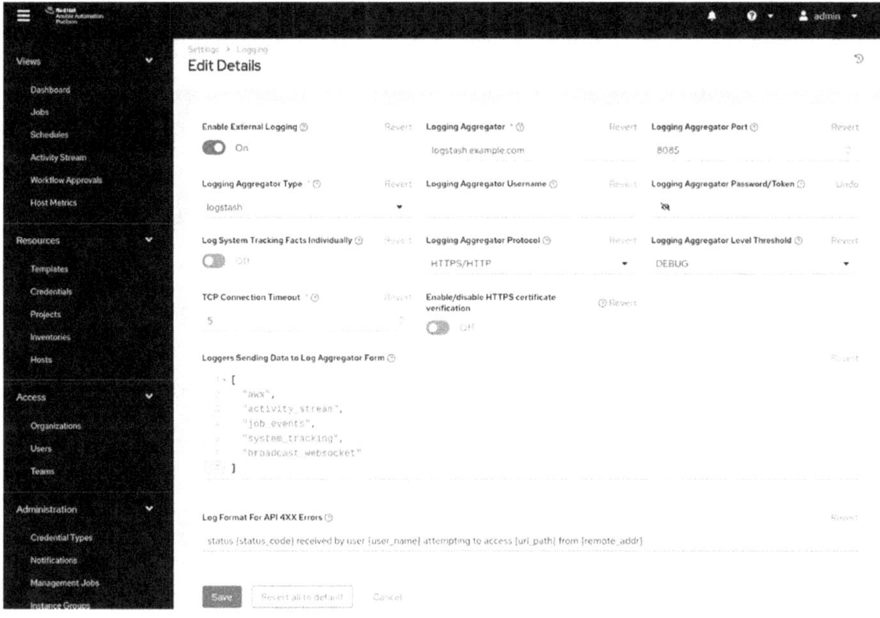

Figure 6.10: *Logstash UI integration*

When the integration is successfully configured, the events are successfully sent to Logstash, and we can visualize using the Kibana dashboard, as shown in *Figure 6.11*:

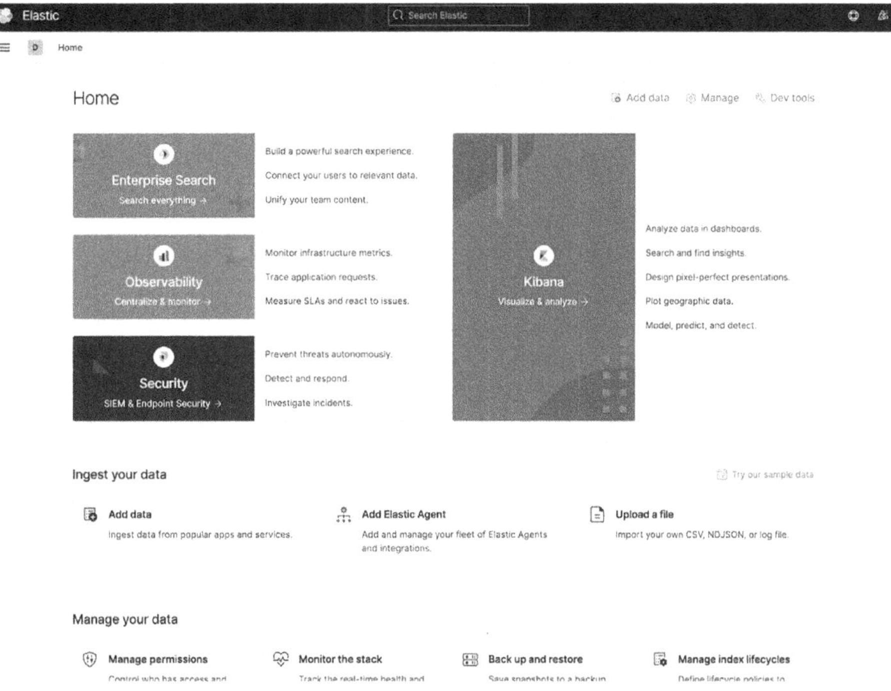

Figure 6.11: *Kibana Dashboard*

Note on compatibility: It is important to know that the Elastic Stack has undergone changes, including backward-incompatible ones introduced with Elastic version 5.0.0 and beyond. The provided configuration example is tailored to ensure compatibility with Logstash and Elastic Stack versions. Depending on the versions we are utilizing, adjustments may be required.

Integrating the Elastic Stack with an automation controller can elevate wer log management and analysis capabilities to new heights. By effectively configuring Logstash to handle JSON log data, we pave the way for enhanced data processing and visualization through Elasticsearch and Kibana. As we embark on this journey of seamless integration, keep in mind that the Elastic Stack offers a versatile solution to not only manage log data but also derive actionable insights from it. In the ever-evolving landscape of IT operations, the Elastic Stack stands as a reliable ally in the quest for log data mastery. The ELK Stack empowers organizations to manage and analyze their log and event data effectively, improving operational efficiency, faster issue resolution, and better decision-making.

Metrics

Monitoring the health and performance of an IT infrastructure is crucial for ensuring its smooth operation and timely identification of potential issues. Automation controller integrates a metrics API endpoint that offers real-time data about the controller's performance. By integrating with Prometheus, an open-source monitoring and alerting toolkit, system administrators can leverage this data to create comprehensive monitoring solutions.

The metrics endpoint, located at **/api/v2/metrics/**, presents instantaneous metrics related to the Ansible automation controller. The data can be consumed by system monitoring software, with available content types being **"text/plain"** and **"application/json"**. These metrics offer valuable insights, including the count of active user sessions and the number of jobs actively running on each controller node.

Prometheus

The Prometheus software is an open-source monitoring and alerting toolkit designed for capturing and analyzing time-series data in real-time. Developed by the **Cloud Native Computing Foundation (CNCF)**, Prometheus is widely used in modern IT environments to monitor the performance and health of applications and systems. It is particularly popular within cloud-native and containerized architectures due to its flexibility and scalability:

Figure 6.12: *Prometheus logo*

Key features and concepts of Prometheus include:

- **Data collection**: Prometheus collects metrics data from various sources, such as applications, services, and infrastructure components. It uses a pull-based model, where data is collected by periodically querying target endpoints called **"exporters."** These exporters expose metric endpoints that Prometheus scrapes to retrieve data.

- **Time-series data**: Prometheus organizes collected data as time series, where each data point is associated with a timestamp. Time-series data provides insights into how metrics change over time, enabling performance analysis, trend identification, and troubleshooting.

- **Data storage**: Metrics data is stored in a local time-series database designed for efficiency and speed. This allows Prometheus to handle a high volume of data while ensuring fast query response times.

- **Query Language**: **Prometheus Query Language (PromQL)** is used to query and aggregate metrics data. PromQL supports various operators and functions for data manipulation, transformation, and filtering. It enables users to create custom queries and expressions to extract specific insights from the collected data.

- **Alerting and alert manager**: Prometheus includes a built-in alerting mechanism that enables the creation of alert rules based on defined thresholds and conditions. When an alert rule is triggered, Prometheus can send alerts to an external alert manager, which then routes notifications to various channels like email, chat platforms, or incident management systems.

- **Visualization and dashboards**: While Prometheus itself provides basic graphing capabilities, it is often used in conjunction with visualization tools like Grafana. Grafana can connect to Prometheus to create rich, interactive dashboards and visualizations for monitoring data.

- **Service discovery**: Prometheus supports service discovery mechanisms that automatically detect and monitor new instances of services as they are added or removed from the environment. This is particularly useful in dynamic and containerized environments.

- **Scalability and federation**: Prometheus can be deployed in a federated architecture, where multiple Prometheus instances collect and store data from different parts of an environment. This allows organizations to scale their monitoring infrastructure while maintaining a unified view of metrics.

- **Integration and ecosystem**: Prometheus has a vibrant ecosystem with a wide range of exporters, libraries, and integrations. It can be integrated with other tools like Kubernetes, Docker, and cloud providers to gather and monitor data from various sources.

- **Community and support**: Being open source, Prometheus benefits from an active and growing community of contributors, users, and developers. This community-driven approach ensures continuous improvement, documentation, and support.

Prometheus provides observability and monitoring capabilities that enable IT teams to proactively identify and address issues, optimize performance, and maintain the health of their applications and systems in dynamic and complex environments.

Prometheus serves as a leading choice for time-series-based monitoring solutions. To set up Prometheus, administrators need to install it on a virtual machine or container. The process involves the following steps:

1. **Install Prometheus**: Begin by installing Prometheus on a suitable host system. Detailed instructions can be found in the Prometheus documentation. We can install Prometheus via the **prometheus.prometheus** Ansible collection.

2. **Configure Prometheus**: The Prometheus configuration file, typically named prometheus.yml, requires specific settings to scrape metrics from the Ansible automation controller. For accessing the metrics endpoint, a valid user/password pair is needed for a controller user account. An alternative is using an OAuth2 token that we can find in the user interface or generated via the API endpoint **/api/v2/users/<id#>/personal_tokens/**. The example configuration below assumes using OAuth2.

```
scrape_configs:
  - job_name: 'controller'
    tls_config:
        insecure_skip_verify: True
    metrics_path: /api/v2/metrics
    scrape_interval: 5s
    scheme: https
```

```
bearer_token: <token_value>
static_configs:
    - targets:
        - <controller_host>
```

3. **Prometheus Service Restart**: After modifying the Prometheus configuration, a service restart is necessary to apply the changes.

With Prometheus up and running, administrators can access its user interface at **https:// prometheus.example.com:9090/graph**. The interface allows executing queries to explore the collected metrics visually. For instance, one can query the current number of active controller user sessions using the query: **awx_sessions_total{type="user"}**.

The metrics endpoint in the controller API offers various ways to query data, enabling administrators to tailor their monitoring solution according to their specific requirements.

Prometheus, when combined with Grafana or Metricsbeat, enables the creation of stunning visualizations and dashboards for efficient data analysis. Administrators can craft comprehensive views of the infrastructure's health, job performance, and user activity. Moreover, they can set up alerts to be notified of critical events promptly.

Integrating Ansible automation controller with Prometheus empowers IT operations with a robust monitoring solution. The metrics endpoint in the controller API provides real-time data that can be scraped by Prometheus and stored in a time-series database. This data can be analyzed, visualized, and used to set up alerts, facilitating proactive system management and swift issue resolution. With these monitoring tools in place, administrators can ensure the stability and efficiency of their Ansible-powered infrastructure.

Grafana

Integration between automation controller, Prometheus, and Grafana creates a robust and comprehensive monitoring and visualization ecosystem for managing and optimizing IT operations:

Figure 6.13: Grafana logo

These three tools together provide valuable insights into the performance, health, and efficiency of our infrastructure and automation processes. Grafana is an open-source analytics and visualization platform that allows us to create customizable and interactive dashboards, as shown in *Figure 6.14*:

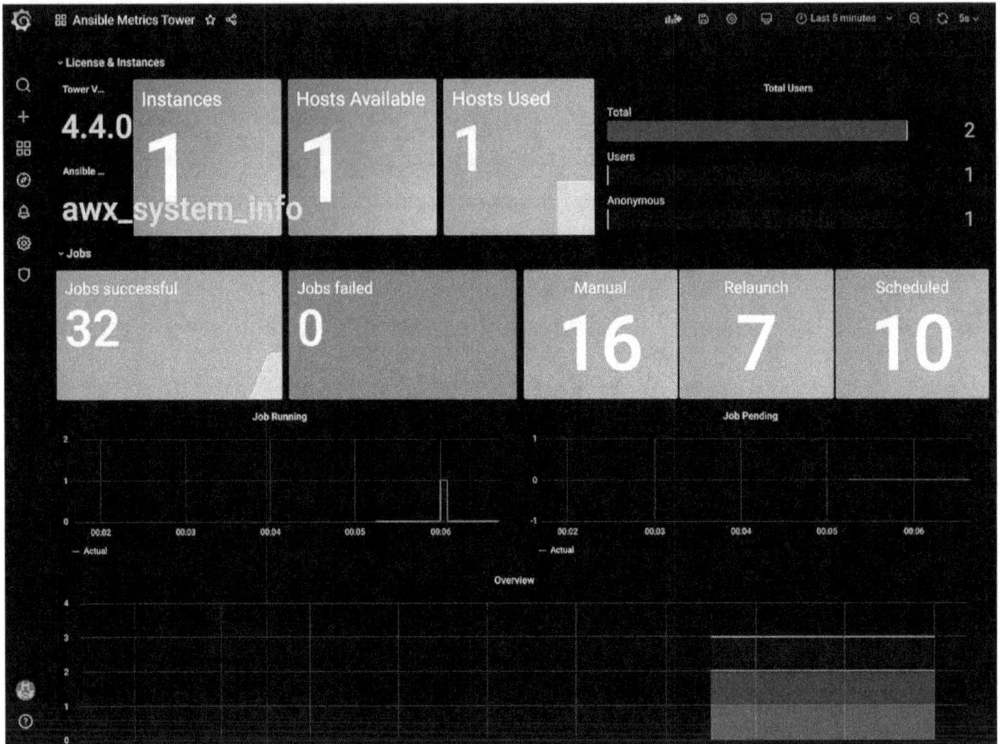

Figure 6.14: Grafana dashboard

Grafana supports various data sources, including Prometheus, and offers a wide range of visualization options and alerting capabilities.

These are the benefits of the integration between automation controller, Prometheus, and Grafana:

- **Comprehensive monitoring:** The integration provides a holistic view of our automation tasks and infrastructure, allowing us to identify issues and trends across our environment.

- **Real-time insights**: Prometheus collects real-time metrics, enabling us to monitor the performance of automation jobs and infrastructure components as they happen.

- **Customized visualization**: The flexible Grafana dashboards let us create visualizations tailored to our specific monitoring needs, improving data interpretation.

- **Alerting and notifications**: we can set up proactive alerting in both Prometheus and Grafana, ensuring we were promptly notified of critical issues or anomalies.

- **Data-driven decisions**: By combining automation-related metrics with infrastructure metrics, we gain actionable insights that drive informed decision-making and optimization.

- **Historical analysis**: The time-series database in Prometheus allows us to analyze historical data, helping us identify patterns and long-term trends.

In summary, integrating automation controller, Prometheus, and Grafana offers a powerful solution for monitoring, analyzing, and visualizing automation tasks, infrastructure performance, and resource utilization. This synergy enhances our ability to manage IT operations efficiently and proactively address challenges.

Backup and restore

In the dynamic realm of IT management, having a robust backup and restoration strategy is akin to having a safety net under the tightrope of operations. The Ansible Automation Platform, an integral part of efficient system administration, offers an integrated backup and restoration mechanism to ensure our digital landscape remains secure, resilient, and ready for unforeseen challenges. In this article, we delve into the intricacies of this vital feature, exploring its setup, execution, and best practices.

In the ever-evolving landscape of IT infrastructure, the ability to safeguard our systems with effective backup and restoration strategies is paramount. automation controller acknowledges this necessity and seamlessly integrates a comprehensive backup and restoration system into its platform setup playbook. Whether it is to mitigate unforeseen incidents or to ensure a smooth migration to new environments, this functionality serves as our digital insurance policy. Before embarking on our backup and restoration odyssey, we must acquaint ourselves with a few key pointers. First and foremost, when restoring, ensure that we are returning to the same version from which the backup was taken. This ensures compatibility and stability throughout the process. Moreover, it is advisable to utilize the latest minor version of a release for backup and restoration, enhancing the efficiency and reliability of the procedure. It is worth noting that backup and restoration operations are tied to the version of PostgreSQL supported by our current platform version. Be sure to check the System Requirements documentation for compatibility details.

The Ansible Automation Platform installer includes the backup and restores capability via the **setup.sh** command. It is the heart of the backup and restoration process. This versatile script takes center stage, accepting a range of arguments that orchestrate the backup and restoration actions. Here are the two pivotal arguments:

- **-b**: Initiates the platform backup, ensuring that critical data is preserved for future restoration.

- **-r**: Triggers the platform restoration, rejuvenating our system from a previously stored backup.

As the captain of this ship, the root user holds the helm. Executing `setup.sh` with the appropriate parameters guides our system through the exhilarating waves of backup and restoration.

```
# ./setup.sh -b
# ./setup.sh -r
```

The time needed for the backup and restoration process depends on the amount of data stored in our Ansible Automation Platform. By default, backup files materialize in the same directory as the **setup.sh** script, as shown in *Figure 6.15*:

```
root@localhost:/home/luca/Downloads/ansible-automation-platform-setup-bundle-2.4-1-aarch64
ah.example.com              : ok=68    changed=29   unreachable=0    failed=0    skipped=110   r
escued=0     ignored=0
localhost                   : ok=2     changed=0    unreachable=0    failed=0    skipped=0     r
escued=0     ignored=0

The setup process completed successfully.
[warn] /var/log/tower does not exist. Setup log saved to backup.log.
[warn] Provided path does not exist or is not accessible. Setup log saved to ./backup.log.
[root@ah ansible-automation-platform-setup-bundle-2.4-1-aarch64]# ls
automation-platform-backup-2023-08-03-14:45:33.tar.gz
automation-platform-backup-latest.tar.gz
backup.log
bundle
certified_collection_seed_2023-07-09-10-31-21.log
collections
group_vars
inventory
README.md
setup.log
setup.sh
validated_collection_seed_2023-07-09-10-38-20.log
[root@ah ansible-automation-platform-setup-bundle-2.4-1-aarch64]# du -hs automation-platform-
backup-*
581M    automation-platform-backup-2023-08-03-14:45:33.tar.gz
0       automation-platform-backup-latest.tar.gz
[root@ah ansible-automation-platform-setup-bundle-2.4-1-aarch64]# less backup.log
[root@ah ansible-automation-platform-setup-bundle-2.4-1-aarch64]# █
```

Figure 6.15: Ansible Automation Platform Backup

Successful execution of the backup creates a tarball with the date of execution:

```
581M   automation-platform-backup-2023-08-03-14:39:23.tar.gz
```

The utility also creates a soft link named **automation-platform-backup-latest** pointing out to the latest backup file in the current directory.

However, flexibility is at our fingertips. Using **EXTRA_VARS**, we can tailor the destination of our backups to align with our preferences.

```
# ./setup.sh -e 'backup_dest=/path/to/backup_dir/' -b
```

Moreover, restoration paths can be sculpted similarly. When restoring, we can specify a non-default path for where we restore the backup file.

```
# ./setup.sh -e 'restore_backup_file=/path/to/nondefault/backup.tar.gz'
-r
```

Alternatively, when we are not specifying the name of the backup file, the setup procedure looks for the **automation-platform-backup-latest.tar.gz** file in the current directory. The best practice is to create a symlink to our file before starting the restore process.

```
# ln -s automation-platform-backup-2023-08-03-14:39:23.tar.gz automation-
platform-backup-latest.tar.gz
```

```
# ./setup.sh -r
```

As we explore the realm of backup and restoration, the orchestration is handled by a trio of playbooks. These virtuoso scripts encompass:

- **backup.yml**: Initiates a comprehensive backup, embracing our database, **SECRET_KEY** file, custom user config files, and manual projects.

- **restore.yml**: Breathing life into our backup, this playbook artfully restores our precious system resources to a fresh instance of the automation controller.

The restoration process diligently checks for the existence of the backup file before embarking on its transformative journey. Ensure that our system credentials are in harmony, granting us the necessary access and privileges for a seamless restoration, as shown in *Figure 6.16*:

Figure 6.16: Ansible Automation Platform Restore

It is necessary to have a fully installed Ansible Automation Platform or only the components that we need in order that the restore operation can succeed.

As we prepare for the exhilarating voyage of backup and restoration, a few considerations illuminate our path:

- **Disk space**: Ensure our vessel is well-equipped for the journey. Review disk space requirements to accommodate backups and relevant data.

- **System credentials**: Secure the keys to our systems. Be armed with the right credentials, whether we are sailing the seas of a local or remote database.

For clustered environments, the backup and restoration process harmoniously aligns with the abovementioned principles. Whether restoring an existing cluster or embarking on a new one, the essence remains the same—safeguarding our digital IT fleet.

When sailing the clustered seas, a few additional notes become were guiding stars:

- Ensure the old cluster is at anchor before restoring to a new one, preventing conflicts.

- Per-node backups gracefully find their homes only on nodes sharing the same hostname as the backup.

- Restoring to a different cluster preserves manual projects and settings, ensuring a seamless transition.

As we steer our ship through the clustered tides, the restoration process remains our steadfast ally, enabling us to chart new courses and secure our digital dominion.

In the ever-evolving landscape of IT management, mastering the art of backup and restoration is a journey every adept administrator embarks upon. Automation controller stands by our side, providing the tools and guidance to navigate this crucial endeavor. So, hoist our sails, invoke `setup.sh`, and embark on a voyage of digital resilience and preparedness. Were systems' safety and longevity await our skilled hands and the power of the automation controller's backup and restoration prowess.

Security

In the ever-evolving landscape of cybersecurity, where threats loom large and data breaches are a constant concern, the role of automation becomes paramount. Ansible, a powerful and versatile automation tool, takes center stage in fortifying our organization's defenses. We are going to delve into two critical aspects of security automation: firewall policy management and the automation of **Intrusion Detection and Prevention Systems (IDPS)**.

Firewall Policy Management

A network's firewall stands as a digital guardian, shielding our organization from cyber threats and unauthorized access. As a security operator, managing firewall policies is not merely a task—it is a strategic imperative. Ansible security automation provides the means to create, modify, and delete firewall rules, ensuring that our network's fortress remains impenetrable.

The complexities of managing multiple firewall rules across diverse products and vendors can overwhelm security teams. Manual workflows, prone to errors, are not an option in the fast-paced world of cybersecurity. Ansible's security automation comes to the rescue, providing a unified language and framework to automate tasks across a spectrum of products, leading to unparalleled efficiency.

Incorporating Ansible roles, such as the acl_manager role, empowers us to seamlessly manage **Access Control Lists (ACLs)** for various firewall devices. Whether it is blocking or unblocking IP addresses or URLs, Ansible's automation prowess ensures that our network is shielded from threats. Leveraging Ansible's capabilities, the creation and execution of firewall rules have become a streamlined process. A typical incident response scenario showcases Ansible in action—upon receiving an intrusion alert, a playbook with the acl_ manager role is triggered, effectively blocking the attacker's IP address. Ansible security automation has become our steadfast ally in investigations, threat hunting, and incident response. The Red Hat Ansible Automation Platform offers certified content collections that facilitate seamless integration and reuse within our security team, enabling a harmonious synergy between human expertise and technological efficiency.

Network Intrusion Detection and Prevention Systems

In the realm of cybersecurity, **Intrusion Detection and Prevention Systems (IDPS)** stand as sentinel guardians, detecting and thwarting threats in real time. Ansible's transformative power extends to IDPS automation, offering an elegant solution to managing these critical systems. Before embarking on our journey of IDPS automation with Ansible, ensure that our groundwork is solid. This entails having Ansible 2.9 or later installed, SSH connections and keys configured, and chosen IDPS software (for example, Snort) properly set up.

With the stage set, Ansible is the orchestrator of our IDPS automation. Utilizing the **ids_ rule** role, we gain the ability to create and modify rules and signatures for our IDPS. Snort, a renowned player in the IDPS arena, becomes a seamless extension of our cybersecurity arsenal.

A simplified lab environment paints the picture of Ansible security automation integration. The process involves crafting and executing IDPS rules to detect potential attacks, demonstrating Ansible's dexterity in safeguarding our digital realm.

Leveraging Ansible's **ids_rule** role, we embark on a journey of automated IDPS management. For example, let us consider creating a new Snort rule to detect specific attack patterns. This process involves installing the **ids_rule** role, crafting a playbook, and executing it.

By following this path, we empower our cybersecurity infrastructure to identify and thwart potential threats autonomously. Ansible's role as the conductor of our IDPS symphony ensures that our digital domain remains vigilant and secure.

In the ever-evolving cybersecurity landscape, automation is a beacon of efficiency and resilience. Ansible, with its remarkable security automation capabilities, empowers security operators to manage firewall policies and automate IDPS systems effectively. As threats multiply and cyber adversaries grow more sophisticated, Ansible stands as a stalwart ally, ensuring our organization's defenses remain strong and vigilant. Through Ansible's orchestration, cybersecurity transcends from a challenge to a triumph, where human expertise and automation harmoniously coexist to safeguard the digital realm.

Key learning

In this chapter, we learned how to manage, monitor and support the Ansible Automation Platform services taking care from the first start to analyze log and system status and to execute backup and restore of the service successfully.

Points to remember

- We can control the status of the automation controller using the **automation-controller-service** script, and we can handle the controller services.

- We can aggregate log files using tools like Splunk, Loggly, Sumologic, and Elastic Stack (formerly ELK Stack).

- We can monitor in real-time the performance of our automation controller by using Prometheus and Grafana Dashboard.

- We can backup and restore our Ansible Automation Platform using the Installer utility.

Multiple choice questions

1. **How can we start, stop and restart the automation controller?**

    a. The **automation-controller-service** script

    b. The service command

    c. The Ansible Automation Platform installer

    d. It is not possible

2. **What directory contains the log files of the automation controller?**

    a. `/var/log/aap/`

    b. `/var/log/controller/`

    c. `/var/log/tower/`

    d. `/var/log/automation/`

3. **What are the most used logging aggregator services?**

    a. rsyslog

    b. Splunk and ELK Stack

    c. Datadog and Sumo Logic

    d. None of the previous options

4. **What is the metrics API endpoint of the automation controller?**

    a. `/api/v2/ping`

    b. `/api/v2/data`

    c. `/api/v2/controller`

    d. `/api/v2/metrics`

Answer

1. a

2. c

3. b

4. d

Questions

1. How can we start, stop and restart services for automation controller and automation hub?

2. What are the log files paths in automation controller and automation hub?

3. What are the options to aggregate log files?

4. How can we monitor in real-time the performance of the automation controller?

5. How can we back up and restore our Ansible Automation Platform?

6. What are the most common use cases for security?

Key terms

- **Rsyslog** is an open-source software utility used for forwarding, filtering, and processing log messages in a Linux or Unix-based system.

- **Pulp** is a platform for managing repositories of software packages and other content, enabling efficient distribution and management of content across different systems.

- **Security Information and Event Management** (**SIEM**) is a comprehensive cybersecurity solution that centralizes and analyzes security data from various sources to detect and respond to potential threats in real-time.

- **Splunk** is a powerful data platform that enables organizations to collect, analyze, and visualize machine-generated data from various sources for insights and operational intelligence.

- **ELK Stack**, now known as the Elastic Stack, is an integrated open-source software suite consisting of Elasticsearch, Logstash, and Kibana, used for collecting, storing, and visualizing large volumes of data.

- **Prometheus** is an open-source monitoring and alerting toolkit, while **Grafana** is a visualization platform; both are commonly used together for monitoring and analyzing system metrics and performance data.

- **Network Intrusion Detection and Prevention Systems** (**IDPS**) are cybersecurity solutions designed to monitor, detect, and respond to unauthorized or malicious activities within a network in real time.

Join our book's Discord space

Join the book's Discord Workspace for Latest updates, Offers, Tech happenings around the world, New Release and Sessions with the Authors:

https://discord.bpbonline.com

CHAPTER 7

App Deployments

Introduction

Ansible Automation Platform orchestrates playbook and rulebook in our organization. In this chapter, we dive deep into our Ansible resource and discover tips and tricks to organize our content better and streamline our automation journey.

Structure

In this chapter, we will discuss the following topics:

- Create Ansible Playbooks and content
- Ansible Lightspeed
- Automate application deployments
- Event-driven automation
- Distribute containerized applications

Objectives

Learn how to write an effective Ansible Playbook and Rulebook to solve problems in our organization.

Create Ansible Playbooks and content

We will embark on a journey to understand the art of crafting Ansible Playbooks and generating content, unlocking the potential to orchestrate tasks with precision and scalability. Ansible Playbooks are the foundation upon which Ansible's automation capabilities are built. These YAML-formatted files serve as the vehicle to express automation tasks in a human-readable and easily maintainable manner. Ansible Playbooks are coded in the YAML format that follows the Ansible language. An Ansible Playbook typically consists of the following components:

- **Hosts and inventory:** Define the target systems or hosts for executing the tasks. Ansible's inventory system allows us to group hosts based on various attributes.

- **Variables and facts:** Set variables that can be used within the playbook. Additionally, Ansible gathers facts about target hosts, which can be utilized during playbook execution.

- **Tasks:** Specify the individual tasks to be performed. Tasks can range from installing packages and managing files to running scripts and restarting services.

- **Handlers:** Define tasks triggered only if specific conditions are met. Handlers are often used to manage services or perform actions based on changes made by tasks.

- **Roles and modules:** Utilize Ansible's extensive library of modules - small units of code that perform specific actions. Roles provide a way to organize tasks, handlers, and variables into reusable components.

Each node of the Ansible Automation Platform includes the latest version of Ansible and the necessary running tool, so we do not need to worry about the installation in our production and testing environment. For the development environment, we still need to install the necessary software in our development machine manually. We can develop Ansible Playbook using any text editor, even a textual (VIM, Emacs, Pico, Nano, and so on.) or graphic user interface (Geany, Sublime Text, and so on.). Nowadays, most Ansible developers prefer to use Visual Studio Code (VSCode).

Visual Studio Code

Developing Ansible resources in **Visual Studio Code** (**VSCode**) can greatly enhance our productivity and streamline the automation process. VSCode offers rich features, extensions, and tools that make writing, testing, and debugging Ansible playbooks and configurations more efficient. Here is a step-by-step guide on how to develop Ansible code in VS Code:

1. **Install Visual Studio Code:** The first step is to actually download and install Visual Studio Code from the official website: **https://code.visualstudio.com/** as shown in *Figure 7.1*. The packages are available for the most known operating systems:

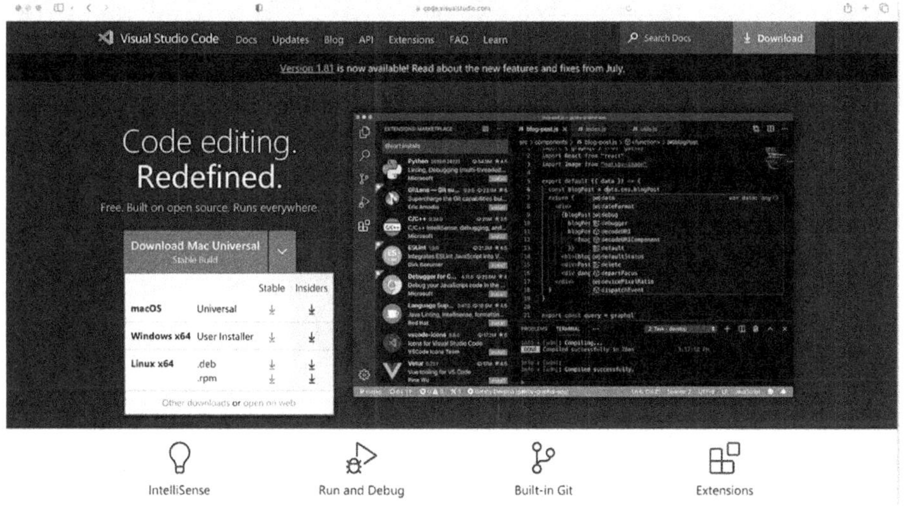

Figure 7.1: Visual Studio Code website

2. **Install Ansible extension:** The Visual Studio Code's extensibility comes from its vast collection of extensions. To develop Ansible code, we need to install the Ansible extension. We need to launch VSCode and go to the Extensions view by clicking on the square icon in the sidebar on the left or by pressing *Ctrl + Shift + X*. Search for **Ansible** and install the official Ansible extension provided by Red Hat, as shown in *Figure 7.2*:

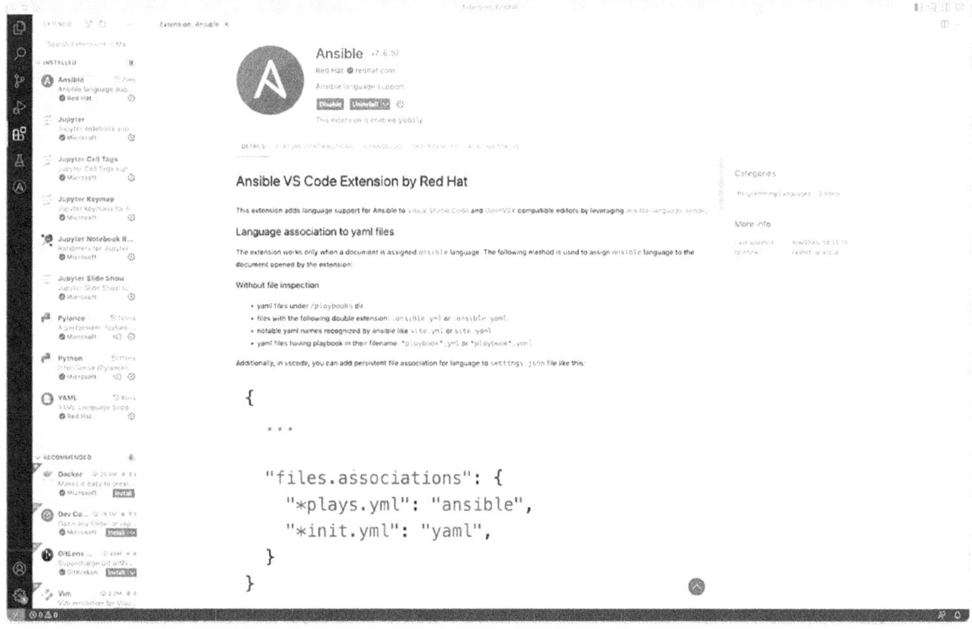

Figure 7.2: VSCode Ansible extension

When editing an Ansible resource, the VSCode status bar displays information about the current file and the currently loaded profile. When the Ansible extension is successfully enabled, we see the details about the current and Python versions. *Figure 7.3* shows Ansible version 2.15.2 in Python 3.11.4 with the Ansible Lightspeed feature enabled:

Ln 1, Col 1   Spaces: 2   UTF-8   LF   Ansible   {} 2.15.2   Python 3.11.4   Lightspeed

Figure 7.3: VSCode status bar

Visual Studio Code (VS Code) speeds up the development process of Ansible resources. First, we should either open an existing Ansible project or create a new one, organizing playbooks, roles, and configurations in a dedicated directory. Usually, a project includes Ansible Playbooks in YAML files within the project directory, utilizing VS Code's built-in YAML support for syntax highlighting and auto-completion. The IntelliSense technology offers context-aware suggestions, automatic formatting of YAML files for consistency, and linting/validation to catch syntax errors and enhance playbook structure. Execution of Ansible Playbooks directly from the integrated terminal in VS Code is detailed, along with debugging capabilities such as setting breakpoints and inspecting variables. There is also a Git integration for version control and collaboration, supporting the integration with additional extensions based on workflow preferences. The VS Code Ansible extension offers additional integration and stays updated with the latest features and best practices through the Ansible documentation. By following these steps and taking advantage of VS Code's features and extensions, we can streamline our Ansible development process, write more efficient and reliable code, and accelerate our automation projects.

Ansible Playbook

Ansible Playbook is the key component in our automation journey. In order to be able to develop our Ansible code successfully, we need to follow these steps:

1. **Installation:** Ensure we have Ansible installed on our development system. Use our operating system package manager or the latest version using the Python package manager (**pip**) for Ansible or Ansible Core packages plus any additional collections. Additional development utilities are useful to expand the syntax check with linter (**ansible-lint**), Ansible role testing (**molecule**), collection creator (**ansible-creator**) and changelog management (**antsibull-changelog**)

2. **Playbook Structure:** Create a new directory for our playbook. Inside this directory, create a YAML file (for example, **playbook.yml**) as the first Ansible Playbook.

3. **Defining Hosts**: Begin our Playbook by specifying the target hosts or host groups under the **hosts** section referring to our Ansible inventory.

4. **Tasks:** Add tasks to our playbook. Each task includes a **Fully Qualified Collection Name (FQCN)** with each module (for example, **ansible.builtin.apt, ansible.builtin.yum, ansible.builtin.copy**) and relevant parameters. For instance, to

install a package, use the **ansible.builtin.yum** module and define the package name. Since Ansible 2.10 is strongly suggested to use the FQCN to avoid collisions between modules with the same name stored in different collections.

5. **Execute the playbook:** Run the playbook using the **ansible-playbook** command, followed by the playbook filename. Watch as Ansible executes each task on the designated hosts.

Our first Ansible playbook usually begins with the **ansible.builtin.ping** module for Linux and Unix target, **ansible.windows.win_ping** for Windows target, and **ansible. netcommon.net_ping** for network target. This module test for connectivity to our target hosts. The following **ping.yml** Ansible Playbook tests the connection between the Ansible controller and the target node:

```
---

- name: Test connection
  hosts: all
  tasks:
    - name: Test target
      ansible.builtin.ping:
```

We can type the **ping.yml** Ansible Playbook in our Visual Studio Code editor as shown in *Figure 7.4*:

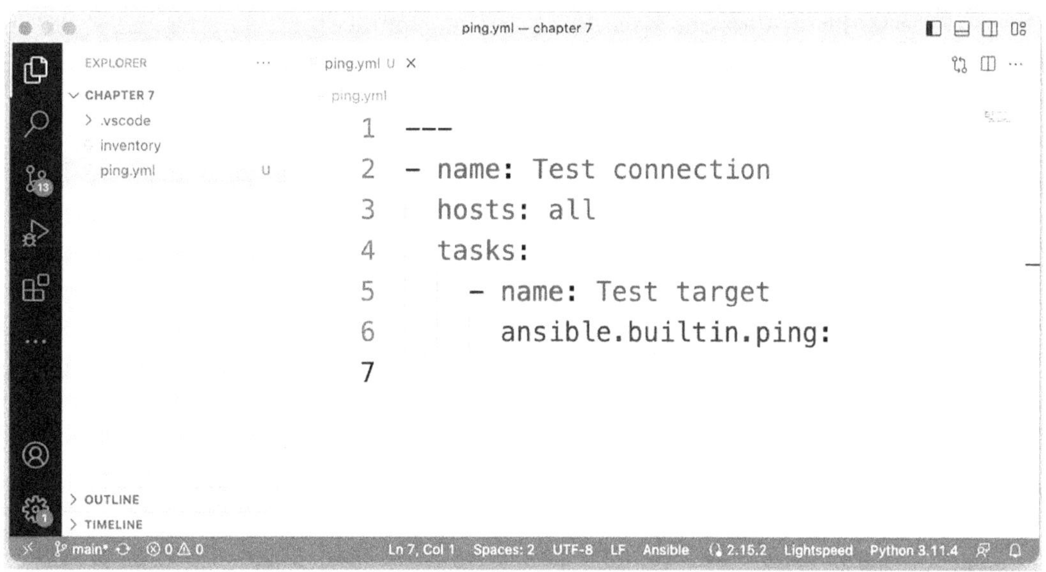

Figure 7.4: ping.yml in VSCode

We can manually execute our code using the **ansible-playbook** command:

```
ansible-playbook ping.yml
```

We can also specify an inventory file using the "**-i**" parameter of the **ansible-playbook** command:

```
ansible-playbook -i inventory ping.yml
```

The inventory file supported formats are INI, YAML, and JSON. The simplest format is INI. For example, the following file is used to connect to the server **server01.example.com**:

```
server01.example.com
[all:vars]
ansible_connection=ssh
ansible_user=ansible
ansible_password=password
ansible_host=192.168.0.99
```

With:

- **ansible_connection**, the protocol of the connection - **"ssh"** in this case.

- **ansible_user**, the username for the initial authentication - **"ansible"** in this case.

- **ansible_password**, the password for the authentication - **"password"** in this case.

- **ansible_host**, (optional) the IP address of the host - **"192.168.0.99"** in this case.

The output of the verbose execution shows us the **"ping": "pong"** message on the screen:

```
PLAY [Test connection] ****************************************************************

TASK [Gathering Facts] ****************************************************************
ok: [server01.example.com]
TASK [Test target] ****************************************************************
ok: [server01.example.com] => {"changed": false, "ping": "pong"}
PLAY RECAP ****************************************************************

server01.example.com                 : ok=2    changed=0    unreachable=0
failed=0    skipped=0    rescued=0    ignored=0
```

We can use the Ansible **ping** module to test the connection, along with different scenarios involving the **data** parameter. This module verifies the connection and execution capability of target hosts in an Ansible Playbook.

- **Ansible ping module**: The Ansible **ping** module, named **ansible.builtin. ping**, is used to test the availability of target hosts. It verifies Ansible's ability to log in to the managed host and whether a Python interpreter can execute Ansible code.

- **Default behavior**: By default, the **ping** module does not require any parameters to be specified. When executed, it tests the connection and returns the response **"ping": "pong"** when the connection is successful.

- **Customizing output**: The `data` parameter allows us to customize the output message. We can change the default `"pong"` response to a custom message. For example, setting `data: "ready for connections"` would change the response to `"ping": "ready for connections"`.

- **Simulating Errors**: We can use the `data` parameter with the value **"crash"** to simulate an exception. This can be useful for testing how our playbook handles errors.

- **Verbose Execution**: Using the amount of from **-v** to **-vvvv** parameter (from one to four) with the **ansible-playbook** command allows us to see the detailed output, including the actual responses from the **ping** module.

- **Windows Hosts**: The **win_ping** module should be used instead of the **ping** module with the same parameters and behaviors for Windows hosts.

We learned how to use the Ansible **ping** module to test host availability and customize its behavior. This information is helpful for beginners and those looking to understand the basics of using Ansible to interact with target hosts.

GitOps

A successful Ansible journey does not begin and end with the playbooks themselves – an optimized directory layout plays a pivotal role in ensuring smooth navigation, maintainability, and scalability. The following two directory structures are usually used in enterprise projects for our Ansible projects. We are going to explore the standard structure as well as an alternative approach for larger and more complex environments.

At the heart of every Ansible project lies a well-structured directory layout that fosters clarity and organization, as shown in *Figure 7.5*:

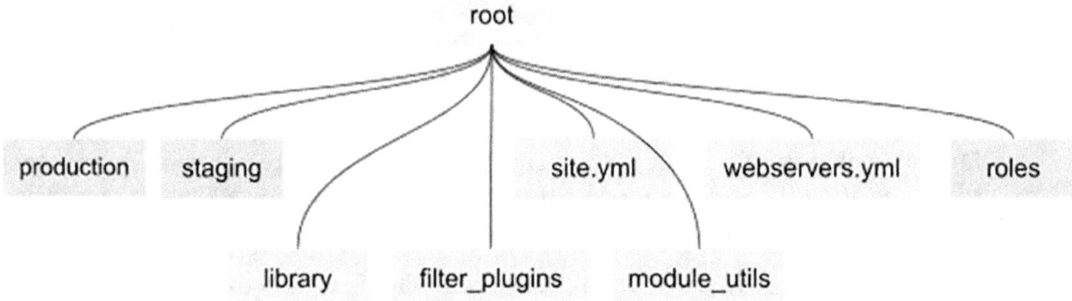

Figure 7.5: Ansible directory structure

Let us unravel the anatomy of this structure:

- **Inventory Files:** (blue color) The **production** and **staging** files are inventory files that list the target servers for deployment in their respective environments. These files provide a clear inventory of systems that Ansible will interact with.

- **Group Variables**: The **group_vars** directory contains YAML files (**group1.yml**, **group2.yml**, and so on.) that assign variables to specific groups of servers. This allows we to define common attributes and settings for sets of servers.

- **Host Variables**: The **host_vars** directory contains YAML files (**hostname1.yml**, **hostname2.yml**, and so on.) that assign variables to individual systems. This is useful for configuring specific attributes unique to each server.

- **Library, Module Utils, and Filter Plugins**: These directories (**library, module_utils, filter_plugins**) provide locations for adding custom modules, utility scripts, and filter plugins to extend Ansible's capabilities.

- **Playbooks**: The **site.yml** and **webservers.yml** files are playbooks written in YAML format. **site.yml** serves as a master playbook, whereas the **webservers.yml** is a specific playbook targeting web servers.

- **Roles**: The **roles** directory is a core component, encapsulating self-contained roles that organize and modularize our tasks.

For larger environments with diverse group and host variables, an alternative directory layout can provide greater flexibility, as shown in *Figure 7.6*:

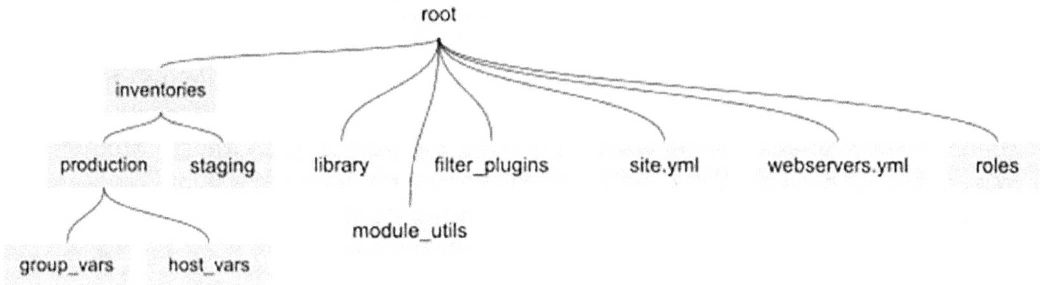

Figure 7.6: *Alternative Ansible directory structure*

This approach involves grouping inventory files, **group_vars**, and **host_vars** into separate directories. The benefits of this layout include:

- **Granular environment management**: The **inventories** directory houses subdirectories for different environments, such as **production** and **staging**. Each environment contains its own inventory file, **group_vars**, and **host_vars**, ensuring a clear separation of variables.

- **Customization and scalability**: This approach facilitates a higher degree of customization based on the unique requirements of each environment. Variables specific to a particular environment remain isolated, promoting modularity.

- **Reduced complexity**: Separating variables into distinct directories streamlines maintenance by providing a clear overview of variables associated with each environment.

- **Enhanced collaboration**: When multiple teams collaborate on a project, this layout minimizes conflicts and simplifies version control for variable definitions.

Selecting the most suitable directory layout depends on our Ansible project's size, complexity, and needs. The standard structure provides a cohesive approach that is straightforward to manage, making it an ideal choice for smaller projects. On the other hand, the alternative layout shines in larger environments, ensuring a granular and organized approach to variable management.

Whichever path we choose, a well-designed directory layout serves as the foundation for a successful Ansible automation journey. It fosters order, modularity, and efficiency, allowing us to focus on the core goal – automating our IT operations precisely and easily. As we embark on our Ansible adventure, remember that an optimized directory layout is our compass, guiding us through the complexities of automation and paving the way for streamlined, scalable, and successful deployments.

Ansible modules

Ansible modules are standalone scripts or code snippets that perform specific tasks on target hosts. They act as the building blocks of Ansible automation by encapsulating functionality to manage resources, services, configurations, and more. Modules are written in various programming languages, including Python, and they follow a specific interface to communicate with Ansible. Each module typically corresponds to a single action, such as managing packages, creating files, restarting services, and more. Ansible modules provide a consistent and declarative way to describe the desired state of a system. When we run an Ansible Playbook, we are essentially instructing Ansible to apply a set of modules to the target hosts to achieve the desired configuration or state.

For example, the `"ansible.builtin.yum"` module can be used to manage packages on a Red Hat-based system, and the file module can be used to create or manage files and directories. As Ansible evolved and its ecosystem grew, the number of modules, plugins, and other content also increased. Ansible collections were introduced to organize and package these pieces of content more effectively. A collection is a distribution format that bundles related content together, including modules, plugins, playbooks, and more, all under a common namespace. Ansible collections make it easier to share and distribute Ansible content, and they provide a structured way to manage reusable automation code. Collections can be installed from various sources, such as Ansible Galaxy (a public repository for Ansible content) or private sources. By using collections, we can better organize our automation code, share it with others, and keep it up-to-date. For example, the community could create a collection for managing specific networking devices, bundling together modules, plugins, and playbooks tailored for that purpose. Ansible modules are the individual building blocks of tasks that Ansible performs on target hosts, while collections are a higher-level packaging mechanism that organizes and distributes modules, playbooks, and other Ansible content, making it easier to manage and share automation code within the Ansible ecosystem.

For Linux, modules like `ansible.builtin.command`, `ansible.builtin.shell`, `ansible.builtin.apt`, and `ansible.builtin.yum` enable the execution of commands and package management. Additionally, modules such as `ansible.builtin.file`, `ansible.builtin.user`, and `ansible.builtin.systemd` facilitate file and user account management, as well as handling `systemd` services. On Windows, corresponding modules like `ansible.windows.win_command` and `ansible.windows.win_shell` execute commands, while `ansible.windows.win_copy` handles file copying. Management of services is achieved through `ansible.windows.win_service`, and updates are managed by `ansible.builtin.win_updates`. Other modules cater to tasks like repository management, template rendering, and archive extraction, with examples including `ansible.builtin.apt_repository`, `ansible.builtin.template`, and `ansible.builtin.unarchive`. Please refer to the Index of all Modules[1] webpage for the full list of modules and documentation.

---

[1] https://docs.ansible.com/ansible/latest/collections/index_module.html

Note: The availability of specific modules may vary depending on the Linux distribution or version of Windows being used.

These are the most common Ansible modules used:

- **Command module (`ansible.builtin.command`)**: Executes arbitrary shell commands on the target hosts and returns the command's output.

- **Shell module (`ansible.builtin.shell`)**: Similar to the command module, but provides additional features like environment variable handling and shell command arguments and full feature pip, redirection like a full terminal.

- **Raw module (`ansible.builtin.raw`)**: Runs raw shell commands on the target hosts without requiring Python to be installed on the remote machine.

- **Copy module (`ansible.builtin.copy`)**: Copies files from the control machine to the target hosts and can set file attributes like permissions and ownership.

- **Fetch module (`ansible.builtin.fetch`)**: The opposite of the copy module. It retrieves files from the target hosts and copies them to the control machine.

- **File module (`ansible.builtin.file`)**: Manages files and directories on the target hosts, allowing us to create, delete, and modify files and directories.

- **Template module (`ansible.builtin.template`)**: Generates configuration files using Jinja2 templates and copies them to the target hosts.

- **Package module (`ansible.builtin.package`)**: Manages packages on the target hosts. It can install, update, or remove packages using the appropriate package manager.

- **Lineinfile module (`ansible.builtin.lineinfile`)**: Manages lines in text files on the target hosts. We can add, modify, or remove lines.

- **Service module (`ansible.builtin.service`)**: Manages system services on the target hosts. We can start, stop, restart, enable, or disable services.

- **Package module (`ansible.builtin.package`)**: Manages packages on the target hosts. It can install, update, or remove packages using the appropriate package manager.

- **User module (`ansible.builtin.user`)**: Manages user accounts on the target hosts. We can create, modify, or remove user accounts and set attributes like passwords and shell.

- **Group module (`ansible.builtin.group`)**: Manages groups on the target hosts. We can create, modify, or remove groups and manage their attributes.

- **Mount module (`ansible.builtin.mount`)**: Manages mounts and filesystems on the target hosts. We can mount, unmount, and manage mount options.

- **Debug module (`ansible.builtin.debug`)**: Prints variables and expressions for debugging purposes.

- **Wait_for module (`ansible.builtin.wait_for`)**: Waits for a specific condition to be met on the target hosts, such as a port being open or a file appearing.

- **Yum module (`ansible.builtin.yum`)**: Manages packages on Red Hat-based systems using the yum package manager.

- **Apt module (`ansible.builtin.apt`)**: Manages packages on Debian-based systems using the apt package manager.

- **Systemd module (`ansible.builtin.systemd`)**:** Manages systemd services and units on the target hosts.

- **Firewalld module (`ansible.builtin.firewalld`)**: Manages firewalld rules on the target hosts, allowing us to add, modify, or remove firewall rules.

- **Copy Module (`ansible.builtin.copy`)**: Copies files from the control machine to the target hosts and sets attributes like permissions and ownership.

- **Docker container module (`community.docker.docker_container`)**:** Manages Docker containers on the target hosts.

- **Docker images module (`community.docker.docker_image`)**:** Manages Docker images on the target hosts.

- **Slurp module (`ansible.builtin.slurp`)**: Reads files on the target hosts and returns their contents as a Base64-encoded string.

- **Async_status module (`ansible.builtin.async_status`)**: Checks the status of asynchronous tasks and retrieves their results.

- **Setup module (`ansible.builtin.setup`)**: Gathers facts about the target hosts, including details about the operating system, hardware, and network.

- **Assert module (`ansible.builtin.assert`)**: Defines conditions that must be met for a playbook to continue executing.

- **Template module (`ansible.builtin.template`)**: Generates configuration files using Jinja2 templates and copies them to the target hosts.

- **Synchronize module (`ansible.builtin.synchronize`)**: Syncs files and directories from the control machine to the target hosts using rsync.

- **Uri module (`ansible.builtin.uri`)**: Performs HTTP requests and can be used to interact with REST APIs on the target hosts.

- **Debug module (`ansible.builtin.debug`)**: Prints variables and expressions for debugging purposes.

- **Include_vars module (`ansible.builtin.include_vars`)**: Loads variables from external files and includes them in the playbook.

- **Subversion module (`ansible.builtin.subversion`)**: Manages subversion repositories on the target hosts.

- **Script module (`ansible.builtin.script`)**: Executes scripts on the target hosts, copying them from the control machine.

- **File module (`ansible.builtin.file`)**: Manages files and directories on the target hosts, enabling us to create, delete, and modify files and directories.

- **Pip module (`ansible.builtin.pip`)**: Manages Python packages using the pip package manager on the target hosts.

- **Git module (`ansible.builtin.git`)**: Manages Git repositories and performs Git operations on the target hosts.

Most of the specified Ansible recourses are part of the **`ansible.builtin`** collection that is present in all the Ansible installations as part of the Ansible Core platform. The Ansible Core is the minimal part of the Ansible platform with the main components, tools, and the internal Ansible collection.

Code reuse

Creating Ansible Playbooks and content empowers system administrators and DevOps professionals to automate a wide array of tasks, from server provisioning and configuration management to application deployment and maintenance. By harnessing the flexibility of YAML-based playbooks, leveraging modules, and organizing tasks with roles, we can achieve efficient, consistent, and scalable automation that adapts to the evolving needs of our IT environment. To streamline the creation of playbooks and ensure reusability, Ansible offers three powerful features:

- **Templates**: Ansible allows us to use templates to generate configuration files dynamically. By incorporating variables, conditions, and loops, templates enable us to generate content tailored to each target host.

- **Roles**: Roles provide a structured way to organize our playbooks, making them more modular and maintainable. Create roles for specific tasks (for example, web server setup, database configuration) and reuse them across different playbooks.

- **Collection**: An Ansible collection is a curated and shareable package that contains playbooks, roles, modules, and plugins, enhancing the capabilities and extensibility of Ansible automation.

Figure 7.7 shows the directory structure of an Ansible Role:

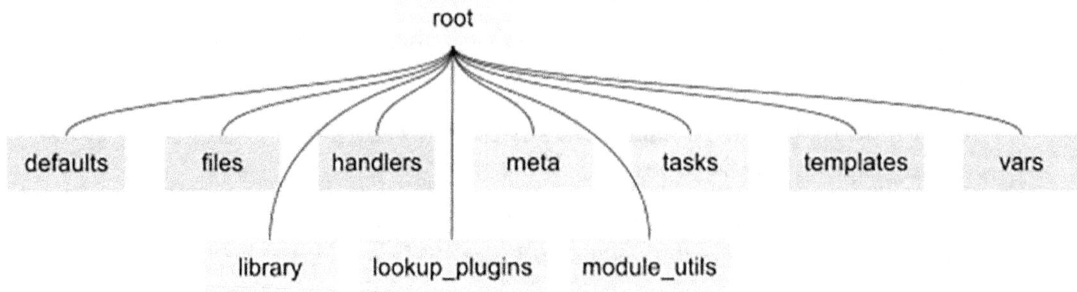

Figure 7.7: Ansible Role directory structure

Each Ansible role has a structured hierarchy:

- **tasks**: Contains **main.yml** or smaller task files defining actions to be executed.

- **handlers**: Includes **main.yml** for defining handler tasks to be triggered by events.

- **templates**: Stores template files (with **.j2** extension) for use with the template resource.

- **files**: Contains files to be copied to the target servers using the copied resource.

- **vars**: Houses **main.yml** for role-specific variables.

- **defaults**: Stores **main.yml** for default lower-priority variables.

- **meta**: Contains **main.yml** defining role dependencies.

- **library** and **module_utils**: Optional directories for custom modules and utilities.

- **lookup_plugins**: An optional directory for custom lookup plugins.

Whether we're automating routine maintenance or orchestrating intricate workflows, Ansible Playbooks act as our toolset to embrace the future of IT operations. Begin your exploration of Ansible's automation capabilities and unlock the potential to revolutionize the way you manage and maintain systems. When integrating a role into our Ansible Playbook, it's crucial to grasp the sequence of execution. Special statements exist to execute code either before or after the Ansible role, providing flexibility and control over the automation process. The full breakdown is like the following:

- **pre_tasks**: This section contains tasks that are executed before role execution.

- **roles**: This section specifies the role named **role1** to be executed.

- **tasks**: This section contains tasks that are executed after the role execution.

- **post_tasks**: This section contains tasks executed after the role execution and tasks in the **tasks** section.

- **handlers**: This section defines handlers triggered by tasks using the **notify** keyword.

The sequence of execution of every Ansible Playbook is **pre_tasks**, **roles**, **tasks**, **post_tasks**, and **handlers**.

Collections

Ansible collections are curated and packaged sets of Ansible content, including playbooks, roles, modules, plugins, and documentation. Collections enhance Ansible's functionality by providing a structured way to organize and distribute content for various use cases. Here are explanations of the most commonly used Ansible collections:

- **ansible.builtin**: This is the default collection that ships with Ansible. It contains essential modules and plugins that provide core functionality for managing systems, configuration, and applications.

- **community.general**: Formerly known as **"ansible"** on Ansible Galaxy, this collection offers a wide range of additional modules contributed by the Ansible community. It covers various use cases, such as cloud management, networking, and more.

- **community.docker**: This collection simplifies the management of Docker containers and services, allowing users to create, manage, and configure Docker containers and related resources.

- **community.kubernetes**: Focused on Kubernetes, this collection offers modules to interact with Kubernetes clusters, manage resources, and perform operations related to deployments, services, and more.

- **ansible.aws** and **community.aws**: Designed for **Amazon Web Services (AWS)**, this collection provides modules to automate tasks like provisioning EC2 instances, managing S3 buckets, working with security groups, and more.

- **community.vmware**: Aimed at VMware environments, this collection includes modules to manage virtual machines, data centers, clusters, and various VMware resources through Ansible automation.

- **ansible.windows** and **community.windows**: Tailored for Windows environments, this collection offers modules to automate tasks on Windows systems, covering tasks like user management, service control, file manipulation, and more.

- **cisco.ios**: For Cisco network devices running IOS, this collection includes modules to configure, manage, and monitor networking equipment, facilitating automation of network infrastructure.

- **netmiko.netmiko**: Netmiko is a popular library for managing network devices. This collection wraps Netmiko, allowing Ansible users to automate network configuration and administration tasks across various devices.

- **redhat.cloudforms**: This collection integrates Ansible with Red Hat CloudForms, enabling management and automation of hybrid cloud environments, including private and public clouds.

- **awx.awx**: This collection is built around Ansible AWX, an open-source platform that provides a web-based interface for managing Ansible playbooks, inventories, and job execution. This is similar to `ansible.controller`.

- **ibm.ibm_zos_core**: Targeting IBM Z systems, this collection offers modules for managing resources on mainframes, including job submission, data set management, and system configuration.

- **google.cloud**: Tailored for **Google Cloud Platform** (**GCP**), this collection offers modules to interact with GCP resources, including VM instances, storage buckets, and network configurations.

- **azure.azcollection**: Microsoft Azure users can leverage this collection to automate tasks within Azure, such as provisioning resources, managing virtual machines, and working with Azure services.

These collections showcase the versatility of Ansible in managing various environments and technologies.

We can install additional Ansible collection manually using the **ansible-galaxy** command line tool. For example for installing the **containers.podman** collection we need to execute the following full command:

```
ansible-galaxy collection install containers.podman
```

We can verify a successful installation using the command:

```
ansible-galaxy collection list containers.podman
Collection         Version
----------------- -------
containers.podman 1.10.2
```

By utilizing collections, users can leverage pre-built modules and content to streamline automation tasks and simplify infrastructure management.

Ansible Utils

Ansible Utils is a collection of utility plugins and modules that simplify various tasks and operations within Ansible Playbooks and roles. These utilities help users manipulate data, convert between different data formats, work with inventory data, and perform other common automation-related tasks. These are the key components and examples we mentioned from the Ansible Utils collection:

1. **Filter plugins:** Filter plugins allow us to modify or filter data during playbook execution. While not explicitly mentioned in our examples, filter plugins can be used in various places within Ansible to manipulate and filter data.

2. **Modules**: Ansible modules are reusable, standalone scripts that can automate specific tasks on managed nodes. **Ansible Utils** may include additional modules to perform specific utility tasks.

3. **Lookup plugins**: Lookup plugins are used to retrieve data from external sources and make it available within Ansible. They can fetch data from various locations and integrate it into our playbooks.

4. **Test plugins**: Test plugins evaluate certain conditions or properties. They can be used to verify data or check if specific conditions are met before proceeding with tasks in our playbook.

Now, let us look at the specific examples we provided:

- `ansible.utils.from_xml`: This utility can convert XML data into a Python dictionary, making it easier to work with XML data in Ansible Playbooks. For example, we can parse XML data from a file or a variable and convert it into a dictionary for further processing.

- `ansible.utils.to_paths`: This utility can flatten a complex object into a dictionary of paths and values. It helps deal with nested data structures and convert them into a more accessible format.

- `ansible.utils.cli_parse`: This utility is used to parse command-line output or text using various parsers. It is helpful when we need to extract specific information from a command or text file output within our playbook.

- `ansible.utils.private`: This utility can test whether an IP address is within the private IP address ranges defined by RFC 1918. It helps us determine if an IP address is internal or external.

These utilities are part of the `Ansible Utils` collection to simplify common automation tasks and data manipulation operations within Ansible. We can include them in our playbooks to streamline our automation workflows.

Ansible Lightspeed

Ansible Lightspeed is the generative AI created by Red Hat with IBM Watson code assistant technology. It was introduced in October at Ansible Fest 2022 as Project Watson and unveiled in May 2023 at Red Hat Summit 2023. The most famous ChatGPT and

Google Bard are more generic versions of Generative AI; Ansible Lightspeed is specifically designed and trained for Ansible code. The development team's intent is to provide the most accurate code prediction, taking advantage of the vast community Ansible code published on the Ansible Galaxy. A planned feature request is to populate content from the private Automation Hub. A typical developer journey starts with typing the name of the task that we would like to achieve, and Ansible Lightspeed creates code predictions based on the IBM Watson AI model. Ansible Lightspeed's most significant features include significant productivity improvement that enables faster and more efficient Ansible code development. Ansible Lightspeed offers significant performance improvements, enabling faster and more efficient automation tasks and enhanced scalability and resource utilization to handle large-scale automation environments. Ansible Lightspeed is a promising Ansible code assistant, aiming to deliver faster performance, increased scalability, and improved automation capabilities to simplify IT automation tasks in various environments. The target user of the Ansible Lightspeed is a developer creating some Ansible code using the Visual Studio Code **Integrated Development Environment** (IDE). Once the Ansible Extension is in the IDE, we need to enable the Lightspeed settings and are ready to create the code assistant. The tool works with traditional code validation tools such as **ansible-lint** to adhere to the Ansible best practices. We interact with the Generative AI when we create a new task, as it suggests the code based on our request once we hit the *Enter* button. We can confirm the suggestion using the *Tab* key on the keyboard or skip using the *Esc* button. Let me enter the same request as before and obtain the result displayed in *Figure 7.8* that create an AWS EC2 server on the "**us-east-1**" region deploying the **Ubuntu Jammy 22.04** AMI image:

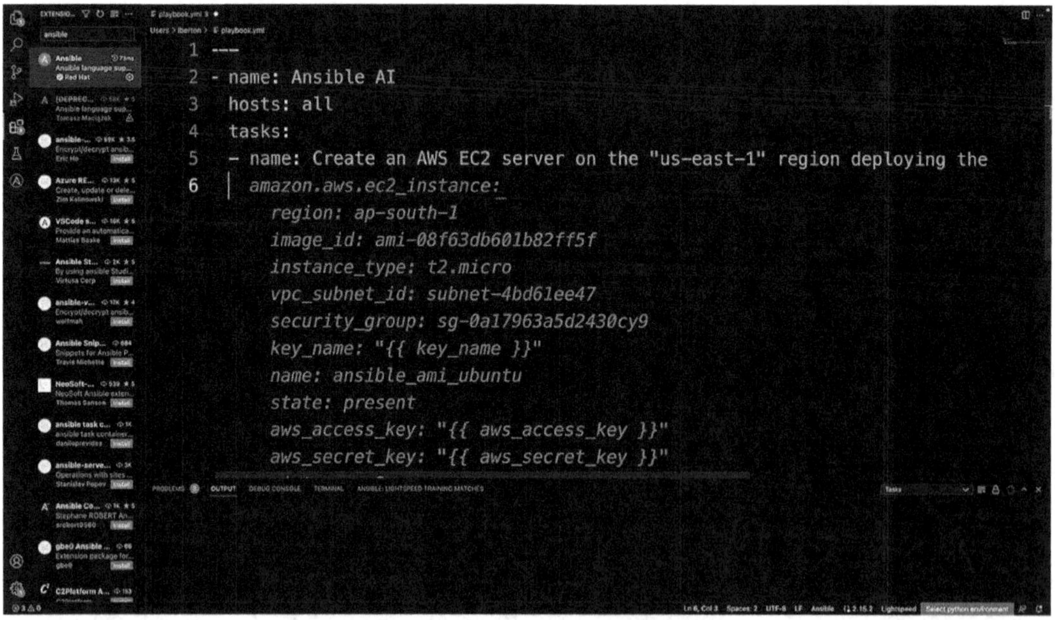

Figure 7.8: Ansible Lightspeed

Ansible Lightspeed creates a code suggestion. The code meets the latest best practices but might require manual rework. Ansible Lightspeed shows transparency and accountability, displaying the Ansible resource used by the AI model in the "Ansible Lightspeed training matches" area. This also gives credit and attribution to the original creator of the code, and we can understand how the decision process. At the moment, Ansible Lightspeed is available free of charge as in the Technical Preview software release phase. The technical preview aims to show users the upcoming features and improvements in Ansible Lightspeed. The technical preview is open to users who want to explore the new features and capabilities of Ansible Lightspeed and provide feedback to improve the platform before its full release. It is necessary to link our GitHub account to access the software. We can also influence the future of the Ansible Lightspeed project by providing feedback via the Matrix chat. Installing Ansible Lightspeed requires just downloading the Ansible Extensions and enabling the Ansible Lightspeed in the Settings sections of the VSCode. The future for Ansible Lightspeed is shining. The team would like to improve the tool to become more efficient.

Automate application deployments

Ansible ushers in a new era, allowing us to script, codify, and automate deployment processes. The shift from manual to automated deployments accelerates the release cycle and drastically reduces the risk of configuration errors. At the heart of automated deployments lie Ansible Playbooks, which orchestrate routines and define every deployment step. These playbooks encapsulate tasks, configurations, and dependencies, ensuring that every deployment adheres to a standardized and auditable process. Ansible's roles provide a structured approach to organizing and reusing deployment tasks. With roles, we can modularize our deployments, creating standardized building blocks that can be easily shared, reused, and extended across projects. This not only enhances consistency but also simplifies maintenance. Ansible seamlessly integrates with DevOps pipelines, bridging the gap between development and operations. By embedding Ansible playbooks within our CI/CD pipelines, we ensure that each code change triggers automated deployments, fostering a culture of continuous integration and deployment. In the world of Ansible, deployments become artifacts defined in code. This **configuration as code (CaC)** approach offers traceability, version control, and repeatability. It allows us to manage infrastructure as well as application configurations, ensuring that our deployments are not just efficient but also consistent. As we embark on the journey of automating application deployments with Ansible, remember that we are shaping a future of efficiency, agility, and excellence. Ansible empowers us to unleash the full potential of our applications, ensuring that each deployment is a meticulously choreographed symphony of precision and success.

Launching jobs via API

The Ansible Controller API brings a world of automation possibilities to our fingertips, allowing us to initiate jobs and tasks seamlessly. In this guide, we will walk through the process of launching jobs using the powerful curl tool. Whether we are seasoned Ansible users or just getting started, these examples will help us harness the potential of the Ansible Controller API for efficient job execution. Launching jobs through the Ansible Controller API is a straightforward process, and the curl tool provides a convenient way to interact with the API. Let us dive into some easy-to-follow examples to help us kickstart our job execution journey. Assuming we have our Job Template ID as identifier '**1**', our controller is identified by the hostname "**ac.example.com**", and we use valid login credentials (**admin:redhat**). We can create a new job by sending the request to the Ansible Controller API to launch a job based on the specified Job Template ID. The response is expected in a JSON format that contains various details about the job. We can extract the '**id**' field from this JSON object, which corresponds to the ID of the newly created job. The Ansible Controller API allows us to pass extra variables to our job templates, enhancing flexibility in customizing job execution. Here is an example of how we can achieve this using **curl**:

```
curl -f -k -H 'Content-Type: application/json' -XPOST \
    -d '{"extra_vars": "{\"foo\": \"bar\"}"}' \
    --user admin:redhat http://ac.example.com/api/v2/job_templates/1/launch/
```

In this command, the '**-d**' flag is used to include the extra variables as part of the request data. Make sure to structure the **extra_vars** parameter as a string containing valid JSON. This capability lets us dynamically modify job behavior by passing specific variables when launching jobs. We can access the automation controller API documentation to understand further and explore the capabilities of the Ansible Controller API. Log into our Ansible Controller instance through a web browser by navigating to **http://ac.example. com/api/**. This interactive documentation provides insights into the available objects and endpoints, allowing us to navigate and experiment with the API's features. When using the **extra_vars** parameter, it is important to note that the parameter value should be a string containing valid JSON, not just a JSON dictionary. Take care when escaping quotes and formatting the parameter value to ensure proper parsing by the API.

Launching jobs using the Ansible Controller API and curl tool opens a realm of automation possibilities. Whether we are initiating tasks, managing configurations, or orchestrating complex workflows, the API's flexibility and curl's simplicity provide us with the tools to accomplish our automation goals. By leveraging these techniques, we can enhance the efficiency, scalability, and customization of our Ansible-driven operations, unlocking a new level of automation prowess.

Event-Driven automation

In the dynamic landscape of IT operations, event-driven automation, exemplified by the integration of Ansible, stands out as a transformative force. Ansible, a powerful automation tool, seamlessly aligns with event-driven workflows, ushering in a new era of operational efficiency. This paradigm shift operates on the principle of triggering actions not by schedules but by real-time events such as system changes, alerts, user interactions, or data updates. Ansible modules serve as efficient executors, responding to events, while event handlers act as vigilant responders ready to initiate specific actions. This approach brings agility and responsiveness to the forefront, allowing instantaneous reactions to dynamic scenarios. Event-driven Ansible finds application in diverse areas, ranging from infrastructure scaling to security responses and continuous deployment, offering the ability to dynamically adjust infrastructure based on events like resource spikes and respond swiftly to security alerts or configuration drift events. The benefits of event-driven Ansible include agility, enabling rapid adjustments to infrastructures and applications; efficiency, automating responses to events and reducing manual intervention; consistency, ensuring standardized actions across diverse scenarios; and scalability, allowing the seamless scaling of resources in response to demand spikes without delay. Automation is driven by real-time triggers, a symphony composed by the cadence of events. With Ansible as our conductor, we can create harmonious automation that adapts, evolves, and responds – all orchestrated by the rhythm of events. The Ansible Rulebook is a YAML document used in Event-Driven Ansible. The syntax is similar to an Ansible Playbook, the Ansible automation script. It is basically a set of procedures to execute the automation when an event happens. There are five building blocks of our Ansible Rulebook:

- **source**: where the event is being generated

- **event**: any changes from the source

- **rule**: evaluated for every event

- **conditional**: the event expression that triggers the action

- **action**: what to execute (playbook, modules, tasks)

In the rulebook, we can define the sources of events, hooks, Alertmanagers, URLs, and files to listen to that are the most popular. At the moment of writing this book, nine source plugins are available:

- **alertmanager**: receive webhook events from Alertmanager

- **azure_service_bus**: receive Azure Service Bus events

- **kafka**: receive Apache Kafka topic messages

- **url_check**: poll URLs and send events based on their statuses

- **watchdog**: send events when a file status changes

- **webhook**: receive events from a webhook

- **file**: load facts from YAML files and reload when any file changes

- **tick**: generate events with an increasing index

- **range**: generate events with an increasing range

We can define and perform some action for each of them according to the rule we write. Each rule defines the condition that triggers the action. Each rule has some conditionals. Conditionals evaluate some event status logically and define when to trigger an action. For example, it could be an event from the **alertmanager** or when a specific HTTP status code is obtained, a newly created file, or just received a message from the webhook. When a condition is reached, one or more actions can be triggered. The most common action is **run_playbook**. Each source of event determines the type of event in the rulebook. A very interesting source of events is Apache Kafka as a message bus or webhook. The following **eda.yml** Ansible Rulebook exposes a webhook on port 8000 that is listening for messages.

```yaml
---

- name: Listen for webhook events
  hosts: all
  sources:
    - ansible.eda.webhook:
        host: 0.0.0.0
        port: 8000
  rules:
    - name: Webhook
      condition: event.payload.message != ""
      action:
        debug:
```

Each time we receive a non-empty message (**condition**), it triggers the execution of the Ansible module debug that simply displays the message on the screen, like a hello world. The Ansible Event Driven tool is going to listen on the address **0.0.0.0**, which is a special placeholder for all the network interfaces on our system. As we can see, we use a YAML manifest syntax, so be very careful about indentation. This is the simplest way to implement the source, event, rule, and action. In the real world, for example, we can combine with a Git repository, GitHub, or GitLab pipeline to deliver JSON messages as an event when a push operation happens. In the **rules** section, we can specify as many conditions as we want and apply some filters to messages before processing. For example, we can exclude some messages based on keys or apply some transformation like **dashes_to_underscore**. The easiest action is using the Ansible **debug** module to display messages on the screen. But we can do so much more. Combined with the powerful Ansible Playbook, the actions are limitless. Just change the **debug** line with **run_playbook** and specify the playbook name.

Drift configuration

Configuring systems with Ansible in a brownfield environment with ad-hoc legacy deployments poses a notable challenge in managing configuration drift. It is efficient the usage of Event-Driven Ansible to detect and correct configuration drifts. This drift, resulting from inconsistencies among systems, poses uncertainty and complexity when attempting to standardize configurations using Ansible. Various techniques are possible to audit configuration drift, such as running playbooks with **--check** and **--diff** options, using **'assert'** tasks with **changed_when** or **failed_when**, employing **'stat'** tasks to compare files, utilizing the **'backup'** parameter for template or copy tasks, and leveraging the **ansible.utils.fact_diff** module. Usually, the Ansible playbook extracts configuration files, compares them against a reference host, generates diff reports, and offers insights into addressing configuration drift during role and playbook development.

Distribute containerized applications

In the modern IT, the distribution of applications within containers has emerged as a cornerstone of efficiency and scalability. Ansible's versatility shines as it effortlessly bridges the gap between operations and development, enabling teams to collaborate seamlessly. Containerization has revolutionized the way applications are packaged, distributed, and executed. Containers encapsulate applications and their dependencies in a portable and consistent environment. DevOps teams are empowered to create reproducible deployments, scale applications effortlessly, and achieve operational consistency across environments. We can codify complex deployment processes with Ansible's playbooks, collections, and roles, transforming them into repeatable and auditable tasks. Regarding distributing applications in containers, Ansible Playbooks can guide the deployment of applications within containers. Its extensive module library, which empowers us to interact with container orchestrators like Kubernetes or Docker, ensures precise execution and management. Container registries, like Docker Hub, Amazon ECR, and private automation hub, store container images for distribution. Ansible seamlessly integrates with these registries, enabling us to pull, tag, and push container images effortlessly. Ansible's prowess extends beyond mere deployment as we can configure containers, manage their state, and ensure their adherence to desired configurations with Ansible. This holistic approach ensures that our containerized applications are deployed, maintained, and optimized for peak performance. As applications evolve and requirements change, Ansible keeps pace, allowing us to easily update, scale, and modify our containerized applications. This agility translates into quicker responses to market demands, improved resource utilization, and enhanced innovation. There are multiple different container engines. We can interact with Docker using the **community.doker** collection for Docker and the **containers.podman** for Podman. The **community.doker.docker_image** module can build images using a **Dockerfile**. It can also load and save images to archive files, as well as interact with image registries. The following **docker.yml** Ansible Playbook deploys a Docker container **python:bullseye**, connect to it, and install the **apache2** package.

```
---

- name: Deploy Docker image
  hosts: localhost
  ansible_connection: local
```

```
tasks:
- name: Start container
  community.docker.docker_container:
    name: apache
    image: python:bullseye
    command: sleep infinity
- name: Connect to Docker container
  hosts: apache
  connection: docker
  tasks:
  - name: Test connection
    ansible.builtin.ping:
  - name: Install apache
    ansible.builtin.apt:
      name: apache2
      update_cache: true
```

Key learning

Ansible Playbook and Ansible Rulebook enable us to deploy our application using a human-readable format. We are able to automate most of our Linux and Windows workflow. In the next chapter, we are going to implement a hybrid cloud environment taking advantage of the Kubernetes technology.

Points to remember

- Ansible Playbooks are coded in YAML format, enabling automation using **modules**, **plugins**, and **roles**.

- Ansible collections expand the modules available in the **ansible.builtin** collection.

- Event-Driven Ansible uses rulebook to execute automation that reacts to events.

- Ansible Lightspeed uses Generative AI to speed up and propel our development.

- Containers are a great way to distribute our applications, taking advantage of Ansible, the pipeline, and CI/CD.

Multiple choice questions

1. What is the most used graphical IDE to create Ansible resources?

   a. VIM

   b. Emacs

   c. Geany

   d. Visual Studio Code

2. What Ansible module is used to test the connection to Linux target hosts?

   a. `ansible.builtin.debug`

   b. `ansible.builtin.command`

   c. `ansible.builtin.ping`

   d. `ansible.builtin.shell`

3. How can we distribute Ansible Playbooks, roles, modules, plugins, and documentation?

   a. Ansible Playbook

   b. Ansible Collection

   c. Ansible Role

   d. Ansible Rulebook

4. What Ansible collection interacts with Docker technology?

   a. `community.doker`

   b. `containers.podman`

   c. `ansible.docker`

   d. `linux.container`

Answer

1. d

2. c

3. b

4. a

Questions

1. What are the most used Ansible modules for Linux?

2. What are the most used Ansible modules for Windows?

3. What are the two most famous Ansible directory layouts?

4. What software can we use to validate our Ansible Playbook best practices?

5. How can we create a script for Event-Driven Ansible?

6. What are the most used Ansible collection to interact with containers?

Key terms

- **VS Code**: Visual Studio Code is a versatile and free source-code editor known for its extensibility and robust features, catering to various programming languages and development tasks.

- **IntelliSense:** IntelliSense is a code editor feature that provides context-aware suggestions, autocompletion, and information to enhance the coding experience and accuracy.

- **GitOps**: a software development approach that uses Git as the single source of truth to manage and automate the deployment and operation of applications and infrastructure.

- **Ansible Lightspeed**: a Generative AI developed by Red Hat using IBM Watson code assistant technology, specifically designed for Ansible code to enhance productivity, offering suggestions for code creation and adhering to best practices, currently available in technical preview for users to explore and provide feedback for further improvement.

- **Ansible Playbook**: A declarative configuration file that defines a series of tasks to be executed on remote hosts, enabling automation and orchestration of IT infrastructure.

- **Ansible Rulebook**: The Ansible Rulebook is a YAML document used in Event-Driven Ansible that outlines procedures to execute automation when specific events occur, involving components like sources, events, rules, conditionals, and actions, such as running playbooks or modules, based on event triggers from sources, URLs, files, or other plugins.

- **CaC**: Configuration as Code refers to the practice of defining and managing system configurations using code and automation tools to ensure consistency, version control, and reproducibility in infrastructure and application setups.

- **IaC**: Infrastructure as Code is the approach of managing and provisioning IT infrastructure through code and automation tools to ensure consistency and efficient management of resources.

## CHAPTER 8

Hybrid Cloud and Kubernetes

Introduction

Hybrid cloud and Kubernetes with Ansible Automation Platform refers to using Ansible's automation capabilities to manage and orchestrate complex infrastructure and applications across both on-premises and cloud environments while leveraging Kubernetes for container orchestration and management. This enables seamless application deployment, scaling, and management in a hybrid cloud architecture using the Ansible powerful automation framework combined with Kubernetes for containerized workloads.

Structure

In this chapter, we will discuss the following topics:

- Cloud infrastructure
- Hybrid cloud
- Kubernetes
- Scale containerized applications

Objectives

By the end of this chapter, we are going to provision, configure, deploy, and manage hybrid cloud infrastructure with Red Hat Ansible Automation Platform leveraging all the modern technologies and Kubernetes.

Cloud infrastructure

Automated infrastructure provisioning using Red Hat Ansible Automation Platform is beneficial to speed up productivity in our organization. Red Hat Ansible Automation Platform is a tool that facilitates the automation of various tasks involved in managing and maintaining IT infrastructure. It uses a common, powerful language to define automation tasks in a human-readable way. Modern IT environments are complex and diverse, consisting of various operating systems, databases, applications, and cloud solutions. Managing such complexity manually can lead to errors and consume a lot of time. To address this challenge, the text suggests that a simplified and holistic approach is needed to manage this mix of components:

Figure 8.1: Software deployment

Automating critical infrastructure becomes crucial for effectively deploying, managing, and scaling workloads across different environments, including on-premise data centers, private and public clouds, and network edge locations, as shown in *Figure 8.1*. Red Hat Ansible Automation Platform is the solution to automate infrastructure tasks. It offers a way to automate IT system provisioning, deployment, and ongoing management. By doing so, Ansible can ensure consistent configurations across different parts of the infrastructure, simplify operational tasks, and minimize downtime. Moreover, the platform's capabilities extend to orchestrating complex workflows and assisting with day-to-day infrastructure management. Let us break down the key points:

- **Automated infrastructure provisioning**: Automated infrastructure provisioning automatically creates and sets up the computing resources and services required to run applications. It is the first step in the operational lifecycle of applications and involves deploying servers, networking, storage, and other components without manual intervention.

- **Provisioning across different platforms**: Ansible Automation Platform supports provisioning across various types of infrastructure platforms:

  o **Bare metal**: This refers to physical servers without virtualization. Ansible can automate provisioning on bare metal using data center management tools.

o **Virtualized**: Ansible can manage hypervisors, virtual storage, and virtual networks, making cross-platform management more efficient.

o **Networks**: Ansible can configure and manage physical network devices, ensuring compliance and reducing manual processes.

o **Storage**: Ansible can provision and manage storage, whether it is software-defined, cloud-based, or hardware storage appliances.

o **Public cloud**: Ansible includes modules for major public cloud platforms, allowing direct provisioning of compute, storage, and networking services.

o **Private cloud and OpenStack**: Ansible can be used to deploy, configure, and manage private cloud and OpenStack private cloud environments, including provisioning infrastructure and adding services.

- **Centralized automation controller**: Ansible Automation Platform provides an automation controller that helps centralize and control IT automation. It offers a visual dashboard, role-based access control, job scheduling, notifications, and inventory management. The platform's REST API and CLI make it easy to integrate into existing tools and processes.

- **Transition to configuration management and beyond** Automated provisioning with Ansible Automation Platform is just the starting point. Once the infrastructure is provisioned, Ansible can seamlessly transition into configuration management, orchestration, and application deployment using the same automation language. This means that the same tool and language can be used throughout the entire lifecycle of IT operations.

Automated infrastructure provisioning with Ansible Automation Platform simplifies setting up and managing various types of IT environments, from bare metal servers to public and private clouds, while also providing a foundation for further automation tasks beyond provisioning.

The good news is that automation controller already includes integration with the most common cloud providers and technologies in the field. Specifically, the Ansible automation controller includes dynamic inventories that updates are managed and configured using dynamically generated YAML files and inventory plugins. The inventory plugins are responsible for parsing and processing these YAML files to gather information about various resources in different environments. This feature applies to the following inventory sources:

- Amazon Web Services EC2

- Google Compute Engine

- Microsoft Azure Resource Manager

- VMware vCenter

- Red Hat Satellite

- Red Hat Insights

- OpenStack

- Red Hat Virtualization

- Red Hat Ansible Automation Platform

The inventory source configuration under the hood changed versions over version (3.8, 3.7, and so on.). To ensure compatibility between different versions, the automation controller uses templates for each of these sources. These templates are designed to guide the output of inventory plugins into a legacy format, preserving compatibility with older versions. For guidance on how to migrate to the new style inventory plugin output, we can refer to the *Supported Inventory Plugin Templates* section of the provided guide. With the release of automation controller version 4.4.0 / Ansible Automation Platform 2.4, a new feature has been introduced where users can directly configure the new style inventory plugins for certain inventory sources through the controller. This configuration is done using the **source_vars** parameter. The guide also highlights how **source_vars** containing a **plugin: foo.bar.baz** as a top-level key will be dynamically replaced with the appropriate fully qualified inventory plugin name at runtime based on the selected **InventorySource**. For instance, if the **ec2** source is selected for the **InventorySource**, the plugin will be set to **amazon.aws.aws_ec2** during runtime. In summary, the Ansible automation controller handles inventory updates and introduces a new feature for configuring inventory plugins directly through the controller.

Amazon Web Services

Ansible is a great tool for automating **Amazon Web Services** (**AWS**) cloud services and resources:

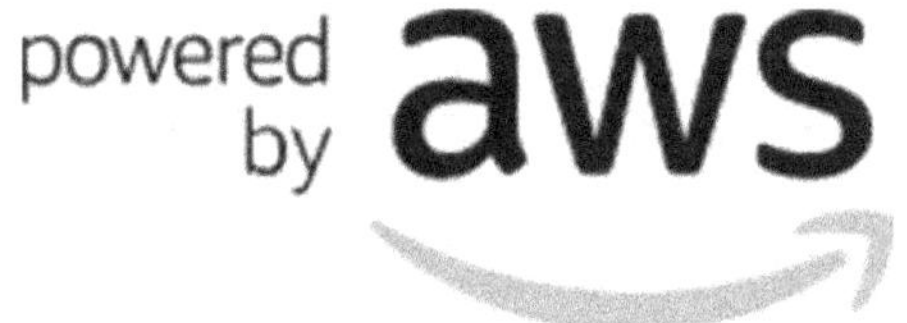

Figure 8.2: The Amazon Web Services (AWS) logo

In this section, we are going to explore the key Ansible modules for AWS, the importance of idempotence, configuration considerations, and running Ansible with AWS. It also mentions the use of AWS info modules to gather information about existing resources.

Ansible AWS collections:

Ansible modules can be used to manage various AWS resources, making it easier to automate tasks. There are two main collections for AWS within Ansible:

- **amazon.aws collection**: This contains modules directly supported by the Ansible cloud team. This collection is already included in the Ansible Execution Environment.

- **community.aws collection**: This collection includes additional modules supported by the broader Ansible community.

Ansible resources

Table 8.1 lists some important Ansible modules for managing AWS resources, along with the resources they manage. Examples include managing security groups, SSH keys, virtual networks, instances (virtual machines), load balancers, and more:

Module	Description
`amazon.aws.ec2_group`	Security groups
`amazon.aws.ec2_key`	SSH keys
`amazon.aws.ec2_vpc_net`	Virtual networks
`amazon.aws.ec2_instance`	EC2 instances (virtual machines)
`amazon.aws.elb_classic_lb`	Network Load Balancers
`amazon.aws.elb_application_lb`	Application Load Balancers
`community.aws.elb_target_group`	Target groups for load balancers

Table 8.1: Ansible Key Modules for AWS

- **Idempotence with AWS and Ansible**: Idempotence is crucial when automating cloud deployments. It ensures that running Ansible will maintain existing infrastructure and create duplicate resources. Each module has its way of finding existing resources to manage. It is important to configure modules correctly to prevent unnecessary resource duplication.

- **Configuring for AWS modules**: Ansible modules for AWS have unique installation and configuration requirements. They use the **boto3** Python library as Amazon SDK, which is the official Python library for the AWS API. Both **amazon.aws** and **community.aws** collections provide a requirements.txt file for installing necessary Python packages using the Python Package Manager (**pip**).

- **AWS credentials and configuration**: Credentials for AWS modules should not be stored in plain text in automation, as this poses a security risk. AWS credentials can be managed through environment variables or the **.aws** config directory used by the AWS command line. AWS region settings can also be inherited from these configurations or specified as a module parameter.

- **Running Ansible with AWS**: When working with cloud deployment modules, the concept of **target machine** is less relevant, as modules interact with APIs.

Typically, cloud deployment modules are run against localhost with the local connector, which means they run directly on the control machine. This approach ensures that only the control machine requires the necessary Python installation and configuration.

- **AWS dependencies and info modules**: Cloud resources often rely on other resources. Ansible helps in automating the creation of dependent resources. Info modules are available to query existing resources without taking any action. These modules are helpful for gathering information about resources that are already in place.

- **Instances and AWS info modules**: Creating virtual machine instances in AWS requires multiple dependencies like SSH keys, networks, security groups, and so on. Info modules like **ec2_instance_info** can be used to collect data about existing instances.

- **Cleanup and deletion**: Info modules can be especially useful when cleaning up cloud resources. They help in identifying and collecting data about connected resources, which may need to be deleted before removing a parent resource.

Info modules

Several Ansible info modules for AWS provide information about different types of resources, as shown in *Table 8.2*, such as machine images, security groups, instances, networks, Auto Scaling Groups, and more.

Module	Description
`amazon.aws.ec2_ami_info`	Amazon Machine Images
`amazon.aws.ec2_group_info`	Security groups
`amazon.aws.ec2_instance_info`	Instances (virtual machines)
`amazon.aws.ec2_vpc_net_info`	Networks and subnets
`amazon.aws.autoscaling_group_info`	Auto Scaling Groups
`amazon.aws.iam_user_info`	AWS Identity and Access Management

Table 8.2: Ansible Key Info Modules for AWS

Integrating Ansible with AWS via Ansible modules enables the idempotence to deploy and configure an AWS infrastructure environment for our workload. Moreover, we can use the info modules for gathering information about existing resources. It is important to emphasize the importance of automation for managing AWS resources efficiently and consistently.

Dynamic inventory

We can configure the dynamic inventory in the automation controller to create an inventory source for **Amazon Web Services (AWS) Elastic Compute Cloud (EC2)** instances. We can create an AWS inventory via the Dashboard in the Inventories section and then add a new **Inventory source**, as shown in *Figure 8.3*:

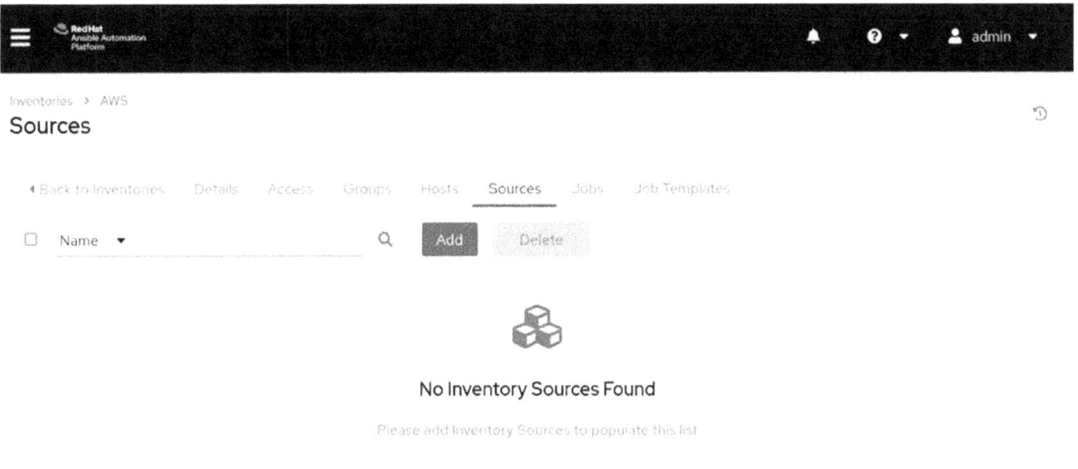

Figure 8.3: Inventory Source

Select the appropriate Inventory Source for Amazon Web Services using the **Amazon EC2** option in the scroll-down menu, as shown in *Figure 8.4*:

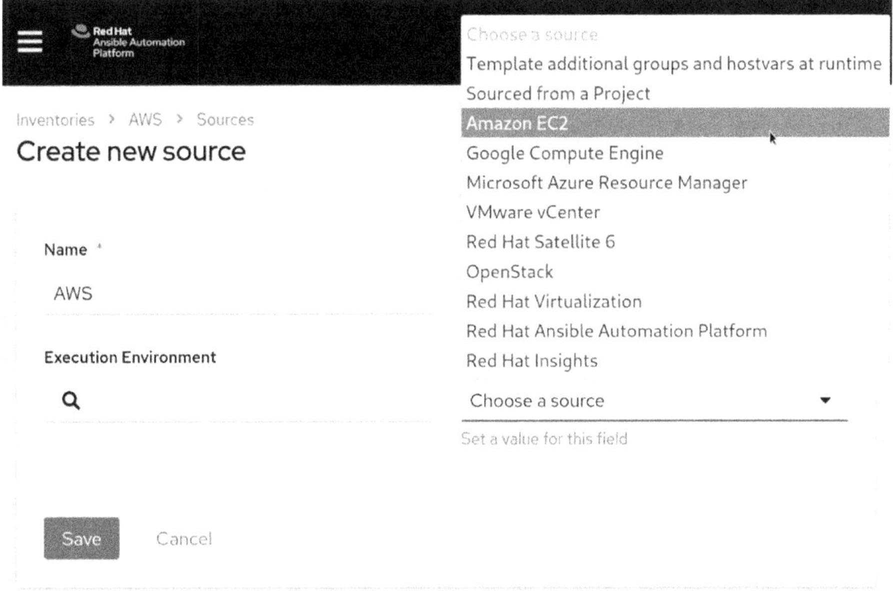

Figure 8.4: AWS Source

This is the step-by-step procedure to set up the inventory source for managing AWS EC2 resources in the automation controller.

- **Selecting the source**:

  To configure an inventory source based on AWS EC2, we need to select **Amazon EC2** from the **Source** field within the **Create Source** window, as shown in *Figure 8.3*.

- **Entering details**: After selecting **Amazon EC2** as the source, the **Create Source** window expands, revealing additional fields that need to be filled out, as shown in *Figure 8.4*. Here are the details to enter:

- **Credential**: We have the option to choose an existing AWS credential. This credential is required to authenticate and access our AWS resources. If the automation controller runs on an EC2 instance with an assigned IAM Role, we may omit this credential. Instead, the security credentials associated with the instance metadata will be utilized. IAM Roles enhance security and simplify the management of AWS credentials.

- **Other options**: We can specify additional options, such as verbosity, host filtering, enabled variable/value, and update options. These options provide control over how the inventory source is configured and maintained.

- **Source variables**: The **Source Variables** field allows us to override variables used by the **aws_ec2** inventory plugin. This plugin collects information about our AWS EC2 instances and creates the inventory. We can enter these variables using either JSON or YAML syntax, and there is a toggle button to switch between the two formats. We can refer to the documentation for the **aws_ec2** inventory plugin for a comprehensive understanding of these variables.

Note: if we use `include_filters`, the AWS plugin will always return all the hosts. To utilize this properly, the first condition in the `or` logic must be based on `filters`, and then we can build additional `or` conditions on a list of `include_filters`. This helps us use filtering more effectively to manage and retrieve specific hosts from our AWS EC2 inventory.

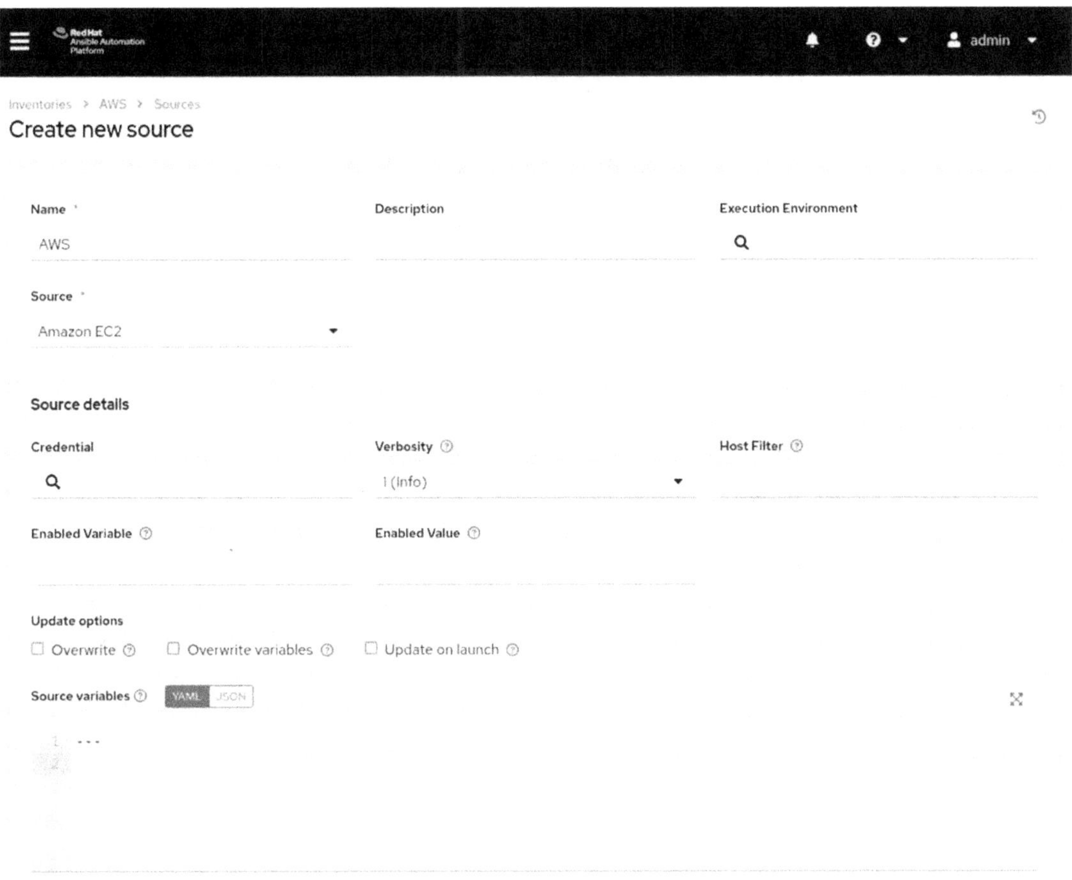

Figure 8.5: AWS Source details

We successfully configured an AWS EC2-sourced inventory within the Ansible automation controller with the appropriate credentials or IAM Roles, used the source variables, and enabled filtering to optimize our inventory management.

Microsoft Azure

Ansible Automation Platform has joined with Microsoft Azure to offer a seamless solution for deploying and managing our IT resources. This partnership combines the power of Ansible's automation capabilities with the reliability and scalability of Microsoft Azure's cloud infrastructure, delivering a comprehensive platform for organizations to streamline their operations. Please refer to the following figure:

Figure 8.6: The Microsoft Azure logo

With the integration of the Ansible Automation Platform on Microsoft Azure, organizations gain access to a fully managed application that brings automation to the heart of their Azure cloud environment. Red Hat's extensive support network backs this, ensuring businesses have the tools to implement and maintain enterprise-wide automation seamlessly. One of the standout features of Red Hat Ansible Automation Platform on Microsoft Azure is its close integration with native Azure services. This includes seamless compatibility with Azure Active Directory, Azure Virtual Machines, Azure Database Services, Azure Container Registry, Azure Key Vault, and more. This integration ensures that the cloud environment does not limit our automation strategy and extends to various Azure services. Ansible Automation Platform on Azure provides the freedom and flexibility to automate any application across diverse landscapes. The platform can be extended to meet our specific automation needs, whether it is an on-premise datacenter, regional footprint, global enterprise network, or edge nodes. This scalability allows us to automate tasks across a hybrid cloud environment easily. Red Hat handles the intricate details by managing, servicing, and supporting the Ansible Automation Platform on Azure. This means that our IT team can focus on designing and implementing automation strategies without worrying about managing the underlying infrastructure. The result is an environment that is efficient, streamlined, and designed for growth. Ansible introduces a dynamic inventory feature, allowing us to fetch inventory directly from Azure resources. Tagging our existing Azure deployments enables us to manage these resources efficiently through Ansible. Integrated billing provides a unified perspective of our expenses. If our organization has a spending agreement with Microsoft, the costs associated with the Ansible Automation Platform offering count toward that total. This streamlined billing approach ensures transparency and efficient financial management. Ansible Automation Platform on Azure combines the agility of cloud computing with the convenience of a managed application. Deploying the platform takes only minutes, and with integration into Azure services, we can begin automating our Azure resources swiftly. For those looking to explore the capabilities further, a self-paced lab and a technical expert demo are available to guide our journey.

Azure's microservices, such as Azure Functions and Kubernetes on Azure, can be harnessed seamlessly through Ansible. This empowers us to automate the deployment and management of cloud-native applications with precision and speed. This enables the deployment of Cloud-Native Applications.

The partnership between Red Hat for the Ansible Automation Platform and Microsoft Azure brings the world of automation to the cloud in an unprecedented manner. The managed application, integration with Azure services, seamless scalability, and comprehensive support make this offering a compelling choice for organizations seeking to optimize their operations through automation. Whether we are in North America, Australia, Singapore, India, Korea, New Zealand, or the EMEA region, the benefits of the Ansible Automation Platform on Microsoft Azure are within our reach, with global availability coming soon. Embrace the future of automation with confidence and embark on a journey of efficiency and growth. Ansible's rich matrix of modules for Azure spans across various provisioning and configuration tasks. This matrix encompasses virtual machines, scale sets, networking services, and container services. It offers a comprehensive guide to Ansible's capabilities within the Azure ecosystem, detailing the modules available and their compatibility with specific Ansible versions.

Ansible Resources

The **azure.azcollection** collection in Ansible encompasses a set of modules specifically designed to interact with various Azure services and resources. These modules simplify the process of provisioning, configuring, and managing Azure resources through Ansible automation. Here are some of the top modules within the **azure.azcollection** collection:

- **azure_rm_resourcegroup**: This module enables the creation, update, and deletion of Azure resource groups. Resource groups are logical containers used to manage and organize related Azure resources.

- **azure_rm_virtualmachine**: This module is used to manage **Virtual Machines (VMs)** in Azure. It allows for tasks such as creating, updating, starting, stopping, and deleting VM instances.

- **azure_rm_virtualnetwork**: With this module, we can automate the management of virtual networks in Azure. Virtual networks enable communication between Azure resources and on-premises networks securely.

- **azure_rm_storageaccount**: This module facilitates the management of Azure Storage accounts, which are used to store various types of data, including blobs, files, queues, and tables.

- **azure_rm_securitygroup**: Security groups are essential for controlling inbound and outbound network traffic to Azure resources. This module helps automate the configuration of security groups.

- **azure_rm_keyvault**: Azure Key Vault is a secure management system for keys, secrets, and certificates. This module allows us to manage key vault resources, including creating and managing keys and secrets.

- **azure_rm_dnsrecordset**: Automate the management of Azure DNS record sets using this module. It enables the creation, update, and deletion of DNS records within Azure DNS zones.

- **azure_rm_sqlserver**: This module deals with the automation of Azure SQL Server instances, allowing us to create, update, and manage these database server resources.

- **azure_rm_webapp**: Automate the deployment and management of Azure Web Apps using this module. It supports tasks such as creating, updating, and deleting web applications.

- **azure_rm_lb**: Load balancers distribute incoming network traffic across multiple resources for better availability and responsiveness. This module facilitates the management of Azure Load Balancers.

- **azure_rm_networkinterface**: This module handles network interfaces in Azure, which enable network connectivity for virtual machines. It supports tasks such as creating, updating, and deleting network interfaces.

- **azure_rm_cosmosdbaccount**: Azure Cosmos DB is a globally distributed, multi-model database service. This module helps manage Cosmos DB accounts, including creation, updates, and deletions.

- **azure.azcollection.azure_rm_aduser** module allows for modifying Azure Active Directory users, rebranded as Microsoft Entra ID, while **azure. azcollection.azure_rm_adgroup** module enables the management of Azure Active Directory groups.

These modules are just a subset of the offerings within the **azure.azcollection** collection. They demonstrate the versatility and capability of Ansible when it comes to provisioning and managing a wide range of Azure resources, from virtual machines and networks to databases and security groups. Utilizing these modules can greatly enhance our automation workflows in Azure environments.

Info modules

In the same way as Amazon Web Services, Microsoft Azure has some info modules to search for resources, as shown in *Figure 8.3*.

Module	Description
azure.azcollection.azure_rm_ resourcegroup_info	Azure resource groups: names, locations, and tags
azure.azcollection.azure_rm_ virtualmachine_info	Azure virtual machines: name, location, size, and configuration
azure.azcollection.azure_rm_ virtualnetwork_info	Azure virtual networks: Virtual network names, addresses, subnets, and associated resources
azure.azcollection.azure_rm_ storageaccount_info	Azure Storage: names, types, and resource group associations

Module	Description
`azure.azcollection.azure_rm_securitygroup_info`	Azure Network Security Groups (NSGs): Names, rules, and associations.
`azure.azcollection.azure_rm_keyvault_info`	Azure Key Vault instances
`azure.azcollection.azure_rm_dnsrecordset_info`	Azure DNS record: Names, types, and associated IP addresses
`azure.azcollection.azure_rm_sqlserver_info`	Azure SQL Server instances: Server names, versions, and firewall rules.
`azure.azcollection.azure_rm_webapp_info`	Azure Web Apps: Names, resource group associations, and configurations
`azure.azcollection.azure_rm_lb_info`	Azure Load Balancers: Names, frontend IP configurations, and backend pools
`azure.azcollection.azure_rm_networkinterface_info`	**Azure Network Interfaces** (**NIC**) names, IP configurations, and associated resources
`azure.azcollection.azure_rm_cosmosdbaccount_info`	Azure Cosmos DB: Names, database types, and consistency policies

Table 8.3: *Ansible Key Info Modules for Microsoft Azure*

Dynamic inventory

We can populate an Azure dynamic inventory in the same way that we configured an AWS. After creating a new inventory we can select the **Microsoft Azure Resource Manager** from the new source window as shown in *Figure 8.6*:

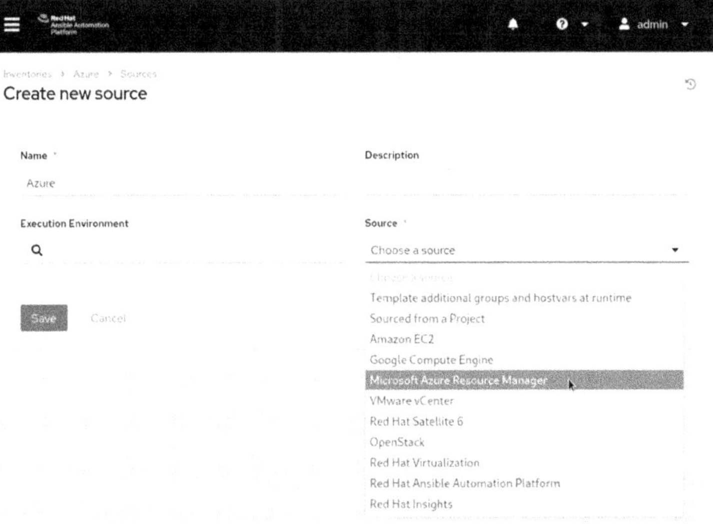

Figure 8.7: *Azure source*

After selecting **Amazon EC2** as the source, the **Create Source** window expands, revealing additional fields that need to be filled out as shown in *Figure 8.7*. The fields reflects the same as for Amazon Web Services. Please refer to the following figure:

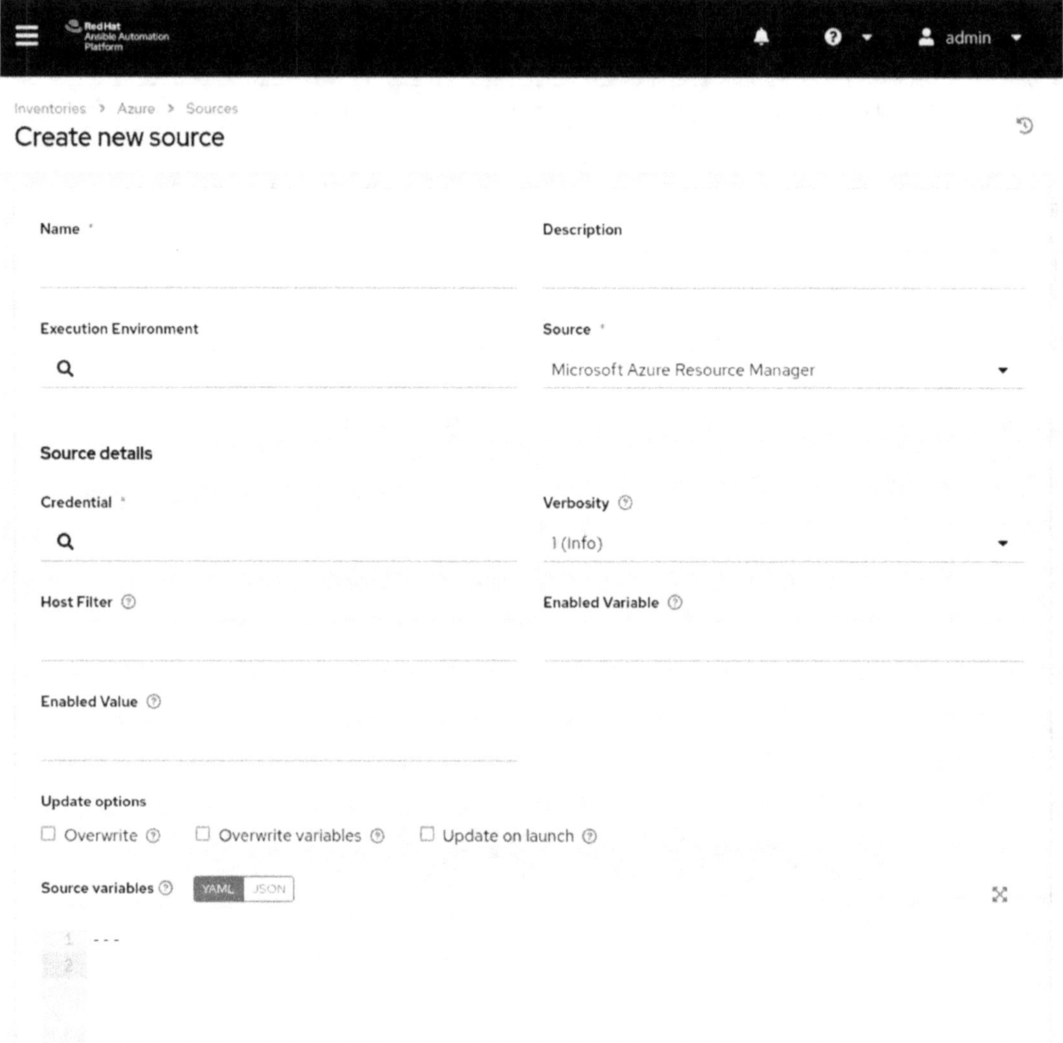

Figure 8.8: Azure source details

Google Cloud Platform

The **Google.Cloud** Ansible collection consists of a set of modules designed to interact with various **Google Cloud Platform** (**GCP**) services and resources. These modules enable users to automate tasks related to provisioning, configuration, and management of GCP resources through Ansible:

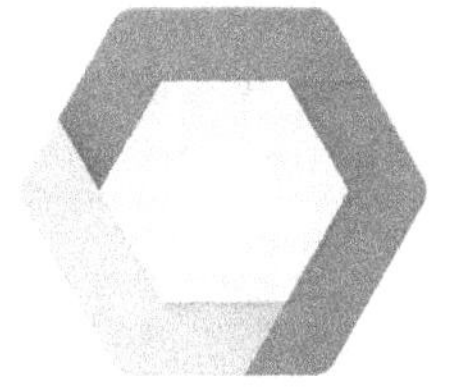

Google Cloud Platform

Figure 8.9: The Google Cloud Platform (GCP) logo

Ansible resources

The **Google.Cloud** Ansible collection also includes a set of info modules designed to gather information about various resources within the **Google Cloud Platform** (**GCP**). These modules allow users to retrieve metadata, status, and configuration details without changing the actual resources. These info modules provide valuable insights into GCP components like instances, networks, storage, and more, enabling administrators to make informed decisions and efficiently manage their Google Cloud infrastructure through Ansible automation.

Here are some of the top modules within the **google.cloud** collection:

- **gcp_compute_instance**: This module allows us to manage Google Compute Engine instances, including tasks such as creating, updating, starting, stopping, and deleting virtual machine instances.

- **gcp_compute_disk**: Automate the management of Google Compute Engine disks using this module. It supports actions such as creating, resizing, and deleting persistent disks.

- **gcp_compute_network**: With this module, we can manage Google Compute Engine networks. It facilitates tasks like creating and deleting networks, subnets, and firewall rules.

- **gcp_compute_address**: Automate the allocation and management of Google Compute Engine IP addresses using this module. It supports both regional and global IP addresses.

- **gcp_storage_bucket**: This module enables the management of Google Cloud Storage buckets. It allows us to create, update, and delete storage buckets to store and manage data.

- **gcp_pubsub_topic**: Google Cloud Pub/Sub is a messaging service for event-driven systems. This module lets us manage Pub/Sub topics, which are channels through which messages are published.

- **`gcp_sql_instance`**: Automate the provisioning and management of Google Cloud SQL database instances using this module. It supports tasks like creating, updating, and deleting database instances.

- **`gcp_bigquery_table`**: Google BigQuery is a fully managed data warehouse service. This module enables the management of BigQuery tables, including schema changes and deletions.

- **`gcp_iam_member`**: **Identity and Access Management (IAM)** is crucial for controlling access to GCP resources. This module allows us to manage IAM members and roles within projects.

- **`gcp_dataproc_cluster`**: Google Cloud Dataproc is a managed Spark and Hadoop service. This module automates the creation, management, and deletion of Dataproc clusters.

- **`gcp_logging_metric`**: Google Cloud Logging provides insights into application and system behavior. This module manages logging metrics that help monitor resource usage and performance.

- **`gcp_container_cluster`**: With this module, we can automate the management of **Google Kubernetes Engine (GKE)** clusters. It supports creating, updating, and deleting GKE clusters.

These modules exemplify the capabilities of "`Google.Cloud`" Ansible collection when it comes to interacting with various GCP services and resources. From managing virtual machines and databases to configuring network settings and access controls, Ansible provides a powerful toolset for automating GCP workflows. Utilizing these modules can significantly enhance our ability to deploy, manage, and scale applications and infrastructure on the Google Cloud Platform.

Google Cloud Ops Agent

Automating the deployment and configuration of software agents across a fleet of **Virtual Machines (VMs)** is crucial for efficient management and observability. We can streamline the process of deploying and configuring the Google Cloud Ops Agent using Ansible. The Ops Agent is the primary agent for collecting telemetry from our Google Compute Engine instances. Metrics collected include CPU, memory, storage, IIS, network interface, GPU, MSSQL, pagefile, swap, processes, and agent self-metrics. By automating these tasks, IT teams can ensure the consistent and reliable collection of telemetry data from VMs. The provided **`gpc_ops_deploy.yml`** playbook exemplifies the process of deploying and configuring the Google Cloud Ops Agent on multiple VMs using Ansible:

```
---

- name: Deploy Google Cloud Ops Agent
  hosts: all
  become: true
```

```yaml
roles:
  - role: googlecloudplatform.google_cloud_ops_agents
    vars:
      agent_type: ops-agent
      version: 1.*.*
      main_config_file: gpc_ops_agent.yaml
    notify:
      - Restart Ops Agent
tasks:
  - name: Install Nginx
    ansible.builtin.package:
      name: nginx
      state: present
  - name: Customize Nginx for telemetry
    ansible.builtin.template:
      src: ansible_templates/status.conf
      dest: /etc/nginx/conf.d/status.conf
    notify:
      - Restart Nginx
  - name: Start nginx
    ansible.builtin.service:
      name: nginx
      state: started
      enabled: yes
  - name: Start Ops Agent
    ansible.builtin.service:
      name: google-cloud-ops-agent
      state: started
      enabled: yes
handlers:
  - name: Restart Nginx
    ansible.builtin.service:
      name: nginx
      state: restarted
      enabled: yes
  - name: Restart Ops Agent
    ansible.builtin.service:
```

```
      name: google-cloud-ops-agent
      state: restarted
      enabled: yes
```

The following **gcp_ops_agent.yaml** customize the Ops Agent to collect metrics and logs from Nginx:

```
logging:
  receivers:
    nginx_default_access:
      type: nginx_access
    nginx_default_error:
      type: nginx_error
  service:
    pipelines:
      nginx:
        receivers:
          - nginx_default_access
          - nginx_default_error
metrics:
  receivers:
    nginx_metrics:
      type: nginx
      stub_status_url: http://127.0.0.1:80/status
      collection_interval: 60s
  service:
    pipelines:
      nginx_pipeline:
        receivers:
          - nginx_metrics
```

The **status.conf** template under the **templates** folder looks like this:

```
location /nginx_status {
    stub_status;
    allow 127.0.0.1;
    deny all;
  }
```

Let us break down the playbook step by step.

1. **Deploying the Ops Agent role**: The playbook specifies the role **googlecloudplatform.google_cloud_ops_agents** responsible for deploying the Ops Agent. It sets variables such as the agent type, version, and main configuration file (**gpc_ops_agent.yaml**). This section ensures the correct agent version and configuration are applied.

2. **Installing Nginx**: Ansible automates the installation of the Nginx web server on target hosts. The **ansible.builtin.package** module installs the Nginx package, ensuring its presence for further configuration.

3. **Customizing Nginx configuration**: In this step, Ansible utilizes the **ansible. builtin.template** module to customize the Nginx configuration for telemetry purposes. A custom configuration file **status.conf** is copied to the appropriate location (**/etc/nginx/conf.d/**) on the target hosts.

4. **Starting Nginx and Ops Agent**: The playbook then initiates Nginx and the Google Cloud Ops Agent on the target VMs. It uses the **ansible.builtin.service** module to start these services and enables them for automatic start up.

5. **Handling restarts**: Ansible employs handlers to restart both Nginx and the Ops Agent to ensure changes take effect. Handlers are executed only when necessary, optimizing efficiency.

The result of the GCP resource monitor is shown in *Figure 8.8*:

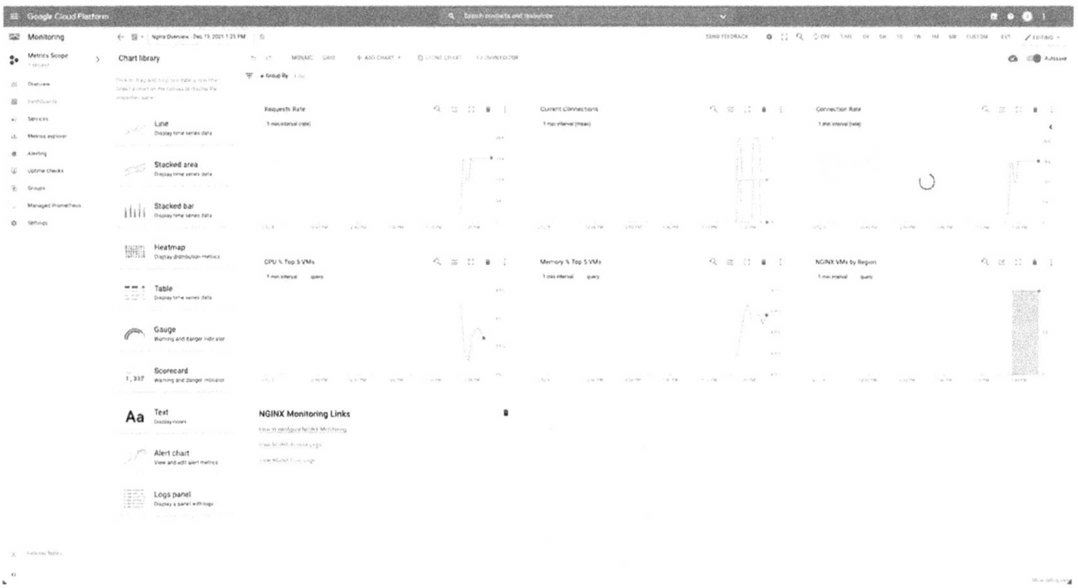

Figure 8.10: Google Cloud Ops Agent

Automating the deployment and configuration of the Google Cloud Ops Agent using Ansible simplifies the management of telemetry data collection on VMs. By following the provided playbook, IT teams can achieve consistent results across their infrastructure, reducing manual efforts and ensuring reliable monitoring and troubleshooting capabilities. This approach enhances operational efficiency and supports the seamless management of virtualized environments in the Google Cloud ecosystem.

Dynamic inventory

We can populate a Google Cloud dynamic inventory like we configured an AWS and Azure. After creating a new inventory, we can select the **Microsoft Azure Resource Manager** from the new source window, as shown in *Figure 8.9*:

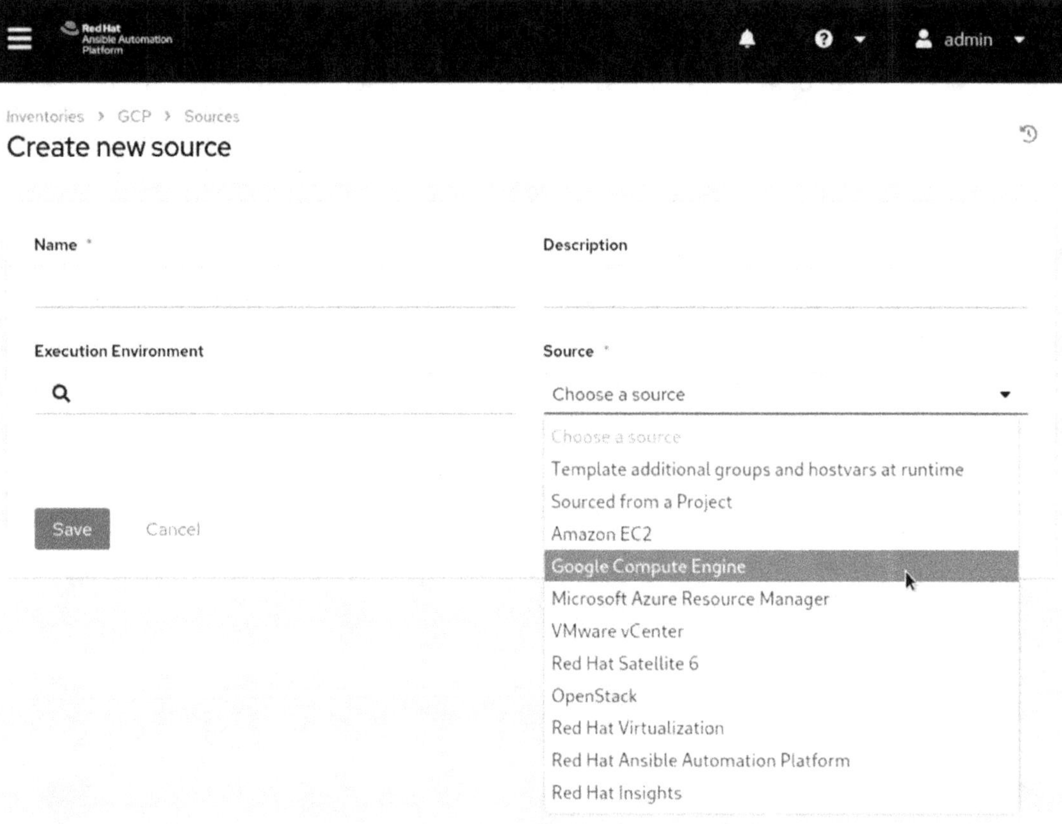

Figure 8.11: GCP source

After selecting **Google Compute Engine** as the source, the **Create Source** window expands, revealing additional fields that need to be filled out as shown in *Figure 8.10*. The fields reflects the same as for Amazon Web Services or Azure:

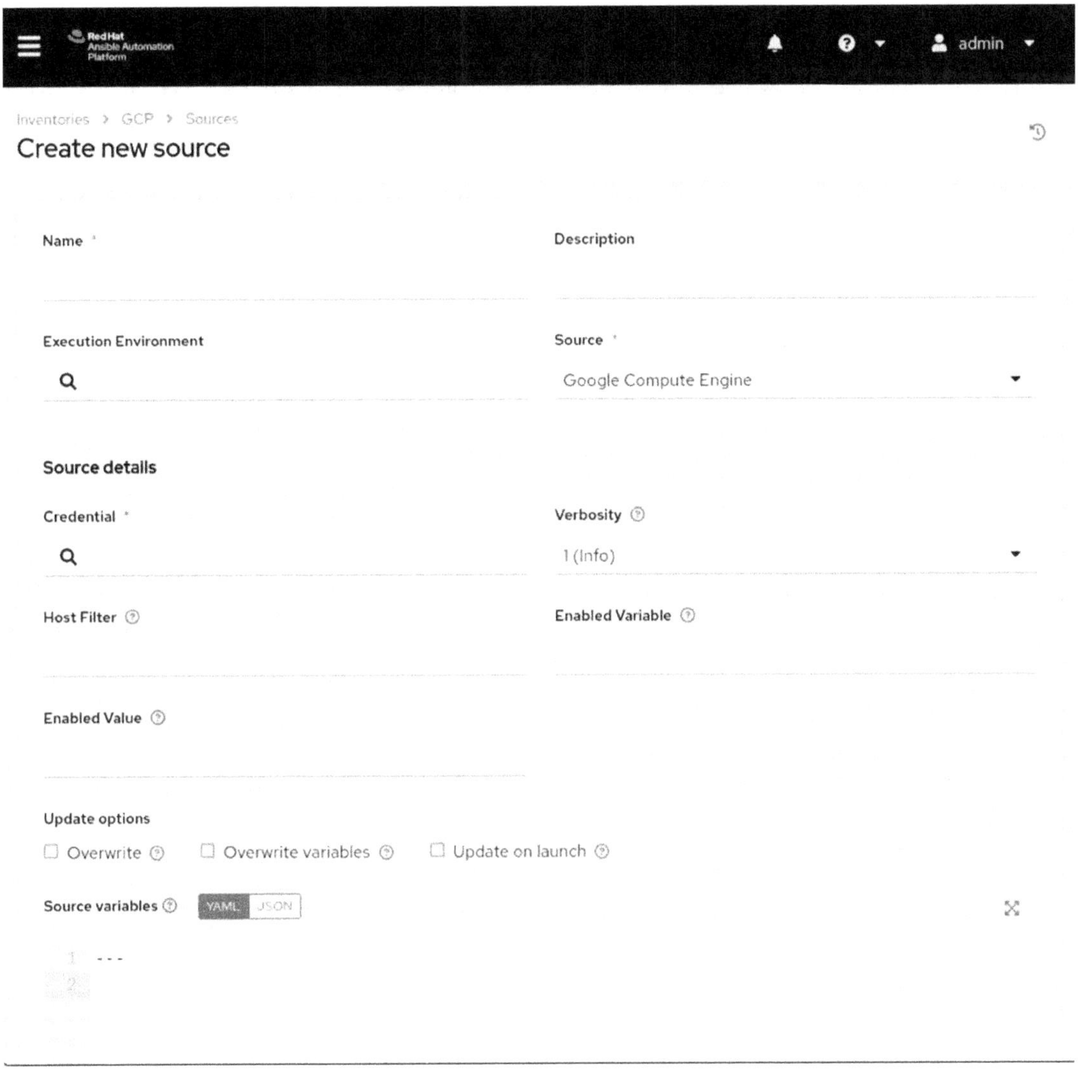

Figure 8.12: GCP source details

Hybrid cloud

A hybrid cloud could be implemented using on-premise and cloud computing resources to match the demand of our cloud-native applications. We can decide, for example, to take advantage of the low latency of global-distributed cloud infrastructure and the security of a tiered network in the on-premise one. Nutanix and AgnosticD are useful platform tools to set up combined on-premises and cloud infrastructure environments, allowing seamless integration between private and public clouds, enabling workload portability, and ensuring compatibility across diverse cloud environments.

Nutanix

Nutanix is a company that specializes in **hyper-converged infrastructure** (HCI) solutions for enterprise data centers and cloud environments:

Figure 8.13: The Nutanix logo

The core idea behind Nutanix's technology is to simplify and streamline data center infrastructure by consolidating compute, storage, and networking components into a single, integrated solution. This approach is designed to enhance scalability, ease of management, and overall efficiency in data center operations.

Key features and concepts associated with Nutanix include:

1. **Hyperconverged Infrastructure (HCI)**: Nutanix's primary offering is its HCI platform. HCI combines computing, storage, and networking resources into a single appliance or software-defined solution. This consolidation eliminates the need for separate silos of infrastructure components, making it easier to manage and scale the data center.

2. **Virtualization:** Nutanix supports various virtualization technologies, including VMware vSphere, Microsoft Hyper-V, and its own built-in hypervisor called AHV (Acropolis Hypervisor). This allows businesses to run virtualized workloads on the Nutanix platform.

3. **Scalability**: Nutanix solutions are designed to be easily scalable. Organizations can start with a small cluster of nodes and expand as their needs grow. New nodes can be added to the cluster seamlessly without disrupting ongoing operations.

4. **Software-defined storage**: Nutanix's storage architecture is based on a distributed file system that spans across all nodes in the cluster. This provides a unified storage pool and eliminates the need for external storage arrays. The distributed nature of the storage system contributes to high availability and data redundancy.

5. **Management and automation**: Nutanix provides a centralized management interface, often referred to as Prism, that allows administrators to monitor and manage the entire HCI infrastructure. Prism offers features for performance monitoring, capacity planning, and configuration management. It also supports automation and orchestration tasks.

6. **Data protection and disaster recovery**: Nutanix offers data protection features like snapshots, replication, and backup solutions. These tools help safeguard data and provide options for disaster recovery strategies.

7. **Multi-Cloud and hybrid cloud**: Nutanix provides solutions for managing workloads across various cloud environments, including private, public, and

hybrid clouds. This allows organizations to deploy and manage applications seamlessly across different cloud platforms.

8. **Enterprise applications**: Nutanix is known for its support of running enterprise applications, including databases, **virtual desktop infrastructure** (**VDI**), and various line-of-business applications. The goal is to provide consistent performance and reliability for critical workloads.

Overall, Nutanix is the solution for the hyper-converged infrastructure that simplifies IT infrastructure management, reduces operational complexity, and improves the agility of data center operations. The company has gained popularity in enterprise IT circles for its innovative approach to modernizing data center architecture.

AgnosticD

The AgnosticD software, also known as Ansible Agnostic Deployer or AAD, is a fully automated deployer designed for building and deploying various types of environments, from basic infrastructure setups to fully configured application environments. It is capable of deploying on public cloud providers and OpenShift clusters. While it is not exclusively an OpenShift deployer, it is often used to deploy OpenShift and OpenShift-related workloads. It enables efficient and reproducible deployments through its automation capabilities. Please refer to the following figure:

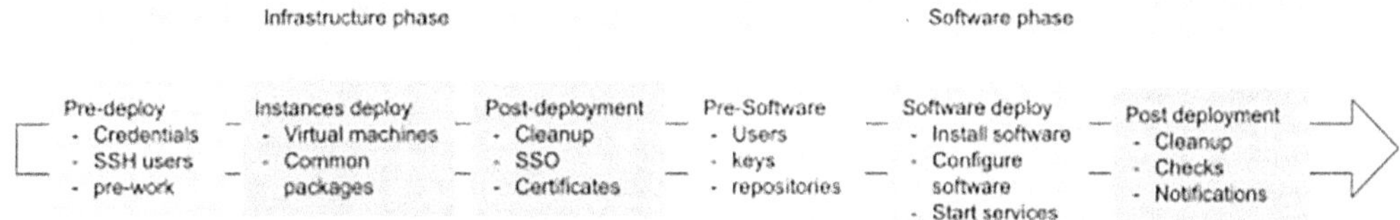

Figure 8.14: AgnosticD deployment phases

Here is an overview of key points about AgnosticD:

1. **Deployment flexibility**: AgnosticD is versatile and can deploy diverse types of environments, not just OpenShift-related ones. It can handle everything from simple node deployments to complex multi-tier application setups.

2. **Supported environments**: It supports deployment on public cloud providers like AWS, Azure, OpenStack, and so on., and on OpenShift clusters.

3. **Phases of deployment**: AgnosticD follows a two-phase deployment process. In the first phase, it deploys infrastructure components, and in the second phase, it configures and deploys applications on top of the infrastructure.

4. **Ansible roles**: For OpenShift workloads, AgnosticD uses Ansible roles to interact with existing OpenShift clusters. These roles are designed to deploy and configure various aspects of the application environment.

5. **Configurations**: AgnosticD uses configuration files that define the desired deployment. These configuration files include deployment playbooks, supporting files, and any necessary cloud provider tools. These configurations can be designed for specific use cases and easily abstracted for deployment across different cloud environments.

6. **Reproducibility**: AgnosticD emphasizes reproducibility by enabling consistent deployment of environments across different clouds and clusters.

7. **Community contribution**: AgnosticD offers an extensive set of documentation and guides for contributors. This includes guides on creating OpenShift workloads, creating configurations, and extending the capabilities of AgnosticD.

8. **Use cases**: AgnosticD is suitable for various use cases, including deploying simple node setups, multi-tier applications, OpenShift clusters, and other application workloads on various cloud platforms.

9. **Automation**: AgnosticD leverages the power of Ansible for automation, allowing users to define deployment steps and configurations as code.

10. **Open Source**: AgnosticD is open source and community-driven, meaning that it benefits from contributions and improvements from a community of users and developers.

Overall, AgnosticD is a tool designed to simplify and automate the deployment of diverse environments using Ansible. It is particularly useful for those looking to deploy on various cloud providers and OpenShift clusters while maintaining a high degree of automation and reproducibility.

Kubernetes

Kubernetes is an open-source container orchestration platform that automates the deployment, scaling, and management of containerized applications. Kubernetes architecture consists of control plane components for management and worker nodes for running containers; the control plane includes API server, etcd, controller manager, and scheduler, while worker nodes host containers, kubelet, and container runtime, collectively enabling containerized application deployment, scaling, and management:

Figure 8.15: The Kubernetes logo

Managing and automating Kubernetes clusters with Ansible involves using the Ansible automation capabilities to streamline the deployment, configuration, and management of Kubernetes resources. Here is how to do it:

1. **Preliminary checks**: Ensure we can access the Kubernetes clusters we want to manage.

2. **Inventory configuration**: Define our Kubernetes cluster nodes in the Ansible inventory using a dynamic inventory script or manually specifying host details.

3. **Playbook creation**: Write Ansible playbooks to define the desired state of our Kubernetes resources. Use the Ansible Kubernetes collection of modules to interact with Kubernetes API to create, modify, or delete resources such as pods, services, deployments, and namespaces.

4. **Authentication**: Configure authentication methods to access our Kubernetes clusters. This may involve using **kubeconfig** command line utility, files, or tokens.

5. **Secrets management**: Utilize Ansible Vault or other secrets management tools to store sensitive information like API tokens or credentials securely.

6. **Variables and templates**: Utilize variables and templates in our playbooks to make them reusable and adaptable across different environments.

7. **Playbook execution**: Run our Ansible playbooks to apply changes to our Kubernetes clusters. Ansible is going to ensure the current state matches the desired state defined in our playbooks.

8. **Automation**: Set up scheduled tasks or trigger playbooks based on events to automate routine tasks like scaling, updates, or backups.

9. **Error handling and idempotence**: Design our playbooks to be idempotent, ensuring they can be safely run multiple times without unintended side effects. Implement error handling and recovery mechanisms in our playbooks to handle potential issues.

10. **Testing and validation**: Test our Ansible resources in a controlled environment before changing production clusters. Use Ansible's dry-run mode to preview changes without making actual modifications.

11. **Monitoring and logging**: Integrate monitoring and logging tools to track the status and performance of our Kubernetes clusters.

12. **Version control**: Store our playbooks in version control systems like Git to track changes and collaborate with team members.

13. **Documentation**: Maintain clear and concise documentation for our playbooks, including explanations of their purpose and usage.

By following these steps, we can effectively manage and automate our Kubernetes clusters using Ansible, ensuring consistency and efficiency and reducing manual intervention in cluster management tasks. The module **kubernetes.core.k8s_info**.

Kubernetes, with its unparalleled orchestration capabilities, aligns with DevOps objectives of scalability and resilience. Ansible, a masterful automation tool, amplifies Kubernetes' efficiency by maintaining the desired state of clusters. This powerful synergy empowers organizations to embrace DevOps practices confidently and achieve operational excellence in managing containerized applications.

Scale containerized applications

Providing scalability failover for containers or hosts is the key reason for adopting Kubernetes. As applications become more complex and user demands increase, the need for scalable, resilient, and efficiently managed deployments has become paramount. DevOps teams ensure applications can handle varying loads and recover from failures seamlessly. This article explores how Kubernetes and Ansible address these challenges by providing container orchestration and streamlined management, allowing applications to thrive in dynamic environments. In the world of containers, achieving scalability and resilience requires managing multiple containers distributed across various physical or virtual machines while load balancing between them. While Docker or Podman can achieve this, implementing manually can quickly become complex and overwhelming.

Kubernetes emerges as a powerful solution to container orchestration challenges. Designed to distribute, monitor, and update containers across multiple worker nodes, Kubernetes creates a unified cluster that efficiently manages containerized applications. This level of orchestration ensures applications can scale up or down as needed, even in the face of hardware or software failures.

Kubernetes operates on a declarative model, where users specify desired container states, quantity, and interconnections. Ansible's strengths align seamlessly with this approach. It ensures that the configuration specified for a Kubernetes cluster is maintained accurately.

The Kubernetes API server is central to managing a Kubernetes cluster. It enables querying the current configuration creating, updating, and deleting cluster resources. While **kubectl** is the command-line tool to interact with the cluster, Ansible can also communicate with the API server, streamlining management tasks.

The **kubernetes.core** Ansible collection offers modules to interact with Kubernetes, including the pivotal "**k8s**" module. This module applies resources to the cluster, accommodating both creation and updates. Notably, it supports different methods of defining resources, such as inline definitions, separate files, and Jinja2 templates.

Ansible extends its capabilities to Kubernetes with modules like **k8s_cp**, facilitating file copying to and from containers, and **k8s_log**, fetching container logs. Management tasks like fetching cluster info and node draining also find their corresponding Ansible modules. Furthermore, Ansible's integration with Helm, the Kubernetes package manager, allows managing containerized applications through Helm charts.

While various tools like Kustomize and Helm exist for Kubernetes resource management, Ansible offers a cohesive approach, especially for teams already invested in Ansible for automation. By utilizing Ansible's capabilities, DevOps teams can streamline Kubernetes deployments and maintain consistency and reliability across their entire infrastructure. In the pursuit of scalable and resilient application deployments, the ability to deploy, manage, and configure cloud-native applications is crucial for enabling world-scale scalability and beginning the business of tomorrow.

Key learning

Cloud computing is a powerful resource for scaling up our environment and delivering cloud-native applications to our target audience. Take advantage of Amazon Web Services, Microsoft Azure, and Google Cloud Platform to create an automatic environment to enable a hybrid cloud strategy in our organization.

Points to remember

- We can automate any workload on Amazon Web Services using the `amazon.aws` and `community.aws` Ansible collections.

- Workload on Microsoft Azure can be automated using the `azure.azcollection` collection.

- The `Google.Cloud` Ansible collection automates the management of resources in the **Google Cloud Platform** (**GCP**).

- Each collection for cloud providers offers info modules to create dynamic reporting of the resources.

- We can implement a hybrid cloud strategy using Nutanix and AgnosticD services and tools.

Multiple choice questions

1. **What are the Ansible collection(s) for Amazon Web Services?**

    a. amazon.aws

    b. community.aws

    c. amazon.aws and community.aws

    d. amazon.amazon

2. **What type of Ansible modules can we use to create dynamic reports?**

    a. Info modules

    b. Lookup plugin

    c. Filters

    d. Dynamic inventory

3. **What is the best technology to orchestrate containers between different Cloud providers?**

    a. Docker

    b. Kubernetes

    c. Podman

    d. Red Hat Enterprise Linux

4. **What is the best way to monitor resource usage in the Google Cloud Platform?**

    a. CloudWatch

    b. Azure Monitor

    c. Prometheus

    d. Cloud Ops Agent

Answer

1. c

2. a

3. b

4. d

Questions

1. What are the major public cloud providers?

2. What are the most used Ansible collections to manage cloud resources?

3. How can we create dynamic documentation for cloud providers using Ansible?

4. How can we retrieve dynamically the allocated resources in a cloud provider?

5. What are the best tools to implement a hybrid cloud strategy in our organization?

Key terms

- **NIC**: Network Interface Card, a hardware component that enables a computer to connect to a network and communicate with other devices.

- **IAM:** Identity and Access Management, a framework used to manage and control user access to resources and services within a system or organization.

- **AWS**: Amazon Web Services is a comprehensive cloud computing platform that offers a wide range of services for computing, storage, databases, networking, analytics, machine learning, and more.

- **Azure** is a cloud computing platform by Microsoft that provides a variety of services for building, deploying, and managing applications and services through datacentres around the world.

- **GCP**: Google Cloud Platform is a suite of cloud computing services provided by Google, offering infrastructure, storage, analytics, machine learning, and more for building, deploying, and managing applications.

- **Dynamic inventory**: Using Ansible plugin we automatically gathers and updates information about our infrastructure, such as hosts and their attributes, to enable dynamic and automated configuration management.

Join our book's Discord space

Join the book's Discord Workspace for Latest updates, Offers, Tech happenings around the world, New Release and Sessions with the Authors:

https://discord.bpbonline.com

CHAPTER 9

Automate IT Processes

Introduction

Automating IT processes with Ansible is a transformative approach that empowers organizations to streamline, standardize, and accelerate a wide range of tasks, from provisioning servers to configuring network devices and orchestrating complex workflows. In this guide, we'll explore how Ansible, an open-source automation tool, can be harnessed to simplify IT operations, enhance efficiency, and ensure consistency across our IT infrastructure.

Structure

In this chapter, we will discuss the following topics:

- IT Processes
- Ansible Network
- Managing Fleets
- Monitor and Respond to Threats
- Develop Ansible Resources
- XLAB Steampunk Spotter

- Ansible-Lockdown

- Good Practices for Ansible

Objectives

This chapter provides a comprehensive overview of effectively automating IT processes using Ansible. It covers the essential concepts, best practices, and practical examples to enable organizations to achieve greater efficiency, scalability, and reliability in their IT operations.

IT Processes

Every successful organization relies on an organized IT department. A clear understanding of the IT processes by all the stakeholders enables a clear track of the ongoing priorities and faster incident response and resolution, leading to a more reliable IT infrastructure and more satisfactory efficiency of the IT operation team. Automating the most recurrent operation with Ansible enables us to manage the assets and resources in our organization more efficiently. The networking is usually underestimated but is as crucial as our compute nodes because it is heavily involved whenever we retrieve information from a data lake and process it via our cloud-native application.

Ansible Network

Network infrastructure ensures seamless communication and data exchange across organizations in today's rapidly evolving digital landscape. However, managing the intricate web of physical and virtual networking devices and their diverse configurations can take time and effort. This is where Ansible Network Automation steps in as a game-changing solution enabling **Software Defined Networks (SDN)**. In the previous chapter, we learned how to set up network resources in a public cloud provider using the Ansible collections specific to each provider.

Ansible Network Automation is a powerful and versatile automation framework designed to streamline the management and orchestration of network devices and services. Under the Ansible Network umbrella, it is possible to manage switches, routers, enterprise firewalls, load balancers, controllers, and IP address management (IPv4 and IPv6). It offers an efficient means of configuring, provisioning and monitoring an extensive array of networking components, including but not limited to the following brands and technologies: OpenvSwitch, Pureport Fabric, Cisco IOS, Dell OS9, Dell OS10, SONiC, F5 BIG-IP, Cisco NX-OS, Cisco IOS-XR, VyOS, Nvidia, Cumulus Linux, Juniper Junos, Arista EOS, SDN Controllers, Cisco ACI, A10 ACOS, Infoblox NIOS, Cisco DNA Center, Cisco NAE, and Cisco MSO, etc. Successfully managing network operations is paramount in today's interconnected world. Efficient network operations bring about several high-level benefits that contribute to the overall stability and effectiveness of an organization's IT infrastructure. Here are three key benefits:

- **Configuration Management:**

  o **Backup & Restore**: Network configurations are crucial and can be prone to errors or accidental changes. Successful network operations utilize automation to regularly back up configurations, ensuring quick recovery in case of issues or failures.

  o **Scoped Configuration Management**: Effective configuration management involves applying changes consistently and securely across the network. Scoped configuration management ensures that configuration changes are targeted and well-defined, minimizing the risk of unintended consequences.

- **Infrastructure Awareness (NetOps):**

  o **Dynamic Documentation**: Keeping track of network changes and configurations is challenging. Infrastructure awareness provided by network automation tools creates dynamic documentation that reflects the network's real-time state, helping administrators have an up-to-date view of their infrastructure.

  o **Compliance and Traceability**: Compliance with industry regulations and internal policies is essential for many highly regulator industries. Automation facilitates compliance by ensuring that configurations adhere to established standards. Additionally, it provides traceability, allowing organizations to audit and track configuration changes for accountability.

- **Network Validation:**

  o **Operational State Validation**: Successful network operations go beyond initial configuration. They continuously validate the network's operational state to ensure it meets performance, security, and reliability goals. They are automating the configuration and management of VLANs, ACLs, and SNMP services. The automation tools can run periodic checks to confirm that the network remains in a desired and stable state, introducing the source of truth concepts storing our **Infrastructure as Code (IaC)**.

  o **Rollback when Configuration Changes**: If configuration changes lead to unexpected issues or negatively impact network performance, network validation mechanisms can automatically roll back to a known good configuration, minimizing downtime and potential disruptions.

These high-level benefits highlight the critical role of network automation in ensuring that network operations are efficient, resilient, and aligned with the organization's objectives. Organizations can proactively manage their networks, reduce risks, and deliver consistent and reliable network services to support their business needs by automating configuration management, enhancing infrastructure awareness, and implementing network validation processes. With Ansible Network Automation, organizations can achieve numerous critical objectives, such as reducing operational overhead, ensuring network security and compliance, accelerating network provisioning, and enabling rapid adaptation to changing business needs. Automating routine network tasks empowers IT teams to focus on strategic initiatives, enhance network reliability, and respond promptly to network issues, ultimately driving efficiency, agility, and innovation in the ever-evolving realm of network infrastructure management. In this introduction, we will explore the key capabilities and benefits of Ansible Network Automation, shedding light on how it transforms the way organizations handle their network resources and services.

The Ansible Network meta collection is a collection of Ansible roles, modules, and plugins specifically designed for network automation tasks. In this context, "`ansible.network`" refers to the namespace or prefix used for organizing and categorizing network-related automation content within the Ansible ecosystem.

Here's a breakdown of what this statement means:

- **Ansible Network Meta Collection**: This is a collection of Ansible content focused on network automation. It includes various roles, modules, and plugins that are tailored for configuring, managing, and automating network devices and infrastructure.

- `ansible.network`: is a namespace or prefix used to categorize and organize the network-related automation content within the Ansible Network Meta Collection. It helps users easily identify and access the specific network automation modules and roles available in the collection.

For example, if we want to configure a network switch or router using Ansible, we would typically use modules and roles from the "`ansible.network`" namespace. These modules and roles are specifically designed to interact with network devices and perform tasks such as device provisioning, configuration changes, and gathering network information.

The "`ansible.network`" is a way to label and group network-focused Ansible automation content within the Ansible Network Meta Collection, making it easier for users to find and utilize these resources for network automation tasks.

Network Automation is different from server automation because module code is executed locally on the Ansible Controller node in order to connect to the Network Devices or the Network API Endpoint, resulting in a Local Execution. Whereas in the traditional Ansible server automation, the Ansible module is copied to the target node, executed, and then removed by the end of the execution. This behavior is usually called Remote Execution.

The connection between the Ansible Controller node and the final Network Device is performed via a Network Connection Plugin set via the "`ansible_connection`" variable in the Ansible Inventory. The most common connection plugins are:

- **netconf**: XML over Netconf – used to connect to the Juniper Junos.

- **network_cli**: Command line over OpenSSH used for the Cisco IOS-XE, Arista EOS

- **httpapi**: The connection is performed via the vendor API service for the Arista eAPI, Cisco NX-API.

- **ssh** : Many vendors embed a version of the OpenSSH for secure remote administration of their devices.

Each vendor has a specific Ansible collection to interact with the network device(s), as summarized in *Table 9.1*.

Vendor	Ansible Collection
Arista EOS	`arista.eos`
Cisco IOS/IOS-XE	`cisco.ios`
Cisco NX-OS	`cisco.nxos`
Cisco IOS-XR	`cisco.iosxr`
F5 BIG-IP	`f5networks.f5_bigip_bigip`
Juniper Junos	`junipsnetworks.junos`
VyOS	`vyos.vyos`
Cisco Meraki	`cisco.meraki`
Arista Validated Designs (AVD)	`arista.avd`

Table 9.1: *Most common Ansible Network Collection*

The interaction between Ansible and the Network Devices is performed, setting the Inventory and Playbook according to the resource available for our vendor. The following **cisco_inventory.ini** Ansible Inventory connects to a Cisco NXOS router using the **network_cli** Ansible connector.

```
[cisco]
rtr1 ansible_host=1.2.3.4 private_ip=10.0.0.250
[cisco:vars]
ansible_user=devops
ansible_network_os=ios
ansible_connection=network_cli
```

Once successfully connected using the Ansible Inventory, we can execute our **cisco_vlan.yml** Ansible Playbook to create and verify the VLAN id **10** with the label **WEB** is present in our IT infrastructure. We can easily customize the VLAN ID and name, setting the **vlan_id** and **vlan_name** variables in the code or via a Job Template Survey.

```
---
- name: Cisco Configure VLAN
  hosts: cisco
  gather_facts: false
  vars:
    vlan_id: 10
    vlan_name: WEB
  tasks:
    - name: Ensure VLANs is present
      cisco.nxos.vlans:
        config:
        - vlan_id: "{{ vlan_id }}"
          name: "{{ vlan_name }}"
```

We can execute the **cisco_vlan.yml** Ansible Playbook with the **cisco_inventory. ini**, creating a Job Template referencing the Ansible Inventory via the Ansible Controller Dashboard.

ansible-navigator

A content creator can locally test the execution of the Playbook using the following **ansible-navigator** command:

ansible-navigator run cisco_vlan.yml --mode stdout

The **ansible-navigator** command simplifies the development when dealing with Ansible collections, inventories, and execution environment via a **text-based user interface (TUI)** or **command line (CLI)** interface. The TUI interface is the default when the omit the "**--mode**" or "**-m**" argument is not specified.

Note: that we can enable the debug execution in the same way as the traditional ansible-playbook command. We can specify and increase the level of verbosity by adding the "v" parameters from "-v" to the most verbose "-vvvv".

In the same way the following **cisco_snmp.yml** Ansible Playbook sets or verifies some specific configuration in a Cisco Device(s):

```
---
- name: Cisco Configuration
  hosts: cisco
  gather_facts: false
  vars:
    snmp_config:
```

```
      - snmp-server community ansible-public RO
      - snmp-server community ansible-private RW
  tasks:
    - name: Cisco Configuration present
      cisco.ios.config:
        lines: "{{ snmp_config }}"
```

network.base

The **network.base** Collection is an essential component of Ansible's ecosystem, tailored specifically for network automation tasks. It provides a robust foundation for network engineers and administrators to automate and manage network devices across various vendors. This collection acts as a bridge between the network devices and Ansible, simplifying the process of automating network configurations. Let's delve deeper into the key features and capabilities that make the **network.base** Collection a game-changer in the realm of network automation:

- **Resource Manager:** The heart of the **network.base** Collection is the Resource Manager, a platform-agnostic entry point for managing network resources. It offers a structured and efficient approach to device configuration management, making it easier to maintain and update configurations across diverse network devices. Resource Manager serves as a critical component for all other Ansible validated content in the network automation domain.

- **Build Brownfield Inventory** The `persist` action within the `network.base` Collection allows users to obtain facts about network resources and store them as inventory **host_vars**. This dynamic inventory acts as a single source of truth for network configurations, ensuring that engineers have accurate and up-to-date information about the network's state. In today's dynamic network environments, having a reliable source of inventory data is invaluable.

- **Supported Resource Query** Network administrators often work with a wide range of network devices from different vendors. The list action in the **network. base** collection simplifies the process of identifying which resource modules are supported for a specific network operating system. This capability streamlines the automation workflow, ensuring that the right modules are used for each device.

- **Display Structured Configuration** The `gather` action in the collection enables users to collect and display facts for specified network resources. This feature is essential for network troubleshooting, auditing, and documentation. It provides a structured view of the network's configuration, making it easier to analyze and understand.

- **Deploy Changes** The `deploy` action is a powerful tool for making configuration changes to network devices. It allows users to apply **host_vars** facts changes to the devices efficiently. Network administrators can use this action to ensure that configuration changes are consistent across the network, reducing the risk of errors and ensuring compliance with network policies.

To illustrate the practical use of the **network.base** Collection, let's consider a few scenarios:

Building Ansible Inventory

Using the `persist` action, we can gather configuration facts for a specific resource and create a dynamic inventory. This inventory serves as a reliable source of information for other automation tasks.

Suppose we start with the following Cisco IOS configuration:

```
R1#show ip interface br | ex una
Interface              IP-Address        OK? Method Status                    Protocol
GigabitEthernet0/0     10.254.254.220 YES DHCP    up                            up
GigabitEthernet0/1     1.0.1.1           YES manual administratively down down
```

The full Ansible Playbook **ios_persist.yml** look like the following:

```
---
- name: Building Ansible Network Inventory
  hosts: ios
  gather_facts: false
  tasks:
    - name: Network Resource Manager
      ansible.builtin.include_role:
        name: resource_manager
      vars:
        action: persist
        resources:
          - 'interfaces'
          - 'l3_interfaces'
```

We can execute our playbook via **ansible-navigator**:

```
ansible-navigator run ios_persist.yml
```

The execution produces the following directories and files on the file system:

```
├── inventory
│   ├── host_vars
│   │   └── 10.254.254.220
│   │       ├── interfaces.yaml
│   │       ├── 13_interfaces.yaml
```

The content of the generated file **inventory/host_vars/10.254.254.220/13_interfaces.yaml**

13_interfaces match the output of the initial Cisco IOS configuration:

```
-   ipv4:
    -   dhcp:
            enable: true
    name: GigabitEthernet0/0
-   ipv4:
    -   address: 1.0.1.1/29
    name: GigabitEthernet0/1
-   name: GigabitEthernet0/2
-   name: GigabitEthernet0/3
```

Querying Supported Resource Modules

The `list` action simplifies the process of identifying which resource modules are supported for a given network operating system. This information is crucial when designing automation workflows.

```
---
-   name: Listing Ansible Network Inventory
    hosts: ios
    gather_facts: false
    tasks:
      - name: Network Resource Manager
        ansible.builtin.include_role:
          name: resource_manager
        vars:
          action: list
```

We can execute our playbook via **ansible-navigator** in the command line or via Ansible Controller Job Template:

```
ansible-navigator run ios_list.yml
```

Produce the following output:

```
ok: [10.254.254.220] => {
    "msg": {
        "ansible_connection": "ansible.netcommon.network_cli",
        "ansible_network_os": "cisco.ios.ios",
        "changed": false,
        "failed": false,
        "modules": [
            "acl_interfaces",
            "acls",
            "bgp_address_family",
            "bgp_global",
            "hostname",
            "interfaces",
            "l2_interfaces",
            "l3_interfaces",
```

Deploying Configuration Changes

The `deploy` action enables network engineers to apply configuration changes consistently across network devices. This ensures that network configurations remain up-to-date and compliant with organizational standards.

Let's begin with our Ansible Brownfield Inventory file **inventory/host_vars/10.254.254.220/l3_interfaces.yaml**

l3_interfaces with the following configuration:

```
-   ipv4:
    -   dhcp:
            enable: true
    name: GigabitEthernet0/0
-   ipv4:
    -   address: 1.0.1.1/29
    name: GigabitEthernet0/1
-   name: GigabitEthernet0/2
-   name: GigabitEthernet0/3
```

Now that we have our Ansible inventory, we can use the **deploy** action as shown below:

```
---
- name: Deploy Ansible Network
  hosts: ios
  gather_facts: false
  tasks:
    - name: Deploy Network Resource Manager
      ansible.builtin.include_role:
        name: resource_manager
      vars:
        action: deploy
        resources:
          - 'interfaces'
          - 'l2_interfaces'
          - 'l3_interfaces'
          - 'ospfv2'
          - 'ospfv3'
          - 'ospf_interfaces'
```

We can execute our playbook via **ansible-navigator** in the command line or via Ansible Controller Job Template:

ansible-navigator run ios_deploy.yml

We can confirm the application of our Ansible Brownfield Inventory directly on the network appliance via the Cisco IOS terminal:

```
R1#show ip interface br | ex una
Interface              IP-Address      OK? Method Status                    Protocol
GigabitEthernet0/0     10.254.254.220 YES DHCP    up                        up
GigabitEthernet0/1     1.0.1.1         YES manual administratively down down
```

network.interfaces

The **network.interfaces** Ansible collection is a collection of Ansible roles and modules designed for managing network interfaces on networking devices. It is part of Ansible's validated content ecosystem, which provides best practices and guidance for performing operational tasks in the network automation domain. This collection is particularly useful for network engineers and administrators who want to automate tasks related to network interfaces on various networking devices.

Here are some key features and capabilities of the **network.interfaces** Ansible collection:

- **Build Brownfield Inventory (persist operation)**: The persist operation allows users to collect data about network interfaces and store it as host variables (YAML format). This dynamic inventory can serve as a single source of truth for network operations.

- **Display Structured Configuration (gather operation)**: The gather operation enables users to retrieve and display facts about network interfaces in a structured format, making it easier to work with and analyze the data.

- **Deploy Changes (deploy operation)**: The deploy operation allows users to apply changes to network interface configurations based on the facts stored in host variables. It can push configuration changes to network devices.

- **Detect Network Configuration Drift (detect operation)**: The detect operation helps users identify configuration drift in network interfaces. It compares the current configuration with the stored facts and reports any discrepancies.

- **Remediate Network Configuration Drift (remediate operation)**: The remediate operation is used to rectify configuration drift in network interfaces. It overrides the running configuration with the stored facts to align it with the intended state.

- **Health Checks (health_check operation)**: The **health_check** operation allows users to perform health checks on network interfaces. It provides information about interfaces' administrative and operational status and offers various checks, such as ensuring all interfaces are operational or a minimum number of interfaces are administratively up.

The collection is designed to be platform-agnostic, meaning it can be used with different network platforms, making it versatile for managing network interfaces across various devices.

Here's a brief overview of how we can use some of these operations:

- **Persist Operation**: This operation collects data about network interfaces and stores it as host variables. This data can be stored locally or published to remote repositories for further use in deployment, remediation, or drift detection tasks.

- **Deploy Operation**: We can use the deploy operation to apply changes to network interfaces by updating the host variable facts. This operation can help maintain the desired state of interfaces.

- **Gather Operation**: The gather operation is useful for retrieving and displaying structured information about network interfaces. It provides detailed facts that can be used for analysis and reporting.

- **Detect Operation**: The detect operation is used to identify configuration drift in network interfaces. It checks for discrepancies between the stored facts and the current device configuration.

- **Remediate Operation**: The remediate operation is employed to rectify configuration drift. It overrides the running configuration with the stored facts to ensure consistency.

- **Health Check Operation**: The `health_check` operation lets us perform health checks on network interfaces. We can use various checks to verify the status of interfaces, and the results can be detailed to provide insights into interface health.

Overall, the `network.interfaces` Ansible collection streamlines the management of network interfaces, making it easier to automate tasks, maintain configuration consistency, and monitor interface health across a diverse range of networking devices.

network.ospf

The "`network.ospf`" Ansible collection is a set of pre-built Ansible roles and modules designed to help automate the management of **Open Shortest Path First** (**OSPF**) routing protocols in a network infrastructure. OSPF is a widely used dynamic routing protocol that helps routers and network devices communicate and determine the best paths for data traffic within a network. This collection provides a structured and automated way to configure, monitor, and maintain OSPF configurations across various network devices.

Here's an overview of the key components and functionalities of the "`network.ospf`" Ansible collection:

- **Resource Manager**: The "`network.ospf`" collection includes a platform-agnostic role called Resource Manager. This role serves as an entry point for managing OSPF configurations across different network **operating systems** (**OS**). It provides several operations for OSPF management, including:

  o **Build Brownfield Inventory**: The "`persist`" operation gathers information about OSPF configurations, such as OSPFv2, OSPFv3, and OSPF interfaces, in a structured format (JSON). This data can be stored as YAML-formatted `host_vars` files locally or in a remote repository to serve as a single source of truth for network operations.

  o **Supported Resource Query**: The "`list`" operation retrieves a list of all resource modules supported for a specific network OS.

  o **Display Structured Configuration**: The "`gather`" operation collects and displays facts for specified network resources, making it easier to manipulate and process the data.

  o **Deploy Changes**: The "`deploy`" operation reads facts from inventory and deploys changes onto network devices' running configurations.

  o **OSPF Health Checks**: The "`health_check`" operation performs health checks for OSPF neighborship, providing details about the OSPF neighborship status.

- o **Detect Drift and Remediate**: The "**detect**" operation identifies configuration differences between provided and running configurations, while the "**remediate**" operation allows us to apply changes to network devices based on the facts gathered.

- **Use Cases**: The collection offers various use cases for managing OSPF, including building an Ansible inventory, deploying configuration changes, displaying structured configurations, detecting configuration drift, remediating drift, and running OSPF health checks.

  Here's a brief overview of how these operations can be used:

  - o **Persist Operation**: Use this to build an Ansible inventory by gathering OSPF configuration information and storing it as YAML-formatted **host_vars** files.

  - o **Deploy Operation**: Deploy configuration changes to network devices by reading facts from inventory.

  - o **Gather Operation**: Display structured OSPF configuration facts for specified network resources.

  - o **Detect Operation**: Identify configuration differences between provided and running configurations.

  - o **Remediate Operation**: Apply configuration changes to network devices based on gathered facts.

  - o **Health Check Operation**: Run health checks on OSPF neighborship, including checks for all neighbours being up or down, a minimum number of neighbors being up, and OSPF status summary.

Overall, the "**network.ospf**" Ansible collection provides network engineers with a powerful toolset for efficiently managing OSPF routing protocols, automating common tasks, and ensuring the reliability and optimization of network performance. This collection simplifies the process of configuring and monitoring OSPF on diverse network devices, making network management more efficient and consistent.

network.bgp

The **network.bgp** Ansible collection is a collection of Ansible roles and modules specifically designed for managing **Border Gateway Protocol (BGP)** resources in network devices. BGP is a crucial routing protocol used in internet and enterprise networks, and the **network.bgp** collection provides automation capabilities for BGP management tasks. Here's an overview of its capabilities and how to use them:

- **Build Brownfield Inventory (persist** action): This action allows users to gather BGP global and address family configuration facts from network devices and store them as inventory **host_vars** in YAML format. This dynamic inventory acts as a single source of truth for other BGP management actions. It helps in quickly obtaining an updated inventory for BGP resources. This action can be executed using the persist action, and it's useful for creating an initial inventory.

- **Display Structured Configuration (`gather` action):** The gather action enables users to retrieve and display BGP global and address family facts from network devices. This action helps network administrators understand the current configuration of BGP resources. It can be executed using the gather action.

- **Deploy Changes (`deploy action`):** The deploy action allows users to deploy changes made to BGP configuration by applying the **host_vars** facts stored in the dynamic inventory onto the network devices. For example, we can use this action to modify BGP parameters and then apply those changes to the devices. This can be especially useful for ensuring consistency in BGP configuration across devices.

- **BGP Health Checks (`health_check action`):** This action provides capabilities for checking the health and status of BGP neighborships. It includes various health-check options:

  o **all_neighbors_up**: This check returns "successful" only when all BGP neighbors are up and running.

  o **all_neighbors_down**: This check returns "successful" only when all BGP neighbors are down.

  o **min_neighbors_up**: This check returns "successful" only when a minimum number of BGP neighbors specified by **min_count** are up and running.

  o **bgp_status_summary**: This check provides a summary of the BGP status.

- **Detect Configuration Drift (`detect action`):** The detect action reads the facts from the provided/default inventory and detects if there are any configuration changes on the network devices. It helps in identifying discrepancies between the desired state and the actual state of BGP configurations.

- **Remediate Configuration Drift (`remediate action`):** The remediate action reads the facts from the provided/default inventory and applies remediations to align the device configuration with the desired state. It overrides the running configuration with the facts from the inventory to correct any detected configuration drift.

To use the **network.bgp** collection, we would typically create Ansible playbooks that include the relevant roles and tasks for our desired BGP management actions, set the appropriate variables, and execute the playbooks using **ansible-navigator** or other Ansible execution methods.

This collection simplifies the automation of BGP management tasks, making it easier to maintain BGP configurations, monitor BGP neighborships, and ensure the overall health of BGP routing in our network infrastructure.

LibSSH

Libssh and Paramiko are two different libraries used for **Secure Shell (SSH)** connectivity in network automation, each with its own advantages and use cases. Understanding the benefits of libssh over Paramiko for network automation requires considering the specific requirements and scenarios in which each library excels. Here are some key advantages of libssh over Paramiko in the context of network automation:

- **FIPS 140-2 Readiness for Enhanced Security Compliance**: Libssh is designed with FIPS 140-2 readiness in mind. This means it meets the stringent security requirements mandated in environments that require FIPS compliance. For organizations operating in such regulated industries (e.g., government, finance, healthcare), libssh becomes a preferred choice due to its ability to ensure security and compliance.

- **Performance and Efficiency**

  o **Better Performance**: Libssh is known for its performance improvements over Paramiko. When dealing with a large number of network devices or frequent SSH connections, libssh can offer faster connection setup and reduced latency, leading to more efficient network automation tasks.

  o **Lower Resource Consumption**: Libssh typically consumes fewer system resources compared to Paramiko, making it more suitable for resource-constrained environments or scenarios where efficient resource utilization is critical.

- **Libssh Integration for Seamless Integration**: Libssh is tightly integrated into the Ansible network automation ecosystem through the **ansible-pylibssh** library. This integration simplifies the adoption of libssh as an SSH connection option in Ansible playbooks and roles.

- **Compliance and Security Standards**:

  o **Support for Security Standards**: Libssh's FIPS readiness aligns with security standards and regulations, making it an appropriate choice for organizations that need to adhere to specific security protocols and certifications.

  o **Security Auditing and Compliance**: Libssh's adherence to FIPS standards allows organizations to better audit and ensure compliance with security policies, reducing potential security vulnerabilities in their network automation processes.

- **Future-Proofing**: Long-Term Viability: As security standards evolve and compliance requirements become more stringent, libssh's focus on security readiness positions it as a more future-proof option for network automation. Organizations can be confident that their automation infrastructure will remain secure and compliant.

It's important to note that while libssh offers these advantages, the choice between libssh and Paramiko should be based on our network automation environment's specific needs and constraints. If FIPS compliance, performance optimization, or resource efficiency are critical factors for our organization, libssh may be the better choice. However, Paramiko remains a viable option for many network automation tasks and is widely used in the industry. Ultimately, the selection of the SSH library should align with our organization's security, performance, and operational requirements.

Managing Fleets

Managing a large fleet of machines or instances in the IT infrastructure efficiently is daunting for businesses in various industries. These fleets can consist of servers, routers, switches, and numerous other devices that keep our business operations running smoothly. To simplify this complex task and ensure seamless performance we can use Ansible as our best ally. Ansible can revolutionize the management of a large fleet of machines, making our business operations more efficient, cost-effective, and reliable.

Before delving into the Ansible purpose in fleet management, let's understand the challenges that come with overseeing a vast array of machines:

- **Configuration Consistency**: Ensuring that all machines are correctly configured with the latest software updates and security patches can be time-consuming and prone to human error.

- **Scalability**: As our fleet grows, manually managing configurations and updates becomes increasingly unmanageable.

- **Diverse Environments**: Large fleets often include a mix of operating systems, making uniform management even more complicated.

- **Continuous Monitoring**: Tracking the performance and health of each machine is essential for proactive maintenance.

Ansible excels in fleet management by providing a streamlined, consistent, and scalable approach. Ansible tackles the challenges of managing a large fleet of machines:

- **Infrastructure as Code (IaC)**: Ansible leverages the concept of Infrastructure as Code, allowing us to define our machine configurations in human-readable YAML files. This approach ensures that our configurations are consistent across our entire fleet and can be easily version-controlled.

- **Scalability**: Ansible is designed to handle large fleets effortlessly. By creating reusable playbooks and roles, we can consistently deploy configurations, updates, and applications to all our machines, regardless of their number.

- **Cross-Platform Compatibility**: Ansible offers built-in support for various operating systems, making it a versatile choice for managing diverse environments. We can write platform-agnostic playbooks to accommodate different machine types and configurations.

- **Continuous Monitoring and Remediation**: Ansible enables us to set up automated monitoring and alerting for our fleet. If any machine deviates from the desired state, Ansible can automatically trigger remediation actions to restore it to the correct configuration.

We can implement the Ansible fleet management by applying the following steps in our organization:

- **Inventory Management**: Start by defining our machine inventory in Ansible. We can categorize machines into groups based on their roles and characteristics, making it easier to apply configurations and updates selectively.

- **Playbook Creation**: Write Ansible playbooks to define the tasks we want to automate, such as software installations, configuration updates, and security patching. These playbooks are reusable and can be applied to specific machine groups.

- **Task Execution**: Use Ansible to execute our playbooks across our fleet. Ansible's agentless architecture ensures that we can manage machines without needing to install additional software on them.

- **Continuous Integration and Continuous Delivery (CI/CD)**: Integrate Ansible into our CI/CD pipelines to automate the deployment of configurations and updates as part of our software release process.

- **Monitoring and Reporting**: Implement monitoring tools that integrate with Ansible to keep track of our fleet's health and performance. Ansible can automatically respond to issues by running remediation playbooks.

Managing a large fleet of machines can be a complex and challenging task, but Ansible simplifies it by providing a flexible, scalable, and automated solution. By adopting Ansible for our fleet management, we can achieve consistency, reliability, and efficiency across our entire machine fleet. With the right setup and practices, Ansible can revolutionize the way we manage our machines, enabling our organization to thrive in the digital age and take full advantage of Ansible.

Rolling Updates

In the fast-paced world of information technology, keeping software and systems up to date is critical. Traditional methods of manual installations, deployments, upgrades, and management can be time-consuming, error-prone, and inefficient. Ansible can streamline these processes and enable rolling updates. We are going to explore how we can make our lives easier by automating and accelerating installations, deployments, upgrades, and everyday system management tasks.

Before diving into Ansible's role in rolling updates, let's understand why they are essential:

- **Minimized Downtime**: Rolling updates allow us to update software or configurations on a system while it's still running, reducing downtime and ensuring continuous service availability.

- **Improved Reliability**: Automation minimizes human errors during updates, resulting in more reliable and consistent deployments.

- **Scalability**: Ansible's automation capabilities make it easy to apply rolling updates across a large number of systems simultaneously, ensuring uniformity and efficiency.

- **Simplified Maintenance**: Routine tasks like software patching, configuration management, and monitoring can be automated, freeing up valuable time for IT teams to focus on more strategic activities.

Ansible simplifies rolling updates by offering a declarative approach to infrastructure as code. Here is how Ansible can help:

- **Playbooks and Roles**: Ansible uses playbooks and roles to define and execute tasks. We can create playbooks that describe the desired state of our systems, including the software versions, configurations, and settings we want to apply.

- **Idempotence**: Ansible ensures idempotent execution, meaning running a playbook multiple times has the same result as running it once. This helps maintain system consistency.

- **Inventory Management**: Ansible allows us to manage an inventory of our systems, ensuring we can target specific hosts or groups of hosts for updates and maintenance.

- **Dynamic Updates**: Ansible can dynamically determine which hosts require updates by querying our inventory, making it easy to automate rolling updates based on system criteria.

- **Role-Based Updates**: Create roles for specific tasks, such as database updates, web server deployments, or security patches. These roles can be reused across different playbooks and scenarios.

Use the following step-by-step guidelines to create an action plan guide in our organization to implement rolling updates using Ansible:

1. **Define the Desired State**: Create playbooks that describe the desired state of our systems, including the software versions, configurations, and settings we want to enforce.

2. **Inventory Configuration**: Set up an inventory file that lists all the hosts we want to manage with Ansible. The group hosts logically to simplify playbook targeting.

3. **Develop Roles**: Create roles for specific tasks or services. Roles are reusable and can be shared across playbooks, making updates and maintenance more efficient.

4. **Execute Playbooks**: Run our Ansible playbooks to apply rolling updates. Ansible will check the current state of each host and apply changes as needed, ensuring idempotent and efficient updates.

5. **Monitoring and Reporting**: Implement monitoring and reporting tools to track the progress and success of our rolling updates. Ansible can integrate with various monitoring solutions to provide real-time insights.

6. **Continuous Improvement**: Regularly review and update our playbooks and roles to accommodate changing requirements, new software versions, or security updates.

Rolling updates are essential for keeping our IT fleet up-to-date, reliable, and secure while minimizing downtime and errors. Ansible's automation capabilities, combined with its declarative approach to infrastructure as code, make it an ideal tool for implementing rolling updates efficiently. By integrating Ansible into our deployment and management workflows, we can simplify installations, deployments, upgrades, and everyday system management, ultimately saving time and ensuring our IT infrastructure remains agile and resilient.

Red Hat

Using the "**yum**" Ansible module, we can execute a successful complete system upgrade on a Red Hat-compatible operating system (RedHat Enterprise Linux, CentOS, CentOS Stream, Fedora, ClearOS, Oracle Linux, Amazon Linux, Rocky Linux, Amalinux, EuroLinux, Fermi Linux, EulerOS, ROSA Linux, Springdale Linux, Asianux, etc.).

```yaml
---
- name: Rolling update YUM
  hosts: all
  become: true
  tasks:
    - name: Updated YUM system
      ansible.builtin.yum:
        name: "*"
        state: latest
        update_cache: true
```

Let us break down the playbook step by step:

1. `---`: This is the YAML document separator at the beginning of every YAML document.

name: Rolling update Red Hat: This is a description for the first play within the playbook. It's a human-readable name that helps us understand the purpose of this play.

2. **hosts: all**: This line specifies the target hosts for this play. In this case, the play will be executed on all hosts that are part of the Ansible inventory (all means all hosts).

3. **become: true**: This indicates that Ansible should use privilege escalation to execute tasks with elevated privileges (typically using the sudo command) on the target hosts. The tasks can be executed as a superuser or another privileged account.

4. **tasks:**: This is the beginning of the list of tasks to be executed within this play. Each task is defined as a dictionary within this list.

5. **name: Updated Red Hat system**: This is the description for the first task within the play. It's a human-readable name for the task.

6. **ansible.builtin.yum**: This is the Ansible module used in this task. The **ansible.builtin.yum** module is used to interact with the YUM package manager on Red Hat-based Linux systems. It allows us to manage package repositories and perform package-related tasks. Since Red Hat Enterprise Enterprise Linux 8, we can use the **ansible.builtin.dnf** module. Newest releases can take advantage of the performance from the latest DNF5 using the latest **ansible.builtin.dnf5** module.

7. **name: "*"**: This specifies the package's name to update. In this case, the wildcard "*" is used to update all installed packages on the target system.

8. **state: latest**: This specifies the desired state for the package. Here, it's set to "latest," which means Ansible will ensure that all packages specified (in this case, all packages with the wildcard *) are updated to their latest available versions.

9. **update_cache: true**: This option instructs Ansible to update the package cache before performing any package management tasks. This ensures that Ansible works with the most up-to-date information about available packages.

This Ansible playbook is designed to perform a rolling update on Red Hat-based Linux systems. It uses the YUM package manager to update all installed packages to their latest available versions while ensuring the package cache is updated before the updates are performed. The **become: true** directive indicates that privilege escalation will be used if necessary to execute these tasks with elevated privileges.

Debian

We can automate the rolling update on Debian-based Linux systems (Debian, Ubuntu, Linux Mint, MX Linux, Deepin, AntiX, PureOS, Kali Linux, Parrot OS, Devuan, Knoppix, AV Linux Linux, etc.) using a simple Ansible Playbook.

```
---
- name: Rolling update APT
  hosts: all
  become: true
  tasks:
    - name: Updated APT system
      ansible.builtin.apt:
        name: "*"
        state: latest
        update_cache: true
```

Let us break down the playbook step by step:

1. `---`: This is the YAML document separator at the beginning of every YAML document.

2. **name: Rolling update Debian**: This is a description for the first play within the playbook. It's a human-readable name that helps you understand the purpose of this play, which is to perform a rolling update on Debian systems.

3. **hosts: all**: This line specifies the target hosts for this play. In this case, the play will be executed on all hosts that are part of the Ansible inventory (all means all hosts).

4. **become: true**: This indicates that Ansible should use privilege escalation to execute tasks with elevated privileges (typically using the sudo command) on the target hosts. It allows the tasks to be executed as a superuser or another privileged account.

5. **tasks:**: This is the beginning of the list of tasks to be executed within this play. Each task is defined as a dictionary within this list.

6. **name: Updated Debian system**: This is the description for the first task within the play. It's a human-readable name for the task, indicating that it's responsible for updating the Debian system.

7. **ansible.builtin.apt**: This is the Ansible module used in this task. The **ansible.builtin.apt** module is used to interact with the APT package manager on Debian-based Linux systems. It allows you to manage package repositories and perform package-related tasks.

8. **name: "*"**: This specifies the package's name to update. In this case, the wildcard * is used to update all installed packages on the target system.

9. **state: latest**: This specifies the desired state for the package. Here, it's set to "latest," which means Ansible will ensure that all packages specified (in this case, all packages with the wildcard *) are updated to their latest available versions.

10. `update_cache: true`: This option instructs Ansible to update the package cache before performing any package management tasks. This ensures that Ansible works with the most up-to-date information about available packages.

This Ansible playbook is designed to perform a rolling update on Debian-based Linux systems. It uses the APT package manager to update all installed packages to their latest available versions while also ensuring that the package cache is updated before performing the updates. The become: true directive indicates that privilege escalation will be used if necessary to execute these tasks with elevated privileges.

Apply Security Patches

In today's digital landscape, cybersecurity is of paramount importance. Organizations must take proactive measures to protect their systems and data from ever-evolving threats. One crucial aspect of cybersecurity is ensuring that systems are up-to-date with the latest security patches. However, manually applying these patches across a large infrastructure fleet can be a time-consuming and error-prone process. Ansible is useful for this use case. Ansible can streamline the process of applying security patches, helping organizations enhance their cybersecurity posture. Security patches are software updates designed to fix vulnerabilities and address potential security risks in operating systems, applications, and libraries. Regularly applying these patches is essential for several reasons:

- **Protecting Against Exploits**: Unpatched systems are vulnerable to cyberattacks, as attackers often target known vulnerabilities.

- **Compliance**: Many regulatory frameworks and industry standards require organizations to keep their systems up-to-date with security patches.

- **Strengthening Defences**: Patching helps organizations proactively strengthen their security defenses, reducing the risk of data breaches and downtime.

- **Maintaining Reputation**: Timely patching demonstrates a commitment to security, which can enhance an organization's reputation.

Ansible simplifies the process of applying security patches by automating the entire lifecycle, from assessment to deployment. Here is how Ansible can help:

- **Inventory Management**: Ansible allows us to maintain an inventory of all our systems, enabling us to organize and target specific hosts for patch management.

- **Playbooks**: Ansible uses playbooks, which are written in human-readable YAML format, to define tasks and the desired state of our systems. We can create playbooks that specify which security patches to apply and how to apply them.

- **Role-Based Patching**: Roles in Ansible enable us to categorize systems and apply patches based on their roles, ensuring that the right patches are applied to the right systems.

- **Dry Runs**: Before actually applying patches, Ansible allows us to perform dry runs, which simulate the patching process without making any changes. This helps us identify potential issues before they affect production systems.

- **Idempotent Execution**: Ansible ensures that patching is idempotent, meaning running a playbook multiple times has the same result as running it once. This prevents unintended changes and maintains system consistency.

- **Reporting** Ansible provides detailed reporting and logging, allowing us to track the progress of patching tasks and verify that patches were successfully applied.

- **Scheduling**: We can schedule patching tasks to occur during maintenance windows, reducing the impact on production systems and ensuring continuity of service.

This is a checklist about implementing Ansible for applying security patches:

- **Inventory Setup**: Create an inventory file listing all the systems we want to manage with Ansible. Organize them into groups based on their roles or functions.

- **Playbook Creation**: Develop Ansible playbooks that define the tasks required to apply security patches. Specify which patches to apply, how to apply them, and any required system reboots.

- **Role Definition**: Organize our systems into roles based on their functions (e.g., web servers, databases, application servers). Create role-specific playbooks for patching.

- **Dry Run**: Before applying patches to production systems, perform dry runs to identify and address any potential issues.

- **Execution**: Run our Ansible Playbooks to apply security patches. Monitor the progress and check the logs for any errors or warnings.

- **Validation**: After patching, validate that the patches were successfully applied and that systems are functioning as expected.

- **Scheduling**: Schedule patching tasks during maintenance windows to minimize disruption to services.

Applying security patches is a critical component of maintaining a strong cybersecurity posture. Ansible's automation capabilities simplify the patch management process, making it efficient, reliable, and consistent across our infrastructure. By integrating Ansible into our security patching workflows, we can proactively protect our systems from vulnerabilities, reduce the risk of cyberattacks, and demonstrate a commitment to cybersecurity best practices.

Red Hat

We can apply the security update in a Red Hat compatible system using the **ansible. builtin.yum** module specifying the additional parameter **security: true**. This parameter tells Ansible to consider security updates when checking for package updates. It ensures that only security-related updates are applied.

Windows

The following playbook, when executed, applies critical and security updates to all Windows hosts specified in the inventory and handles reboots if necessary. It will also log the update process to "**C:\ansible.txt**" for reference. It's important to note that this playbook assumes Ansible is properly configured to manage Windows hosts and that the necessary **Windows Remote Management** (**WinRM**) settings are in place for communication with the Windows hosts.

This Ansible playbook is designed to automate the process of installing critical and security updates on Windows hosts. It specifically targets all hosts defined in the Ansible inventory (specified by the **hosts: all** line).

```
---
- name: Windows Security
  hosts: all
  tasks:
    - name: Install all critical and security updates
      ansible.windows.win_updates:
        category_names:
          - CriticalUpdates
          - SecurityUpdates
        state: installed
        reboot: true
        log_path: C:\ansible.txt
```

Here is a breakdown of the playbook:

- **Playbook Header**:

    `---` The three dashes at the beginning are YAML markers, indicating the start of a YAML document.

- **Play Name**:

    - name: Windows Security

This is the name of the playbook, which is windows rolling update. Playbook names are primarily for human readability and documentation purposes.

- `hosts: all`

  This line specifies the target hosts for this playbook. In this case, it targets all hosts defined in the Ansible inventory (all). You can modify this to target specific groups of hosts or individual hosts as needed.

- `tasks:`

  This section defines the list of tasks that Ansible should execute on the target hosts.

- **Task**: Install all critical and security updates:

  `- name: Install all critical and security updates`

  This task has a name for identification and documentation purposes.

  `ansible.windows.win_updates:`

This is a module provided by Ansible for managing Windows updates. We are using the following parameters for the **win_updates** module:

- **category_names**: Specifies the categories of updates to install. In this case, it targets updates in the "**CriticalUpdates**" and "**SecurityUpdates**" categories. This ensures that only critical and security updates are installed.

- **state**: Sets the desired state of the updates. Here, it is set to "**installed**," indicating that Ansible should ensure the specified updates are installed on the target Windows hosts.

- **reboot**: This parameter is set to true, which means that if a reboot is required after installing updates, Ansible will initiate a reboot on the Windows hosts. This is often necessary to complete the installation of certain updates.

- **log_path**: Specifies the path where Ansible should log information about the updates. In this case, it's set to "**C:\ansible.txt**," so the log will be written to that file on the target Windows hosts.

Monitor and Respond to Threats

In today's interconnected digital landscape, cybersecurity threats are an ever-present concern for businesses and organizations of all sizes. Rapid detection and swift response to these threats are crucial to safeguarding sensitive data and maintaining operational integrity. Ansible offers an effective way to monitor and respond to threats triggering automated scripts. We will explore how Ansible can bolster our cybersecurity strategy by helping us detect and mitigate threats in real-time. Cybersecurity threats come in various forms, from malware and ransomware to vulnerabilities and unauthorized access. These threats can exploit weaknesses in our infrastructure, applications, and configurations, potentially causing significant damage to our organization. Manual threat detection and response processes are often too slow and error-prone, leaving us vulnerable to attacks. Ansible provides a robust framework for automated threat detection and response, enabling organizations to fortify their cybersecurity posture. These are the main advantages of using Ansible:

- **Real-time Threat Monitoring**: Ansible can integrate with various monitoring tools, such as **intrusion detection systems (IDS)** and **security information and event management (SIEM)** solutions. These integrations allow Ansible to continuously monitor system logs, network traffic, and other data sources for signs of potential threats.

- **Custom Playbooks**: Ansible's strength lies in its ability to create custom playbooks that define specific response actions for various threats. Playbooks are written in human-readable YAML format, making them easy to understand and modify as needed.

- **Automated Response**: When Ansible detects a security threat, it can trigger a predefined playbook to respond immediately. This might include isolating affected systems, blocking malicious IP addresses, or initiating incident response procedures.

- **Scalability**: Ansible's scalability is well-suited for large and complex environments. Regardless of scale, we can apply the same automated threat response workflows consistently across all our systems and devices.

- **Remediation**: Ansible can also automate the process of remediating vulnerabilities or misconfigurations identified during threat detection. It can apply security patches, update configurations, and ensure systems comply with security policies.

To effectively use Ansible for automated threat response, consider the following steps:

1. **Identify Threat Vectors**: Begin by identifying potential threat vectors within our environment. Understand the types of threats we want to monitor and the corresponding response actions.

2. **Integrate Monitoring Tools**: Set up integrations with monitoring and alerting tools to feed threat data into Ansible. Ensure that our data sources are well-configured and continuously updated.

3. **Develop Playbooks**: Create Ansible playbooks that outline the steps to take in response to different types of threats. These playbooks should be thoroughly tested and regularly updated to adapt to evolving threats.

4. **Automation**: Configure Ansible to automatically execute the appropriate playbook in response to detected threats. Ensure that the playbook execution is monitored and logged for auditing purposes.

5. **Continuous Improvement**: Regularly review and refine our automated threat response workflows to enhance their effectiveness. Stay informed about emerging threats and adjust our playbooks accordingly.

Cybersecurity threats are an ongoing concern for organizations, and timely detection and response are paramount. Ansible offers a powerful solution by automating threat detection and response processes. By integrating Ansible into our cybersecurity strategy, we can enhance our organization's ability to protect against threats, reduce response times, and minimize potential damage. As the threat landscape continues to evolve, leveraging Ansible's automation capabilities can provide a significant advantage in safeguarding our digital assets.

Develop Ansible Resources

The private Automation Hub provides a platform to showcase and share these custom creations with the world. In this section, we are going to craft our custom Ansible Collection, named "`test.test`," and publish it on Ansible Automation Hub.

Code Inclusion

Including code from other files in automation scripts can greatly enhance the reusability and maintainability of Ansible Playbooks. Ansible provides two methods for this purpose: static import and dynamic include. These mechanisms allow us to incorporate individual tasks, handlers, or entire playbook files into our scripts, enabling better modularization and organization.

- **Static Import**:

  Static import involves using import statements such as `import_playbook`, `import_tasks`, etc. These import statements are processed during playbook parsing. When using static imports, the parent task options are inherited by all child tasks within the import. This means that the task options of the parent are applied to each child's task.

  Consider the following code examples to understand the distinction between import and include when combined with a loop statement:

```
- import_tasks: example.yml
  with_items: [1, 2]
```

In this case, the `example.yml` file is imported only once. However, the imported tasks are executed in a loop for each element (1 and 2) in the sequence [1, 2].

- **Dynamic Include**:

  On the other hand, dynamic include involves using statements like `include_tasks`, `include_role`, etc., which are processed as they are encountered during playbook execution. Unlike static imports, the parent task options are not copied to child tasks in dynamic includes. The parent task options only apply to the dynamic task as it is evaluated and won't be propagated to the child tasks.

In the same way the following code:

```
- include_tasks: example.yml
  with_items: [1, 2]
```

In this example, the `example.yml` file is included twice. Each time it is included, the 'item' iteration variable is set to 1 and then 2, respectively, from the sequence [1, 2].

In summary, static import and dynamic include ways to integrate external code into our Ansible playbooks. Static import processes statements during playbook parsing and inherits parent task options, while dynamic includes processes statements during playbook execution and does not propagate parent task options to child tasks. Choosing between the two depends on our specific use case and the behaviour we intend to achieve.

Plugins & Modules

Regarding extending Ansible, two avenues take center stage: plugins and modules. These building blocks are crafted in Python, and each plays a crucial role in shaping Ansible's capabilities. While plugins operate on the Ansible controller machine, modules execute on the Ansible target machines.

Ansible plugins are like the hidden magicians behind the curtain, orchestrating the core functionality. These Python snippets come alive on the Ansible control machine, enhancing its capabilities. They come in various flavors, each contributing a distinctive facet to Ansible's prowess.

Ansible's plugin landscape is diverse, serving specific purposes that optimize automation workflows. Here are some major plugin types that contribute to Ansible's comprehensive toolkit:

- **Action Plugins**: These assist with controller-side tasks for modules like copying and templating, enhancing module functionality.

- **Become Plugins:** Elevate privileges for executing tasks, granting administrator capabilities.

- **Callback Plugins**: Craft the format of Ansible's output, shaping the information presented.

- **Connection Plugins**: Establish connections to target machines, a crucial link in the automation chain.

- **Filter Plugins**: Transform and manipulate data, offering a dynamic edge to automation processes.

- **Inventory Plugins**: Fuel inventory data, whether it's static or dynamically evolving.

- **Test Plugins:** Create logical expressions to evaluate true or false conditions within playbooks.

Action plugins, in particular, are remarkable agents of enhancement. When a module is specified, Ansible first checks for an action plugin with the same name. If found, the action plugin is invoked before the module, performing tasks on the controller side. It's like the behind-the-scenes choreographer preparing the stage for the main performance.

While Ansible comes bundled with a host of plugins, it's also possible to fashion our own to suit unique requirements. These plugins can find their home in playbooks, roles, and collections. Speaking of collections, it's an ideal habitat for these custom creations, enabling streamlined management and sharing.

Ansible's plugin discovery mechanism involves specific directories. Within the playbook and role directories, subdirectories named "**type_plugin**" store plugins. Additionally, "**plugins/type**" directories within collection directories serve as plugin repositories. To ensure seamless publishing, management, and reuse, embracing Ansible collections as the repository of choice is recommended.

In the realm of automation, Ansible's extensibility shines through plugins and modules. These components empower us to fine-tune our automation workflows, transforming complex tasks into elegant solutions. As we delve into the world of Ansible customization, remember that plugins and modules are our allies, enabling us to orchestrate intricate automation symphonies with precision and finesse.

Custom Test Plugin

In the world of Ansible, plugins are the craftsmen behind the magic, contributing their expertise to orchestrate seamless automation. While they resemble regular Python code, they require a specific structure that Ansible can decode to unleash its power. Let's dive into the intricate structure of Ansible plugins using a "test" plugin example as our guide.

In our exploration, we'll dissect a "**test**" plugin – a versatile tool that evaluates conditions and returns either true or false based on input. Specifically, we'll craft a plugin that inspects our "**aws_instances**" dictionary to ascertain if an instance qualifies as "**large**."

```
from ansible import errors
from collections.abc import MutableMapping
def is_large(item):
    '''Determine if instance_type is large, 2xlarge, etc.'''
    if not isinstance(item, MutableMapping):
        raise errors.AnsibleFilterError("The 'is_large' test expects a
dictionary")
```

```python
    if not 'value' in item:
        raise errors.AnsibleFilterError("Unexpected dictionary")
    value = item.get('value', {})
    if not 'instance_type' in value:
        raise errors.AnsibleFilterError("No 'instance_type' was found")
    return 'large' in value.get('instance_type', '')
class TestModule(object):
    ''' Custom Ansible tests '''
    def tests(self):
        return {
            'is_large': is_large,
        }
```

Test plugins follow a well-defined blueprint. They should contain a "**TestModule**" class encompassing a "tests" method, which returns a dictionary of available tests. This structure ensures Ansible can seamlessly interpret and execute the plugin.

As we embark on crafting plugins, keep these important considerations in mind:

- **Exception Handling**: Plugins should gracefully handle errors by raising specific Ansible exceptions. This ensures that the automation process remains smooth and comprehensible.

- **Python Abstract Base Collections**: Ansible utilizes specific types from Python's Abstract Base Collections. This includes **MutableMapping** for dictionaries and **MutableSequence** for lists. Adhering to these types ensures compatibility and consistency.

- **Key-based Plugin Discovery**: Ansible's plugin discovery hinges on keys, represented as strings. Ensuring our plugin aligns with this naming convention ensures it's found and executed effectively.

"Why write a plugin like this?" we might wonder. After all, the same functionality could be directly implemented in YAML using conditional statements. The answer lies in the balance between YAML's readability and plugin maintenance.

While the "**test**" plugin example might seem simple, it offers enhanced readability to our YAML playbooks. It's a small step towards maintaining cleaner, more comprehensible automation scripts. With the advent of easy integration of plugins into Ansible collections, the overhead of creating and maintaining a plugin becomes significantly smaller.

In essence, Ansible's plugin architecture offers a powerful trade-off. By investing in the creation of these components, we simplify complex YAML playbooks and elevate the overall quality of our automation. As Ansible collections pave the way for streamlined plugin management, the barrier to entry for utilizing this extensibility feature has never been lower.

Custom Filter Plugin

Ansible understands this implicitly and introduces us to a versatile tool for shaping and enhancing data: the filter plugin. Let's venture into the realm of filter plugins, understanding their purpose, structure, and the art of using them to create elegant automation solutions. Filter plugins, true to their name, are the virtuosi of data transformation. They perform the role of the master sculptor, molding raw data into refined structures that align with our automation objectives. These plugins aren't confined to Ansible YAML alone – they also extend their magic to Jinja 2 templates.

As we immerse ourselves in the world of filter plugins, consider these guiding principles to harness their power effectively:

- **Focused Transformation**: When crafting filter plugins, lean towards transforming individual elements. While we can use the Python **"map()"** function to apply filters to multiple items within lists or dictionaries, remember that singular transformations often lead to cleaner, more comprehensible code.

- **Consistency in Output Type**: The golden rule in filter plugin creation is to ensure that the output remains consistent with the input's data type. Unless the filter's purpose is to intentionally change data types (e.g., the Python **"join()"** filter), uphold this principle to maintain clarity.

- **Composing Filters**: Crafting composite filters that elegantly string together multiple filters can be a wise approach. This technique simplifies YAML scripts, making them more manageable and comprehensible.

- **Journey Beyond YAML**: While filter plugins are gems within Ansible YAML, remember that their influence extends into Jinja 2 templates. Consider their utility in both realms to create solutions that transcend platforms.

Filter plugins follow a clear structure, anchored by a **"FilterModule"** class housing a **"filters"** method. This method should return a dictionary containing the available filters. This architecture ensures seamless integration with Ansible's internal workings.

Let's unveil the might of filter plugins with an example. Imagine a filter plugin that extracts the AWS instance class from a given AWS instance type. This seemingly modest plugin carries significant potential, streamlining automation scripts and enhancing data comprehension.

```
def instance_class(instance_type):
    '''Extract the instance class (e.g. t2, t3) from the full instance type'''
    return instance_type.split('.',1)[0]
```

```
class FilterModule(object):
    ''' Custom Ansible tests '''
    def filters(self):
        return {
            'instance_class': instance_class,
        }
```

As we navigate this realm, keep in mind that Ansible must be installed on our Ansible Controller machine, and the example files for this exploration are conveniently available in our current directory.

Using Callback Plugin

Ansible's output is a symphony of information in the grand orchestration of automation. But what if we could fine-tune that output, creating a customized harmony that aligns with our needs? Enter Ansible's callback plugins – the conductors of output orchestration. Let's delve into the world of callback plugins, exploring their structure, special variables, and the magic they bring to shaping Ansible's output. Some particular callback plugins are aggregate callback that adds additional console output next to the configured stdout callback.

The following snippet we provided is a portion of an Ansible configuration file (`ansible.cfg`) where certain settings are configured under the `[defaults]` section. Ansible configuration files are used to customize.

```
[defaults]
```

```
callback_whitelist=ansible.posix.timer,ansible.posix.profile_tasks,ansible.posix.profile_roles
```

```
callbacks_enabled=ansible.posix.timer,ansible.posix.profile_tasks,ansible.posix.profile_roles
```

The behaviour of Ansible contains various settings that affect how Ansible executes tasks and plays. Let us break down the settings in our snippet:

1. `callback_whitelist`: This setting is used to specify a whitelist of Ansible callback plugins that are allowed to be executed during playbook runs. Callback plugins are scripts or modules in Ansible that allow us to customize and extend the output and behavior of Ansible when it runs playbooks. In our snippet, the `callback_whitelist` is set to include the following callback plugins: `ansible.posix.timer`, `ansible.posix.profile_tasks`, and `ansible.posix.profile_roles`. By listing these plugins, we are allowing them to be used during playbook runs, which means they can provide additional functionality or collect specific information about the playbook execution.

2. `callbacks_enabled`: This setting is similar to `callback_whitelist` but specifies a list of Ansible callback plugins that are enabled during playbook runs. Enabling a callback plugin means that it will actively participate in the playbook execution and can perform tasks like profiling, timing, or other custom actions. In our snippet, the `callbacks_enabled` setting is also configured with the same callback plugins as `callback_whitelist`, including `ansible.posix.timer`, `ansible.posix.profile_tasks`, and `ansible.posix.profile_roles`.

In summary, the configuration we provided is enabling and whitelisting specific Ansible callback plugins under the `[defaults]` section of the `ansible.cfg` file. These plugins, such as `ansible.posix.timer`, `ansible.posix.profile_tasks`, and `ansible.posix.profile_roles`, are allowed to participate in playbook runs and provide additional functionality or insights into the execution process. The use of callback plugins can be valuable for tasks like performance profiling, timing, and role-based analysis during Ansible playbook runs. The result is shown in *Figure 9.1* with a more verbose output of the execution time.

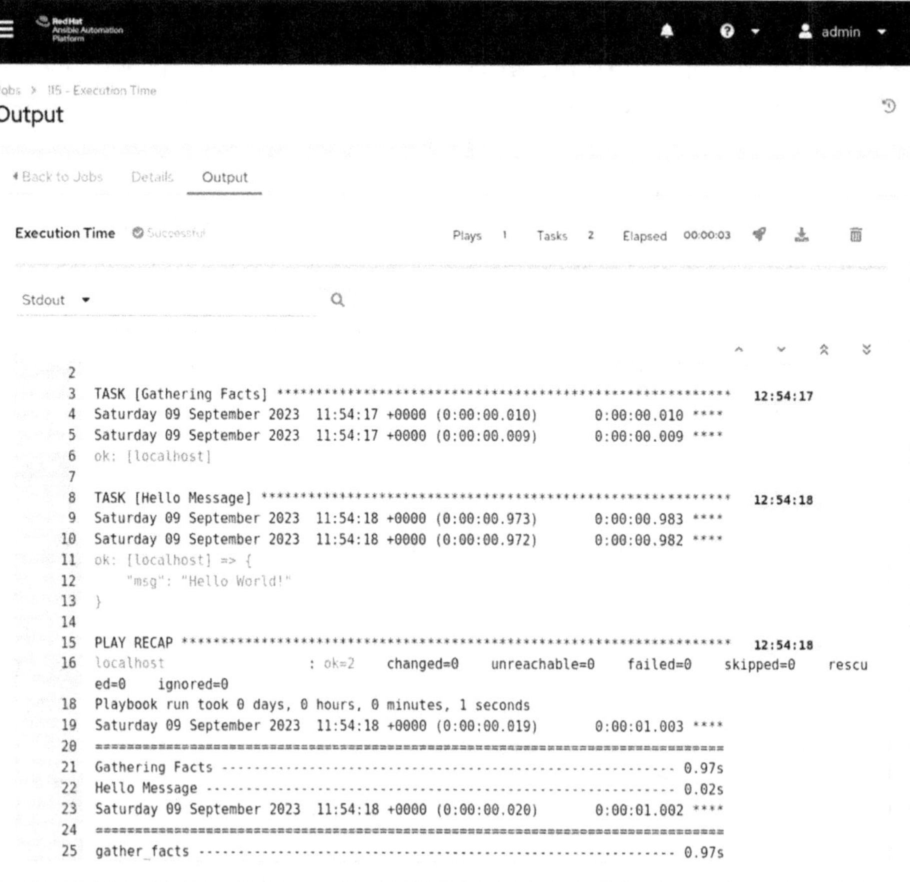

Figure 9.1: Execution with Ansible Callback

As a comparison, *Figure 9.2* shows the same execution without the callback plugins enabled as *Figure 9.1*.

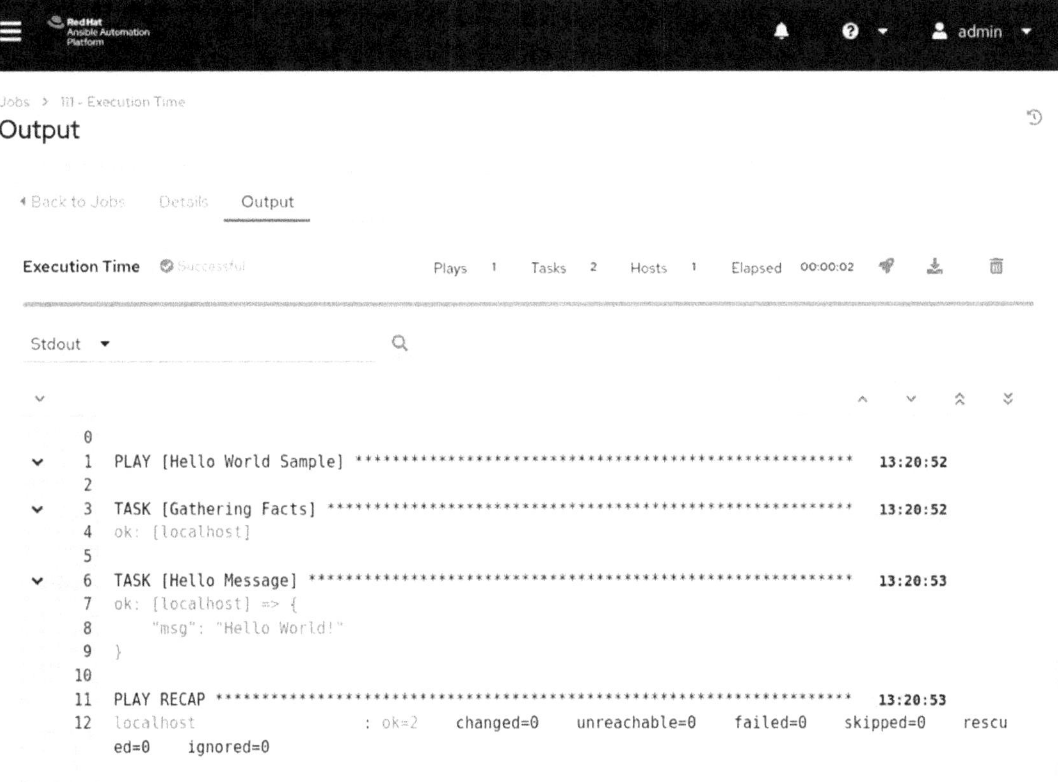

Figure 9.2: Execution without Ansible Callback

The most common Ansible Callback Plugins to enhance output readability are: **community. general.unixy**, **community.general.dense**, **ansible.builtin.tree**.

Custom Callback Plugin

Callback plugins are like the tailor's touch, adding a personal spin to Ansible's output when it takes center stage. These plugins wield the power to augment or entirely replace the default output, offering us the freedom to present automation results in a manner that resonates.

While callback plugins might appear akin to their siblings, they sport a distinct structure. These plugins are defined within a **CallbackModule** class, gracefully inheriting attributes from the **CallbackBase** class. The callback methods within this class can be overridden to dictate output at various stages of an Ansible run.

Callback plugins operate in harmony with Ansible through special class variables, allowing effortless registration and usage. The following *Table 9.2* summarize the special class variables.

Variable	Purpose
`CALLBACK_VERSION`	Informs Ansible of the callback API version used (typically set to 2.0)
`CALLBACK_TYPE`	Dictates the plugin's role – if 'stdout', it replaces the default output
`CALLBACK_NAME`	Assigns a name to identify and specify the plugin's usage
`CALLBACK_NEEDS_ENABLED`	Set to True if the plugin should only be used when explicitly chosen

Table 9.2: Special Class Variables

The selection of callback plugins can be tailored to our preferences. We can define a list of extra callback plugins in an "**ansible.cfg**" configuration file, or utilize environment variables like "**ANSIBLE_CALLBACK_PLUGINS**" and "**ANSIBLE_STDOUT_CALLBACK.**" However, only one "**stdout**" type plugin can be selected.

Experience the enchantment of callback plugins with a JSON summary callback plugin example. In this instance, the plugin crafts a JSON output to summarize Ansible results, replacing the default output. With Ansible installed on our control machine and example files at our disposal, we can witness the JSON summary gracefully supplanting the regular Ansible output.

```
from ansible.plugins.callback import CallbackBase
import json
class CallbackModule(CallbackBase):
    CALLBACK_VERSION = 2.0
    CALLBACK_TYPE = 'stdout'
    CALLBACK_NAME = 'json_stats'
    CALLBACK_NEEDS_ENABLED = True
    def v2_playbook_on_stats(self, stats):
        output = {}
        for h in stats.processed.keys():
            t = stats.summarize(h)
            output[h] = {
                'successful': t['ok'],
                'failed': t['failures'],
```

```
        'skipped': t['skipped'],
    }
    self._display.display(json.dumps(output, indent=2))
```

Callback plugins wield the power to transform automation's output canvas, allowing us to curate an output symphony that resonates with our objectives. By crafting custom callbacks, we are not just shaping information – we are crafting a personalized automation experience that elevates efficiency and comprehension.

Custom Lookup Plugin

The following code is a Python script designed to work as a custom lookup plugin for Ansible. Let us break down what each part of the code is doing:

1. **Python Headers and Documentation**:

   ```
   from __future__ import (absolute_import, division, print_function)
   __metaclass__ = type
   ```

   These are common codes at the beginning of the script, indicating that this is Python version 3 onward code.

2. **Documentation**

   It also includes a documentation block (indicated by triple double-quotes) providing information about the plugin's name, author, version, and a brief description.

   ```
   DOCUMENTATION = r"""
     name: test
     author: Luca Berton <luca@ansiblepilot.com>
     version_added: "0.1"  # same as collection version
     short_description: read API token
     description:
         - This lookup returns the token from the provided API.
   ```

3. **Importing Ansible and External Libraries**:

   ```
   from ansible.errors import AnsibleError, AnsibleParserError
   from ansible.plugins.lookup import LookupBase
   from ansible.utils.display import Display
   import requests
   ```

   The script imports several modules and classes from Ansible and external libraries:

   - **from ansible.errors** imports Ansible-specific error classes.

   - **from ansible.plugins.lookup** imports the base class **LookupBase** for creating custom lookup plugins.

- **from ansible.utils.display** imports the Display class for handling display output.

- **import requests** imports the Python requests library for making HTTP requests.

4. **Initialization:**

```
display = Display()
```

This line of code creates an instance of the **Display** class, which is used for displaying messages or debugging information. It's a part of Ansible's logging and output system.

5. **Custom Lookup Module:**

```
class LookupModule(LookupBase):
```

This line defines a custom lookup module named **LookupModule** that inherits from **LookupBase**, an Ansible base class for creating lookup plugins.

6. **Custom Method (run):**

```
    _URL_ = "https://reqres.in/api/login"
    def run(self, terms, variables=None, **kwargs):
      payload = {
        "email": "eve.holt@reqres.in",
        "password": "cityslicka"
      }
      try:
        res = requests.post(self._URL_, data=payload)
        res.raise_for_status()
        ret = res.json()['token']
      except requests.exceptions.HTTPError as e:
        raise AnsibleError('There was an error getting a token. The
lookup API returned %s', response.status_code)
      except Exception as e:
        raise AnsibleError('Unhandled exception is lookup plugin.
Origin: %s', e)
      return [ret]
```

The run method is a required method in a lookup plugin. It is called when the plugin is invoked in an Ansible playbook.

Inside the run method, the script does the following:

    a. It sets the **_URL_** attribute to a specific API endpoint URL.

    b. It prepares a payload dictionary with email and password data.

    c. It makes an HTTP POST request to the specified URL with the payload.

    d. If the request is successful (HTTP status code 200), it extracts the token from the JSON response and stores it in the ret variable.

    e. If there's an HTTP error, it raises an **AnsibleError** with a specific error message.

    f. If there's any other exception, it also raises an **AnsibleError** with an error message.

7. **Return Value**:

```
return [ret]
```

Finally, the run method returns a list containing the extracted token (**[ret]**).

This custom lookup plugin can be used within Ansible playbooks to fetch an API token from the specified URL. It handles HTTP errors and exceptions gracefully and returns the token for further use in Ansible tasks or roles. The plugin's name is "test," and it's used like other Ansible lookup plugins within playbook tasks.

Please note that by design, Ansible Lookup plugins are historically usually used to pipe results into loops. Ansible expects a list as a return type. A common walkaround is to wrap our return value into a list, like:

```
return [ret]
```

Ansible automatically enables all available lookup plugins. To activate a custom lookup plugin, we can do so by placing it in one of the following locations:

- **Adjacent to Our Playbook**:

  We can include our custom lookup plugin in a directory called `lookup_plugins` located next to our playbook file.

- **Inside a Collection**:

  We can place our custom lookup plugin in the `plugins/lookup` directory within that collection.

- **Within a Standalone Role**:

  Custom lookup plugins can also be included within a standalone Ansible role. Place the plugin in the appropriate `lookup_plugins` directory within the role.

- **Configured Directory Sources:**

  If we have configured custom directory sources in our `ansible.cfg` configuration file, we can place the lookup plugin in one of those directories. The setting key is `lookup_plugins` under the `[defaults]` section or `ANSIBLE_LOOKUP_PLUGINS` environmental variable

By following these methods, we can activate and use custom lookup plugins in Ansible to extend its functionality according to our specific automation requirements. *Figure 9.3* show the output of the execution of the custom lookup plugin in the Ansible Controller via a Job Template. As expected, we obtained the `QpwL5tke4Pnpja7X4` token on the screen due to the API request.

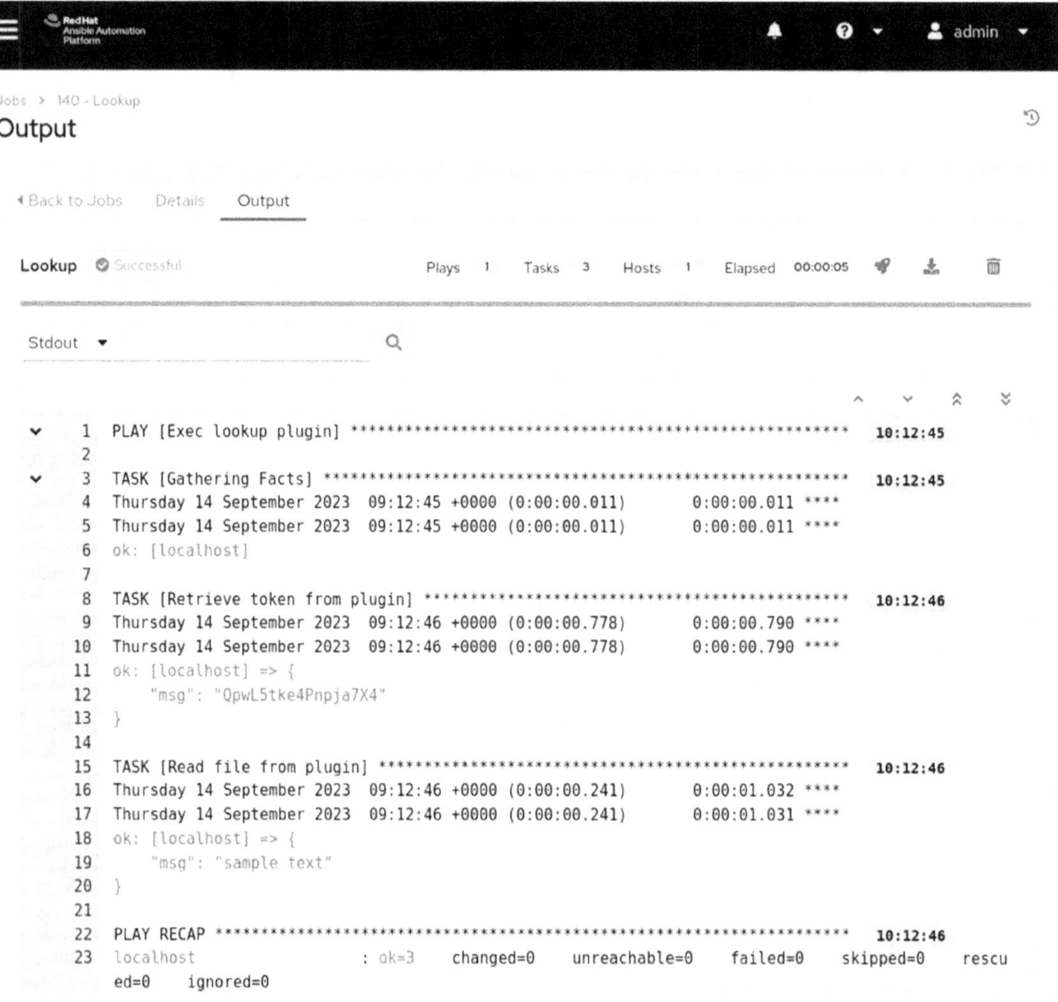

Figure 9.3: Custom lookup plugin execution

Custom Module

In the realm of automation, Ansible modules are the master craftsmen, donning their Python code robes to orchestrate change on the target machines. These modules are the key to transforming the automation landscape, the exclusive conduit through which Ansible can influence its subjects. Let us delve into the realm of Ansible modules, unraveling their essence, tips for crafting them, and a glimpse into creating a custom module.

Picture Ansible modules as the artisans on the ground, executing tasks directly on target machines. These Python-powered entities encapsulate the commands and logic required to effect change – whether it's installing software, managing configurations, or orchestrating complex tasks. Without modules, Ansible's power would remain dormant.

As we embark on our journey to create Ansible modules, consider these guiding principles to sculpt modules that stand the test of time:

- **Dependency Delicacy**: Since modules operate on target machines, they must carry their Python dependencies. Opt for widely used dependencies, but steer clear of custom or hefty ones. Action plugins can be a suitable alternative in such cases.

- **Check Mode Support**: "**Check mode**" is a valuable capability that lets us simulate changes without implementing them. Modules should support check mode by checking the existing state and reporting changes accurately.

- **Idempotence Excellence**: A hallmark of modules is their ability to maintain idempotence. This entails making changes only when necessary and ensuring the "changed" field in the results dictionary is accurate.

- **Exception Handling Grace**: Rather than causing a storm with exceptions, modules should handle failures gracefully. Utilize the **fail_json()** function from the **AnsibleModule** class to convey failures.

Integrating a module into a collection is a straightforward endeavor – a simple placement within the "plugins/modules" directory. Let's embark on a journey to understand the intricacies of creating custom modules, unraveling their structure, leveraging the **AnsibleModule** class, and mastering the art of handling arguments and results.

A custom module is akin to a standalone script, often scripted in Python. Its purpose revolves around ingesting arguments, generating JSON-formatted output, and signaling completion with a return code. This elegant simplicity underpins the essence of custom modules.

Custom modules are graced with the presence of the **AnsibleModule** class on the target machine. This class is a formidable ally, automating the intricacies of argument reading, JSON output generation, and return code establishment. By leveraging this class, custom modules are liberated from reading arguments from external files, resulting in a significant performance boost.

A pivotal facet of custom modules is their argument specification, which dictates the expected arguments, their types, and any default values. This specification, passed to the **AnsibleModule** instance, empowers Ansible to effortlessly parse and validate arguments, minimizing errors and enhancing the user experience.

The dialogue between Ansible and a module culminates in the results dictionary. Modules orchestrate this dictionary, ensuring it carries crucial information. The **"changed"** field, a sentinel of transformation, indicates whether changes were made. The **"msg"** field provides a user-friendly error message to communicate errors effectively, fostering a coherent interaction between automation and users.

As we witness the creation of a custom module, remember that the essence lies in integrating our application components through open APIs, creating a harmonious symphony of automation. In a world where orchestration reigns, Ansible modules are the conductors, guiding the automation ensemble to a harmonious performance. By embracing these Python-powered envoys, we unlock the potential to wield change on target machines with precision and finesse. It's a journey of crafting transformation, one module at a time.

Custom Collection

Packing all filters within a custom Ansible collection streamlines plugin management, enhances collaboration, and ensures efficient maintenance, fostering a cohesive and efficient automation ecosystem.

1. **Create the Custom Collection**

   Begin our journey by creating the **"test.test"** collection using the ansible-galaxy command-line utility:

   ```
   ansible-galaxy collection init test.test
   ```

   We will receive a confirmation that the **"test.test"** collection has been successfully created.

   ```
   - Collection test.test was created successfully
   ```

   The command generates the following directory tree in the current directory:

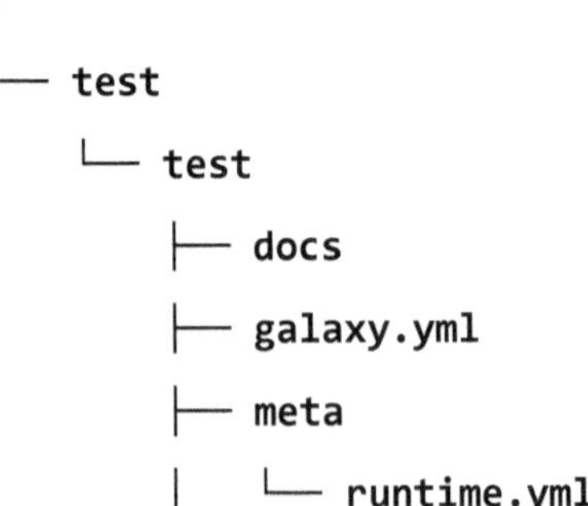

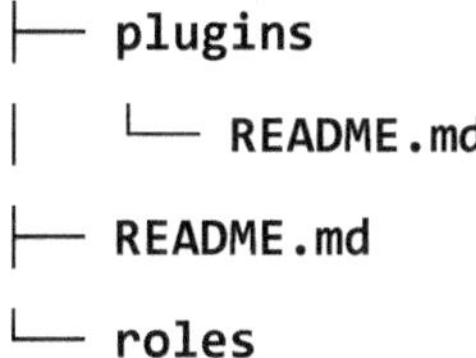

```
├── plugins
│   └── README.md
├── README.md
└── roles

6 directories, 4 files
```

2. **Customize the Collection Contents**

   Navigate into the collection directory and modify the "**runtime.yml**" file located at "**test/test/meta/runtime.yml**". We can customize by adding additional modules, plugins, roles, etc.

   Here, set all the necessary parameters. Between all of these, the "**requires_ansible**" parameter specifies the minimum Ansible version required:

```
---

requires_ansible: '>=2.9.20'
```

3. **Build the Ansible Artifact**

   The following command creates the "**test-test-1.0.0.tar.gz**" archive that we can publish in Automation Hub. Generate the "**test-test-1.0.0.tar.gz**" archive using the following command:

```
ansible-galaxy collection build
```

   Upon execution, the generated archive is ready to be published on Automation Hub.

```
Created collection for test.test at /home/user/collection/test/test/
test-test-1.0.0.tar.gz
```

Automation Hub

Creating and publishing our custom Ansible Collection on Automation Hub signifies our dedication to innovation and collaboration. It's an opportunity to make a lasting impact on the automation landscape while joining a community that thrives on creativity. The following step-by-step guide publishes our custom Ansible "**test.test**" collection in the private Automation Hub. Feel free to substitute with a meaningful name for the namespace and collection in the real world.

1. **Create a Namespace**

   Access the Automation Hub interface and navigate to **Collections** > **Namespace** > **Create**. Enter "**test**" as the namespace name. Create the "**test**" namespace via the **Collections** > **Namespace** > **Create** menu and insert the "**test**" in the name pop-up window as shown in the following *Figure 9.4*:

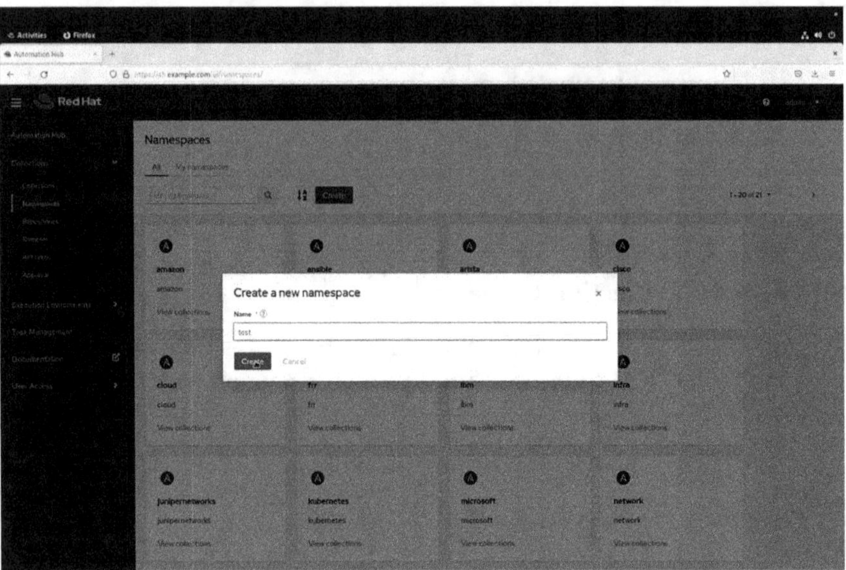

Figure 9.4: Automation Hub Create a Namespace

2. Create the Collection

Within the newly created namespace, select the "**Upload collection**" button. Proceed by uploading the "**test-test-1.0.0.tar.gz**" file, created earlier with the **ansible-galaxy** command. Inside the namespace, select the "**Upload collection**" button to populate the "**test.test**" collection with the generated file as shown in *Figure 9.5*:

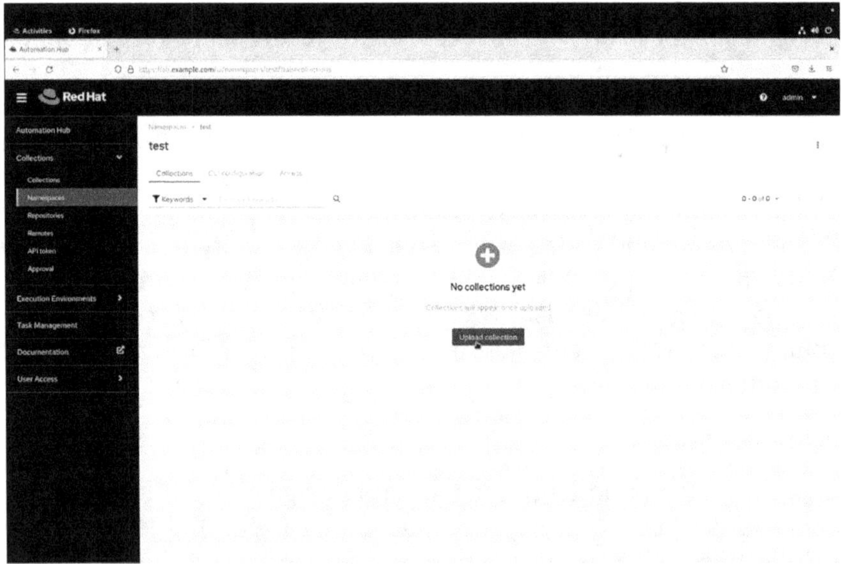

Figure 9.5: Automation Hub New Collection

Upload the "**test-test-1.0.0.tar.gz**" file generated by the ansible-galaxy command, as shown in *Figure 9.6*:

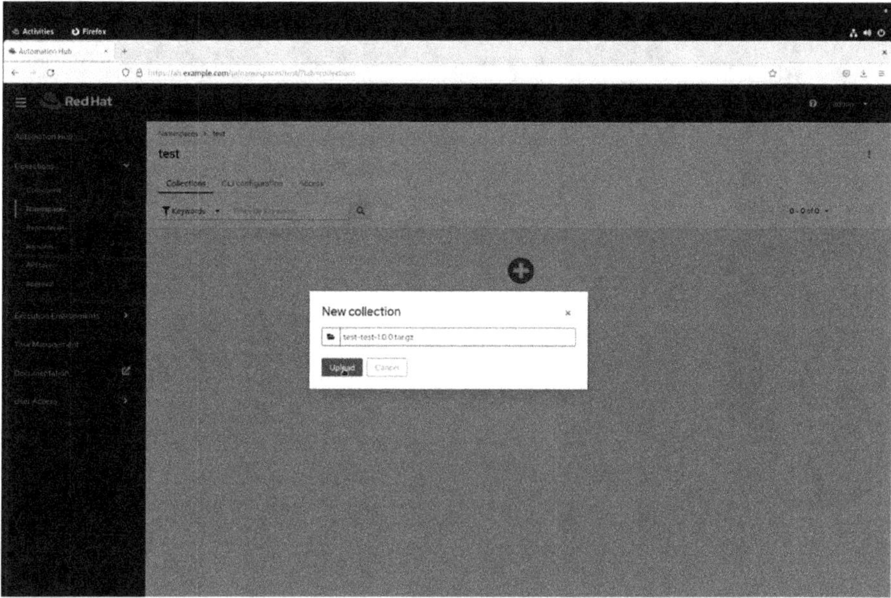

Figure 9.6: *Automation Hub Upload Collection*

An automatic procedure is going to check the correctness of our artifact as shown in *Figure 9.7*:

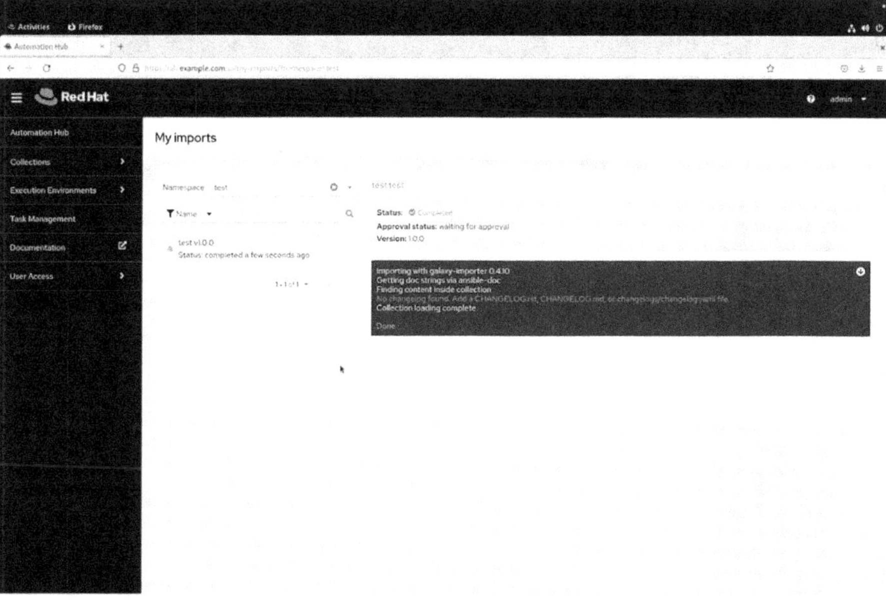

Figure 9.7: *Automation Hub Collection Check*

The "**test.test**" collection is in the "**staging**" area, as shown in *Figure 9.8*:

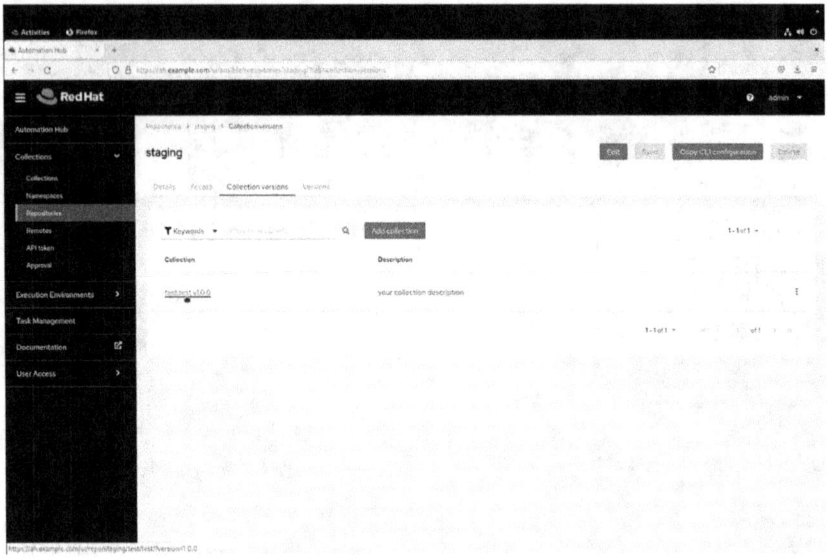

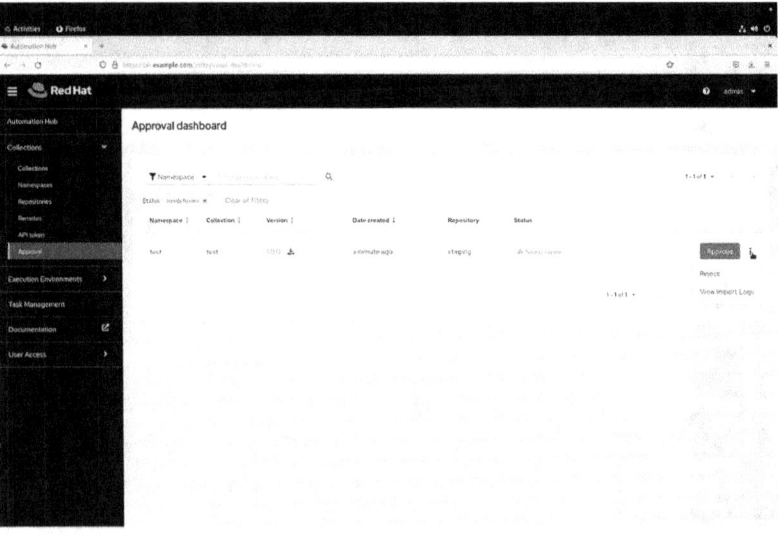

Figure 9.8: Automation Hub Staging

3. **Approval Process**

   At this point, our "**test.test**" collection resides in the "**staging**" area. Automation Hub administrators hold the power to approve or reject it. Admins can navigate to **Collections** > **Approval** to make their decisions. An Automation Hub administrator can approve or reject the "**test.test**" collection in the staging area using the **Collections** > **Approval** menu, as shown in the following *Figure 9.9*:

Figure 9.9: Automation Hub Approval

4. **Publish and Share**

   With approval granted, our "**test.test**" collection is now available for usage in the "**published**" repository. From now onward, our collection is available to be consumed in our organization via the private Automation Hub, as shown in *Figure 9.10*:

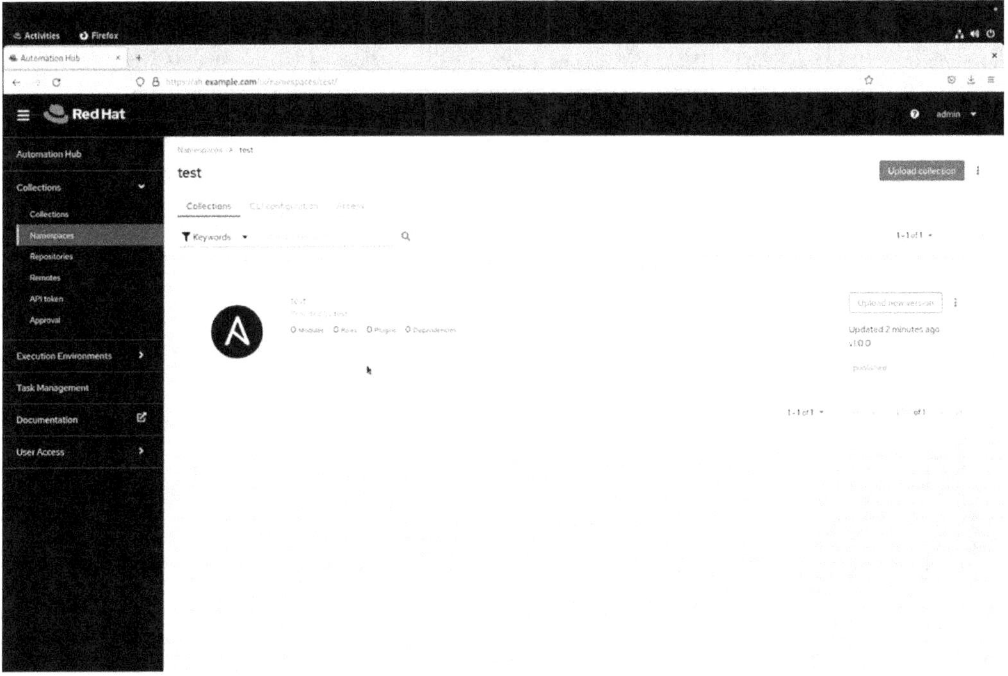

Figure 9.10: *Automation Hub Published*

Once approved, the "**test.test**" collection is available for usage in the "published" private Automation Hub repository. Now, we can use in our Automation Controller the "**test.test**" collection.

XLAB Steampunk Spotter

In the enterprise automation world, managing Ansible playbooks and ensuring they adhere to best practices, remain secure, and are compatible with the latest Ansible versions can be a daunting task. That's where XLAB Steampunk Spotter comes in as part of our development journey, integrating into our development workflow or in the validation pipeline, an Ansible playbook scanning tool designed to streamline and enhance our Ansible automation workflow.

XLAB Steampunk Spotter is an innovative Ansible playbook scanning tool that has made waves in the IT automation community, offering trustable automation that significantly reduces risks and accelerates automation processes. Organizations across the globe trust this remarkable tool, and it has been used successfully by DevOps Engineers, Consultants, System Engineers, Infrastructure Engineers, Automation Developers, and Technical Account Managers.

Reduce Risks and Speed Up Automation

Spotter's primary objective is to optimize our automation process by providing a comprehensive analysis of our Ansible playbooks and offering recommendations for improvement. With Steampunk Spotter, our can:

- Identify hard-to-catch and time-consuming errors within our playbooks.

- Improve the quality, reliability, and security of our playbooks.

- Reduce development and test time.

- Ensure that we follow automation best practices.

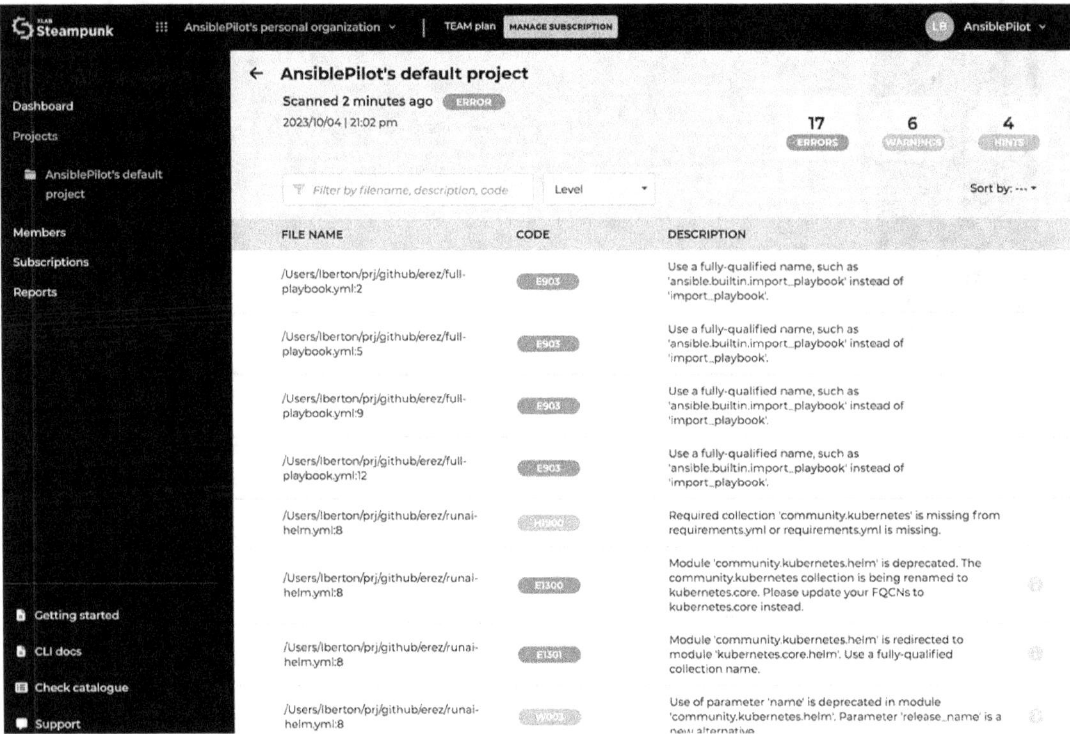

Figure 9.11: Spotter Project

One of the standout features of Spotter is its ability to ease the transition to the latest Ansible versions. It checks our playbooks for compatibility with specific Ansible versions, identifies issues that need to be addressed, provides advice on how to ease migrations, and facilitates playbook upgrades in minutes, sparing our hours of manual work.

XLAB Steampunk Spotter and Ansible Lint may seem similar on the surface, as both tools check Ansible Playbooks for errors and offer recommendations. However, they complement each other rather than duplicate functionalities. Ansible Lint is excellent for catching programming errors stylistic mistakes, and enforcing best practices, ensuring our playbooks are easy to understand and consistent. In contrast, Steampunk Spotter goes beyond syntax checking, delving into the content, spotting hard-to-catch issues, and offering specific suggestions for modules, roles, and collections. While Ansible Lint identifies some issues, Spotter takes it further by catching elusive errors, addressing deprecated modules, and facilitating smoother Ansible version upgrades. By using both tools together, we can ensure comprehensive and reliable automation. Ansible Lint is the first step to eliminate common errors, and Spotter picks up where it leaves off, addressing more complex issues and automating many fixes. It's the perfect combination to streamline our Ansible playbook management and upgrade processes.

Playbook Secure Execution

Security is a top priority in IT automation. Spotter adds an extra layer of security by helping us understand what will happen when we run our playbooks. It also guides us in following security best practices to minimize security risks, downtime, and costs. With Steampunk Spotter, we can:

- Prevent misconfigurations, security vulnerabilities, or policy violations.

- Proactively evaluate runtime security threats and prevent security breaches.

- Ensure compliance with security standards.

- Include custom policies to ensure automation meets our specific security requirements and internal team rules.

Customization is a key aspect of Spotter. we can define our own rules and policies to meet our organization's or industry-specific regulations, standards, or compliance requirements. This enables us to specify playbook standards, allowed modules and collections, and naming conventions tailored to our unique needs.

Spotter offers a range of checks to ensure the quality and integrity of our Ansible playbooks:

- **Best Practice Checks**: These checks help structure our playbooks for readability, collaboration, and ease of use.

- **Validation Checks**: These checks verify that modules, parameters, and parameter values within our playbooks are correct and accurate.

- **Upgrade Checks**: These checks ensure that our playbooks are compatible and supported with the latest versions of Ansible and Ansible Collections.

- **Custom Checks**: Customize rules and policies to meet our specific organizational, industry, and security requirements.

- **Security Checks (Coming Soon)**: Spot security misconfigurations within our playbooks and ensure compliance with security best practices in addition to that, Spotter checks Pythin-based Ansible Modules to see if they are safe to use in production environments.

Spotter takes convenience to the next level by offering time-saving features:

- **Automatic Issue Resolution**: Fix issues automatically with suggested changes, saving us time and effort.

- **Module Documentation**: Get instant help with module documentation, complete with direct links to specific module versions.

- **Requirements File Generation**: Generate missing requirements files (requirements. yml) with all the collections we need for the installation.

Insights and Reporting

Spotter is equipped with an intuitive reporting feature that allows us to analyze and scan data, spot trends, monitor progress, and create custom reports. With these insights, we can focus on delivering results and making data-driven decisions.

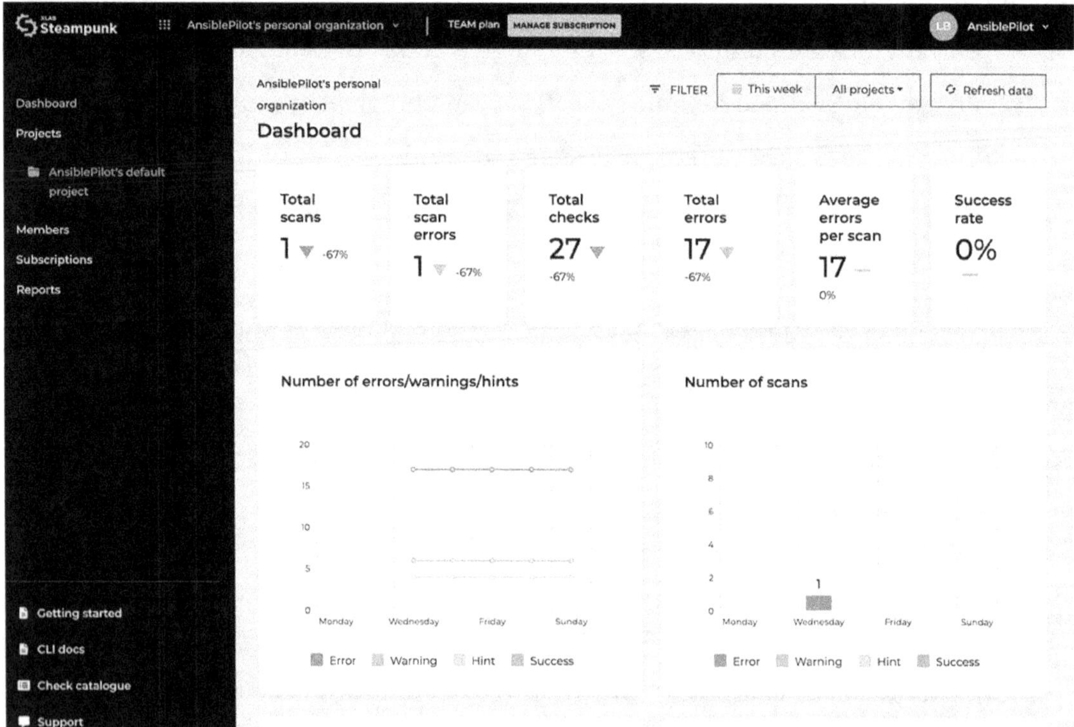

Figure 9.12: Spotter Dashboard

The product has seamless Integration and cross-platform compatibility, taking advantage of Python and pipeline integration. XLAB Steampunk Spotter is versatile and caters to a variety of users:

- Scan playbooks from the command line using the steampunk-spotter CLI tool.

- Check the quality of public Git repositories with the Spotter app.

- Integrate Spotter with GitHub Actions, GitLab, and other CI tools to scan content within CI/CD workflows.

- Analyze and get recommendations for our playbooks directly within Visual Studio Code.

- Spotter is fully compatible with Windows operating systems, allowing seamless integration with other Windows applications to streamline our workflow.

Integrating XLAB Steampunk Spotter with GitLab CI/CD is very simple as it only requires adding one file to an existing GitLab repository to enable the automatic scan of every Ansible content. Once our GitLab repository has been created, we need to set up a YAML file with the test playbook, configure API token authentication for Spotter in CI/CD, and create a "`.gitlab-ci.yml`" file to initiate Spotter scans. From now onward, every code submission is going to be validated using the Spotter in GitLab CI/CD, including generating reports for scan results. The integration process is very simple and enables the seamless validation of every Ansible content using a CI/CD pipeline.

Custom Policies

Spotter's custom policies enable us to craft automation solutions that adhere to internal or industry-specific regulatory standards. With the ability to specify permitted modules, establish naming conventions, and impose constraints on various elements like exposed ports and virtual machine sizes, we gain control over our automation's behavior. Whether we are striving to meet the **Center for Internet Security (CIS)**, **Health Insurance Portability and Accountability Act (HIPAA)**, or **General Data Protection Regulation (GDPR)** standards, custom policies offer the versatility to mold automation according to our goals. Custom policies in Spotter adhere to the **Open Policy Agent (OPA)** [**https://www.openpolicyagent.org/**] engine's standards, leveraging Rego, a rule-based language. Rego rules analyze Spotter's extracted data from Ansible tasks or playbooks, ensuring compliance with the defined conditions and delivering the desired outcomes. Users can conveniently house all their OPA-compliant policies in one location, even incorporating **Keeping Infrastructure as Code Secure (KICS)** policies that follow the same guidelines.

Furthermore, Spotter streamlines the use of KICS policies, providing access to a wealth of pre-written Ansible policies that can be effortlessly imported alongside our custom policies. To apply our custom policies, we can conveniently upload them to Spotter via the **Command Line Interface (CLI)**. The results of these custom policy checks are presented alongside the native check results, providing a comprehensive playbook scan all in one place.

Moreover, we have the option to selectively apply custom policies to playbooks within an organization or a single project, enabling us to cater to the specific requirements of each project, thus enhancing our efficiency. For example, consider a playbook that defines the provisioning of **Amazon Web Services (AWS)** resources. Before importing any policies, a preliminary scan may yield some hints. Once custom Rego policies are imported, Spotter scans the playbook again, quickly identifying issues and guiding us toward resolving them. With the errors identified by custom policies addressed, the playbook is transformed into a successful and compliant automation solution. Tailored according to our needs, it meets the desired standards, ensuring functionality and security.

Custom policies within Spotter allow us to craft automation that perfectly aligns with our specific business objectives and regulatory demands. By incorporating OPA-compliant policies, KICS policies, and custom policies, we can trust that our automation is not only efficient but also secure and compliant. Spotter streamlines this process, making it accessible to organizations of all sizes. If we're seeking to achieve corporate standards and security compliance for our Ansible Playbooks, Spotter is here to help.

Who is it for?

XLAB Steampunk Spotter is designed to meet the diverse needs of professionals in the IT automation and infrastructure management fields:

- **Development**: Playbook Developers can verify templates, check Ansible core and Collection version compatibility, and understand the implications of Ansible upgrades.

- **Quality Assurance**: QA Managers can understand what will happen when running playbooks, perform QA automation without errors, and comprehend best practices and what-if scenarios for testing.

- **Operations**: Operations Managers can identify potential vulnerabilities, receive quality reports and recommendations for improvements, and achieve reliable execution of automation.

- **Security**: IT Security Specialists can use Spotter to prevent misconfigurations and security breaches, ensure corporate compliance standards, and achieve secure execution of automation.

In a rapidly evolving IT landscape, XLAB Steampunk Spotter offers a lifeline for organizations seeking to streamline their Ansible automation processes, enhance security, and ensure compliance. By reducing risks, speeding up automation, and enabling customization, Spotter is poised to become an indispensable tool for those dedicated to efficient, secure, and reliable IT automation.

The team around the XLAB Steampunk Spotter is actively involved in the community, contributing to the quality assurance of popular repositories such as Ansible Lockdown.

Ansible-Lockdown

It is an open-source project sponsored by MindPoint Group. In the ever-evolving landscape of cybersecurity, ensuring the hardening of systems is of paramount importance. Compliance with industry standards and benchmarks is a fundamental step in establishing a secure foundation for an organization's IT infrastructure. Ansible Lockdown is used to achieve recognized security benchmark compliance for CIS (Center for Internet Security) or **Secure Technical Implementation Guides** (**STIG**). Recognized and recommended by Mitre, it is a must-have to meet PCI, HIPAA, NIST, CMMC, FedRAMP, and other regulatory compliance requirements. One such standard is the **Center for Internet Security** (**CIS**) Benchmark, which provides a comprehensive set of baselines for securing and applying good practices to various operating systems. Many of these baselines have already been converted to Ansible Playbooks and are regularly maintained and updated by the Ansible-Lockdown project.

Red Hat Enterprise Linux (**RHEL**) 9 is renowned for its stability and security features. By harnessing the power of Ansible automation, organizations can automate the implementation of CIS Benchmark guidelines, thereby fortifying their systems against potential threats. The following example delves into the significance of automating security compliance using the Ansible-Lockdown project and the role of the RHEL 9 CIS Benchmark.

Automation with Ansible

Automating the implementation of CIS benchmarks with Ansible and ansible-lockdown offers numerous advantages:

- **Standardization and Consistency**: Manually implementing CIS benchmarks across multiple systems is a complex and time-consuming endeavor. Ansible, with its declarative language, allows organizations to consistently apply security controls, minimizing human errors and ensuring adherence to the CIS benchmark guidelines. This standardized approach forms the bedrock of a robust security posture.

- **Time and Resource Efficiency**: Implementing CIS benchmarks manually on each system is labor-intensive. Ansible automation significantly reduces the time and effort required to apply security configurations. With a single playbook, organizations can automate the hardening process across numerous systems simultaneously, saving valuable time and freeing up resources for other critical tasks.

- **Highly configurable:** Not all suggested controls contained within a baseline can be implemented on all systems. Utilizing ansible-playbooks and the highly configurable ansible-lockdown, with the use of ansible variable precedence, roles can be adapted to run across many types or groups of servers, allowing different configurations to be deployed to differing systems where applicable.

- **Scalability and Manageability**: Ansible's scalability makes it an ideal tool for applying CIS benchmarks across large and distributed environments. Whether managing a handful of systems or hundreds of servers, Ansible allows for efficient and centralized management of security configurations. Updates and changes to the benchmark can be effortlessly implemented across the infrastructure, ensuring ongoing compliance.

- **Consistent Auditability and Compliance**: Compliance with CIS benchmarks often necessitates periodic audits and assessments. Ansible provides built-in capabilities to track and document changes made during the automation process, ensuring a clear audit trail. Organizations can generate reports demonstrating compliance with the CIS benchmarks, simplifying the compliance and audit processes.

- **Rapid Response to Security Threats**: Automating CIS benchmark configurations with Ansible enables organizations to respond swiftly to emerging security threats. Ansible playbooks can be updated and re-executed in real time to enforce new security controls or remediate vulnerabilities identified in the CIS benchmark. This agility ensures systems remain protected and aligned with the latest security best practices.

- **Continuous Monitoring and Enforcement**: Ansible allows for continuous monitoring and enforcement of CIS benchmark configurations. Playbooks can be scheduled to run periodically or triggered by events, ensuring that systems remain hardened. If any deviations from the benchmark are detected, Ansible can automatically remediate the issues, restoring systems to a secure state.

Automating the implementation of CIS benchmarks using Ansible-Lockdown simplifies the process, saves time and resources, ensures consistency and compliance, and enhances an organization's ability to respond to security threats. By leveraging Ansible's automation capabilities, organizations can strengthen their security posture, improve operational efficiency, and maintain ongoing adherence to industry-recognized security standards.

Implementation Steps

To effectively implement the automation of the CIS Benchmark hardening for RHEL 9 with Ansible, organizations can follow these steps:

Step 1: Familiarize ourself with the CIS Benchmark

Start by obtaining the latest CIS Benchmark for RHEL 9 and thoroughly review the guidelines and recommendations for securing our RHEL 9 systems.

Step 2: Install and Configure Ansible.

Ensure that Ansible is installed on our control machine, which will execute the hardening tasks on the target RHEL 9 systems.

Step 3: Download the Ansible-Lockdown Resources.

The Ansible-Lockdown project has created a series of Ansible roles that correspond to the necessary tasks for hardening RHEL 9, aligning with the CIS Benchmark recommendations.

```
$ ansible-galaxy install git+https://github.com/ansible-lockdown/
RHEL9-CIS.git
```

The expected output look like:

```
Starting galaxy role install process
- extracting RHEL9-CIS to /Users/devops/.ansible/roles/RHEL9-CIS
- RHEL9-CIS was installed successfully
```

Step 4: Create an Ansible Playbook

Enhance the flexibility and reusability of the playbook by defining the "RHEL9-CIS" role where appropriate. An example playbook is often provided with the Ansible role, which can be used as a starting point.

```
-                              -                              -
- name: Run RHEL9-CIS role
  hosts: all
  become: true
  roles:
      - role: "RHEL9-CIS"
```

Step 5: Create Our Ansible Inventory

Define the list of target hosts and how to connect to them in our Ansible inventory. This includes specifying host names, connection methods, and user credentials. In my case, connecting to the **rhel.example.com** host in my network:

```
rhel.example.com
```

Step 6: Execute the Ansible Playbook

Use the **ansible-playbook** command to execute the playbook on the development machine or via the Automation Controller Job Template. The playbook should automate the tasks that align with the CIS Benchmark recommendations, such as restricting root access, configuring network parameters, enabling auditing, and securing system services.

The output of the execution summarize the findings according to the CIS report document:

```
[...]
TASK [RHEL9-CIS : If Warnings found Output count and control IDs
affected] *******************
ok: [rhel.example.com] => {
    "msg": "You have 16 Warning(s) that require investigating that
are related to the following benchmark ID(s)  [1.1.2.1] [1.1.3.1]
[1.1.4.1] [1.1.5.1] [1.1.6.1] [1.1.7.1] [1.1.8.1] [1.2.3] [1.6.1.6]
[2.4] [4.3] [6.1.10] [6.1.11] [6.1.13] [6.1.14] [6.1.15]"
}
PLAY RECAP ***************************************************************
************************

rhel.example.com                 : ok=343    changed=4      unreachable=0
failed=0     skipped=173  rescued=0    ignored=0
```

Step 7: Test and Verify

Thoroughly test the playbook in a test environment before deploying it in production. Utilize Ansible's dry-run mode to preview changes without making actual modifications to the systems. Develop a verification process to ensure that the desired hardening configurations have been successfully applied to our RHEL 9 systems.

Step 8: Schedule and Monitor

Schedule the execution of our Ansible playbook periodically to enforce continuous hardening and compliance with the CIS Benchmark. Implement monitoring mechanisms to alert us to any deviations from the desired security configurations. Ansible provides various reporting and logging options to facilitate this monitoring process.

Automating the hardening process for Operating systems using Ansible and the CIS Benchmark allows organizations to establish a robust security posture efficiently. By following the approach outlined in this example, we can leverage the power of Ansible's automation capabilities to enforce security configurations consistently across their RHEL 9 systems. Staying up to date with the latest CIS Benchmark recommendations is crucial to staying ahead of emerging security threats. Using those playbooks provided by the ansible-lockdown project takes away a lot of the overhead in updating and maintaining the role content. Implementing CIS Benchmark hardening with Ansible not only strengthens the security of RHEL 9 infrastructure but also saves valuable time and resources by automating repetitive manual tasks.

Good Practices for Ansible

The **Good Practices for Ansible (GPA)** is a worldwide initiative by the Red Hat Automation Community of Practice. Many hours of automation experts from different Red Hat organizations have flown into it, and all this massive experience is open to use by anybody. Eric Lavarde and Moritz Schönwetter are the main contributors and shared with me the importance of standardizing Ansible best practices during the Ansible Community Day Berlin 2023. They recognized that while individual consultants, engineers, and support personnel had their own effective methods, there was a need to establish a unified approach. This approach ensures that everyone involved in Ansible-related activities follows a common set of guidelines and practices. The initiative called "**Good Practices for Ansible (GPA)**" began by adopting GitOps principles, treating best practices as code. Collaborative efforts led to the development of a repository that encompasses best practices for Ansible. These recommendations extend beyond the scope of Ansible Linter, addressing code organization, role structure, inventory management, and more.

This best practices initiative goes beyond Ansible Linter. While Ansible Linter primarily focuses on checking code for formatting and field usage, this project extends its scope to cover broader aspects of Ansible playbook development. It encompasses considerations related to code organization and playbook structuring, areas where Ansible Linter may not provide direct guidance. The project's future, Eric and Moritz expressed their aspiration to compile a comprehensive Ansible community book. This book would serve as a valuable resource for Ansible practitioners worldwide. While the vision is ambitious, it aligns perfectly with the collaborative and community-driven spirit of Ansible. The project is open to contributions from the Ansible community and encourages users to get involved. Read more on the website: **https://redhat-cop.github.io/automation-good-practices/**

Key learning

We can organize, simplify, and scale up IT processes using Ansible automation. The "**ansible.network**" meta collection is specifically created for network infrastructures and devices. Managing a large fleet implies adopting a strategy for rolling updates and rapidly and consistently applying security patches to monitor and respond to threads. When the appetite for automation grows in our organization, we might need to create some custom Ansible resources, such as plugins and modules, and distribute them as a collection via the Automation Hub.

Points to remember

- Use the **persist, list, deploy, gather, detect,** and **remediate** operations in some "**ansible.network**" collection when managing our network devices.

- Managing a large fleet and organization requires organizing some IT processes to automate as much as possible to quickly respond to security threats and rapidly apply any software update via rolling upgrades.

- Use the **TestModule, FilterModule, CallbackModule, LookupModule**, and **AnsibleModule** to create out custom Ansible resources.

Multiple choice questions

1. **What Ansible namespace we need to use to automate our network?**

    a. `network.base`

    b. `ansible.network`

    c. `network.ospf`

    d. `network.bgp`

2. **What SSH library is the most used in Ansible Network automation?**

    a. libSSH

    b. Paramiko

    c. OpenSSH

    d. Not possible

3. **What Ansible applies rolling updates on Red Hat Enterprise Linux?**

    a. `ansible.builtin.yum`

    b. `ansible.builtin.apt`

    c. `ansible.builtin.file`

    d. `ansible.builtin.debug`

4. **How can we create a new collection in the Automation Hub?**

    a. Use the "`Upload collection`" button

    b. Create namespace

    c. Authorize via the Approval section

    d. It's not possible

Answers

1. b

2. a

3. d

4. a

Questions

1. What are the four most used common connection plugins for Ansible Network?

2. What is the strategy to protect our organization from security threads?

3. What are the key Ansible modules for applying rolling updates?

4. What is the difference between an Ansible module and a plugin?

5. What are the special class variables for a custom Ansible callback plugin?

6. How can we distribute custom Ansible resources between our organization>

Key terms

- **NetOps:** NetOps, short for Network Operations, is a set of practices and methodologies aimed at efficiently managing and optimizing network infrastructure to ensure its reliability, performance, and security.

- **Brownfield Inventory**: A Brownfield Inventory is a dynamic inventory of existing network configurations and resources, serving as a single source of truth for automation and management purposes in network infrastructure.

- **IaC**: **Infrastructure as Code (IaC)** is the practice of managing and provisioning IT infrastructure using code and automation tools to achieve consistency, efficiency, and scalability.

- **Local Execution**: Local Execution refers to the process of running commands or scripts directly on a local computer or device, typically without the need for network connectivity or remote access.

- **Remote Execution**: Remote Execution refers to the process of running commands or scripts on a remote computer or device, often facilitated through network connectivity or remote access tools, allowing for management and automation of remote resources.

- **TUI**: A **Text-based User Interface** (**TUI**) is a computer interface that utilizes text characters and menus to interact with and control software applications, typically in a terminal or console environment.

- **CLI**: A **Command Line Interface** (**CLI**) is a text-based user interface that allows users to interact with a computer or software by entering text commands, typically in a terminal or console, for performing various tasks and operations.

Join our book's Discord space

Join the book's Discord Workspace for Latest updates, Offers, Tech happenings around the world, New Release and Sessions with the Authors:

https://discord.bpbonline.com

CHAPTER 10

Wrap-Up

Introduction

Red Hat Ansible Automation Platform is important in strategic automation within an enterprise context. It encourages collaboration across different teams within our organization, such as developers, operations, IT, and security. It enables these teams to work together in automating tasks.

Structure

In this chapter, we will discuss the following topics:

- Review of Ansible Automation Platform
- Use cases
- Administration
- Ansible SDK
- Ansible validated contents
- The future

Objectives

In this chapter, we are going to capitalize on and summarize the success of the previous chapters and understand the holistic impact that the Ansible Automation Platform can have on our organization.

Review of Ansible Automation Platform

Ansible is a powerful automation tool that simplifies and streamlines various IT tasks for every modern organization, offering numerous benefits through the enterprise its Ansible Automation Platform. This platform empowers organizations to achieve efficiency, consistency, and scalability in IT operations. To harness the power of Ansible, it's essential to understand its fundamental workings. Ansible operates based on playbooks, which consist of plays, tasks, and modules. These playbooks use inventories and the main Ansible configuration file to define the target systems and configuration details. Ansible also leverages variables, allowing users to customize automation processes and gain insights into their tasks through the debug module and Ansible facts.

Additionally, Ansible introduces key constructs like conditionals, handlers, and loops to control automation flow. Templating using Jinja2 and the template module enables the creation of dynamic configuration files. Roles and Collections are two fundamental concepts in Ansible that provide a structured way to organize and reuse Ansible resources. Roles contain only playbooks and tasks, whereas Collections can contain any Ansible resources, especially modules, and plugins that significantly expand the Ansible capabilities. The latest releases of Ansible take advantage of containers to guarantee the same experience from the Ansible Creator to the final consumer. The execution in a container of our playbook and Ansible resources is called the Ansible Execution Environment. We can build our custom Execution Environment with the Ansible resources, Collections, and Python dependency for a completely customizable experience. Often, the custom execution environments are used in enterprise environments where custom certification authorities are involved to validate content internally in our organization.

The Automation Hub, part of the Ansible Automation Platform, further enhances role, collection, and execution environment management in a common interface that all the stakeholders could use.

Ansible offers an Automation Controller for operationalizing automation that facilitates job execution, inventory management, and credential handling. This leads to creating automation jobs using job templates, which can be tailored with surveys to enable self-service IT. Role-based access control ensures security and restricts access to specific organizations and teams. Finally, Ansible enables the visualization of automation workflows through its workflow visualizer, allowing users to understand convergence and divergence points in complex automation processes. Ansible is a comprehensive automation solution that empowers organizations to streamline their IT operations efficiently and securely. Complex network topologies are handled via the Ansible Mesh technology with hop nodes. We can interact with the Automation Controller using the web user interface, the RESTful API endpoints, or the command line utility.

Ansible is a robust automation platform that simplifies IT management and enables the efficient execution of various tasks. The Ansible Automation Platform encompasses essential concepts and functionalities crucial for automation. One can install the platform to start, setting the foundation for automation excellence. The heart of Ansible lies in playbooks, which consist of tasks executed on managed hosts. These playbooks are fueled by inventories, listing the managed hosts, and variables that facilitate playbook management. Ansible offers precise task control mechanisms, including handlers for event-based responses and error management.

Moreover, Ansible streamlines file deployment on managed hosts, allowing for seamless file management. As automation tasks become more intricate, Ansible equips users with the ability to craft complex plays and playbooks efficiently. The platform further enhances efficiency through roles, enabling the reuse of Ansible code and expediting playbook development. Dynamic inventories in Ansible provide real-time information about the infrastructure, making it easier to manage and automate. This feature ensures that changes in the infrastructure are reflected in the management process.

The latest generative artificial intelligence is powered inside the Ansible Lightspeed product. A typical development journey involves using these tools: Visual Studio Code with Ansible extension, language server, ansible-lint, molecule, ansible-navigator, and potentially other development goodies.

Troubleshooting is made simpler with Ansible's built-in debugging capabilities, verbose execution and traceback output, and some additional tools.

Finally, Ansible's prowess extends to automating and orchestrating Windows, Linux, and Cloud automation administration tasks, making it a valuable tool for simplifying common system administration processes. With these capabilities at one's disposal, Ansible becomes an indispensable asset in automation and IT management.

Installation scenarios

There are many installation scenarios for the Ansible Automation Platform according to the resilience, reliability, and workload capability that our organization requires. Various installation scenarios exist for the Automation Controller, private Automation Hub, and the complete Ansible Automation Platform. The various scenarios include standalone setups, internal and external PostgreSQL databases, and Kubernetes-based deployments. The various options are:

- Single-machine installations for the Automation Controller and Automation Hub are the simplest and most useful for labs, development environments, or minimal setups.

- An Automation Controller or Automation Hub with an internal PostgreSQL database is the easiest scenario.

- High-availability installations of the Automation Controller and Automation Hub with external PostgreSQL databases are the most complex, supporting active-active nodes.

Role management

The Ansible Automation Platform has many customizable settings to enhance the management of user permissions, security, and authentication methods. These are just representative of the features included that enable fine-tuning for our workflows:

- **Automation Controller Settings**: Contains many options to optimize Ansible job execution and customization.

- **Users, Teams, and RBAC**: Apply role management to Users, Roles, and Teams in orchestrating and securing automation processes, emphasizing **role-based access control (RBAC)**.

- **Role-Based Access Controls (RBAC)**: We can apply Roles, Resources, and Users in RBAC, highlighting the role hierarchy and its application in various aspects of the Automation Controller.

- **Authentication Integrations**: Large organizations benefit from integrating external authentication mechanisms (e.g., LDAP, Active Directory, SAML, Open) into the Ansible Automation Platform to enhance security and user management.

- **Ansible Automation Platform Central Authentication**: Introduces a versatile third-party identity provider solution for streamlined single sign-on and user management within the platform.

Effective service account management requires collaboration across teams. Automation tools can bring teams together by providing a unified platform for managing accounts. Cultural fit is essential in adopting these tools, as it requires people to adapt to new ways of working and bring their expertise to the table. Security is a top priority in service account management. Ansible provides the capability to store credentials securely in the Ansible vault. This ensures that sensitive information is protected while enabling automation.

The Ansible Automation Platform emphasizes the importance of configuring settings to optimize automation processes and manage user access efficiently. It also emphasizes the benefits of RBAC and external authentication integrations in maintaining security and collaboration. Key points to remember include customizing job execution and log-level settings, defining users, groups, and teams for permissions, and integrating authentication services for user credential management.

Integration

Ansible Automation Platform could integrate with all the modern IT infrastructure of our organization. In modern IT ecosystems, organizations use a multitude of services. Managing access to each of these services can take time and effort. Ansible can be employed to connect to various services, abstracting the complexities of access control. This ensures that teams can access services without worrying about the intricacies of permissions. Integration refers to the process of seamlessly incorporating the Ansible Automation Platform into an organization's existing infrastructure and workflows. This integration involves connecting the Ansible Automation Platform with various systems, services, and tools to enhance automation, streamline operations, and improve efficiency. Key aspects of Ansible Automation Platform integration include:

- **Configuration Management**: Integrating Ansible with configuration management tools like Puppet, Chef, or Terraform to automate and manage infrastructure provisioning and configuration. We can achieve this via GitOps using the right Ansible collections.

- **Windows integration**: Enhance compatibility with Windows-based systems.

- **Cloud Services**: Integrating with cloud platforms such as Amazon Web Services, Microsoft Azure, or Google Cloud Platform to automate cloud resource provisioning and management. Each provider could maintain an Ansible-certified collection in the Automation Hub.

- **Provisioning VMs with Automation**: Ansible playbooks can be tailored to create VMs with predefined configurations, ensuring consistency and reducing manual intervention.

- **Container Orchestration**: Integrating with container orchestration platforms like Kubernetes to automate the deployment and management of containerized applications.

- **CI/CD Pipelines**: Integrating Ansible into **continuous integration/continuous deployment (CI/CD)** pipelines to automate application deployment, testing, and release processes.

- **Monitoring and Logging**: Integrating Ansible with monitoring and logging tools like Grafana, Nagios, Prometheus, or ELK Stack for automated monitoring and alerting.

- **Security and Compliance**: Integrating Ansible with security and compliance tools to automate security policy enforcement and compliance checks.

- **Authentication and Authorization**: Integrating with **Identity Management (IDM)**, authentication and authorization systems (e.g., LDAP, Active Directory, SAML) to manage user access and permissions.

- **API Integration**: Leveraging Ansible's RESTful API to integrate with other applications and services, enabling automation of various tasks.

- **Inventory Management**: Integrating Ansible with inventory management systems to dynamically discover and manage hosts and resources. Dynamic inventory enables us to report a fast-pacing enterprise fleet of machines.

- **Custom Modules and Plugins**: Developing custom Ansible modules and plugins to extend functionality and adapt to specific integration requirements.

- **Governance Control with ServiceNown**: Maintaining governance and control over changes is paramount in regulated markets. Integrating Ansible with ServiceNow enables organizations to create change records and validate changes within the designated windows. This integration helps maintain compliance and security.

- **Trust and Privilege Access**: Trust is essential in service account management. Organizations can maintain a high level of trust in their operations by controlling privileges and ensuring elevated rights like **Power Distribution Unit (PDU)** access. Automation tools facilitate this by granting access only when needed.

Overall, Ansible Automation Platform integration empowers organizations to achieve greater automation, orchestration, and control across their IT infrastructure. It enables the automation of repetitive tasks, improves operational efficiency, and promotes consistency and reliability in IT operations.

AWX community

Choosing the right service account management solution is crucial in every organization, but especially in regulated industries. AWX represents a powerful solution for small businesses and hobbits seeking to harness the full potential of automation in their IT operations. It offers a user-friendly interface, robust feature set, and vibrant open-source community. AWX offers a path to increased efficiency, improved security, and enhanced agility. However, it doesn't have Red Hat Award-winning support and integration of commercial plugins. It might be an alternative for a small business looking to streamline IT processes. AWX is a valuable tool to consider on our journey toward automation excellence or to build a laboratory compatible with Ansible and Automation Controller quickly. AWX, supported by Red Hat, misses some integrated authentication and plugins from the Automation Controller. If our organization is looking for a complete solution is better to evaluate the Ansible Automation Platform that it is ready to use from day one, supports multi-cloud environments, spreads costs efficiently, and encourages community participation in platform improvements.

Use cases

Ansible Automation Platform has a relevant importance of IT automation and the role it plays in transforming businesses. The following six common automation use cases are the most prominent and used in the context of the Ansible Automation Platform:

- **Infrastructure Automation**: Ansible can automate the provisioning, configuration, and management of servers, virtual machines, and cloud resources. This use case helps organizations scale their infrastructure efficiently, reduce manual tasks, and ensure consistent configurations.

- **Network Automation**: Ansible can automate network device configuration and management, making it easier to deploy and manage network infrastructure. It helps in ensuring network reliability, security, and compliance.

- **Security Automation**: Security automation with Ansible involves automating security tasks such as vulnerability scanning, patch management, and incident response. This helps organizations enhance their security posture by reducing the time it takes to detect and respond to security threats.

- **DevOps Automation**: Ansible is widely used in DevOps practices to automate software deployment, application provisioning, and **continuous integration/ continuous deployment (CI/CD)** pipelines. It accelerates software delivery and improves collaboration between development and operations teams.

- **Hybrid and Multicloud Automation**: Ansible provides a consistent automation framework for managing resources across hybrid and multi cloud environments. It allows organizations to automate tasks across various cloud platforms and on-premises infrastructure.

- **Edge Automation**: Edge automation involves managing and automating edge computing devices and infrastructure. Ansible can help in configuring and maintaining edge devices efficiently, ensuring reliable edge computing operations.

These everyday use cases demonstrate the versatility and applicability of the Ansible Automation Platform across various domains, from IT infrastructure to security and DevOps. By implementing automation in these areas, organizations can save time, reduce costs, enhance the quality of their services, and increase employee satisfaction. The provided customer success stories also showcase real-world examples of organizations benefiting from Ansible automation.

Administration

The Ansible Automation Platform requires low maintenance from the IT System Administration point of view as Red Hat provides up-to-date packages and maintains the security patches. A day-to-day journey usually involves:

1. **Service Starting, Stopping, and Restarting**: The essential tasks of starting, stopping, and restarting services within the Ansible Automation Platform are available in a command line utility. These actions are essential in maintaining the overall health and stability of the IT infrastructure.

2. **Log Files**: Log files in IT operations, particularly within the Ansible Automation Platform, are critical to guarantee service observability. Consolidating the log files provides valuable information for monitoring and troubleshooting system performance and issues.

3. **Metrics Endpoint**: The API endpoint has a cornerstone role in monitoring and integrating with tools like Grafana and Splunk.

4. **Connect Ansible Metrics Endpoint to Grafana**: Details the process of connecting the Ansible metrics endpoint to Grafana for visualizing and analyzing system metrics.

5. **Logging Tools**: we can use the most popular logging tools used in modern IT operations, including tools like Splunk, ELK Stack, Datadog, Sumo Logic, Loggly, SolarWinds Log Analyzer, and New Relic Logs.

6. **Connect Ansible Controller Logging to Splunk**: Ansible Controller logging is deeply integrated for centralized log management and analysis.

7. **Backup & Restore**: the backup and restoration mechanisms integrated into the Ansible Automation Platform are important for creating a robust backup and restoration strategy in every IT management and providing best practices for executing these operations, especially in disaster recovery.

We discovered in this book the knowledge and skills to effectively manage IT operations related to the Ansible Automation Platform. Every system administration task is important is daily maintenance, such as starting, stopping, and monitoring services, managing log files, and implementing backup and restoration strategies. Additionally, the integration capabilities with metrics, Grafana, Splunk, and various logging tools enhance system monitoring and analysis, especially in corporate environments.

Ansible SDK

Ansible SDK serves as a programmatic interface to Ansible, allowing users to dispatch and monitor Ansible tasks, roles, and playbooks directly from their Python projects. Whether you're a developer looking to integrate Ansible into your application or a system administrator seeking to automate tasks with precision, Ansible SDK has you covered. The key features of Ansible SDK are:

- **Access and control**: Ansible SDK provides access to Ansible operations and enables fine-grained control over automation tasks. This means you can programmatically trigger and manage Ansible tasks as needed.

- **Parameter marshalling**: You can marshal parameters for Ansible operations into various formats, making it easier to pass data to and from Ansible. This flexibility ensures compatibility with different data structures.

- **Native Python data**: Ansible SDK allows you to work with native Python data structures when interacting with Ansible. This simplifies data manipulation and integration with your Python projects.

Ansible SDK operates within your Python application, accepting inputs such as projects, credentials, and inventories. These inputs define the scope of your automation tasks. Ansible SDK then makes asynchronous calls to execute these tasks against your defined project payload.

There are two primary modes of execution:

- **Local Execution**: In this mode, Ansible SDK utilizes Ansible Runner to run automation tasks locally. Ansible Runner is responsible for pulling execution environments, running jobs, and reporting back to Ansible SDK.

- **Remote Execution**: Here, Ansible SDK communicates with an Automation mesh controller node to execute automation tasks remotely. The controller node oversees the execution of jobs across a distributed mesh.

Similarly, we might see any Ansible Automation Platform-compatible devices emerging in the industry.

Running Automation Jobs with Ansible SDK

Ansible SDK provides tools to run automation jobs directly from your project. You can execute Ansible content using **AnsibleJobDef**, which defines jobs, and JobExecutor, which runs these jobs. Here's a simple example of running an automation job using Ansible SDK:

```
from ansible_sdk import AnsibleJobDef
from ansible_sdk.executors import AnsibleSubprocessJobExecutor

# Declare the job executor to use.
executor = AnsibleSubprocessJobExecutor()
# Configure the job definition.
jobdef = AnsibleJobDef('datadir', 'pb.yml')
# Run the job with the executor.
job_status = await executor.submit_job(jobdef)
```

Running Automation Mesh Jobs

Automation mesh is a scalable cluster of Receptor nodes that execute Ansible playbooks. Ansible SDK enables you to invoke jobs directly on nodes in the automation mesh. This allows for distributed automation tasks with ease.

To run an automation mesh job with Ansible SDK, you'll need to set up a locally running cluster of Receptor nodes and then use Ansible SDK to connect to and execute tasks across this mesh.

Ansible SDK is a valuable addition to the Ansible ecosystem, offering programmatic control and automation capabilities that extend beyond the traditional command-line interface. Whether you're looking to streamline your automation workflows or integrate Ansible seamlessly into your Python projects, Ansible SDK provides the tools you need to achieve your automation goals. As IT environments become more complex, tools like Ansible SDK become essential for efficient management and automation.

Solutions using Ansible SDK can use the Ansible inside logo, allowing the developer to embed it inside their application. This allows us to spin up the playbook locally or activate the Ansible mesh to spread the execution.

Ansible validated content

Announced during AnsibleFest 2022, Ansible validated content is a game-changer for automation enthusiasts. Ansible validated content is a key component of Ansible Content Collections, introduced in 2019 for packaging, distributing, and utilizing Ansible content, such as playbooks, roles, modules, plugins, tests, and documentation. It is distributed as YAML-based collections that complement Red Hat Ansible Certified Content Collections. Initially, Ansible validated content can be found as a pre-loaded option within the private automation hub of Ansible Automation Platform 2.3, emphasizing supply chain security. In the future, it will be accessible on console.redhat.com's Ansible automation hub, and more validated content will be developed over time through contributions from Red Hat and partners. This initiative aims to enhance automation and is open to feedback and input from customers and users in shaping its future, providing new opportunities for the Ansible community.

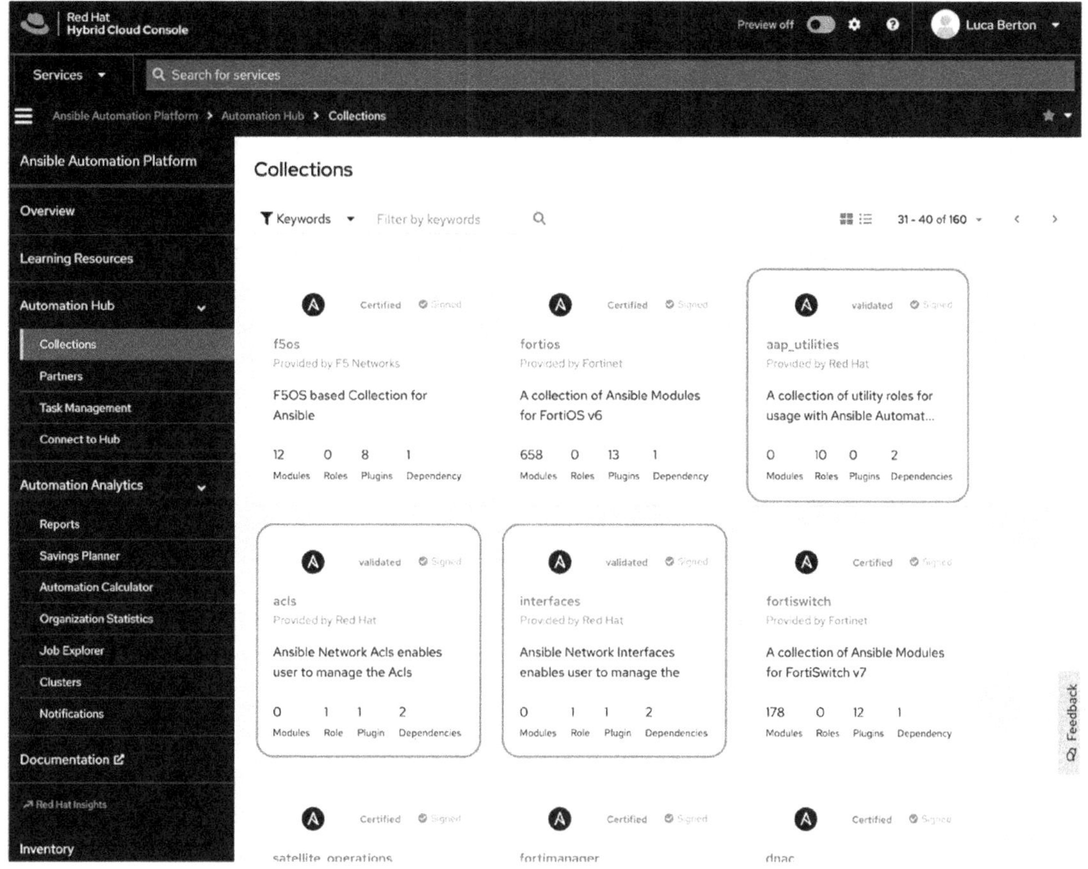

Figure 10.1: Ansible Validated Content

The future

Ansible Automation Platform is a vibrant framework for every organization that wants to propel their business with Ansible automation. The future of the Ansible Automation Platform is set to be a dynamic and robust ecosystem, marked by the introduction of key features and capabilities. With an emphasis on Collections, Ansible users will gain the ability to create, manage, and scale automation solutions, accompanied by Certified content to ensure its quality and reliability. The integration of signed content and cyber assessment tools like Sonarcloud, Raven, and Fortify, together with Pentester capabilities, will fortify the security aspects of automation. Secure supply chain management is being addressed with tools such as Backstage.io, sigstore, Devspace for OpenShift, and Prodsec DigiCert integration. Furthermore, Ansible is focusing on enhancing Identity Access Management and establishing a Red Hat trusted supply chain.

The importance of Certified Content cannot be overstated. Certified Content assures users of the quality, reliability, and compatibility of automation resources distributed via

Automation Hub. It undergoes rigorous testing and validation to ensure that it meets the highest industry standards. This approach provides peace of mind to users by offering a curated selection of automation assets that are ready for immediate deployment in various environments. Moreover, the platform emphasizes the integration of Validated Content, which goes through a comprehensive validation process to ensure its correctness and effectiveness. This content is thoroughly examined to verify that it functions as intended and aligns with best practices. By incorporating Validated Content, Ansible continues to uphold its commitment to delivering trustworthy and dependable automation solutions. To further enhance the security and trustworthiness of automation resources, Ansible has introduced the concept of Signed content. Signed content is digitally signed to confirm its authenticity and origin, assuring users that the content hasn't been tampered with. This adds an extra layer of security, making sure that the automation assets in use are coming from trusted sources, thus bolstering the overall reliability of the Ansible Automation Platform. Together, Certified, Validated, and Signed content represent Ansible's dedication to providing a secure and dependable automation ecosystem for its users.

Developers can look forward to leveraging the Developer containerized experience, implementing Policy as Code, and ensuring policy enforcement at all stages, including Exadata support for granular automation control before, during, and after the automation process. This vision underscores Ansible's commitment to delivering an all-encompassing automation platform for the modern world.

In the present landscape of the Ansible Automation Platform, it is paramount to note the inclusion of hyperscale deployment options, which enable seamless integration with major cloud providers, ensuring the platform's versatility and adaptability. Additionally, the integration of Direct LDAP support in **Role-Based Access Control** (RBAC) reinforces security and governance measures, facilitating the management of user privileges.

In the near term, Ansible is geared towards introducing a fresh and intuitive new web user interface, making automation more accessible and user-friendly. This will be complemented by integrating advanced automation analytics, which provides valuable insights into the performance and efficiency of automation workflows. Furthermore, introducing usage and subscription visibility offers transparency and control over the platform's consumption and billing, streamlining its use in enterprise settings.

Looking towards the long term, Ansible envisions a Unified **User Experience** (UX) that seamlessly blends different platform components, ensuring a consistent and efficient user journey. The containerized **Ansible Automation Platform (AAP)** will enhance its portability and scalability, aligning with modern container orchestration technologies and best practices. This long-term perspective underscores Ansible's commitment to continuous innovation and providing an automation platform that evolves to meet the ever-changing demands of the automation landscape.

Conclusion

We are still determining what the future is going to bring to our automation journey. The future is going to happen whether we want it or not. We, as humans, are going to evolve. Obviously, the tools are evolving as well. The ability to execute innovative projects is so much more. It's important to upskill ourselves and keep track of the changes in the products and in the market. We live in a very unique time because all the information about the world is available at our fingertips. Think how many tools entered and exited in our lifespan: card catalogs, rotary phones, payphones, rolodexes, etc.

At the moment, there is a rise in the market of generative artificial intelligence technologies that are going to help and assist our human life.

Our automation journey is always evolving. We are orchestrating workflows better in any organization and in different ways. Remember that automation is a journey, and all the stakeholders in our organization should embrace and capitalize on the success. There are many commonalities in many automation cases, and we can all learn from each other.

Nowadays, An IT professional must bridge the gap between the operations and the business.

The journey to becoming an automation expert is flexible, with many paths to success. Studying ourselves and being actively involved in the community to equip ourselves for success is a key component. When it comes to climbing the corporate ladder or starting our own business, networking is very crucial. An insatiable need to understand how things work is very useful and doesn't rely only on academic qualifications. Intellectual curiosity to understand how things work with hands-on experience leads to automation success. The best approach is to keep it simple!

Mastering the basics is key for an organization to improve the automation journey. Share with all the stakeholders the automation goals and simple measures. Instead of getting lost in the newest technological advancement, organizations can save time and reduce human burdens by focusing on simple tasks. Such as patching software vulnerabilities, limiting the user's account, implementing CI/CD pipelines for software deployment, and preventing security breaches. Prioritizing these basics saves time to focus on more interesting challenges.

Embracing the joy of learning to keep up on the latest opportunities to save time, optimize our workflows, and navigate the fascinating world of automation.

I encourage all newcomers to leverage the plethora of resources available about Ansible Automation and education and to embrace continuous learning.

Stepping outside the traditional path and engaging with a broader community helps us navigate the vast landscape of system automation.

Humans are not a liability in system automation, and usually, they are willing to change how they operate daily. Rather, we should empower the users to suggest automation challenges.

It's a beautiful reminder of human decency: be genuinely kind and respectful to others as it leads to success. This approach fosters positive outcomes in life.

Automation Experts should comprehend the business they serve, advocating for a balance between operations and automation, prioritizing basic and short-term wins to complex automation scenarios, and capitalizing on success. Step by step, we can achieve wonderful results.

Pursue our tomorrow, shaping our career. Use automation as a vessel to shape the future business and transform nothing into something. Technology has the power to elevate humanity. The total system produces extraordinary results by using the technology to enhance human ingenuity, not replacing it. By steadfastly optimizing the system, not discrete metrics, Ansible sets the benchmark for automation excellence.

Key learning

Effective service account management is essential for maintaining security, compliance, and operational efficiency in every industry, especially in highly regulated markets. By leveraging IT integration and automation tools like Ansible, organizations can streamline service account provisioning, improve access control, and enhance collaboration among teams. Furthermore, integrating ServiceNow, optimizing performance, and choosing the right platform, like Ansible Automation Platform, can help organizations navigate the complexities of service account management in regulated environments.

Points to remember

- AWX is an open-source automation platform sponsored by Red Hat that simplifies and enhances IT automation through a user-friendly web interface, role-based access control, and job scheduling capabilities.

- ServiceNow integration involves connecting ServiceNow, a popular IT service management platform, with other systems and applications to streamline processes, automate tasks, and improve efficiency in managing IT services and operations.

- Ansible SDK is a Python-based interface that allows users to programmatically trigger, control, and manage Ansible tasks, roles, and playbooks, making integrating Ansible automation into their Python projects easier.

Multiple choice questions

1. **What is not a supported installation scenario?**

    a. Single-machine

    b. Machine with internal database

    c. Machine with external database

    d. All components in one machine

2. **What is not a feature to manage roles in the Automation Controller?**

    a. Single user

    b. Users

    c. Teams

    d. RBAC

3. **How can we create a disaster recovery environment?**

    a. Starting, Stopping, and Restarting feature

    b. Ansible SDK

    c. Backup & Restore feature

    d. None of the previous options

4. **What is not a typical Ansible Use Case?**

    a. Infrastructure Automation

    b. Network Automation

    c. Software development

    d. Security Automation

Answer

1. d

2. a

3. c

4. c

Questions

1. How can we integrate Ansible in a highly regulated environment with Service Now?

2. What are the enterprise authentication options for the Ansible Automation Platform?

3. What are the most common Ansible administration operations?

4. How can we use the Ansible SDK?

Key terms

- **Software Development Kit (SDK)** is a collection of tools, libraries, and documentation that simplifies and accelerates the development of software applications for a particular platform, framework, or technology.

- **AWX** is a community-driven open-source project supported by Red Hat that provides a user-friendly interface and robust automation capabilities to simplify and enhance IT processes and workflows.

- **Validated Content** in the Ansible Automation Platform refers to automation resources that have undergone rigorous testing and assessment to ensure their correctness and alignment with best practices.

- **Certified Content** in the Ansible Automation Platform refers to automation resources that have been extensively tested, validated, and endorsed by Ansible to meet the highest quality and reliability standards, ensuring their suitability for various use cases.

- **Signed Content** in the Ansible Automation Platform is automation resources that have been digitally signed to confirm their authenticity and integrity, providing an additional layer of security and trust for users.

Join our book's Discord space

Join the book's Discord Workspace for Latest updates, Offers, Tech happenings around the world, New Release and Sessions with the Authors:

https://discord.bpbonline.com

Index